# BENEATH THE WAVES

# Beneath the Waves

## A History of HM Submarine Losses

## A.S. Evans

Periscope Publishing Ltd.

First Published in 1986 by
William Kimber & Co Ltd.


Republished in 2007 by
Periscope Publishing Ltd.
33 Barwis Terrace
Penzance
Cornwall TR18 2AW
www.periscopepublishing.com

A CIP record for this book is available from the British Library


ISBN No 1-904381-41-3

*Printed in England by CPI Antony Rowe*
*Eastbourne*

This book is respectfully dedicated to the officers and men who crewed the submarines of the Royal Navy during the two World Wars

# Contents

# List of Illustrations

Percy Farley, survivor of the loss of *Poseidon*
The dazzle painted *M1* at speed
*M2* prepares to fly off her Parnell Peto seaplane
The launch of *Thetis*
*Thetis*, the picture that shocked the nation

*Between pages 224-5*

Able Seaman Campbell distributes Red Cross parcels in Oflag IXA
*Thistle* at speed on builder's trials
The *Shark*, lashed to a German anti-submarine vessel
Able Seaman Miller of the *Unity*
Lt-Cdr Ener Bettica, who sank the *Grampus*
The *Odin*
Rear-Admiral Peter Buckley
Lt-Cdr E.O. Bickford at the periscope of the *Salmon*
*Oswald* in pre-war days
Lt-Cdr Bandino Bandini of the *Enrico Toti*
The *Enrico Toti* and *Rainbow* do battle
*Triad* on trials

*Between pages 256-257*

The wreck of *Swordfish*
    *Martin Woodward, Bembridge Maritime Museum*
*Cachalot* after a peacetime ramming by an Italian merchant ship
ERA Whyte, lost in *Perseus*
*Tempest* on the surface
A visiting Russian delegation in *P38*
The only survivor from *U374*
The captain of the *Pegaso*
*Urge* and *Upholder*
*P36* on the surface at Malta
The crew of *Upholder* give three cheers to their captain

*Between pages 288-289*

Lt J. Edgar of *Thunderbolt*
Lt-Cdr C.B. Crouch, lost in *Thunderbolt*
*Thetis* after being salved and repaired
Lt Augusto Migliorini in command of the corvette *Cicogna*
*Thunderbolt* rescues survivors from a sunken ship
Commander J.W. Linton, VC
Lt R.G. Sampson, DSC, lost in *Tigris*
*Turbulent* in Algiers 1943
*Regent* at Algiers
The crew of HM Submarine *Splendid*
Germans attending to survivors of the *Splendid*
The destroyer *Hermes* which sank the *Splendid*
Cdr J.H. Bromage, captain of the *Sahib*
Leading Seaman Briard of *Sahib*, after return from captivity
*P514* under way in Placentia Bay
    *US National Archives*
Lt G.M. Noll of the *Tribune* oversees the coxswain on the hydroplanes

*Between pages 320-321*

Lt E.P. Tomkinson with his wife
Two survivors of *Olympus*
*Thorn* in September 1941
Lt-Cdr M. Willmott lost in *Talisman*
The *Talisman*
*Traveller* ties up in Beirut after a successful patrol
*Utmost* comes home after a successful commission
Submarine hatch
Lt-Cdr Crouch of *Thunderbolt* with Cdr Cayley of *P311*
*P311* en route to Holy Loch for her working up period
The *Trooper* leaves Malta

*Between pages 354-355*

Able Seaman Webb lost in *Parthian*
Lt C.A. Pardoe lost when in command of *Parthian*
Lt Michael Lumby of the *Saracen* at Algiers
Rear-Admiral Mario Baroglio, CO of the *Minerva*
Lt H.B. Turner of the *Porpoise*
Midshipman R.F. Drake, third hand of *Stonehenge*
*Turbulent* doing a trot fob in Alexendria harbour
*Sickle* in Algiers harbour

*Between pages 384-385*

The *Truculent*
*Sidon* gradually sinks
Surgeon Lieutenant C.R. Rhodes of *Sidon*
Sub-Lt J. Blackburn who became captain of the *Affray*
The top of the fin of the *Artemis*
Captain H.P.K. Oram at HMS *Dolphin* in February 1986
The luckiest man in the Submarine Service

# Acknowledgements

This history has been written with the general reader in mind. The encouragement and goodwill experienced during the course of research has been most gratifying and, at risk of offending by omission, I would like to express my thanks to the following individuals and organizations: R.W. Auckland, A.G.E. Briard, Cdr J.H. Bromage, Rear-Adm B. Bryant, Rear-Adm P.N. Buckley, Lt M.V.H. Caplat, S.J. Cox, P. Farley, E. Gray, B.D. Head, R. Hedgecock, D.B. Hemingway, D. Hill, B. Hudson, F.K. Hutchings, G.H. Jagger, G.T.W. Kimbell, F. Luca, Capt M.G.R. Lumby, R.R. McCurrach, Vice-Adm Sir I.L.M. McGeoch, F. Mathews, Sir Iain Moncreiffe of that Ilk, J. Murdoch, Capt E.H.M. Orme, G.H.F. Painter, M. Perratt, F.E. Rumsey, Capt R.E.D. Ryder, VC, T.B. Shacklock, J. Townsend, D.A. Tull, Cdr F.C. van Oosten, R. Neth N, R. Walton, C.E.T. Warren, D.C.R. Webb, Miss B. Wilson of the Public Archives of Canada, Lt-Cdr M.R. Wilson of the Naval Historical Branch (MOD), M.J. Woodward, W.G. Wright.

I would also like to extend sincere thanks to the following retired officers of the Royal Italian Navy for their generosity in replying to my questions: Captain The Baron Francesco Acton, Cdr Bandino Bandini, Rear-Adm Mario Baroglio, Rear-Adm Alfredo D'Angelo. I would especially like to thank Rear-Adm Gino Galuppini of the Italian Naval Historical Branch for his assistance during my research of Italian material.

I am indebted to the Hutchinson Publishing Group Ltd for permission to quote from *Straws In The Wind* by Cdr H.G. Stoker, published by Herbert Jenkins 1925.

The whole of Appendix II, which includes figures 1, 2, and 3, is reproduced from *Subsunk** by kind permission of Mrs W.O. Shelford, widow of the late Capt W.O. Shelford, RN, FRSA, the book's author.

I extend thanks to the staff of the Royal Navy Submarine Museum, HMS *Dolphin*, Gosport, for their unfailing kindness and

_____

\* *Subsunk*, Harrap 1960.

assistance. In particular I wish to thank the museum's Assistant Director, Mr Gus Britton, a World War II submariner, for allowing me unrestricted access to the museum's research facilities and for assembling the photographs contained herein.

In conclusion I would like to express my admiration of the Royal Navy Submarine Service.

A.S.E.

# PART I

## THE EARLY YEARS

# The Early Years

News that the Royal Navy was about to form a Submarine Service
was made known to Parliament in March 1901 when Lord Selborne,
the First Lord of the Admiralty, in his introductory statement to the
Naval Estimates for 1901-2 expounded:

> Five submarine vessels of the type invented by Mr Holland have been
> ordered, the first of which should be delivered next autumn. What the
> future value of these boats may be in naval warfare can only be a matter
> of conjecture. The experiments with these boats will assist the Admiralty
> in assessing their true value.

The John P. Holland Torpedo Boat Company had been formed as
far back as 1883. In July 1898 Holland, then fifty-seven, had cause to
meet the businessman Isaac L. Rice. The wealthy Rice, whose stor-
age battery company was the largest in the United States, had
supplied Holland's latest submarine with batteries. Isaac Rice was
taken for a run in the *Holland*, as the submarine was called, and was
so impressed by the experience that he later formed his own submarine construction company. In February 1899 Rice's new firm
(Electric Boat Company) took over all of Holland's patents. Rice
was a well-known figure in the business world and had many influen-
tial contacts. Armed with a letter of introduction from the New York
banker Augustus Belmont (a director of Electric Boat) to Lord
Rothschild in England, Rice sailed for Europe in July 1900. Ten
weeks later the Admiralty had agreed to the purchase of the five *Hollands*.

An agreement between Electric Boat and the giant ship-building
and armaments firm of Messrs Vickers, Sons, & Maxim, Ltd, was
reached which allowed for the five *Hollands* to be built under licence
at Barrow-in-Furness. The launching, with a minimum of ceremony,
of HM Submarine *No 1* took place on Wednesday 2 October 1901.
The second of the *Hollands* was launched a few months later (21 February 1902), with a further two launchings following in May. The

fifth and final boat took to the water in June. By the beginning of
1903 the builders had delivered all five boats.

Having entered the Navy in 1877 as a youngster of thirteen, Captain (later Admiral Sir) R.H.S. Bacon was already an old hand when
at the age of thirty-eight he was appointed on 20 August 1901, as the
first Inspecting Captain of Submarine Boats and installed in an
office in the Controller's Department at the Admiralty. A determined and forceful officer, his qualities and technical ability made
him an ideal choice to command the new Submarine Service.

As few wanted anything to do with submarines – they were very
much the poor relation of the Navy – Captain Bacon found that he
had the field more or less to himself, a situation which suited Bacon
down to the ground as it enabled him and Vickers between them to
get on with the job of building the Submarine Service with a
minimum of official interference.

By September 1901 Bacon had recruited the first ten submariners.
The officer selected to command *Holland 1* was a slim 26-year-old
lieutenant of unquestionable ability: Forster D. Arnold-Forster.*
When in 1890 Lieutenant Arnold- Forster entered *Britannia* he could
hardly have foreseen that he would one day command the Navy's
first submarine. His first practical move towards submarine duty
occurred in March 1901 when he volunteered his services because
'Somebody will be wanted to do preliminary experiments and it
might be a useful experience'. Five months later he was on his way to
Barrow-in-Furness to take command of *Holland 1*, which at that time
was still under construction.

In the early years of the Submarine Service everything to do with
boats (submarines are always called boats by submariners) appears
to have involved risk and hardship to some degree. With the *Hollands*
having a very small conning tower, even normal surface running in a
choppy sea was not to be taken too lightly. And the use in such a confined space of a petrol engine for surface propulsion was an accepted
hazard that was considered sheer madness by most non-submarin-
ers. Not only was the risk of fire or an explosion a very real danger,
but petrol vapour had a tendency to make eyes water and to cause
the most fearsome headaches. The small, dank and foul-smelling
interior, crammed with noisy and temperamental machinery, was no
place for the faint-hearted; it took first-class men to withstand the

---

* Rear Admiral Arnold-Forster died at his daughter's home at Iwerne Minster in
April 1958.

unsavoury conditions and to perform skilled work with efficiency and with at least a modicum of cheerfulness. So, from the very beginning submariners had to be 'submarine types'.

At first the new boats which came into service were prone to breakdown; but as their crews gained in experience the pitfalls and snags were gradually overcome and by 1904 the *Hollands* and their seven-men crews had reached a standard of efficiency which enabled them to participate in the annual Naval Manoeuvres for the first time.

Though certain of Their Lordships were disgruntled at having submarines in the Service, once the *Hollands* had been purchased the Submarine Service began to grow rapidly. The *Hollands* were still under construction when agreement was reached on the design for a larger and more advanced class of boat, to be known as the 'A' class. The *A1* was laid down on 19 February 1902 and launched on 9 July of that year. Along with the *Hollands* the *A1* was assigned a role in the Naval Manoeuvres of 1904. This imposing event was to be marred by the first-ever submarine disaster of the Royal Navy's new Submarine Service.

On the final day of the manoeuvres (Friday 18 March) several *Hollands* and *A1* left harbour for an attack on the cruiser *Juno*, due to arrive at Portsmouth on completion of her part in the exercises. In the early afternoon the *Juno* was detected off the Nab Tower steaming blissfully towards Portsmouth.

First to chance an attack was *Holland 2*. At about 1400 her captain fired a dummy torpedo which missed the target. This attempt was followed by an attack from 400 yards by *Holland 3*. To the dismay, and possibly surprise, of *Juno*'s officers *Holland 3*'s torpedo found its mark.

Lieutenant Mansergh, the captain of *A1*, had been observing the mock attacks with interest. In accord with the captains of the *Hollands*, Mansergh was keen to put himself, his crew and his boat to the test. Then came the chance he had been waiting for: Captain Bacon, from the submarine tender *Hazard*, signalled *A1* to join the attack.

Born in Bridgetown, County Cork, on 2 March 1873, Loftus Charles Ogilvy Mansergh had entered the Navy as a cadet. Resolute and hard working, Mansergh, the eldest son of an Army officer, had four busy years before he was able to sport on his sleeve the single gold ring of a sub-lieutenant. Two years later (1895) he was promoted lieutenant. The infant Submarine Service had been in existence for no more than a year when Loftus Mansergh was transferred to submarines as promising material. Now, with eighteen years' service to call on, the 31-year-old lieutenant found himself in command of one of the Navy's most recent acquisitions to its Submarine Service.

The only other commissioned officer of *A1* was John Preston Churchill. Promoted sub-lieutenant in September 1902, John Churchill had not spared himself in order to become a thoroughly efficient officer. His appointment to HMS *Thames** 'For instruction in submarine boats' dated from 1 January 1904, so he was a comparative newcomer to submarines. At twenty-one years of age, Sub-Lieutenant Churchill was ten years younger than his captain.

Now that the moment for an attack was upon them *A1*'s crew was eager to get on with it. Lieutenant Mansergh, in common with all submariners of this period, was out to prove to the senior officers who still actively disliked the idea of submarines in the Royal Navy that the small, and seemingly ineffective, submarines were capable of causing the larger surface ships quite a headache.

Even in ideal conditions the firing of a torpedo in the early years of submarines was an ordeal that demanded the utmost concentration if any success was to be achieved by the officer peering through the primitive periscope, one of the problems of which was that the periscope presented an inverted view in its lens. Aware that in these manoeuvres the Submarine Service was very much on trial, *A1*'s captain was taking every possible care that his torpedo would run straight and true.

When the *Berwick Castle* sailed Southampton, her master was unaware that the ship was about to sail into the history books. For the passengers of the liner to whom the sight of a warship was something of a rarity the *Juno* provided a certain amount of interest. On the liner's bridge the duty officers were also taking an interest in the goings-on of the vessels in the vicinity – the ones on the surface that is – as in the Channel the unexpected is inclined to happen more frequently than anywhere else.

Lieutenant Mansergh was so absorbed in conducting a successful attack on the *Juno* that he failed to notice, so it is assumed, the *Berwick Castle* on a collision heading with *A1*.

From the liner's bridge the barely-visible *A1* was sighted, but not identified as being a submarine. Starboard helm was immediately applied and full astern called for. But it was too late. The liner struck *A1* a mortal blow. In a matter of seconds the small submarine was on her way to the seabed.

* An old cruiser fitted-out as the first submarine depot ship.

It was assumed in *Berwick Castle* that the ship had struck a practice torpedo. This assumption was not unreasonable, bearing in mind that the submarine was still in its infancy and many seafarers had never encountered one. Making a signal that *Berwick Castle* had struck a practice torpedo the liner continued her journey to Hamburg in complete ignorance of having sent eleven men to their death.

There was no immediate anxiety when *A1* failed to return to harbour. It was assumed that Mansergh (who rarely passed up an opportunity to further his skill and knowledge of submarine tactics) was putting himself and crew through some form of drill to round off the day. However, when after several hours the submarine had still not made an appearance Captain Bacon set out from Portsmouth with *Hazard* to search for the missing boat.

When *Hazard* eventually located the position where *A1* lay on the seabed there was no doubt that some kind of dreadful accident had taken place: created by air-bubbles escaping from *A1*, a large expanse of white water was grim testament that the Submarine Service had suffered its first serious accident. There was little that *Hazard* could do but circle the area in hope that the submariners, if any were still alive, would somehow find a means of escape. Another gunboat (*Seagull*) was dispatched from Portsmouth to accompany *Hazard* on her silent vigil. With the onset of darkness the watch was maintained with the help of the gunboats' powerful searchlights plying to and fro across a sea that remained disappointingly empty of survivors.

By the following morning (Saturday 19th) no survivors or dead bodies had risen to the surface. Divers put on their cumbersome suits and went down into the murky water to examine *A1*. They discovered that *Berwick Castle* had struck *A1* on the starboard side near the conning tower and that she was lying on her port side. There was no sign of life. On a brighter note it was thought that with some luck there was an outside chance that before the day was over it might just be possible to raise *A1* sufficiently to tow her to harbour.

At the end of the day the submarine was still resting on the bottom. Wire hawsers had been passed beneath the stricken vessel but these had parted in the attempt to raise her. This disappointing, but not entirely unexpected, set-back meant that the only satisfactory course of action was to proceed with a full-scale salvage operation – a possibly lengthy affair as it entailed repairing the collision damage and then forcing air under high pressure into the submarine; only when this had been satisfactorily completed could the actual raising of *A1* be tackled. Strong spring tides were expected to add to the difficulties.

And difficulties there certainly were. The *A1* was not raised until the morning of Monday 18 April, exactly one month to the day of the accident. Hawsers had been passed beneath the bow and stern of *A1* and at 1100 the attempt to lift the submarine off the seabed was begun. Although there was at one time a period of concern as to whether the steel hawsers would withstand the strain (*A1* was being held on the bottom by strong suction) the salvage team risked a few tentative smiles when a sudden slackening of the hawsers suggested that *A1* was no longer a captive of the deep.

Berthed in Portsmouth at the time of the accident, the salvage vessel *Belos*, owned by the Swedish Neptune Company of Stockholm, had at once been pressed into service. In the care of *Belos* and a lighter, *A1* was taken towards the shelter of the Isle of Wight. Her arrival in St Helen's Roads placed *A1* within a few feet of the bottom. At one o'clock that afternoon the small flotilla came to anchor for the purpose of raising *A1* a little higher (but not so high as to make her visible to a curious public which followed the operation in a variety of small boats) so as to ensure her entry into harbour.

Work on docking and removing the bodies from *A1* occupied most of the night. Secrecy was much in evidence and hardly anyone who was not actually engaged in the work was permitted anywhere near the dock. Sub-Lieutenant Churchill's father, a naval officer, arrived to see his son's body removed to Haslar Hospital. The inquest was to take place the following day.

When the inquest opened, the plain oak coffins, draped with Union Flags, lay in two rooms at Haslar Hospital. It was stated that the body of Lieutenant Mansergh had been found in the conning tower, and that of John Churchill at the foot of the conning tower. It was the opinion of Captain Bacon that:

> Although the conning tower had suffered damage the leak was so small that it could have easily have been stopped from inside if the crew had not been stunned. It appeared that no attempt had been made to blow any of the ballast tanks.

The captain went on to say that *A1*'s periscope had been bent to port and a ventilator broken.

Since that Friday in 1904, more than 5,000 submariners have given their lives in the service of their country. These were the first:

Lieutenant Loftus Mansergh and Sub-Lieutenant John Churchill; Petty Officers George Baker, William Dudgeon, and Vivian Roberts; Chief Engine Room Artificer William Parkinson and ERA Clinton Baly; Chief Stoker Albert Fleming and Stoker Albert Ellis; Able Seamen Charles King and Peter Wallace.

The unexpected sinking of *A1* was of course a cruel blow for the relatives of the dead. ERA Clinton Baly's 22-year-old wife said that her husband had always been fond of life in submarines. His main reason for volunteering for the Submarine Service was that it enabled him and his wife to spend more time together, they having been married only six months. Although Baly had once been rendered unconscious by petrol fumes, his wife had never known him to express doubts as regards the safety or efficiency of *A1*.

Chief ERA William Parkinson was one of the best ERAs in the flotilla. Parkinson was devoted to his work and *A1*, and never had anything but praise for the boat.

Chief Stoker Fleming seems to have had thoughts of leaving submarines, even though he was keen on his work. It appears that fumes from the petrol engine were at times the cause of violent pains in his head and a loss of appetite. His wife recalled that:

> On days when the gasoline engine had not been working properly and the fumes had been allowed to escape, his condition was very bad. It was only on Wednesday last, however, that he came home in a more happy mood and said that the 'old boat' had been running much better than usual and if she continued to behave as well as she had done that day, he would not mind sticking to his job.

*A1*'s sinking was the second naval disaster to affect Mrs Fleming, her brother having been lost when the battleship *Victoria* was rammed and sunk by HMS *Camperdown* during fleet manoeuvres off Tripoli in June 1893. Chief Stoker Fleming left five children.

Lieutenant Mansergh and Sub-Lieutenant Churchill were buried in adjacent graves at the Royal Naval Cemetery, Haslar.

\*

Even tragedies have their use. As a result of *A1*'s sinking, the fitting of a second watertight hatch at the foot of conning towers came into general use as an additional safety measure. Furthermore, the accident nudged thoughts in the direction of submarine salvage and rescue.

No matter how safety-conscious crews were, with petrol engines in such a confined space explosions took place from time to time. On 16 February 1905 an explosion took place in *A5* while she was moored alongside *Hazard*. Half *A5*'s crew died as a result. Three months later an explosion sank *A8* during exercises. Most of her crew, plus eight other personnel who were aboard for training purposes, did not survive, as will be seen from the following.

On the morning of 8 June the *A8* (Lieutenant A.H.C. Candy) was carrying out a series of exercises in Plymouth Sound in company with *A7* and torpedo boat *No 80*. With the submarines manoeuvring and diving just outside the breakwater, the exercises had been in progress for upwards of an hour when at 1030 an explosion shook *A8*. At the time Lieutenant Algernon Candy, who was twenty-eight, was on the bridge with three of his crew: Sub-Lieutenant Hugh Murdoch, Petty Officer William Waller, and Leading Stoker George Watt. Out of a complement of eighteen Lieutenant Candy and the above named were the only survivors.

Almost simultaneously with the explosion, the submarine began to sink. Lieutenant Candy, Murdoch, Waller and Watt found themselves floundering in the sea and not a little bewildered by the rapid turn of events. In the meantime neither *A7* nor torpedo boat *No 80* was aware that a tragedy had taken place so close to hand.

By chance an outgoing trawler, the *Chanticleer*, happened to be passing just as the explosion took place. *Chanticleer* lowered her boat to aid the survivors. Petty Officer Waller, kitted-out in heavy sea-boots and oilskins, was fighting a losing battle to keep himself from going under. Seeing Waller – who as coxswain of *Holland 1* was the Navy's first submarine coxswain – in such desperate straits Lieutenant Candy took a firm hold on him and kept him afloat until the trawler's boat reached them.

The authorities ashore responded to the sinking by ordering to the scene the tugs *Assurance* and *Perseverance* with diving parties and equipment. Divers from the battleship *Commonwealth* and the cruiser *Carnarvon* were also ordered to the area.

The hope that some of *A8*'s crew were still alive was brutally shattered when an explosion from the sunken boat flung wreckage to the surface. Another, but much quieter, explosion followed and all hopes of any form of rescue were dashed completely.

It took four days to raise *A8*. Beginning at 1040 on the morning of the 12th, the tow to Devonport got underway with the help of the tugs *Assurance*, at the head, and *Trusty* and *Industrious* on either flank.

After a tow lasting two hours *A8* arrived at Devonport without further mishap.

*Tuesday 20 June.* Twelve days had passed since the sinking of *A8*. Lieutenant Candy and the three other survivors boarded the battleship *Empress of India* for an inquiry into the incident. As the proceedings were in the nature of an inquiry, the survivors did not have to plead to any specific charges.

Captain Reginald Bacon was called as an expert witness. Bacon made a long statement embracing many technical details. He stated that one rivet was discovered to be out of the foremost petrol tank but that it was impossible to say whether the rivet was missing before the accident. Such a hole would allow a ton of water to enter the boat in ten minutes. Captain Bacon stated further that the strongest evidence in favour of the leakage he had described was that during the time *A8* was steaming she was gradually going down at the bow. She had settled with twenty to thirty tons of water inside her.

It was considered doubtful that petrol had anything to do with the explosion. The most likely cause in this instance was that chemical action had caused a battery explosion, not an uncommon happening in early submarines. Burns discovered on the dead crewmen were caused before death, and not after. Also, though the crew might have been living at the time of the explosion, they had been rendered insensible for some considerable time beforehand.

Lieutenant Candy went on to complete a highly successful and distinguished career. He had entered the Navy in 1892 and served in submarines between 1904-11. After a period of General Service he returned to submarines and served from 1913-16. Retiring from the Navy in 1927, he was recalled at the outbreak of the Second World War. Rear-Admiral Candy died, aged eighty-one, in April 1959.

*

The year 1905 was not a very satisfactory year for HM Submarine *A4*. On two occasions *A4* almost annihilated her crew.

Lieutenant Martin Nasmith, her CO, was detailed to take part in an experiment in underwater signalling. His task was to submerge *A4* until the top of a narrow ventilating tube was poking just above the surface. Nasmith, another officer destined for high rank, was then to listen for the sound of a bell rung at intervals by a torpedo boat.

The experiment was in progress when a steamer, with no knowledge of what was taking place, came close enough for her wash to engulf the open ventilator tube. Water gushed down the tube so fast that *A4*'s delicate trim was quickly upset; before anything could be done to correct trim, her bow pointed downwards and she went hurtling to the seabed ninety feet below.

Before the base of the ventilating tube could be plugged with whatever came readily to hand, the water had risen enough to reach the batteries. When sea-water and a submarine's batteries get together the result is chlorine gas. In *A4* this deadly greenish-yellow gas was soon very much in evidence.

*A4* was in dire trouble; were it not for the actions of her first lieutenant*, Lieutenant Godfrey Herbert, the Submarine Service might have been mourning the loss of its third boat with, in this case, an entire crew. Fighting to hold onto his senses Lieutenant Herbert struggled through the darkness to the controls and blew the ballast tanks. *A4* rose obediently, if somewhat hesitantly, to the surface. The crew, coughing and choking, scrambled thankfully from the stifling interior and out into the fresh air.

In mid-October 1905 the *A4* was again involved in a near-fatal accident. One report of the incident alleged that:

> Whilst the boat was carrying out exercises in Stokes Bay, her weights shifted. She was submerged at the time and the moving of the weights made her unmanageable. As soon as the mishap occurred the crew tried to raise her to the surface. Fortunately their efforts were successful and the boat came up, though listing heavily to one side instead of being on an absolutely even keel. The water got into the batteries. The crew, fearing an explosion, made their escape with all possible speed.

A gunboat and several submarines were in the vicinity and were able to close *A4* and take off her crew. A signal was dispatched to Portsmouth; in response a number of tugs were sent to conduct *A4* to harbour.

When *A4* arrived back in harbour later that evening, it was suggested that she be sent into a deep dock for examination by experts. Whilst being towed to the dock entrance the *A4* sank in deep water. As all efforts to raise her met with failure it was decided to make a fresh attempt at dawn.

Early the following morning work was continued on raising the

---

* The first lieutenant is second-in-command of a submarine and is known variously as Second Captain, Number One, and Jimmy.

submarine sufficiently to float her over the sill of the dock, from which water was to be pumped as soon as she was in position. The task proved much more difficult than anticipated and it was a considerable time before *A4* was lifted off the muddy bottom and satisfactorily secured in the dock.

The *A4* continued in service until January 1920, she then being sold to a firm of ship breakers after having completed seventeen years' service.

*

The last of the thirteen 'A' class was launched in April 1905. The first of their successors, the 'B' class, had been launched at Barrow in October 1904. Though still small and petrol-engined, the 'B's were quite an improvement on the 'A' boats. Armed with two 18-inch bow torpedo tubes the 'B's had forward as well as after hydroplanes. The 'B's were followed in 1906 by the first of the 'C' class. It was during the construction of the 'C's that the monopoly of submarine building hitherto enjoyed by Vickers came to an end. On 13 March 1908 the Royal Dockyard at Chatham launched the *C17*. Prior to *C17* Vickers had built every Royal Navy submarine, forty-five in all. The Admiralty had deemed it wise that contracts for submarines should be distributed to a wider range of firms. Though Vickers had to bow to this decision, the great firm was still able to dominate submarine construction.

The 'C' class was the last of the petrol-engined submarines. Not unpopular with their crews, thirty-eight of them were built before the last (*C34*) was launched at Chatham in June 1910. Eleven of the 'C's met an untimely end. The first of them was *C11*.

On the afternoon of 15 July 1909 the Admiralty issued the following communiqué: 'Secretary to the Admiralty regrets having to communicate that Messrs Farrar, Groves, & Co's steamer *Eddystone*, bound for Hull, was in collision with submarine *C11* at 1145 last night, 4½ miles north-west of Haisborough Light, off Cromer, and the submarine was sunk.' The accident had taken place in an area widely used by north- and south-bound east coast traffic. Haisborough Light stands at Happisburgh, a small fishing village twelve miles south of Cromer on the Norfolk coast.

On the afternoon of Wednesday 14th the depot ship *Bonaventure* put to sea from Grimsby with eight torpedo boats and nine 'C' class submarines, one of them *C11*, in attendance. The flotilla had done exceptionally well in the recent North Sea manoeuvres by theoretically sinking two cruisers off the Yorkshire coast. The passage south proved quite uneventful until the flotilla encountered the *Eddystone* steaming quietly on her northward course.

At 3,850 tons the *Eddystone*, captained by T.B.Pritchard, was one of the smallest ships in the fleet of Messrs Farrar, Groves, & Co's eleven vessels. She was homeward bound from the Sea of Azov with a full cargo of wheat. Captain Pritchard, who had the pleasure of his wife's company for the voyage, had given the greater part of his life to the sea. His many years as a seafarer had justifiably gained the confidence of *Eddystone*'s owners.

A sailor who witnessed the collision from the deck of a torpedo boat had this to say: 'It was a clear night – a night upon which a disaster would seem impossible. We were steaming at 10 knots towards Lowestoft. *Bonaventure*, the parent ship, was leading. The nine submarines in the flotilla followed in lines of three, *C11* slightly leading, with torpedo boats in line in-shore. All lights were showing – we were like a little town upon the water. We could see the *Eddystone* coming towards us. She tried to pass between the lines of submarines, and in doing so struck *C11*. She hit her well aft and cut her tail clean away. The submarine heeled over and went down like a stone. I heard someone cry "Man overboard!" and in a moment the boatswain's pipe was giving its call: "PIPE, AWAY ALL BOATS' CREWS". The searchlights from *Bonaventure* and the torpedo boats were flashed on, illuminating the scene brilliantly. I was away in our dinghy within three minutes. We rowed about for hours looking for the crew of the sunken vessel. The survivors were picked up by a boat from submarine *C12* and taken to the *Bonaventure*. One boat from *Eddystone* also put off. Once I thought I heard a cry in the night, but we could find no one.'

The survivors numbered just three: Lieutenant (later Rear Admiral) C.G. Brodie, *C11*'s captain; the first lieutenant, Lieutenant G. Watkins; and an Able Seaman Stripes. One report as to how these survivors escaped from *C11* runs as follows: Lieutenant Watkins was on the bridge when *Eddystone* struck the submarine. Brodie was below taking a short rest before going on duty. The majority of the crew were sleeping. After the collision Lieutenant Brodie, despite water rushing in from a huge hole, went round trying to rouse his crew. The water was up to his waist before he scrambled up the ladder and out into the night. Brodie had awakened several of his crew but they could not get out in time to avoid the powerful inrush of sea that poured through the hatch and engulfed them. The submarine sank in less than forty seconds from the time she was struck. Apart from Brodie the only man to escape from inside *C11* had been Able Seaman Stripes.

As he swam round Brodie heard, and then saw, Able Seaman Stripes. 'Are you all right?' Brodie called.

'Don't worry about me, sir,' came the cheerful reply.

The force of the collision had thrown Geoffrey Watkins into the sea. Watkins was wearing a thick duffel coat as well as a sweater and sea-boots. Hampered by his clothing he fought to prevent himself from drowning. Brodie swam to Watkins who was clearly in distress. With the assistance of Charles Brodie, Lieutenant Watkins was able to remain afloat until the boat from *C12* rescued the three men from the sea to take them to *Bonaventure*.

The appearance of *Eddystone* among the submarines was cause for some rapid manoeuvres. In the haste to avoid being rammed by the steamer, the *C16* and *C17* collided with each other. *C16* escaped serious damage but *C17* was not so fortunate; she was damaged to such an extent that the tug *Herculanean* had to take her to Sheerness.

Though at first reluctant to make any statement to reporters at Hull, Captain Pritchard, who lived in the South Wales port of Barry, when pressed said that he was not on deck at the time of the collision. He was called on deck at about midnight and on his arrival was almost blinded by searchlights from the warships, the presence of which no one in *Eddystone* seems to have suspected. 'When I realised that there had been trouble', commented Pritchard, 'I at once put out the boat to search for men, but after a long period I sent to the guardship to see if there was anything I could do further. Being told "No" I proceeded to Hull.'

\*

For two-and-a-half years after the *C11-Eddystone* tragedy the Submarine Service suffered no further losses. Then in 1912 two submarines were sunk within eight months of each other.

The loss of the *A3* (Lieutenant F.T. Ormand) took place on Friday 6 February, a cold blustery day with occasional snow showers which at times were quite heavy. The notice posted at Admiralty House shortly after the loss of *A3* told almost all there was to be told of the unhappy event:

> The Commander-in-Chief regrets to announce that owing to a collision between His Majesty's Ship *Hazard* and the submarine *A3*, the latter

sank near the East Princess Buoy about noon today. It is feared that the submarine was completely flooded, in which case there is very little hope of the officers and crew being saved, though salvage appliances have been sent out.

The *A3* had in fact sunk so quickly that the four officers and ten ratings had stood no chance of escape before she went down, and all perished.

The *A3* had left harbour at about 0930 that morning in company with several 'A' and 'C' class submarines for exercises off the Isle of Wight. The area of operation was off Bembridge. The exercises had been in progress several hours when *A3* blew tanks and surfaced directly in the path of *Hazard*. With a large hole torn in her side *A3* hurtled out of control to the seabed.

It was five weeks before *A3* was raised and taken to Portsmouth. Sunday 8 March had been the first favourable day for salvage operations since the accident, there having been a succession of south-westerly gales which made the divers' work difficult at all times, and for most part impossible. Such headway was made throughout that Sunday with preparations for slinging *A3*, that hope of getting her on the move was high. When the opportunity to lift her off the bottom did eventually arrive she was raised a few feet and taken, slung between two lighters, to St Helen's Bay, a sheltered area near Ryde, Isle of Wight. She was then lowered to the bottom to enable a more permanent securing of the slings for the journey to Portsmouth.

On Thursday 12th the move from St Helen's Bay to Portsmouth got underway. It was hoped to complete the journey on the morning tide but fog put paid to that. The lighter, *A3*, and the attendant tugs remained in the bay to await the afternoon tide.

At 1430 a start was made for Portsmouth. With her ensign at half-mast the tug *Seahorse* led the way. She was followed by a second tug towing the lighter. A third tug had been lashed to the lighter's side to steady it. Bringing up the rear were two destroyers with flags at half-mast.

It was several hours before the small flotilla passed the entrance to Portsmouth Harbour. On passing the submarine base of Fort Blockhouse, the procession received a salute of bugle calls and dipped ensigns. The flotilla continued up harbour to the south lock where *A3* was to be berthed. When the work of pumping out the dock had been completed the fourteen bodies were taken to the mortuary at Haslar Hospital to await burial at the Royal Navy Cemetery.

Lieutenant F.T. Ormand had entered the Navy in May 1904. In May 1909 he joined submarines. At the time of *A3*'s sinking Frank Ormand was in temporary command whilst her regular captain, Lieutenant Craven, was away on leave.

Within weeks of the burial of her crew *A3* was towed out to sea by *Seahorse*. After several experiments had taken place the dreadnought *St Vincent* opened fire at 2,000 yards with her 4-inch guns. At the third shot *A3* buckled up and slid from view.

The second submarine to meet with disaster in 1912 was *B2* (Lieutenant P.B. O'Brien). Her loss occurred during the early hours of Friday 4 October.

The destroyer and submarine flotillas attached to the Home Fleet had for several weeks been involved in a series of tactical exercises in the North Sea. The destroyers and submarines had, in turn, been carrying out manoeuvres off the Scottish coast, the north-east coast, and in the English Channel. Dover had been the base for about forty vessels, a figure which included the submarine parent ships *Forth*, *Hazard*, *Minerva*, and *Sapphire*. At 0430 on the morning of *B2*'s sinking, the destroyers and submarines began to clear harbour. For more than an hour units of the Home Fleet continued outward from Dover to assume their role in the manoeuvres.

Whilst this exodus was taking place the 23,000 tons Hamburg-Amerika liner *Amerika* was in transit between Hamburg and Southampton to receive passengers for her impending passage to New York. Dawn was still some way off when *Amerika*, making good progress down Channel, with surprising suddenness struck *B2* a fatal blow just forward of her conning tower. The submarine, which had been on the surface for some time, was badly holed and sank at once.

On the submarine's bridge at the moment of impact were Lieutenant Richard Pulleyne and a petty officer. Pulleyne could later recall with startling vividness *B2* going down very fast – and he with her. At a hundred feet he felt the submarine touch bottom; the next thing he knew was that he was struggling and kicking from the blackness towards the surface.

After what seemed an eternity Pulleyne arrived on the surface feeling more dead than alive. He then heard a most welcome noise: the sound of a propeller. Less than twenty yards away he saw the black mass of a ship making good time. Pulleyne's relief at the prospect of a speedy rescue was short-lived; the unknown vessel went racing by without the slightest easing of speed. Later another ship and several submarines passed within yards of Pulleyne without noticing his

desperate plight. Too exhausted to cry for help, Pulleyne gave himself up for lost.

With hopes of attracting other vessels to the scene, the *Amerika*
fired off distress rockets. Submarine *C16* sighted the bursting rockets
and set off to investigate. She would rescue the only survivor.

Lieutenant Pulleyne (a submariner for ten months) was very near
death when *C16* arrived. By good fortune a lookout spotted the half-
dead officer floating in the sea. Pulleyne was taken aboard and well
looked after until he could be transferred to the depot ship *Forth*.

Showing hardly a trace of the collision, the *Amerika* arrived in
Southampton Water a few hours later. Captain Knuth, her master,
declined to make any comment on the incident. Some of his crew
were not so reticent. The purser said it was a clear morning when *B2*
cross the liner's bow. The submarine had been about sixty feet ahead
with only her conning tower showing. Her speed was about 10 knots,
whilst that of *Amerika* was perhaps 17 knots. Although the order for
full speed astern had been given, the liner had had too much headway on her. The sudden reversal of *Amerika*'s engines and the force of
the impact on striking *B2* caused the ship to tremble from stem to
stern. Alarmed by the liner's unusual behaviour some of her passengers ran on deck to see what was going on. They saw the crew preparing to lower boats to search for survivors. None was found.

As it was thought there would be little to compensate the effort
required to raise *B2* the decision was made to let her remain a tomb.
It was the first occasion that British submariners of a sunken submarine had not been brought ashore for burial. Percy O'Brien, *B2*'s
captain, left a widow.

A funeral service over the sunken submarine was held the following Thursday. Throughout the morning vessels taking part in the
ceremony assembled at Dover. In the early afternoon they set off in
time for the two o'clock service. The *B2* had been sunk about four
miles north-east of Dover. The depot ship *Forth* anchored over the
spot where she had been located. Other vessels formed into line.
Representatives of the submarines in the flotilla were aboard *Forth*;
and it was from *Forth* that the service was conducted by naval chap-
lains. A haze hung over the water like a pall. All flags of the flotilla
were at half-mast, as were the flags over public buildings at Dover.

Hundreds of people lined the cliffs of Dover in an attempt to see as
much of the ceremony as the misty conditions would allow. The
Hamburg-Amerika line was represented at the funeral by their local
agents aboard the tug *Lady Crundall*, which flew the German ensign

and the company's flag. When the service was over, the vessels made their way to Dover. Lieutenant O'Brien, his crew, and *B2* had become a sad part of naval history.

\*

When the *C14* (Lieutenant G.W.E. Naper) was sunk on the evening of 10 December 1913 it was the first occasion in which the Submarine Service did not have to mourn the death of a single submariner. The *C14* had been on her way to Plymouth with other submarines of the 3rd Flotilla when she was involved in a collision with *Government Hopper 29*. Damaged on her port quarter aft, *C14* began to take in water at a startling rate. Work on stemming the flow with collision mats was immediately put in hand but the effort met with little reward and *C14* began to settle ominously down by the stern even with the pumps working at full capacity. Seeing that the water was gaining the upper hand, and recognizing that his command was beyond recovery, Lieutenant Naper ordered the crew on deck and signalled for assistance. The hopper stood by as a refuge in case the submariners were forced to take to the water before help arrived.

The accident had taken place in Plymouth Sound at a point between Drake's Island and Devil's Point, so help was readily at hand. George Naper, who had joined the 3rd Flotilla three months previously, and his crew of nineteen were taken off the sinking submarine. Just as the last man leapt onto the rescue boat, *C14* sank. It had been little more than ten minutes since the collision. An eye-witness was to report that 'Excellent discipline prevailed throughout'.

It was more than a week before *C14* was raised and docked. On the 18th, hawsers were positioned fore and aft round the submarine. Using a lighter specially designed for salvage, *C14* was raised on a favourable tide during the late evening of the following day. Slung beneath *Salvage Lighter 94* the submarine was taken to Devonport. She survived a further eight years.

A little over a month after the *C14* incident the ageing *A7* (Lieutenant G.M. Welman) failed to surface whilst exercising in Whitsand Bay on 16 January 1914. *A7* had put to sea from Devonport with five other submarines for exercises with the *Onyx* and *Pigmy*. Both ships were to be targets for simulated torpedo attacks by the submarines. The gunboat *Pigmy*, on whom it is proposed to concentrate, and her two submarines (*A7, A9*) took up their designated positions: *A9* at Position A, a point 2½ miles WNW of Rame Head, and *A7* at Position B which was on the same bearing but some two miles farther on.

It was *A9* that began the series of attacks on *Pigmy*. After she had completed her second attack, and had had her spent torpedo recovered by *Pigmy*, the gunboat sighted *A7* about two miles south-east of Position B. *A7* appeared to be trimmed down and waiting for *Pigmy* to start her run. By 1110 *A7* had dived, having observed *Pigmy* at the start of her run. *Pigmy* stayed on course until it became evident that Lieutenant Welman's attack had failed. *A7* could now be expected to surface and prepare for a second attack.

When *A7* remained unsighted *Pigmy* steamed towards Rame Head in search of her. The following was reported by *Pigmy*'s captain:

> Black ball was hoisted at 1155 as a signal to come to the surface, and course from then on was as requisite until 1215 when my attention was called by the crew to a spot where a disturbance on the surface was visible (this I personally could not see but shaped course for it). At 1218 a second disturbance, which I saw, showed itself on the surface in a position 3 miles west-by-north from Rame Church. *Pigmy* was taken over this as nearly as could be judged and the spot buoyed and fixed by cross-bearings. *Pigmy* then returned to harbour and communicated with C-in-C *Forth*.

Surprisingly, although *A7*'s approximate position was known, she defied all efforts to locate her exact position until the 22nd, six days after her sinking. Of all the ships, and even aircraft, involved in the search it was the *Pigmy* that sighted a large patch of oil on the surface. Divers confirmed that the oil was leaking from *A7*; also, they reported that she was lying at an angle of 30° to 40° with her stern buried in mud up to about twenty-two feet from her forward hydroplanes. Her bow was estimated as being more than 30 feet off the bottom.

*Friday 23 January*. The operation to raise *A7* got underway with the arrival of a salvage vessel, the same one that had raised *C14* off the bottom of Plymouth Sound. The weather, which was to cause much frustration over the coming days, was hazy and cold. An attempt by a tug to pull the submarine out of the mud ended in failure. A further attempt, weather permitting, was proposed for the following day.

*Saturday 24th*. As the swell was too heavy for divers to shackle big hawsers to *A7*, no attempt was made to free her from the mud until the 28th, when a 5½-inch hawser was shackled to an eye-plate at the forward end of the submarine's superstructure, the other end being attached to the tug *Exmouth*. This effort to pull *A7* free resulted in the

The first of many! *A1*, seen here entering Portsmouth on a pleasant sunny day, was the first of the Royal Navy's submarines to pay the price of Admiralty. Among the messages of condolence at her loss was one from the Prince and Princess of Wales who had visited the submarine one week before her loss.

(*Left*) A petty officer first class in Queen Victoria's navy, William Waller was the first submarine coxswain, the senior rating responsible for the general running of a submarine. When *A8* sank off Plymouth in 1905 Waller, wearing heavy clothing and large leather boots, was lucky to survive. *Holland 1*, Britain's first submarine, is preserved at HMS *Dolphin*, Gosport, Hampshire.

(*Right*) PO Winstanley, the coxswain of *C11*, poses at the upper deck steering wheel on the bridge of the submarine. He did not survive the sinking.

(*Top left*) Ironically, the *A3* was sunk by a collision with her own depot ship the *Hazard*. No doubt, superstitious members of the crew thought that the number 13 on the conning tower was unlucky, especially as under the strange Admiralty system of numbering, A13 bore the numbers 03!

(*Top right*) *A7* in her early days with Roman numeral markings. Divers who have been down to her in Whitsand Bay say that there is very little damage and she sits upright on the sea bed.

(*Centre*) There was only one survivor from the sinking of B2, Lt Pulleyne, who later commanded the minelayer *E34* with great success, winning the DSO and the DSC. Six years later, with the war nearly finished, *E34* disappeared with all hands off Heligoland.

(*Bottom left*) *C14* in dock in 1913 after being sunk after a collision with a vessel in Plymouth Sound. There were no casualties as the crew swiftly abandoned ship. The boat was restored to service and was not scrapped until 1921.

eye-plate fracturing and the submarine remaining just as before.

Salvage operations were not resumed until the morning of 17 February. On this third day a 6½-inch hawser slipped from under the submarine during the tow to free her. The failure of this attempt, and adverse weather conditions, cast serious doubts on the feasibility of salvaging the submarine. When ten days later another attempt failed, the prospect of raising *A7* from 130 feet was considered impracticable, as to manoeuvre the submarine into a suitable position for slinging would present great difficulties during the winter months when the weather could be relied on to add to the problems. Faced with so difficult and dangerous a task, the operation was abandoned.

Lieutenant Gilbert Welman had been captain of *A7* only a matter of weeks. Prior to his appointment to *A7* he had served in *Forth* since his return from two years' service in Hong Kong.

From the development of the 'A' class in 1903, British submarine design made such good progress that by 1914 Britain was able to enter the war with some of the finest submarines in existence anywhere. As noted elsewhere, the 'A' class gave way to the 'B's which in turn had been bettered by the 'C's. The Naval Estimates of 1907-8 made provision for a new class of submarine – the 'D' class. With the coming of the 'D's the submarine in Britain took on a new dimension in both capability and stature. Prior to the 'D' class British submarines were designed as nothing more than coast defence submarines. The 'D's were the first of the 'ocean-going' class of submarines. At almost twice the displacement of the 'C's, the 'D' boats were in some ways a revolutionary design. First and foremost they were the first British submarines specifically designed for diesel propulsion. The 'D's could claim a number of 'firsts': not only were they the first submarines to have twin screws but they were also the first to be fitted with radio and, from *D4* onwards, with a gun. Another innovation of the class was that their ballast tanks were not inside the hull, as was the case with previous classes, but fitted outside as saddle tanks.

Security during the construction of *D1* was inordinately severe – and for her launching at Barrow in May 1908 there was scarcely any let-up. Immediately after taking to the water she was towed to a wharf and hidden from prying eyes. Only eight 'D's were built but the success of these submarines was so marked that from them developed the famous 'E' class. The 'E's – perhaps one of the most

successful classes of submarine ever built – were formidable submarines and popular with their crews. Though only nine of these fine
submarines were in commission at the outbreak of hostilities in
August 1914, fifty-six of them eventually joined the fray.

# PART II

## THE GREAT WAR

# 1914

Although for many years Britain and Germany had known that some day they would face each other in a war, by 1914 the Royal Navy was still the most powerful navy in the world. For seventeen years Germany had been studiously increasing the strength of her Navy. By the outbreak of war the German Navy had expanded to roughly half the size of the Royal Navy.

On Friday 31 July, August Bank Holiday Weekend, the Royal Navy prepared for sea in anticipation of war. Three days later the Army was mobilised. The feeling throughout the country was one of great excitement. People sensed that the eve of some momentous occasion was upon them. The air was electric. Union Jacks, peddled by hawkers, were snapped up as a great wave of patriotism swept the land. Foreign visitors packed their bags and booked passage to their own countries. The hot sun shone down from a vast clear blue sky. The feeling was widespread that the coming war would show that Britain was the greatest country on God's earth.

With the age of radio still to come, news-vendors could hardly keep pace as the day-to-day clamour for war news intensified. The Bank Holiday mood was still strong when huge crowds gathered outside Buckingham Palace calling for the King and Queen. On Tuesday 4 August Germany invaded Belgium. Before the day was over, Britain had also become a part of what would become known as The Great War.

The first Allied submarine loss of the war was *AE1* (*Australian E1*). Australia had ordered two 'E' class submarines in 1913. On 2 March 1914 the *AE1* and *AE2* set out from Portsmouth on a dismal and overcast morning for the 13,000 mile journey to Australia.

*May 24 1914*. Dawn was breaking as the two submarines entered Sydney Harbour. Australia's first submarines made their way across harbour to tie up at Garden Island. The eighty-three days' journey had been a considerable triumph for such small craft.

The submarines had been in Australia two months when, within hours of Britain declaring war on Germany, the Australian Government offered Britain 'A Force of twenty thousand men, of any desired composition, to any destination desired by the Home Government'.

To the north-east of New Guinea lie the islands of New Britain and New Ireland. Both islands were German possessions. Rabaul was the capital of New Britain and the seat of government of the islands that made up the Bismarck Archipelago. The German Pacific Squadron of five cruisers constituted its sole naval protection. In August 1914, Australian ships, including *AE1* and *AE2*, set off to capture Rabaul.

On their arrival in the area, the leading destroyer found Rabaul Harbour free of German ships. The next day a force of Australian ships entered harbour. Troops were put ashore and fighting ensued. While this action was taking place the two submarines were detailed to patrol St George's Strait, which separates New Britain from New Ireland and through which all shipping making for Rabaul from the south must pass. With a destroyer *AE2* (Lieutenant-Commander H.G.D. Stoker) was first to take up this duty. Stoker returned to harbour later in the day after an uneventful patrol. The following day it would be the turn of *AE1* to patrol the Strait.

At 0700 on 19 September Lieutenant-Commander T.E. Besant, the captain of *AE1*, sailed Blanche Bay, New Britain, with the destroyer HMAS *Parramatta* to patrol off Cape Gazelle. In the hazy conditions visibility was reduced to between two and five miles; consequently *Parramatta* occasionally lost sight of *AE1* as she scouted in advance of the submarine. At 1430 that afternoon, Besant reported all well. An hour later the submarine was sighted by *Parramatta* to the west of Duke of York Island, and apparently *en route* for Blanche Bay in accordance with orders. After this sighting *Parramatta* remained at sea awhile before proceeding to Herbertshohe. This sighting by *Parramatta* was the last time *AE1* was ever seen.

*AE1* was not reported as missing until eight o'clock that evening. The *Parramatta* and *Yarra* put to sea in search of her, using flares and searchlights as an aid. Early the following morning more vessels joined the search. The entire coast of New Britain and New Ireland was searched but not even a tell-tale trace of oil was sighted to give a clue as to *AE1*'s fate. As no claim for her sinking was made by the Germans, a submarine accident might have been the cause of her loss, though this is unlikely.

A favoured hypothesis for the loss of *AE1* is that she dived for practice on approaching Blanche Bay and rolled so close to the coastal reef which formed the edge to the deep entrance channel, that her hull was pierced by sharp coral rock. *AE1*'s crew was a mixture of Australian and British.

*

The first Royal Navy submarine to be sunk during a state of hostilities was *E3* (Lieutenant-Commander G.F. Cholmley). *E3* sailed Harwich with *E8* on 16 October to patrol an area off Borkum. At ten o'clock that night the two submarines parted company. Nothing further was heard of *E3* until the Germans announced her destruction two days later.

The Germans at this time were employing U-boats in the Heligoland Bight to seek out British submarines. On 18 October, *U30* was cruising north of Borkum Reef Light Vessel, whilst to the south *U27* was doing likewise off the mouth of the Ems. At 1025 Lieutenant-Commander Bernhard Wegener (*U27*) sighted an object, which was thought to be a buoy. The 'buoy' was soon made out to be an enemy submarine. *E3* was on the surface with six of her crew on the bridge. The lookout appeared to be concentrated in the direction of the Ems. *U27* was able to approach unobserved from the direction of the sun. About two hours after having first sighted *E3*, Wegener fired a torpedo from 300 yards. *E3* broke in half and sank at once. The Germans saw four men in the sea but, fearing that Lieutenant-Commander Cholmley was not operating alone, they made no attempt to surface and pick them up. Half an hour passed before *U27* closed the position where *E3* had gone down. By then the four survivors were nowhere to be seen. This sinking on 18 October 1914 was the first occasion on which a submarine had sunk one of its own kind by hostile action. Thirty-two years old, Lieutenant-Commander George Cholmley left a widow.

November was not a month in which the 8th Flotilla had much to cheer about. The flotilla, which consisted of 'D' and 'E' class submarines, lost two submarines. On the morning of 3 November, German battle-cruisers unleashed a barrage of gunfire on an east coast town with the object seemingly nothing more than to strike a blow at the civil population. The ships' heavy gunfire on Yarmouth was heard three miles down the coast at Gorleston, where *D3*, *D5*, and *E10* were moored. The submarines were ordered into the roads and at 0815 were instructed to attempt an interception of the enemy off Terschelling. The captain of *D5* was Lieutenant-Commander Godfrey Herbert who, it will be recalled, had been first lieutenant of *A4* when she was almost sunk during underwater signalling experiments. Soon after that incident Herbert left *A4* for duty in surface ships. In 1910 he returned to submarines on being appointed captain of *C36*, which he then took on a record-breaking passage to the China Station. Returning home in 1913, Herbert took command of *C30*. Then came *D5*.

Lieutenant-Commander Herbert was as startled as those with him on the bridge when *D5*'s after end touched off a mine. The submarine gave a violent shudder and in less than a minute had sunk from view, leaving Herbert and about half a dozen of his crew floundering in the sea.

Though he witnessed the explosion, the skipper of the drifter *Faithful* bravely disregarded the danger of mines to rescue the men in the sea. Godfrey Herbert and three of his crew (Sub-Lieutenant Ian McIntyre, Chief Petty Officer Robert Speirs, and Able Seaman Charles Sexton) were hauled aboard *Faithful*. A fifth man, Able Seaman Albert Suttill from Leeds, was later picked up by a fishing smack. For his display of gallantry James Collin, master of *Faithful*, and his crew shared an award of ninety-seven pounds.

The position where *D5* had struck the mine was so far from the track of the enemy ships, which themselves were probably dropping mines in their wake, that it seems possible that the mine had been British and had dragged or broken adrift.

The second of the 8th Flotilla's submarines lost in November 1914 was *D2*. Before this submarine went missing she had a particularly bad stroke of luck.

A naval operation, which included submarines, had been planned for a date towards the latter part of November. The first vessels to leave for the operation were *D2*, *E5* and *E15*. It was 0700 on the 22nd when the trio departed Harwich in weather that looked distinctly unpromising.

By the time the leading submarine arrived in the vicinity of Gorleston her companions were nowhere to be seen. When they failed to reply to repeated calls, the leading submarine put into Yarmouth for instructions; these were received by 1500 and were to the effect that as the weather forecast was favourable, the submarines were to proceed as ordered. By this time the other two boats had entered harbour. All three put to sea again. As it was now too late for navigating the Haisborough Channel they anchored in the Wold in seas which, breaking over their conning towers, caused *E5* to plunge with such force that her hydroplane guards tore her hull, resulting in a bad leak.

At dawn on the 23rd the three submarines proceeded in seas which reduced their speed so markedly that, in conformity with their orders for cancellation, they were forced to return to harbour. It was now that tragedy struck *D2*. In the heavy seas her captain, Lieutenant-Commander A.G. Jameson, was swept overboard. For several hours *D2* searched the area. The chances of survival in a sea whipped into a fury by gale-force winds was very slim. And so it proved to be for Arthur Jameson. *D2* returned to harbour under the command of her first lieutenant.

At twenty-nine years of age Lieutenant-Commander Clement Head, *D2*'s new captain, was two years younger than Jameson. Lieutenant-Commander Head was not to enjoy a long relationship with his new command. On 24 November he put to sea for a patrol in the North Sea. The submarine failed to return to harbour. Her loss is thought to have been due to an encounter with a German torpedo boat.

# 1915

The new year was not a week old when *C31* failed to return from patrol. The British were keen to add to their limited knowledge of German naval activities off the Belgian coast. Of particular interest was the submarine base at Zeebrugge, later to be the scene of an audacious assault by Royal Marines and Bluejackets*. In order for a watch to be maintained in the area, two submarines, *C31* and *C32*, were placed under the command of Commodore Roger Keyes.

With Lieutenant George Pilkington in command, *C31* sailed Harwich on 4 January. She was not seen again. Commodore Keyes set out on the night of 9-10 January with the destroyers *Lurcher* and *Firedrake* in hopes of making contact with Pilkington. When no trace of *C31* was found, the conclusion was that she had struck a mine of a German minefield off Zeebrugge. At the suggestion of Commodore Keyes the Royal Naval Air Service at Dunkirk was ordered to keep a look out for any sign of salvage operations; nothing that could reasonably be assumed to be such was observed however. *C31*'s loss had the effect of suspending the watch on Zeebrugge and *C32* was given other duties.

* Descriptive term for a sailor. Dates from 1858.

Two weeks later the *E10* (Lieutenant-Commander W. St J. Fraser) failed to return from patrol. On 18 January, *E5* (Lieutenant-Commander C.S. Benning), *E15* (Lieutenant-Commander T.S. Brodie), and *E10* put to sea from Harwich as part of a combined air and sea operation in the Heligoland Bight. Benning's *E5* arrived at her position, four miles north of Heligoland, at 0515 on the morning of the 19th. She cruised to the north- east throughout the 19th and 20th. On that first morning two destroyers were sighted near Heligoland and, from time to time, some Zeppelins. Next day the weather closed in.

*E15*, off the Ems, saw a Zeppelin and two submarines on the 19th, but was unable to get close enough for an attack. Neither of these two submarines saw anything of an enemy destroyer force which had been reported active, and for which they were on the look out.

Of Lieutenant-Commander William Fraser's *E10* nothing was seen nor heard. Fraser's billet had been NNW of Heligoland. There is a possibility that she met her fate in an enemy minefield, the existence of which was unknown at the time, that had been laid on 22 December.

Every once in a while British fishing trawlers would come under gunfire from U-boats. This form of attack opened the way for the adoption of a plan to lure German submarines into a position from which they could be destroyed. The scheme called for a trawler, outwardly conducting the business for which it was intended, to tow a submerged 'C' class submarine. The two vessels would remain in contact by means of a telephone line. If a U-boat surfaced to attack the bait, the British submarine would slip its tow and manoeuvre for a torpedo attack on the unsuspecting enemy. Success, after a near miss, came on 23 June when the trawler *Taranaki*, towing *C24*, attracted Lieutenant-Commander Gerhardt Furbinger's *U40*, which was then sunk by Lieutenant Frederick Taylor's *C24*.

On 27 July the trawler-submarine duo scored another success after Lieutenant Colin Cantile, captain of the trawler *Princess Louise*, informed Lieutenant-Commander Dobson (*C27*) that a U-boat had the trawler under observation. The outcome was that at 0811 Claude Dobson torpedoed *U23*.

On 31 July the trawler *Weelsby* (renamed *Malta* for these decoy operations) left Harwich to meet up with *C33* (Lieutenant G.E.B. Carter). Linked up, they were to patrol for two days in the hope of emulating *C24*'s and *C27*'s success. After completing the two-day operation Lieutenant Carter was to return to harbour. The *Malta* would meet up with *C34* and continue cruising for a further two days.

The trawler and *C33* patrolled for the allotted period without attracting any meaningful attention. At 2015 on the evening of 4 August Gerald Carter slipped the tow and started his return to harbour. Nothing further was heard of *C33* except for a few wireless signals: HAVE NOTHING TO COMMUNICATE. These ceased at 2150.

When Lieutenant Carter failed to return to harbour HMS *Firedrake* was dispatched at dawn 5 August to look for him. Apart from rescuing survivors from four sunken fishing smacks, the search proved unrewarding. During the course of the next three days further searches were carried out but no sign of *C33* or wreckage was reported. As the Germans made no claim for her sinking, *C33* is thought to have been mined.

Another 'C' class submarine to run foul of a mine was *C29*. This submarine was also part of a trawler – submarine team when she was lost on 29 August. The *C29* (Lieutenant W.R. Schofield) was actually in tow of the trawler *Ariadne* when she went down with the loss of all hands. The position given (53°59'N 1°25'E), though outside an area prohibited as mined, was really on a minefield that had been laid in January.

Even though none of the British submarines that took part in the Baltic Campaign returned home, the decision to send them to the Baltic seems justified in view of the turmoil their presence caused enemy shipping in that theatre.

British warships had no hope of forcing a passage into the Baltic Sea. For submarines the challenge looked very inviting, although even for them any attempt was bound to be a risky operation. If some submarines could reach the Baltic. . . The trouble they might create would give the Germans plenty to think about. A prime target would be the disruption of the vital iron-ore trade between Sweden and Germany. This alone would make the risks of a breakthrough worthwhile. Furthermore, the consternation of the German Navy, which had been using the Baltic Sea in which to exercise units of its High Seas Fleet, on discovering Royal Navy submarines on its doorstep would be an additional incentive for success.

The most dangerous part of the passage to the Baltic would come on rounding the Skaw. Mines would be a great hazard. So would sea- and air-patrols. Penetrating the Sound, the narrow channel which separates Sweden and Denmark, would be the biggest test of all. In places the Sound was too shallow for diving, and at the Baltic end of the narrow passage enemy destroyer patrols meant almost certain destruction if discovered.

Lieutenant-Commanders Noel Laurence (*E1*), Max Horton (*E9*)

and Martin Nasmith (*E11*) were three of the most experienced submarine captains in the Service. Their skill and daring made them a
fitting choice to pioneer the Baltic offensive. On the night of 15
October 1914 the *E1* and *E9* sailed Gorleston (Nasmith's *E11*
remained behind with engine trouble) and set off across the North
Sea to whatever lay ahead.

To his amazement Lieutenant-Commander Laurence had a relatively easy time. Laurence was able to break through the defences
and enter the Baltic without the Germans gaining the slightest suspicion that he had done so.

For Max Horton in *E9* the complete reverse was the case. An
engine fault forced him to drop behind Laurence and it was not until
the night of the 17th that he reached the entrance to the Sound. As he
had arrived too late to complete the passage through the Sound by
first light, he took *E9* to the bottom to await dusk of the following day.

Darkness was fast approaching when Horton gently raised *E9* for a
look-round before setting off towards the shallows of Flint Channel.
With Horton and his lookout keeping a sharp watch, *E9* made her
way silently through the darkness on one motor. A sudden increase
in destroyer activity gave Horton the uneasy feeling that the Germans were aware that submarines were attempting a breakthrough
into the Baltic.

And this was exactly so: Noel Laurence had inadvertently given
the game away. Laurence had assumed that Lieutenant-Commander Horton had followed him through the Sound and was safely in
the Baltic. This wrongful assumption had prompted Laurence to
chance a torpedo attack, on the German cruiser *Victoria Luise*, at ten
o'clock on the morning of the 18th, at which time Horton was lying
on the bottom waiting for darkness to arrive. As the wake of a torpedo was seen by the cruiser in good time for avoiding action to be
taken, the attack failed. On receipt of a signal from *Victoria Luise* the
Germans at once suspected that the attacking submarine had been
British, Russian submarines having displayed little enthusiasm
hitherto for attacking. From Kiel the Germans hurriedly dispatched
ships to augment patrols in the Sound. It was these reinforcements
which Max Horton was having to contend with.

Lieutenant-Commander Horton was manoeuvring *E9* through
the Sound when, quite suddenly and not a hundred yards to starboard, a German destroyer loomed out of the darkness. *E9*'s bridge
party made a silent but hectic dash below. *E9* had no sooner dived
when there was a thud followed by a loud scraping noise. A quick
check on the depth-gauge told the story. They had tried to dive in a

mere fourteen feet of water! With pounding hearts they waited for the destroyer to come in for the kill.

Nothing happened. It seemed impossible that the Germans could have failed to see *E9*. But this was in fact the case. Half an hour passed before Horton tentatively raised *E9* just sufficient to allow her conning tower to show above surface. Keeping a close watch on the destroyer Horton eased *E9* slowly forward and in a few minutes slipped out of immediate danger. After an encounter with another destroyer *E9* entered the Baltic to do battle.

It was two days before Lieutenant-Commander Nasmith was able to leave Gorleston. Certain that at least one British submarine was in the Baltic the Germans made an all-out effort to ensure that no more submarines breached the defences. Against such extensive precautions Nasmith had little chance. He made a determined attempt but the odds against him at that time were too great and he was obliged to abandon a worthwhile effort in the interest of his crew and submarine.

The sub-zero winter effectively limited the scope of operations for the submarines and it was not until the spring that they were able to extend their efforts with such impact that Prince Henry of Prussia, the German C-in-C Baltic, was positive that at least a flotilla of submarines was operating against the iron-ore trade from Sweden.

The success of *E1* and *E9* was viewed in London as confirmation that Their Lordships had been right in their decision to send submarines to the Baltic. Fighting in extremely difficult conditions the accomplishments of the two submarines was out of all proportion to their number and size. It was, therefore, natural that the small submarine force should be strengthened. To this end, Lieutenant-Commanders Geoffrey Layton and Francis Goodhart sailed Harwich on 14 August 1915.

Lieutenant-Commander Goodhart, the son of a vicar, put to sea in a mood of optimism – which was just as well for he was to experience a harrowing time in the Sound and could consider himself fortunate to meet up with Max Horton's *E9* outside Drageport in the Gulf of Finland. By 2100, on the 22nd, *E8* was safely tucked away in the harbour of Revel (now Tallinn).

For 31-year-old Geoffrey Layton in *E13* the attempt to fox the German defences was nothing short of disastrous. Layton had managed to navigate the Sound without incident until just after 2300 on the 17th when, still in Danish territorial waters, *E13* ran aground on a Saltholm mudbank. A faulty compass and a falling tide appeared to be the cause.

A belligerent warship is allowed sanctuary in neutral waters for up to twenty-four hours, after which the vessel has either to leave or remain interned with her crew. Not wishing to sample the undoubted warmth of Danish hospitality at that time, *E13*'s crew set to work to lighten the submarine for a rapid getaway on the next high tide.

*Thursday 19th*. At dawn *E13* was sighted by Danish and German units. At 0500 the Danish *Narhvalen* closed to within hailing distance and informed Lieutenant-Commander Layton that he would be given twenty-four hours to refloat *E13*. By this time Layton had reached the conclusion that his chances of refloating *E13* were slim; consequently he sent Lieutenant P.L. Eddis, his first lieutenant, across to the *Narhvalen* for transportation to the *Falster*, the guardship at anchor off the west coast of Saltholm. Eddis had been instructed to try and arrange a tow within the twenty-four hours limit. If this failed he was to negotiate terms for internment.

Shortly after *Narhvalen*'s time-limit warning a German destroyer approached *E13* but hauled off when she herself was approached by the Danish 1st Torpedo Boat Squadron (*Storen, Sbaekhuggeren, Soulven*) under the command of Captain E. Haach. The squadron anchored to the north of *E13*.

The crew of *E13* had by now ceased their effort to refloat and were taking things easy on the casing. All seemed peaceful: the German destroyer appeared to have been frightened off and *E13* was safe in neutral waters. But things were not as they appeared. At 0928 two German destroyers were seen closing at high speed from the south. Each vessel was flying the signal: ABANDON SHIP IMMEDIATELY. Before the submariners or the Danes could take action one of the destroyers fired two torpedoes at *E13* and raked her with machine-gun fire. The Danish *Soulven* hoisted a signal of protest. The torpedoes missed their target. The gunfire, however, was devastating. The submariners jumped into the water and struck out for the Danish ships. German gunfire was directed at the swimmers and had it not been for a Danish torpedo boat positioning herself between the desperate men in the water and the German gunners, casualties would have totalled far more than the fifteen men killed. Two of the twenty-three survivors were taken to hospital, while others were billeted in *Peder Skram*, where Captain Carstensen and his crew did everything possible to make the British as comfortable as conditions permitted. The following evening *Peder Skram* put the survivors ashore at Copenhagen for accommodation at the naval barracks.

Although restricted in their radius of movement, the British were well cared for by the Danes. Some of the crew were keen to escape but Layton, waiting for the question of *E13*'s future to be sorted out, forbade any such move.

Negotiations by Denmark for the purchase of *E13* were concluded by the end of August. Once the holes in *E13* had been patched and she had been pumped dry, she was taken to Copenhagen slung between the pontoons *Thor* and *Oden*. Though *E13* was later scrapped, parts of her machinery remained in service for many years. In 1929 her motors were sold to the Aarhus Electric Works. Two years later one of the motors was resold to a firm at Grenan, where it remained in faithful service until 1952.

Neither Layton nor Eddis remained in internment. Lieutenant Layton withdrew his parole and escaped to England. The son of a Liverpool solicitor, Admiral Sir Geoffrey Layton (who was C-in-C Portsmouth when he retired from the Navy in May 1947) died aged eighty in September 1964.

Lieutenant Paul Eddis also escaped. Interned aboard a Danish ship he used a barrel to row out to a British-owned yacht. Layton and Eddis will again feature in this history.

Lieutenant-Commander Layton's misfortune in the Sound did not extend to Lieutenant-Commanders R.C. Halahan (*E18*) and F.N. Cromie (*E19*). Despite the stringent defences both were able to force an entry into the Baltic. With these additions the flotilla was of sufficient strength to cause a major upset to enemy shipping.

In a difficult attack from 1,300 yards, Lieutenant-Commander Goodhart torpedoed the escorted German cruiser *Prinz Adalbert* on the morning of 5 October 1915. The cruiser sank in eight minutes. A few days later (11 October) Lieutenant-Commander Cromie singled out no less than five ships for attention. The first was the ore ship *Walter Leonhardt*.

The *Walter Leonhardt* was stopped by Cromie at 0940 whilst in passage from the northern Swedish port of Lulea to Hamburg with a cargo of iron-ore. After transferring the German crew to a passing Swedish ship, Cromie sank the enemy vessel with a charge of guncotton. Two hours later *E19* was in pursuit of the *Germania*, bound for Settin with a cargo of iron-ore.

*Germania*'s captain had no intention of stopping and, in his anxiety to escape *E19*, he inadvertently ran his ship aground. Cromie took *E19* alongside with the idea of taking off the crew, but they abandoned their ship before he could do so. After a failed attempt to tow

*Germania* off, Cromie left the ship to her fate.

The *Gutrune* was next to fall victim to *E19*. *Gutrune*'s crew was transferred to a neutral ship. *Gutrune* was then sunk.

A Swedish ship, the *Nyland*, was stopped by Cromie and then allowed to continue passage to Rotterdam. Shortly after this the *Direktor Rippenhagen*, a German ore ship, was ordered to stop. Once her crew were safely aboard a Swedish ship, the German ship was sent to the bottom.

The *Nicodemia* was in transit from Lulea to Hamburg when she ran foul of Cromie. The sighting of *E19* acted like a spur. *Nicodemia* made a dash for the Swedish coast in an endeavour to reach the safety of neutral waters. Francis Cromie put an end to this by firing a shot across her bows. *Nicodemia*'s crew was ordered to take to the ship's boat. When this had been completed a boarding party from *E19* set charges to put the ore ship on the seabed. Cromie then towed *Nicodemia*'s boat to the coast to bring an end to a most rewarding day.

The oncoming winter began to curtail submarine operations in the Baltic. By 17 November all five submarines were safely back at Reval (Tallinn), Estonia, to rest and prepare for the spring when the battle would be renewed with vigour. In mid-December Max Horton and Noel Laurence were recalled home.

The spring of 1916 saw the Baltic Flotilla again in the hunt for targets – targets which were now proving to be a good deal more elusive than had previously been the case. The success of the 'E' boats had created a situation whereby they had departed themselves of lone targets by forcing the Germans to introduce a convoy system as a means of reducing losses from submarine attacks. By now the flotilla had been re-inforced by four of the 'C' class submarines: *C26*, *C27*, *C32*, and *C35*.

On 23 May Lieutenant-Commander Robert Halahan (*E18*) fired a torpedo which found the destroyer *V100*. The result was that the destroyer's bow was blown clean away; nevertheless, good seamanship enabled her to limp back to harbour. The next day *E18* was lost without trace. Lieutenant-Commander Halahan, the son of an Army officer, left a widow.

As the summer months drew to a close the score-sheet of sinkings had few entries. The German convoy system was rigidly controlled and a profusion of escorts gave the submarine commanders a frustrating time.

By the spring of 1917 the flotilla was again on the offensive. However, the political situation in Russia was such that the campaign in the Baltic was rapidly drawing to its conclusion. The loss of *C32* (Lieutenant C.P. Satow) came within the dying weeks of the war in Russia.

Perhaps a certain measure of sympathy should be extended to Lieutenant Satow, whose troubles began even before he left harbour on 14 October. Because the Russian liaison officer assigned to *C32* had gone sick, Satow had to sail without such benefit. This being the case, the Russians refused to issue call-signs to *C32* as these and all secret papers had to be held by a Russian officer and were not allowed to be given to a Russian signalman. Furthermore, as the tracings to certain minefields were not readily available, the Russians informed Satow that he would have to sail without these too! Prospects for the patrol were, to say the least, interesting.

*Saturday 20th. C32* had been on patrol for six days. Part of Lieutenant Satow's report for this day states:

> At 1030 Lt Kershaw, being at the periscope, sighted a ship to the west of us. I started to attack her. She proved to be a large transport, with two funnels and one mast, painted grey and escorted by three trawlers with high funnels. One trawler was about half a mile ahead and the other two close in on either quarter. The sea was flat calm. The escorts seem to have been keeping poor lookout, as they did not see me until I fired my second torpedo, which I did at 1115 on the quarter and at a distance of 600 yards. When I put the periscope up to fire on the bow and on the beam, the boat was below her depth and I could not see. I therefore held her for a quarter shot, as I was well within range.
>
> I saw the bubbles of my first torpedo pass under the bows of the starboard escort, which was very close to me (I could almost see the faces of the crew). I then dived to 60 feet and, sixty seconds after firing the first torpedo, heard a loud explosion on my bow, followed fifteen seconds later by a second. The boat was then at 62 feet.
>
> A minute later propellers were heard overhead. A depth-charge was dropped, the explosion of which was very violent and sounded just overhead. After another half-minute, propellers were again heard and a second charge exploded. This seemed to be near my tail. The after diving-gauge broke and the compass light went out, as did several of the lights aft. The conning tower started to leak slightly from the forescuttle. I put the helm amidships, and then managed to get the compass visible once more.

But Lieutenant Satow's compass troubles were not at an end and the following day the faulty compass was to play a major part in his decision to beach *C32*. Lieutenant Satow's report continues:

I sighted Runö Island at 1600 and fixed my position. As soon as I had put the boat on her course again, the compass light went out. I then came to the surface and stripped down the compass. The ball itself was leaking and water was leaking in round the top cover. New lamps were put in and it was thoroughly dried out and the joints tightened up. At 1800 we went to the bottom until dark.

I came to the surface at 2000 hours to find that the compass had gone once more. Water had got into the electric leads and junctions, and the fuse would not hold. We worked on the compass until 2100 but could obtain no satisfaction; we got no reading of the card nor improvement in the earth.

I had now to decide on a definite course of action. I could not hope to round Serrel without a diving compass and I had only two days of provisions left, which could be extended to last for three days. I could find no scheme to save the boat, so considered the only thing I could do was to save the crew.

I had had no communication for about a week. I had no Russian code or call-signs and knew that Russian ships were not supplied with the AFR code. I knew Moon and Oesel were German and credited them with Pernau and all the coast of the Riga Gulf. The night was calm and misty with heavy rain and favourable for a landing. I therefore decided to beach the boat, destroy her, and attempt to break through with the crew to Revel. I had two days' food and might get more *en route*. The crew were to go in parties of twos and threes as it was more probable to avoid capture in this fashion. I selected Vaist Bay as a suitable landing place and was to make it at daybreak. If if I did not start immediately, the weather might break, and also all the food obtainable was necessary for the success of the scheme.

I made the land at 0520, October 21. At 0630 it was light enough to exactly fix my position. At 0730 I beached the boat, going full speed on the motors in order to get as close to the shore as possible. I sent Lt Kershaw in a small raft we had constructed to obtain a boat, while the remainder of the crew set to work to construct rafts out of lockers and woodwork.

Lt Kershaw signalled-off to say he needed assistance with the boat. As the rafts were failures, I called for volunteers to swim in. Four men started: Leading Stoker Selsby, Able Seamen Haynes and Jaggard, and Stoker Nally. The water was very cold, and the distance about 300 yards. Jaggard and Nally had to return on account of cramp, but the other two men reached the shore and launched the boat.

The crew were taken ashore. Lt Kershaw found some Russian soldiers who informed him that Pernau was in Russian hands. I therefore decided to delay destroying the boat and to land myself to obtain information. A sentry was left near the boat. The wooden gear was collected in case it should be possible to get the boat into Pernau.

The crew were taken by soldiers to a nearby farm, where they were billeted. The men were thoroughly tired out. The Russian soldiers, part of a Cossack patrol, rendered them great service and took the greatest pains for their comfort. I met a Russian officer. He knew very little about the situation, but gave me a horse and rode with me to Desdamo. From there I wired to ask for a tug to be sent. A reply came back from the Senior Naval Officer at Pernau to say that a tug would arrive at 2000. I then returned to Vaist, proceeded on board the boat, and got everything ready for the tug.

The tug, a patrol boat of about 150 hp, arrived at 0200. I blew all tanks and got her hawser secured to the towing pendant. The first two attempts she went ahead too quickly and parted the hawsers. Subsequently she took the strain slowly, but could get no movement on the boat. I worked the motors (both stopping and starting and going astern steadily) but without any result.

At 1600, the patrol boat having to return by daylight due to German patrols in the vicinity, arrangements were made to destroy the boat. Two 16-pound charges were placed, one in the crankpit and one by the hydroplane pedestal. As the fuses were uncertain – and at the most five minutes – I dared not use the torpedo heads, having only a leaky boat to get clear in. I did not like to keep the patrol boat in case she should have difficulty in getting clear. The charges fired when I was about a hundred yards clear.

The next morning I sent the crew by road to Pernau and went off to the boat to see if the charges had flooded her. The boat was full of chlorine and I could not see the damage – but she was not flooded. I got to the fore-end and succeeded in flooding through the tube. I then proceeded by road to Pernau. Two German destroyers were patrolling 4 miles or so to the westward, but took no notice of the submarine (probably she was invisible against the land).

The officer of the patrol boat deserves every credit for his services. He had navigated the boat from Pernau without a compass, and with German destroyers in the vicinity.

All the books and papers were destroyed by sinking them on the night of Saturday 20 October. I kept no papers of any sort on landing. Exact courses and times, therefore, cannot be given.

Command of a submarine is always difficult. Working with the Russians in the Baltic, particularly towards the end of the campaign, was for much of the time quite frustrating. Some of the frustrations experienced by COs comes through in Lieutenant Satow's response to questions concerning the beaching of *C32*.

QUESTION: 'You stated that you could not obtain the position of the minefields off Pernau. How long would it have taken you to obtain the tracings?'

LT SATOW: 'If the tracings had been ready in the office of the staff on board the *Libabua*, I could have obtained them at once. But they told me they could not be found, and as the staff required me to leave immediately, the Staff Navigator pointed out that the first minefield ran from a point close to Kuno Island to Gainash and it was impossible to go into Pernau.'

QUESTION: 'Was it possible to obtain clear orders of what you were to do in case you could not get back to Kuivast?'

LT SATOW: 'No – as they wished the boat to leave as soon as possible owing to some cruisers going out an hour later, and there were a great many Russian officers all trying to obtain information. The Russian staff were of the opinion that Kuivast would be open, and so I had difficulty in getting them to discuss any movements should Kuivast fall. Also, they did not appear to think that the question of minefields off Serrel or Pernau of great importance.'

QUESTION: 'Had you a list of signal and telephone stations in the Gulf of Riga?'

LT SATOW: 'Yes.'

QUESTION: 'Why did you not get into communication with them when you were in difficulties?'

LT SATOW: 'Because I believed the coast to be in German hands and I considered that one of the first places the Germans would take possession of would be the signal stations, and so to approach these within visible distance would bring the boat in shallow waters where she would be in a most dangerous position.'

QUESTION: 'Did the Russians made any arrangements whatever in case you had to make a wireless signal?'

LT SATOW: 'No. On a previous occasion, when going on a reconnaissance trip in the Gulf of Riga, I asked to be allowed the use of a temporary code. But after thinking about it they refused to allow this and told me that if I had anything of importance to report I should return.'

Christopher Satow, a popular officer of wide experience, had been a submariner since January 1912.

*

Imperial Russia had entered the war in 1914 with a degree of enthusiasm. But by 1917 a series of defeats and a shortage of military goods and food supplies had produced a state of collapse. In March

1917 there were clashes between strikers and troops in Petrograd (Leningrad). When the Czar abdicated, a provisional government was formed. Part of its programme was to continue the war. The government allowed the return of the Bolshevik leaders from exile; within a few months the Bolsheviks had gained control of the Soviets. The Petrograd Soviet proposed that its executive should seize power. The Soviet formed a Military Revolutionary Committee which ordered an uprising on 6 and 7 November. All public buildings in Petrograd were occupied and the Bolsheviks announced the fall of the provisional government.

In Moscow and elsewhere similar events were taking place. Two important factors for the success of the Bolsheviks was that they had promised they would seize all large estates for distribution among the peasants and make peace with Germany. By 17 November an armistice had been signed with Germany. One of its terms specified the surrender of the British submarines. Francis Cromie, then Senior Naval Officer Baltic, refused to accept the armistice and moved the flotilla to Helsingfors (Helsinki) in Finland.

When the German Army made a landing at Hango, seventy miles from Helsingfors, it was clear that the end was not too far off. There was no hope of the British submarines escaping from the Baltic. As surrender was out of the question the remaining alternative was to render the flotilla useless to the enemy. The following narrative of the destruction of the Baltic Flotilla is by the officer entrusted with the task.

'At 1130 on April 3 I received the following note from Captain Cromie, who had arrived in Helsingfors the previous day:

LANDING TAKING PLACE AT HANGO FROM THREE LARGE TRANSPORTS. MAKE EVERY EFFORT TO GET TUGS, SEIZING THEM IF NECESSARY, AND PROCEED WITH DESTRUCTION.

Having fixed up matters with three Russian officers who had volunteered to help with the destruction, and having given instructions with regard to the submarines for sea, I went to interview the captain of the dockyard regarding the service of an ice-breaking tug. There were, apparently, a score of reasons why a tug could not be provided, and a tug master was called in to corroborate the captain of the dockyard's statement. Realising that argument would be futile I agreed that the provision of a tug was obviously impossible, but said that it was very unfortunate as, of course, the submarines had to be destroyed and we would have to blow them up where they lay, which

I was afraid might cause considerable damage to the dockyard and to ships in the vicinity. They then decided that it might after all be possible to provide a tug, the *Zavtra*, the next day. I told them that this was of no use and started to leave them; they called me back and in a few minutes it was arranged that a tug would be available in half an hour. I discovered subsequently that the tug-master's house was within fifty yards of where the submarines were lying.

'The tug arrived within half an hour and broke up the ice round the submarines. At 1315 I went ahead in *E1*, astern of the ice-breaker, and was followed by *E9*, *E8*, and *E19*, with Russian officers in charge. As I wanted fairly deep water for the destruction, I had chosen a spot off Grohara Lighthouse, about ten miles south of Hel-singfors. When we reached the spot *E1* and *E19* were secured alongside each other. The primers were inserted in the charges and the alarm clocks set for about an hour ahead, allowing for any inac-curacy. The final electrical connections were made and we reboarded the tug and moved ourselves to a respectable distance. *E8* and *E9* came alongside and were prepared for destruction in a simi-lar manner.

'The alarm clocks were fairly accurate; within a few minutes of the hour a sheet of flame shot up from *E1* and *E19*. This was followed by a column of water and a dense cloud of smoke. When the latter had cleared away there was nothing but a large patch of clear water to mark the spot where two submarines had been. The final prepara-tions were made in *E8* and *E9*. This time, having rather more confi-dence in the accuracy of the clocks, we set them only about half an hour ahead. The tug backed away through the ice and we waited for the explosion.

'It came within a few minutes of the half hour – but when the smoke cleared away, whilst there was no sign of *E9*, *E8* was still remaining apparently quite undamaged. We waited another half hour to allow for any inaccuracy in the clocks and then instructed the captain of the tug to go alongside. This he was most unwilling to do but we assured him that there was no danger and I endeavoured to add weight to my argument by toying with my revolver. We went alongside and my first action, on getting down the conning tower hatch, was to cut every wire I could see without pausing to investi-gate the source of the trouble. When we did investigate we found that one of the brushes of the clock was just failing to make contact, only the thickness of a sheet of paper separated it from the connecting strip. We were devoutly grateful that the tug had made a good 'alongside' as a slight bump would, in all probability, have been sufficient to complete the circuit. A spare clock was connected up in *E8* and was again set half an hour ahead. The tug shoved off.

'Half an hour passed and nothing happened . . . Three quarters of an hour . . . An hour. We realised that the circuit had failed again in some way. It was then getting late and as the tug captain was very unwilling to operate in the ice in the dark, it was decided to make no further attempt to destroy *E8* that night but to leave her where she was, stuck in the ice, to be destroyed with the 'C' boats on the following day. We returned at Helsingfors and I arranged for the tug to be available at six o'clock the following morning.

'At 0700 on April 4 we proceeded to sea, the tug towing our torpedo barge with *C26* and *C35* following astern. On our return to harbour the previous night, I had received a message from Captain Cromie asking me to retain one submarine until the last possible moment. He foresaw the possibility of the Russians attempting to prevent our leaving Helsingfors, in which case he proposed that we should make use of the submarine for escaping to Sweden, taking him with us. *C27* had been left behind for this purpose.

'The tug went alongside *E8*. We were unable to find any fault in the circuit or anything to account for the failure. We fitted new fuses and renewed the wiring. *C26* was secured alongside *E8* and both boats were connected to one clock. Again we allowed an interval of half an hour for getting clear and the explosion took place well up to this time. When the smoke cleared away we were relieved to see that both submarines had disappeared. *C35* was then secured alongside the torpedo barge. Two attempts were made to blow them up but on each occasion the circuits failed. After the second failure the tug captain refused to stay out any longer. Short of commandeering the tug there was nothing for it but to return to harbour. I decided to go back and find out how matters stood with regard to the approach of the Germans, and if necessary bring the tug out again with *C27* and complete the destruction.

'At our return I found there was no possibility of the Germans reaching Helsingfors during the following day. I also got information from Captain Cromie that the Russians would not attempt to prevent our departure and, further, that a train would be leaving Helsingfors for Petrograd the following evening. It was therefore unnecessary to complete the destruction until the following morning.

'During the day a small party had been left ashore to destroy some forty of our torpedoes. The swirlers and sinking mechanism of the torpedoes, being considered confidential, had previously been removed and dropped overboard from *E1* when she had proceeded to sea for destruction. The torpedoes were blown through with undiluted sulphuric acid and then the three members of the party got busy on them with sledge-hammers. I hadn't time to see the results of their efforts myself but was informed by the Stoker PO in charge that they had "left a nasty mess for the Russians to clear up".

'Early the following morning I proceeded to sea again in *C27*, accompanied by the ice-breaking tug. There wasn't time to chance a failure of the electrical circuits (particularly as the Germans had advanced more quickly than had been expected and were reported as being only twenty miles away) so it was desired just to sink the two submarines.

'The same procedure was carried out in each case; the boat was trimmed down alongside the tug and the forehatch opened up; the bowcaps and rear doors of both torpedo tubes were then opened slightly and as the water came rushing in we scuttled up the forehatch and jumped on board the tug. In each case, about three minutes after the submarines had disappeared below the surface, a heavy explosion occurred which threw up a column of water about twelve feet high. I image these explosions must have been caused by the rapid formation of chlorine in the battery tanks when the salt-water reached the cells. In any case we had not anticipated anything of this sort happening and the first explosion shook up the tug rather badly. On the second occasion we retired to a respectable distance . . .'

The British contribution to the Baltic Campaign was over; with the exception of Captain Cromie all the submariners were sent home. Cromie became Naval Attaché at the British Embassy in Petrograd. During the remainder of his stay in Russia Captain Cromie worked hard to further the Allied cause against Germany. On 31 August 1918 Francis Cromie lost his life when, entirely alone, he stood on the steps of the Embassy denying entrance to a wild mob intent on plunder. Captain Cromie, thirty-six at the time of his death, has never received adequate recognition for his work during this crucial period.

*

The war had assumed a new dimension when in November 1914 Turkey entered the conflict. In early 1915 the Allies decided to force the Dardanelles in the hope that a successful operation would knock

Turkey out of the war. Subsequent events proved that those who feared the wisdom of such a bold operation were perhaps right to do so. The Gallipoli Campaign was a costly failure, and was to be the cause of much heated controversy for many years. British submarines emerged from the campaign with high honours and the admiration of all.

Great Britain and Turkey had been on cordial relations for many years but this relationship came under severe strain when in September 1914 the British Government, wary that Turkey might one day become an enemy, seized two magnificent dreadnought battleships being built for the Turks in British yards at a cost of nearly four million pounds. Naturally the seizure of the battleships, destined to be the pride of the Turkish Navy, angered the Turks. Germany, however, was delighted with developments and immediately took the opportunity of enhancing friendship with Turkey by making the Turks a gift of the new 22,600 tons battle-cruiser *Goeben*, the fastest and most powerful ship in the Mediterranean, and her consort *Breslau*, a light cruiser of 4,500 tons. The Turks welcomed the gift with open arms. By 10 August the two ships had passed through the Dardanelles and into the Sea of Marmara to take refuge in Constantinople (Istanbul). On 28 October *Goeben*, with other units of the Turkish Navy, bombarded Russian Black Sea ports, thereby making it evident where her allegiance lay.

The Sea of Marmara and the winding straits, known as the Dardanelles, that link it with the Aegean form a water frontier of some 200 miles between Europe and Asia. Events of great historical significance have taken place at this meeting place of East and West. Between October 1914 and January 1916 the Dardanelles would once again be the scene of great importance.

As an insurance against the *Goeben* and *Breslau* venturing back through the Dardanelles the British set up a blockade of the Straits, using as a base of operations Mudros at the Greek island of Lemnos, forty miles from the Dardanelles. In October 1914 the spacious harbour of Mudros thronged with shipping of all types. Submarines, as might be expected, were also in evidence.

An attempt by a submarine to pass through the Dardanelles to the Sea of Marmara was considered by some to be a foolhardy undertaking. Mines were probably the main obstacle. But apart from mines, in early 1915 the defence of the Dardanelles included forts, mobile howitzers, shore-mounted torpedo tubes, and searchlights to discourage night attempts. On both banks of the Straits, the strategically sited forts could muster about 150 guns, some of doubtful vintage, varying in calibre from 6-inch to 14-inch. Patrol craft and, later on, anti-submarine nets were also to be taken into consideration.

The 40-mile-long straits are less than a mile wide at their narrowest point, appropriately called The Narrows, and up to four miles wide at their broadest. From the Sea of Marmara (roughly half the size of Wales) a current varying between two and five knots flowed towards the Aegean. And it was this current, which had protected Constantinople from invaders by sea for centuries, that was to create problems for submarine commanders. Against such a strong current no submarine could hope to cover the entire length of the straits underwater without having to risk coming to the surface to recharge its batteries. Another danger which could, and did, provide some harrowing moments was that at about 60 feet there was a stratum of fresh water which, owing to its different density, made depth keeping no easy matter. To sum up: the Dardanelles was a nasty place to take a submarine.

In the early days at Mudros, the submarine flotilla consisted of three French submarines and three British 'B' class boats: *B9, B10*, and *B11*. The flotilla's main duty was to keep a weather-eye on the entrance to the Dardanelles. But on the morning of 13 December the *B11* (Lieutenant N.D. Holbrook) entered the Straits and after a ten-mile run torpedoed the old battleship *Messudieh* anchored at Sari Sighlar Bay. For this action Norman Holbrook was awarded the Victoria Cross, the first to be gained by the Submarine Service.

Lieutenant Holbrook's success prompted a request for some of the 'E' class to be sent to the Aegean. With the 'E's the way would be open for a possible breakthrough into the Sea of Marmara to attack Turkish communications to Gallipoli during the proposed April landings on the Gallipoli Peninsula.

Four months passed before the requested 'E' boats arrived at Mudros. In the meantime the French submarine *Saphir* arrived off the Dardanelles. The Frenchman had a new battery which her CO, apparently against orders, decided to put to good use by entering the straits on 15 January 1915. *Saphir* managed to get past The Narrows only to run aground off Nagara Point and was lost.

The Australian *AE2* arrived at Mudros in early February. By April she had been joined by *E1, E14*, and *E15*. Lieutenant-Commander Theodore Brodie (captain of *E15* and twin brother of C.G. Brodie, captain of *C11* when sunk in 1909) left Mudros in an attempt to infiltrate the Marmara. *E15* entered the Straits just before dawn on 17 April. Brodie had submerged in preparation for his run beneath the minefield when the treacherous current took a hold of *E15* and swept her ashore at Kephez Point, twelve miles into the straits and directly under the guns of Fort Dardanus. The Turks opened fire at once. Brodie blew tanks and went full astern in an effort to free *E15*. But she was too hard aground and refused to budge. A Turkish torpedo boat closed in. As Brodie opened the conning tower hatch a shell exploded against the hull and killed him. Another shell struck the battery compartment, forcing the crew to make their way topside and surrender.

Aircraft of the Royal Naval Air Service had been in the air since first light, so news that *E15* was aground was soon known at Mudros. At a hastily convened conference aboard the *Hindu Kush*, HQ and parent ship of Allied submarines at Mudros, it was quickly decided that everything possible should be done to prevent *E15* falling into enemy hands. The decision made, there was no time lost in sending *B6* (Lieutenant R.E. Birch) into the Straits to torpedo *E15*.

The Turks were expecting an attempt to be made to destroy *E15*. When Birch put in an appearance he was given a hot reception. Two torpedoes fired by *B6* both missed the target even though Birch had taken *B6* as close to *E15* as was possible.

With the coming of darkness the destroyers *Scorpion* and *Grampus* entered the Straits with the intentions of shelling *E15*. Caught by powerful searchlights the destroyers came under heavy gunfire and had to withdraw before they were able to locate the submarine.

The following morning, 18 April, Norman Holbrook went into the Straits with *B11*. Heavy mist prevented Holbrook from trying to deliver *E15* a fatal blow. Later that day the battleships *Triumph* and *Majestic* were ordered to try their luck. Gunfire from both shores kept the battleships from getting closer than 12,000 yards, a range that was too great for their big guns to bear on *E15* with accuracy. The battleships withdrew.

The destruction of *E15* had now become a matter of some urgency. That the Turks would shortly be in a position to salvage *E15* had become evident. Time had almost, but not completely, run out for the British. Feeling that they were still in with a chance, the Navy decided to make one final daring fling. The officer chosen to lead the enterprise was Lieutenant-Commander E.G. Robinson.

The plan called for two 56-foot steam picket-boats (one from *Triumph* with Robinson and the other from *Majestic* with Lieutenant C. Goodwin in charge) to make a dash into the straits. It was thought that being small the two picket-boats – each equipped with two 14-inch torpedoes carried in 'dropping gear' mounted one either side – would be able to creep towards *E15* unobserved. If they should be sighted it was hoped that the darkness, their speed, and their small size would be their salvation.

The two picket-boats were not detected until searchlights singled them out within a few hundred yards of *E15*. Gunfire came at them thick and fast. blinded by the searchlights 'Kipper' Robinson's first torpedo missed. Suddenly a carelessly directed searchlight beam swept momentarily over *E15*. For Lieutenant Claude Goodwin that was long enough; Goodwin saw *E15* and within seconds his torpedoes were on their way.

A violent explosion indicated that the mission had achieved some measure of success. Both picket-boats were about to clear the area when Lieutenant Goodwin's boat received a direct hit. Without hesitation Eric Robinson took his own boat alongside Goodwin's. The crew were hurriedly transferred. Amid shell bursts which threatened to blast them out of the water, the picket-boat made a shaky retreat. *B6* was able to confirm that the attack had destroyed *E15*.

Next to tempt fate in the Dardanelles was Lieutenant-Commander H.G.D. Stoker with *AE2*. Born in Ireland in 1885, Hew Stoker, with no tradition of the sea behind him, left home at fifteen to join 250 other cadets in *Britannia*. He was twenty-three when appointed CO of his first submarine, *A10*. But it was as captain of one of the 'B' class that he, with other submarines of the class, sailed for Gibraltar to help establish the Navy's first overseas submarine base. Lieutenant-Commander Stoker was still serving in Gibraltar when he heard that Australia was having two submarines built at Barrow. He applied for command of one of them and in due course was informed that he had been appointed captain of *AE2*. Five 'E' class were already in commission when Stoker arrived at Barrow towards the end of 1913. On completion of *AE2*'s trials Stoker, as noted elsewhere, set out for Australia.

Shortly after the disappearance of *AE1* (Lieutenant-Commander Besant) *AE2* had returned to Sydney for a refit. Stoker began persuading the powers that be that his command would be of greater value fighting with the Royal Navy. Permission for *AE2* to leave Home Waters to join British forces was given. On 31 December 1914, *AE2* steamed north, eventually joining shipping at Tenedos Island near the Dardanelles.

*Friday 23 April 1915.* It had been a week since Brodie's abortive attempt to enter the Marmara. As soon as the moon had dipped below the horizon, *AE2* left her anchorage. Shortly after midnight she passed the entrance to the Straits. *AE2* was near the area of the Suandere River before a searchlight at Kephez Point forced her under. She had barely slipped beneath the surface when the shaft which worked the forward hydroplane broke, thus putting any further advance into the Straits out of the question. Stoker could only turn about and make a dash back towards the entrance in an effort to clear the Straits before daylight. Disappointed beyond words, he rejoined the waiting ships before retiring to an anchorage to repair the offending hydroplane shaft.

By noon that same day, the defect had been made good. Stoker was assured that his ill-luck had not altered the situation and that he could try again the following evening.

*Sunday 25 April.* It was 0300 when the Australian boat once again entered the Dardanelles. At about the same time a mass of Allied shipping was advancing towards the enemy coast. The controversial assault on the Gallipoli Peninsula had been launched.

With no moon to point an accusing finger through broken clouds, Hew Stoker was able to hold a steady course up the darkened Straits. From time to time the beam of a searchlight on the eastern (Asiatic) shore swept briefly over *AE2*. The sudden shattering of the stillness by the loud bang of a Turkish gun made Stoker jump. The swish of the shell as it passed overhead was heard by the bridge party. For a fleeting moment Stoker felt angry with himself for allowing the enemy to catch sight of *AE2*. He dived with all speed.

That the submarine was passing through a minefield was made uncomfortably clear by the scraping of the mines' mooring wires along her hull. These tense moments were made even more perilous by Stoker having to snatch an occasional look through the periscope to check progress. It was during one of these 'directional looks' that Stoker noted, not without relief, that he had negotiated the minefield and was about 300 yards below The Narrows.

Should an opportunity present itself, Stoker was under orders to sink any vessel that looked capable of laying mines. When the tip of his periscope broke the mirror-like surface in search of possible targets, it was soon recognised and fired on.

Encountering a small cruiser Stoker fired a torpedo and then ordered 70 feet. A destroyer, intent on ramming, passed directly overhead just as the torpedo hit the target. It was not long after this incident that *AE2* ran aground close to a Turkish fort. She was fired on but as the Turkish gun could not be depressed sufficiently, no hits were registered.

On reaching Nagara Point Stoker observed a variety of vessels searching for him. The Turks were making a concentrated effort, knowing that beyond Nagara Point the straits widened out, thereafter making their task much more difficult. *AE2* was taken to 90 feet. When she was again brought to periscope depth Nagara Point was seen to be astern.

Towards 0730 *AE2* approached the town of Gallipoli. Here Stoker discovered a large number of fishing boats strung out across the Straits from shore to shore. Hew Stoker, not unreasonably, assumed that the boats were there because he was there. Taking *AE2* down to 70 feet he passed under the line without difficulty and at 0900 on the 26th was able to transmit a signal stating that HMAS *AE2* was in the Marmara. The passage through the straits had taken thirty hours.

Back at Mudros the news that *AE2* was in the Marmara acted like a tonic. The landings on the Peninsula had met with greater resistance than anticipated (for a time an evacuation could not be ruled out). With *AE2* now a threat to Turkish supply lines, the situation became slightly more bearable.

Within hours of receiving Stoker's signal the *E14* (Lieutenant-Commander E.C. Boyle) was on her way to join him. After several encounters with the enemy, Courtney Boyle arrived safely in the Marmara on the 29th.

Had *AE2* been armed with a gun, her disruption of shipping to the Gallipoli Peninsula would have been more rewarding, and a lot easier. Nevertheless, Stoker made himself as much of a nuisance as possible and in days sea traffic had reduced noticeably, an indication of the influence a submarine can have on an enemy's shipping.

Hew Stoker had been in the Marmara for four days when he encountered Lieutenant-Commander Boyle. After planning a rendezvous in Atarki Bay for the following morning, the two submarines parted for the night.

*Friday 30 April* Lieutenant-Commander Stoker was proceeding to Atarki Bay for his meeting with Boyle when he sighted what he believed to be *E14* at about five miles. Thirty minutes later *AE2* arrived at the position but as nothing could be seen of *E14* it was assumed that she had dived and was making west to investigate some smoke seen to be coming from a Turkish torpedo boat, the *Sultan Hissar*. As the Turk was on a heading which would take her close to *AE2*'s position, Stoker dived with the intention of remaining submerged until the torpedo boat had cleared the area. Observing another vessel to the south, he set off for a closer look.

*AE2* was making steady underwater progress when quite suddenly, and with no warning that something was about to go drastically wrong, she assumed a bow-up angle and began to rise rapidly towards the surface. Having ignored all attempts to keep her down *AE2* broke surface a mere hundred yards from the *Sultan Hissar*. The Turks opened fire at what would probably be the most lucrative target they would ever encounter. By ordering the flooding of a forward tank Stoker managed to ease the desperate situation. The wayward submarine dived back beneath the surface.

Once under the water *AE2* went down . . . and down . . . and down. There was no stopping her. At 100 feet she reached the limit registered on her depth-gauge. It was not until Stoker ordered full speed astern that *AE2* halted her downwards trend and started to move upwards – slowly at first and then with increasing speed until she broke surface again.

The submarine lay invitingly on the surface. The Turk fired two torpedoes. Both missed. *AE2* dipped her bows and then went careering towards the bottom at a steeper angle and faster than before. The crew had great difficulty remaining on their feet. Nevertheless, they managed to check the alarming descent, again by putting the motors to full astern. As before, *AE2* began to rise towards the surface. The *Sultan Hissar* was waiting. What happened next is told by Hew Stoker in his book *Straws In The Wind*.

> BANG!. . . . . . A cloud of smoke in the engine room. We were hit and holed! And again in quick succession two more holes.
>
> Finished! We were caught! We could no longer dive and our defence was gone. It but remained to avoid useless sacrifice of life. All hands were ordered on deck and overboard.
>
> The holes in the hull were all above water, and therefore not in themselves sufficient to sink the boat, though preventing all possibility of diving. While the crew scrambled up on deck, an officer remained with me below to take the necessary steps for sinking. The third officer, on the bridge, watched the rising water to give warning in time for our escape. A shout from him and we clambered up: but through the conning tower windows I saw there was still a minute to spare. I jumped down again and had a last look round – for, you see, I was fond of *AE2*.
>
> What a sight! Pandemonium – I cannot attempt to describe it – food, clothing, flotsam and jetsam of the weirdest sorts floating up on the fast-entering water in the place which we had been so proud to keep neat and clean. . . .

An anxious shout from above: 'Hurry, sir, she's going down!'

In the wardroom my eye was caught by my private dispatch-case, which contained, I remembered, some money. That was bound to be useful – I ran and picked it up, and darted up the conning tower.

As I reached the bridge the water was about two feet from the top of the conning tower; besides this only a small portion of the stern was out of water. On it were clustered the last half-dozen of the crew, the remainder were overboard.

Curious incidents impress one at such times. As those last six men took the water the neat dive of one of the engine room ratings will remain pictured in my mind for ever.

Perhaps a minute passed, and then, slowly and gracefully, like the lady she was, without sound or sigh, without causing an eddy or a ripple on the water, *AE2* just slid away on her last and longest dive.

Hew Stoker was rescued from the Marmara by the torpedo boat's dinghy. Feeling utterly miserable he clambered over the side of the *Sultan Hissar* to be received by her captain, a pleasant man who assured him that all the crew had been rescued. Thinking that things could have been a lot worse, Lieutenant-Commander Stoker was taken to Constantinople and captivity.

Lieutenant-Commander Boyle remained in the Marmara for three weeks. With the current to his advantage, Boyle made a speedy return to harbour. His place in the inland sea was taken by Lieutenant-Commander Martin Nasmith. Both Boyle and Nasmith were to be awarded the Victoria Cross for their work in the Marmara.

Lieutenant-Commander Nasmith left the Marmara on 5 June. By the 10th, Courtney Boyle was on his way back for a second tour. Eight days later Lieutenant-Commander K.M. Bruce (*E12*) was on his way to join him.

Unknown to Bruce, soon after Boyle's second passage the Turks positioned a net of steel mesh across the narrowest part of the Straits. Bruce ran into it. The line of buoys marking the net's position gave warning to the boats patrolling its length that somewhere below was a submarine.

Ken Bruce's first reaction was to ease *E12* out of the net by going slowly astern. When this failed, Bruce ordered full speed astern, the net still refused to release its captive. Full astern, followed by full ahead, went *E12* until she finally burst through the steel web. Though *E12* reached the Marmara the straining of her electric motors at the net had harmed them sufficiently to cause concern.

After meeting up with Commander Boyle on the 21st, Bruce spent two days working on the electric motors in an attempt to alleviate the

Lt A. G. Jameson (left) and his friend Lt N. Laurence. As a lieutenant-commander, Jameson was destined to be washed off the bridge of his boat, the *D2*, and lost in November 1914. Lt Laurence went on to become one of the legendary names in the British submarine service, being the only person to hit three battleships with torpedoes, the *Moltke, Grosser Kurfürst* and the *Kronprinz.*

Officers and ratings in their No 1 uniforms, proud of their new boat and confident that the six-inch howitzer would make life difficult for the Turks. The *E20* made the difficult passage into the Sea of Marmara but *UB14* finished her very brief career.

*E18* and the officers lost in her: Sub-Lt D. N. Colson RNR, Lt-Cdr R. C. Halahan and Lt W. L. Lansdale. Because they look so clean, it is probable that they are going on patrol.

(*Left*) Signalman W. R. C. Dowsett (who was lost in the *D5*) in his pre-war dress which was usual for submarine ratings of the period. Unlike the Germans the Admiralty paid no regard to comfort or suitable heavy weather dress for submariners who suffered agonies in WWI with bridges protected only by canvas. WWII started with nothing changed but happily Lt-Cdr G. C. Philips persuaded a reluctant Admiralty to order Barbour suits for submarine lookouts and in his honour they were known as Ursula suits after his magnificent boat, the *Ursula*. (*Right*) Lt George Pilkington in command of the *C31*.

*C31* was a very early casualty of the war, being lost off Zeebrugge in January 1915. This photograph was taken in the halcyon days of peace with the submarine arriving on the surface from another port, as bicycles can be seen on the casing!

(*Top*) *B10* in dock at Venice after being sunk in August 1916 by a canvas and wire Austrian air-craft, a harbinger of things to come. Twenty-five years later aircraft became the weapon most feared by the submarine, the weapon that changed the course of the U-boat war. British sub-marines feared the RAF as much as the Germans did! (*Centre*) *K22* (ex-*K13*) dives in slow time. Not content with putting funnels on submarines, the Admiralty also added depth charge throwers to most of the 'K' class submarines. The thrower on *K22* can be seen to the right of the after funnel. Even more bizarre was the fact that *J1* was fitted with internal chutes for dropping depth charges and, incredibly, two days before war ended she attacked a U-boat with them off Gibraltar.

*E43* at Harwich. By the greatest of misfortune on a black, stormy January night, *E43* collided with another submarine, fairly certainly the hapless *E36*.

The ratings of *G9* pose before leaving on their last patrol. The only survivor, Stoker William Drake, is on the extreme right, picked out of the water by the *Pasley*, the ship which *G9* tried to sink.

Soldiers stand and gape at the *K4*, high and dry early on in her life. *K4* had a very brief career, falling victim to Admiralty foolishness; the K boats were sent to sea in darkness, at speed, in company with cruisers, battle-cruisers and battleships, which resulted in the so-called 'Battle of May Island'.

(*Left*) Signalman G. T. W. Kimbell in 1917 when serving in HM Destroyer *Acasta*. Now, aged 91, he is one of the last survivors of the steam-driven 'K' class submarines. Prior to surviving the loss of *K17*, he served in HMS *Caernarvon* in the successful action at the Falklands in December 1914. Chief Yeoman of Signals Kimbell is also a veteran of World War II.

damage caused by their prolonged use at full power. After an adventurous week in the Marmara *E12*, with motors needing the attention of a workshop, made her way through the Straits to Mudros.

At 0200 on 4 September 1915, 33-year-old Lieutenant-Commander A.D. Cochrane (*E7*) set off from Kaphale Bay for a second tour of the Marmara. Confident of success, Cochrane passed Cape Helles at 0500. The night being calm and bright *E7* was dived when abreast of Achi Baba. At 0630 *E7* passed Kilid Baba, the periscope being fired on from 200 yards by the fort. At 0730 Cochrane sighted the buoys of the A/S net off Nagara Point. Altering course to cross the net at right angles, he dived to 100 feet and increased speed to 7½ knots. Shortly after *E7* had reached a hundred feet, her bows were heard cutting the net. The thick wire mesh gave under the powerful thrust of *E7*'s motors and for a time it looked as if Cochrane might break through and continue on to the Marmara. But it was not to be. A torn piece of net snarled the starboard propeller and wound itself round the shaft before the starboard motor could be shut down. Lieutenant-Commander Cochrane takes up the narrative:

'In spite of this the boat's head continued to fall off to port until at the end of ten minutes, by which time the starboard propeller was clear, the boat was lying on the northern side of the net parallel to and much entangled with it. In order to keep the propellers clear of the net I decided to turn the boat's head to the southward and pass through the net. At 0830 a mine exploded a few hundred feet from the boat, no damage being done.'

Assisted by the net's surface marker buoys, which gave warning each time *E7* made a move, enemy patrol craft kept a close eye on the submarine's struggle.

Lieutenant-Commander Cochrane: 'After about two hours of manoeuvring, the boat was turned to the southward and, from depths between 60 to 130 feet, repeated attempts to get clear of the net were made by going alternately full speed ahead and astern. Although several meshes of the net were carried away it was impossible to gather sufficient weight to completely clear the many parts which were holding the boat fore and aft.

'*1030*. A mine was exploded close to the boat. The explosion was violent but no damage was done to the hull. After this explosion the boat was considerably freer than before. In the hope that further attempts to blow up the boat might result in completely freeing her, I decided to remain submerged at a good depth till after dark, when it might be possible to come to the surface and clear the obstruction. Burned all confidential papers.

'By 1400 the battery power was much reduced and further attempts to get clear were given up for the time.

'*1840*. A mine was exploded a few feet from the hull. The explosion was very violent, electric lights and other fittings being broken. The motors were at once started in the hope that the net had been destroyed. But this was not the case. The presence of enemy craft on the surface having made it impossible to come to the surfaace after dark, and so clear the obstruction, I decided to go at once to the surface and remove the crew from the boat before blowing her up.

'The boat was brought to the surface without difficulty and when the conning tower was above water Lieutenant John Scaife went on deck to surrender the crew. Fire was immediately opened on him from light guns ashore and three motor boats.

'As soon as the excitement had died down and the officers had gained control of their men, two motor boats came alongside and the officers and men were taken off without difficulty. This operation was carried out by German submarine officers. The boat was sunk immediately she was clear of men. The time-fuse having been fired, she subsequently blew up.'

A German U-boat commander, Heino von Heimburg, was an observer at the net when *E7* surfaced after thirteen hours. Von Heimburg recalls the incident: 'An explosion, and a column of water shot up. A dark spot appeared on the surface that looked like oil. We were about to let down another mine when a dark form broke the surface. It was the British 'E' boat. Gunboats opened instant fire. A shell went through the conning tower, another pierced the tanks. The boat was sinking. Men came scrambling out of the hatch . . . The water was closing over the conning tower when another figure leaped out of the conning tower and into the water and swam over to a boat. It was the captain, the last man to abandon ship.'

Lieutenant-Commander Cochrane was justly proud of the manner in which his crew had faced up to the ordeal – and an ordeal it undoubtedly was. The fearsome experience of being depth-charged was new to all. 'Throughout the day', Cochrane was to report, 'the discipline and behaviour of the crew was excellent. This was particularly noticeable at the time of the third mine explosion. At this time the crew had been fallen out and many of them were asleep. On being called to their stations every man went quietly to his place although the violence of the explosion was such as to convince everyone that the boat was badly damaged. It was only after receiving reports that the various bilges were dry that I was able to realise that the hull had not received serious damage.'

For the first few days following their capture, the submariners were treated quite well. Then came a move to Constantinople and with it a rude introduction to the more unsavoury aspects of Turkish prison life. For three weeks they were confined in the capital's prison with five hundred criminals for company. Angora (now Ankara, the Turkish capital) was their next destination. Five months were spent at Angora before a move south to the small township of Afion Kara Hissar was ordered. It was there that Cochrane met up with Hew Stoker of *AE2*.

In March 1916 Cochrane, Stoker, and Lieutenant Price of *E15*, escaped. After seventeen days' freedom, all under very harsh conditions, they were recaptured. In August 1918 Lieutenant-Commander Cochrane became involved in another escape, this time from a camp in Yozgat. On this occasion twenty-six officers escaped. In a short time all but a group of eight, led by Cochrane, were retaken. In thirty-eight days the group traversed over 400 miles to reach the coast. Seizing a motor boat they crossed to Cyprus and freedom.

Captain Hon Sir A.D. Cochrane, GCMG, KCSI, DSO, was the second son of the 1st Baron Cochrane of Cults. He had entered the Navy in 1901, when sixteen. Retiring from the Navy in 1922, Captain Cochrane became MP for East Fife (1924-29) and then for Dumbartonshire between 1932 and 1936. Following his Knighthood in 1936, Sir Archibald became Governor of Burma. He returned to naval duty in World War Two and became the commanding officer of an auxiliary cruiser engaged in transatlantic convoy operations. Sir Archibald Cochrane died in April 1958, aged seventy-three.

Hew Stoker remained a prisoner until the end of the war. In 1919 he was promoted to commander and awarded the DSO. Though only thirty-five he retired from the Navy the following year, after twenty years' service, to pursue an acting career, becoming both a successful actor and playwright. With the onset of the Second World War Hew Stoker, whose father was a Fellow of the Royal College of Surgeons in Ireland, returned to the Navy and served in various commands and appointments. Captain Stoker died on his eighty-first birthday, 2 February 1966.

*

Attempts by French submarines to reach the Sea of Marmara were not too successful. The *Bernoulli* tried and failed on 30 April. Early next morning the *Joule* entered the straits. At about 1100 the air-chamber of a torpedo, identified as belonging to *Joule*, was seen floating seawards. The submarine had struck a mine near The Narrows. On 25 July the *Mariotte* got herself tangled in an A/S net and broke surface in the struggle to free herself. As if this was not enough, the situation became even more grave when a mine was discovered attached to *Mariotte*'s bows. Matters reached a climax when gunfire from the shore damaged the submarine and prevented her from diving. After ensuring that his boat would sink, the captain and his crew abandoned ship and became POWs. The *Turquoise* actually reached the Marmara. Unlike *Mariotte* the circumstances surrounding her loss left much to be desired.

*Turquoise* arrived in the Marmara on 22 October. Shortly after her arrival she was sighted by Lieutenant-Commander W.B. Pirie (*H1*) lying on the surface and flying a large tricolour. With a thoughtful stroke of his beard Wilf Pirie decided not to make his presence known.

On 30 October, after little more than a week in the Marmara, Commandant Revenel, *Turquoise*'s captain, decided that he had had enough and made for the Straits. When nearing Nagara Point the Frenchman had the misfortune to run aground. Shore-mounted guns were directed towards the boat. Revenel thought that under such unsavoury conditions the wisest course of action was to abandon ship with all speed. A German report of the incident states that the French were so anxious to get clear of *Turquoise*, they left all lights burning and an alarm bell ringing. This seems likely. When the submarine was searched all her secret papers and documents were found intact in the captain's cabin. The failure to destroy confidential papers contributed largely to the loss a few days later of *E20* (Lieutenant-Commander C.H. Warren).

Lieutenant-Commander Clyfford Warren was due to rendezvous with *Turquoise* on 6 November. This was now known to the Germans, who dispatched von Heimburg to the position marked on Revenel's chart. Lieutenant von Heimburg relates the sequence of events which should never have taken place.

'We left Constantinople at 0010 on 6th November and proceeded on the surface at full speed. At dawn we submerged so as not to be seen and set course for the rendezvous where *E20* was due.

'The sea was as smooth as a mirror and, when the periscope was raised for a moment at 1600, I could see the conning tower of a submarine again five miles away. Half an hour later I looked again and she was still there, which was very nice of her. At 1710, range 550 yards, I fired a torpedo and scored a hit. My men cheered.

'Surfacing immediately, I climbed onto the conning tower and all I could see was a large patch of oil in which a few black spots were moving, which proved to be survivors. I closed them all and called out in English, "How are you?"

'"All right, sir!" one of them replied.

'There were two groups. One consisted of six and the other of three men. We approached the former first and helped them on board, then we went for the other three, who turned out to be the captain supporting two non-swimmers. They were shivering with cold and, like all submariners, very dirty.

'I greeted the captain in a friendly manner, and we exchanged salutes. After cautioning him to refrain from committing any hostile act, I told him that he could take his men down below where they would be given dry clothes and a hot drink.'

The captured *Turquoise* was towed to Constantinople. Having been presented with a submarine in almost perfect working order, the Turks commissioned her into their own Navy. The submarine was renamed *Mustejab Onbashy* (Worthy of Acceptance), which indicates that the Turks have a commendable sense of humour.

On the same day that *E20* was sunk Commander Nasmith returned to the Marmara for a third tour. When Nasmith left the Marmara for the last time, on 24 December 1915, his patrol had spanned a record forty-seven days. Martin Nasmith's departure for Mudros left *E2* (Lieutenant-Commander D. de B. Stocks) as the only Allied submarine in the Marmara. David Stocks remained on the prowl until 2 January 1916. When Stocks received his recall signal the Sea of Marmara was free of British submarines for the first time in more than a year.

As the campaign on the Gallipoli Peninsula came to its inglorious end, so the need for submarines in the Marmara ceased to exist. The Submarine Service had played its part in the campaign with just the right mixture of skill and bravado. More than two hundred enemy vessels of one type or another had been sunk in the Marmara. The stranglehold which Royal Navy submarines had had on enemy shipping had assisted and influenced the military side of the campaign. In penetrating to the very heart of the enemy lair, a task which for capital ships had proved impossible, the submarine had more than proved its worth.

\*

With the struggle to breach the Dardanelles no longer a requirement

British submarines could be spared for other duties. A task for which they were ideally suited was as a first line of attack should the *Goeben* and *Breslau* make a sojourn through the Dardanelles to attack shipping.

It was two years before the ex-German ships entered the open sea. On 19 January 1918 *Goeben* and *Breslau* sailed Constantinople for a raid on shipping in the Aegean. When the ships cleared the Dardanelles there was no submarine (*E2*) waiting to try an attack or give warning of the break out. By an unfortunate coincidence *E2*'s propeller shaft had been giving trouble and she had left station to effect repairs.

At about 0740 the following morning, the ships attacked the monitors HMS *Raglan* and *M28* in Kusu Bay at Imbros Island, sinking both vessels. The aggressors had withdrawn when at 0830 they found themselves in a minefield. *Breslau* hit several mines and was sunk. *Goeben* was also mined but managed to retreat to the Dardanelles. She limped as far as Nagara Point and then ran aground. During the course of the next five days aircraft few 270 sorties over her. Sixteen direct bomb hits were reported.

The Royal Navy was keen to destroy *Goeben*. Courtney Boyle's old boat (*E14*) was ordered from Corfu to do the job. Air reconnaissance of 27 January disclosed that *Goeben* was still aground. That evening *E14*, now captained by Lieutenant-Commander G.S. White, sailed Mudros. Unknown to White, the *Goeben* had been towed to Constantinople that very day.

Breaking through the A/S net at Chanak was no mean feat but White got through to discover that his quarry was gone. Disappointed at not coming to grips with *Goeben*, White turned about and headed back down the straits. At about 0845, it was now the 28th, Geoffrey White fired a torpedo at a Turkish ship. Only eleven seconds after the torpedo had left its tube there was a huge explosion just forward of *E14*: either the torpedo had detonated prematurely or a depth-charge had exploded just ahead. The explosion sprung open the forward torpedo hatch. Water flooded in. When taken to the surface *E14* was met by a fierce barrage of gunfire. A survivor of the ordeal had this to say: 'The captain was the first one up on deck, and then the navigator. I followed to connect up the upper steering gear. We found the spindle to be shot in half. Orders were given to steer from below. We ran the gauntlet for half an hour, only a few shots hitting us . . . The captain, seeing it was hopeless, ran towards the shore. His last words were "We are in the hands of God", and only a few seconds later I looked for him and saw his body, mangled by shellfire, roll into the water and go under. The last shell hit the starboard saddle tank, killing all I believe. By this time the submarine was close to the shore. Soon afterwards she sank, some survivors being picked up by the Turks.'

It was deemed that Lieutenant-Commander White should be posthumously awarded the Victoria Cross. On 2 July 1919, White's birthday, his widow arrived at Buckingham Palace to receive the bronze cross from the King. The father of two young boys, Geoffrey White had a daughter whom he had never seen.

*E14* was the last submarine lost in the conflict with Turkey. From the point of view of the Submarine Service the campaign had been very rewarding. Of particular satisfaction was that submarine crews had been found lacking in neither spirit nor courage nor skill. The Submarine Service, only in being twelve years at the outbreak of war, had set a standard which in the years to come would require the greatest effort to uphold.

Towards the end of December 1915 the Admiralty arrived at the conclusion that U-boats were likely to come out into the North Sea by way of Horn Reefs. On 25 December *E6* (Lieutenant-Commander W.J. Foster) was ordered to the vicinity of Horn Reefs for a possible interception. Weather permitting, Foster was to be relieved after six days by another submarine on the same duty. William Foster, who was thirty, left Harwich on 26 December. *E6* had not long left harbour when, near the Sunk Light Vessel, she struck a mine and sank with the loss of all hands.

The loss of *E6* was all the more unfortunate in that the armed trawler *Resono* had been mined in the same minefield a short time before. The incident is further complicated by the fact that a torpedo boat in the vicinity signalled Foster to keep clear. Although it appeared that the signal had been taken in, *E6* had continued her course and, in full view of the torpedo boat's crew, struck the mine and disappeared.

# 1916

HM Submarine *E17* (Lieutenant-Commander J.R.G. Moncreiffe) was patrolling north of Texel Island when she struck an uncharted sandbank. *E17*, submerged at the time, was badly damaged. Moncreiffe surfaced and, following an inspection of the boat, decided that with luck he might possibly reach English waters.

It was just about this time that a distant cruiser was sighted. As she appeared to be steering directly towards *E17*, no clear identification as to whether she was Dutch or German could be made. When she turned her armament in the direction of *E17*, Lieutenant-Commander Moncreiffe believed, wrongly, that the ship was German. He ordered *E17* dived. The submarine, however, was in no condition to remain submerged and Guy Moncreiffe was forced to surface. He fired off signal flares to attract the warship.

The Royal Netherlands Navy cruiser *Noord Brabant* had first sighted *E17* just prior to the submarine firing off her signal flares. The movement of her armament towards *E17* had been purely coincidental. The cruiser's log for this day reports the incident as follows:

*Thursday 6 January 1916.*

Steaming to sea through Zuiderdiep. Being off Uiterton Schulpengat at 0850 reduced engines to 50 revolutions per minute and shaped course southward at approximately 3° free of the coast. At 0915 changed course northward after receiving wireless orders from Naval Commander-in-Chief. Getting sight of a submarine at 1000, just about in a line with Buoy Middelrug and Buoy Noorderhaaks. While approaching observed distress signals of the submarine (two signal flares accompanied by international signal NC). Position of submarine W by N of Buoy Nooderhaaks, distance 1,600 metres. Came to a stop and lowered the lifeboat and officers' sloop. Took on board the ship the captain, two officers, and thirty members of the crew of the British submarine *E17*. Hoisted the boats and stayed near the submarine until she sank at 1140 in bearing WNW (magnetic) of Buoy Haaksgronden and increased speed to 63 revolutions and 70 revolutions successively . . . At 1545 picket officer and armed escort accompanied crew of *E17* ashore.

The thirty-three survivors were captive for a time at Den Helder before moving on to Groningen (known to its occupants as HMS *Timber*) to join other Royal Navy internees.

Lieutenant-Commander Guy Moncreiffe, thirty-one at the time of *E17*'s loss, had been born in India where his father was a planter. He had joined submarines back in November 1906, a year after serving in the Royal Yacht *Victoria and Albert*. Devoted to the Navy, Commander Sir Guy Moncreiffe, very much admired and respected by his crew, retired from the Service in 1920, a year after his marriage. A fine officer with aristocratic good looks, Sir Guy died in September 1934.

*

At the beginning of World War One naval aviation was very much in its infancy. The Navy commandeered several ferry ships for use as seaplane tenders. In this role a ferry carried about six seaplanes which for take-off were hoisted by a crane onto the sea. On completion of its task the plane would alight near the ship for hoisting back aboard. Both stages of the operation required the ship to be stopped and in fairly calm water. The Isle of Man Steam Packet Company's ferry *Viking* had been requisitioned for naval use in March 1915. Her name was changed to *Vindex*. In the case of *Vindex* it was proposed to construct a platform at her bows to enable a seaplane to take off without the ship having to stop. The seaplane could not of course land back on to *Vindex*.

For some considerable time an air attack on the Zeppelin sheds in the German Bight had been contemplated. The principal factor as to the date the operation would take place was the readiness of HMS *Vindex*. Work on transforming *Vindex* into a primitive aircraft carrier and experiments to test her capacity for flying seaplanes from her platform, and retrieving them, were put in hand. On 3 November 1915 Flight Lieutenant H.F. Towler flew a Bristol Scout from *Vindex*. By 1 January 1916 the tests were completed. It had been several months prior to this that Commodore R.Y. Tyrwhitt had applied for permission to put two operations into effect. The first of the operations (ARH) entailed an attack on the Hage Sheds near Nordeich on the western side of the Bight. The other operation, HRH, was to be against the sheds at Hoyer on the Schleswig coast. Detailed orders for the operations were submitted by Commodore Tyrwhitt. Approval came early in December. The *Vindex* being ready, the commodore was instructed on 5 January to proceed with the HRH operation whenever weather conditions proved suitable.

It was not until 18 January 1916 that a lull in the almost continuous gales presented Commodore Tyrwhitt with the first opportunity for HRH. Part of the operational plan involved a submarine force to deal with any threat from an emerging enemy and to keep a watch for disabled aircraft going to and from the raid. Accordingly, on 18 January the *H7*, *H8*, and *H10* left Yarmouth, and *D3*, *H6*, and *E23* left Harwich for their part in the operation. Captain A.K. Waistell, Captain S8, sailed in support of the submarines with *Firedrake* and four other destroyers, *Medea*, *Melampus*, *Morris*, and *Lavernock*.

At 1615 on the 18th, Commodore Tyrwhitt, in *Arethusa*, put to sea in company with light cruisers, destroyers, and *Vindex*. The weather at that time was ideal, but shortly after passing the position where the force had turned to approach the Heligoland Bight the weather closed in and the commodore found himself in fog.

*Wednesday 19th.* The fog prevented the seaplanes becoming airborne at 0700. By 1000 the fog was still in evidence near the coast; moreover, a wind was blowing fresh from the south-west. It was round 0915 that *Arethusa* received a message from *H6* stating that she was aground off Ameland.

The *H6* (Lieutenant R.N. Stopford) had sailed Harwich at 1035 on the 18th. After clearing the swept channel a course was set to a position which Stopford expected to reach the following morning. At midnight *H6* was stopped and a cast taken, which gave 14 and 15 fathoms. These readings put her southward of her course as laid down on her charts. Stopford remained on his, then, course. A second cast was taken at 0035 which gave 13 fathoms. About this time he was slightly north of Flushing. At 0050 Stopford made a course alteration. At 0105 a cast was taken and 11 fathoms recorded; the tide being half flood, this gave *H6* 10 fathoms. It was decided to stand on until reaching 7 fathoms, when a course would be set which would carry her to her appointed billet.

At 0355 *H6* shuddered and touched bottom. Her engines were immediately stopped. Soundings were taken which gave 3½ fathoms. The submarine's way carried her into 7 fathoms. Course was then altered northward and *H6* proceeded on one engine.

At 0410, and in thick mist, *H6* again ran aground, remaining fast. Soundings taken round her sides indicated a depth of 2¾ fathoms, which made it pretty certain that she was perched on a bank. As *H6* was bumping heavily, all ballast tanks – and two fuel tanks – were blown and the motors worked in agreement with Lieutenant Stopford's orders.

At 0500, while going astern on both motors, *H6* suddenly slithered off but grounded again about fifty yards astern. Soundings gave 7 fathoms. The submarine lay beam-on to a swell and, owing to a falling tide, was rolling heavily from side to side on her bilges. In order to steady her it was decided to fill all tanks. As it was still dark and misty, no point on the shore from which a fix could be taken was seen. The stranding of *H6*, plus the unfavourable weather, prompted Commodore Tyrwhitt to cancel the operation. Detailing two destroyers to escort the *Vindex* to Harwich, he proceeded in search of *H6*.

Lieutenant Stopford had been transmitting news of his grounding since 0900, judging that by then his signals were unlikely to compromise the HRH operation. With the coming of daylight land could, with difficulty, be distinguished on the starboard beam, but nothing so definite could be seen so as to enable their position to be ascertained.

At about 1115 the mist began to thin out. Lieutenant Leslie Brown, *H6*'s navigating officer, was then able to obtain a sighting. A lighthouse on shore could just be seen. This enabled Brown to fix their position at approximately two miles west of Schiermonnikoog Lighthouse.

At noon *H6* was sighted from the shore. Soon, a lifeboat was seen heading towards the submarine. Whilst this was taking place the destroyer *Firedrake* was sighted through the mist and called up.

By now *H6* was in very shallow water and had taken on a big list with her propellers out of the water. When the lifeboat arrived alongside, the submariners were informed that a Dutch naval boat would also be coming out.

*Firedrake* and the other destroyers had made a search for *H6* off Ameland, another of the West Frisian Islands. Captain Waistell had ordered his force to patrol outside neutral waters whilst he closed the shore with *Melampus*. *Firedrake*'s captain noted that: 'It was very misty in shore and I regret to report that *Melampus* touched one of the shoals while following *Firedrake* and damaged a propeller. I ordered her to proceed to Harwich. At 1145, having thoroughly searched all the shores on Ameland and made certain that *H6* was not there, I proceeded to Frieschezee, where on reaching the edge of the shore she was seen.'

It was considered in *Firedrake* that *H6* was too firm aground for any assistance to be effective. Captain Waistell felt that the importance of recovering some of the officers and higher trained ratings from *H6* justified the risk of waiting in such an advanced position; accordingly at 1400 a motor boat from *Medea* was sent to *H6* with instructions that if there was no possibility of her being extricated at high water, Lieutenant Stopford was to send his confidential books, his second and third officers and certain ratings to *Medea*.

The motor boat returned at 1600 with four of *H6*'s officers together with the coxswain, Chief ERA and several ratings – eleven men in all. With the wind and sea rising fast, and a considerable increase in German wireless traffic, it was thought unwise to send the motor boat back to *H6*. Leaving sufficient personnel in the submarine to maintain her, and possibly refloat her at the next high tide, Captain

Waistell proceeded west at 20 knots, which sea conditions later reduced to 8 knots.

*H6* was well and truly stranded on the Dutch shoal. Consequently Robert Stopford and his crew were interned by the Dutch. Bad visibility and drift had been contributing factors in the loss of a submarine which, for a change, resulted in no loss of life.

*H6* was refloated and interned at Niewediep. Negotiations were opened for Dutch purchase of the submarine. Britain agreed terms of sale and *H6* became *O8* in the Royal Netherlands Navy. In the Second World War the *O8* was scuttled by the Dutch at Willemsoord in May 1940. Raised by the Germans she was commissioned into the Kriegsmarine as *UD1*. On 3 May 1945 *UD1* was scuttled at Kiel, where she was later broken up. *H6* had been built in 1915 by Canadian Vickers (Montreal).

How *E5* (Lieutenant-Commander H.D. Edwards) met her end is still something of a mystery. On 4 March four submarines, including *E5*, left for patrol in the Heligoland Bight: *E23* to patrol west of 8°, *E29* between the Ems and Norderney, *H5* between Horn Reefs and List, and *E5* between Ameland and the Western Ems. *E23*, *E29*, and *H5* returned safely on the 10th; Lieutenant-Commander Harrington Edwards, DSO, failed to return. *E29* thought she saw *E5* about seven miles north of Juist Island on the afternoon of 6 March. At 0810 the following morning the German battlecruiser *Seydlitz* and several torpedo boats sighted a submarine in this area and dropped depth-charges without result. A few hours later the German light cruiser *Regensburg* sighted a submarine a little farther east. This area was not far off the deep mines of a German minefield off the Western Ems.

The idea of using submarines as minelayers was first put into operation by the Germans. To design and build minelaying submarines would have been a time-consuming project for the British. Though perhaps not ideal, the next best thing was to convert several existing submarines into minelayers in an effort to regain some lost ground.

The first submarine converted to carry mines was *E41*. Lieutenant-Commander Norman Holbrook, VC, was appointed her captain. *E24* was the next to be converted. In early March *E24* joined the 9th Flotilla at Harwich and on the 21st of that month she put to sea with twenty mines for her second mine-lay – she had already laid a minefield off Heligoland – in enemy waters.

Lieutenant-Commander George Naper, *E24*'s captain, sailed Harwich on the morning of the 21st with orders to enter the

Heligoland Bight, by way of Amerun Bank, during the hours of darkness. Naper was to lay his mines in a zigzag line at a position about three miles to the west of his previous minelay. In view of the danger of mines off Ameland, Lieutenant-Commander Naper had been advised to return by the Amerun Bank route. The submarine failed to return and apart from a positional signal given near the British coast, nothing was heard from her.

It seems unlikely that with several safety arrangements incorporated into the minelayer, *E24*'s loss could have been due to the mines she carried. Lieutenant-Commander Naper had to lay his mines in 12 fathoms; as he had set his mines in 8 fathoms in his previous lay, the possibility of *E24* striking one of the mines she had already laid appears to be slim. Lost with George Naper, who had been CO of *C14* when she sank in Plymouth Sound in December 1913, were three officers and thirty-one men.

Engine Room Artificer F.S. Buckingham was one of only two survivors when on the morning of 25 April the *E22* (Lieutenant-Commander R.T. Dimsdale) was sunk in the North Sea by *UB18*. The following account of the sinking is by ERA Buckingham and was written on 28 July 1918, three months before the war ended.

'At about 1145 I was relieved of my watch on the main engines. The speed of the ship at that time was 9½ knots. The boat was submerged, showing only about 4 or 5 feet of the conning tower above water. All the departments of the boat were in efficient working order as far as came under my notice.

'At 1150 I had occasion to visit the conning tower to examine the air whistle. Whilst on the conning tower I noticed all hands were keeping a sharp lookout. I also saw two of our own submarines, one right ahead nearly out of sight, the other off our port-side. Our escorting destroyer had just disappeared over the horizon. I was looking at Lieutenant Carless coming through the conning tower hatch when a torpedo struck the boat and she immediately sank. Lieutenant Collier was the OOW.

'I regained my senses while under water, and on reaching the surface I saw Stoker Finn's head appear above water. He was very soon in difficulties, being unable to swim. I went over to him and tried to assist him to a piece of splintered wood about 10 or 15 yards distant. Owing to the swell and he being a big man (fully dressed), I was exhausted before I could get him to the wood. I am sorry to report that I had to abandon him. I then secured two pieces of wood myself (the wood was the splintered platform we carried aft for supporting two small hydroplanes).

'Some ten or fifteen minutes after leaving Stoker Finn, I saw Lieutenant Carless, badly wounded about the head and face, clinging to a large piece of wood. I made my way over to him and tried to assist him into a more secure position. I thought there was some chance of our destroyer coming to look for us. I managed to keep Lieutenant Carless on the wood for some time, then he gradually lost consciousness and his slight grip on the wood. I had not sufficient strength to get him back to the wood; owing to the cold and my exertions I was then feeling in a bad way myself. I regret to say Lieutenant Carless drowned.

'After being in the water 1¼ hours the enemy submarine came to the surface and picked me up. I then saw Signalman Harrod for the first time, about a quarter of a mile distant. I was pushed below and after about ten minutes Harrod was picked up. The *UB18* appeared to be an old boat. Her internal fittings looked in bad condition. The crew while at sea seemed to be in a more or less excited state. At 1030, April 26, we were landed at Zeebrugge.

'On arriving at Bruges we were taken before a German naval officer and questioned. I was asked a number of questions to which I replied that it was my first trip to sea and that I was only in the boat for training. I was told not to tell lies. I had already, the day previous, told the captain of the *UB18* that I was the second engineer. I was then asked one question about the Grand Fleet. I replied that before being in submarines I was employed in a workshop and therefore knew nothing about the Fleet. I was then dismissed. Signalman Harrow was then questioned. I believe they did not give him much credit for speaking the truth. Our treatment in the hands of the German sailors was not bad, although the food was very bad. The treatment soon changed on our being handed over to the Army.'

It was sixteen days after the sinking that Ethel Buckingham received a postcard from her 26-year-old husband stating that he was a prisoner at Dulnen in Westphalia. As stated by Frederick Buckingham, who at 5 ft 5 in tall was well suited to submarine life, 22-year-old Signalman William Harrod, from Plumstead, also survived the traumatic event.

Lieutenant Reginald Dimsdale, *E22*'s captain, was thirty years of age. Captain of the *UB18* was Lieutenant-Commander Otto Steinbrinck, one of the ablest of submarine commanders.

Construction of the 'E' class was in the hands of several firms.

Beardmores of Dalmuir was contracted to build four (*E25, E26, E53, E54*). Of these only *E26* (Lieutenant E.W.B. Ryan) failed to survive the war. Originally intended for the Turkish Navy, she was lost during a North Sea patrol.

*E26* had been a unit of the 8th Flotilla. Many of the flotilla's battles took place in, and often with, the North Sea. As a rule, four of the flotilla's submarines would be cruising in the area of Terschelling. On 29 June the *E10, E26, E54*, and *E55* sailed harbour to perform that duty. *E26*'s patrol area was between 53°45'N and the Dutch coast, and east of 5°E, including the approach to the Ems. On 2 July a German outpost boat reported a long trail of oil off the Ems; this oil was apparently coming from a dived submarine. During the following day (Monday 3rd) a British submarine was fired at and also bombed off the Eastern Ems. *E55* was at that time about twenty miles to the north-west and heard the dull explosions which might possibly have eliminated *E26*. Lost with Lieutenant Edward Ryan were two officers and twenty-eight men.

The *H3* was one of the Canadian-built submarines. She was under the command of 27-year-old Lieutenant George Jenkinson when during a patrol off the Austrian naval base of Cattaro (now Kotor in Yugoslavia) on 15 July she struck a mine and went to the bottom of the Adriatic and out of the water. Lieutenant Jenkinson had been described as 'A confident officer for whom the future looked bright'.

HM submarine *B10* was the only one of her class to be sunk during hostilities. Of particular interest is that *B10* was the first submarine to be sunk from an air attack.

On returning to Venice after having taken part in the blockade of Pola in the northern Adriatic, *B10* (Lieutenant K. Michell) tied up alongside the old Italian cruiser *Marco Polo*, *B10*'s parent ship whilst she was operating with the Italian Submarine Service. On the evening of 9 August 1916, aircraft of the Austrian Naval Air Service raided the port area. How *B10* came to be sunk is related, as seen from the depot ship, by one of her officers:

'It was an evening such as the great artist J.M. Turner has immortalised in his *Sunset Over Venice*. On this summer evening an Austrian plane hopped across from Pola, twenty minutes flight away. As far as I can recollect we used to have a ringside seat to see the display. Once I saw a wonderful old church burning like a torch with molten lead cascading like a waterfall.

'On this evening I was standing on deck, in fact lighting my pipe, when there was a red glare. When I had picked myself up I heard someone say "Your old boat has gone" – and so had my pipe! I looked down over the side and saw *B10* settling down for her last dive, and not without a lot of gurgling and protest at the unusual dive.

'After a fortnight the old boat was raised from the bottom and docked. This job was done by Italian divers. It was what happened after that I thought was unusual and interesting. Going to work one morning, I met a crowd of workmen running towards me. They were saying "*B10 tutti fini – fuoci, fuoci*" (*B10* all finished – on fire). As there were 2,000 gallons of petrol, and two torpedoes with their warheads on, I thought it time to have a look; so I went to where the Italians had come from. I saw that the old boat was well and truly alight. The petrol tank had caught fire and was burning like a huge blowlamp very near the torpedoes. Fortunately the vent on the tank was closed, ensuring that no air could get to it, or it would have exploded. The fire was put out by flooding the dock.

'The cause of the fire? It was necessary to put a patch over the hole in the side caused by the bomb. The side of the boat was being drilled with an electric drill. This penetrated the petrol tank, and then either the heat of the drill's point or a faulty electrical connection set fire to the petrol.'

*B10* was written off. By the end of 1919 the remainder of the 'B' class had been sold for scrap.

*

In August 1916 two 'E' class were in collision off Harwich. Of the sixty crewmen involved, over forty-five were lost.

More often than not, attacks by submarines during exercises entailed the use of a surface vessel as target ship; but as submarines occasionally met up with U-boats, it was decided that they would benefit considerably from practising attacks with another submarine acting as a target. With this object in view, *E4, E31, E41,* and *E16* left Harwich on the morning of 15 August for just such an exercise. The plan for this Tuesday was that *E4* and *E31* would attack *E41* and, after an interval, *E16*. When this had been done, the roles would be reversed and the attacking submarines would become targets for *E41* and *E16*. HMS *Firedrake* would be in attendance to keep a watchful eye on the submarines and to recover expended torpedoes.

Lieutenant Alfred Winser's *E41* set off on her run as target ship. As the day was clear with good visibility, Lieutenant-Commanders F.E.B. Feilman (*E31*) and J. Tenison (*E4*) had no trouble in holding a steady depth or observing *E41* through their respective periscopes.

On completing their attacks Julian Tenison and Ferdinand Feilman came to the surface.

At this point *Firedrake* signalled *E41* that *E16* had been delayed and that Winser would have to complete a second run as target ship. The destroyer then signalled Tenison and Feilman to prepare for another attack on *E41*. Lieutenant Winser reports:

> I signalled to *E31*, and afterwards to *E4*, that I intended turning about a mile to the eastwards of the Cork Light Vessel. I actually turned about half a mile to the eastwards of the Cork and reduced speed to 6 knots until *Firedrake* had completed signalling to the attacking boats, and until the attacking boats were both diving, when I increased speed to 12 knots.

The two submarines were then about three miles off *E41*'s starboard bow.

As *E41* steered a steady course, the run appeared to be going pretty much the same as had the first. On the bridge Winser stood close to the voice-pipe which led below to the helmsman, Able Seaman Gaunt. Standing immediately behind Winser was Lieutenant Klemp, a RNR officer; a signalman, standing on the rails, was port side forward. The only other rating on the bridge was Leading Seaman R.S. Ireson, doing duty as a lookout. Visibility was still good. The sea was a little choppy owing to the shallowness of the water and an off-shore wind.

Leading Seaman Ireson saw *E31*'s periscope for some time after she had dived, but of Tenison's *E4* he saw nothing until its sudden appearance ten minutes after *E41* had set off on her run. *E4* was seen by Ireson about 50 yards off *E41*'s starboard bow. She was on a collision course. Ireson at once drew Winser's attention to the sighting. There was no question of avoiding a collision, but there was a chance of minimising it. Lieutenant Winser ordered the engines stopped and, though later he could not remember doing so, the helm hard to starboard. Robert Ireson, his eyes firmly on *E4*'s periscope, noted: 'The periscope was continually rising from the time she was first seen, and at the moment of impact the whole periscope was visible practically down tthe standard.' About thirty seconds after Ireson had sighted her periscope, *E4* struck *E41* at an estimated 5 knots.

*E41* had just stopped engines when *E4* struck 25 feet forward of *E41*'s conning tower. At first Winser thought that *E4*'s periscope and standards would be carried away. Hoping *E4*'s jumping stay would push her under his own submarine, he looked to his stern expecting her to come up; at the same time he ordered the signalman to report the collision to *Firedrake*. Only a slight impact was felt by the bridge party. *E41* had neither pitched nor rolled and Winser believed his submarine was almost unscathed – and even if it was not, the force of the impact suggested that any damage would be minimal.

In *E41*'s control room the first lieutenant, Lieutenant T.F.A. Voysey, first became aware that all was not well when the telegraph rang STOP BOTH and, soon after, he heard a slight noise forward and felt a bump. 'I ran forward at once', Voysey was later to report, 'and shouted out to close the fore bulkhead door. As I shouted this I noticed the water was coming in at the fore-end of the battery, starboard side abreast the bunk. The water was coming in rapidly. I gave the order "Everyone up" and also had the order passed along to the engine room aft. I then waited near the foot of the ladder to the conning tower while the hands were going up. Then there appeared to be a certain amount of jamming in the hatches so I went up into the conning tower where I considered I could best control the crew coming up. While I was there about four more men went up, and then the boat appeared to dive below the surface. The water came down very fast through the upper conning tower hatch. Then shortly after, the upper hatch closed. After the hatch closed it was noticed that the air pressure in the boat was rising. This pressure eventually blew open the hatch and the escaping air carried myself and Sub-Lieutenant Money with it.'

Until the men below began to emerge smartly from the conning tower hatch, the bridge party had no idea that *E41* was sinking. Winser, not aware of the conditions below, ordered the men back down. Lieutenant Winser: 'About the third man up out of the conning tower told me that the water was up over the battery boards. I then allowed the men to continue coming up and called down the voice-pipe to bring up lifebelts. I ordered the signalman to report that we were sinking. The next moment the water was above the conning tower.'

*E41*'s bow took on a downwards inclination and she listed to starboard. Less than ninety seconds after the collision, her conning tower was under water. It was 0940.

At his periscope Lieutenant-Commander Feilman (*E31*) saw *Firedrake* haul down her red flag and hoist a black ball. Three minutes after the collision he surfaced and closed *Firedrake*, only to be told by her captain, Commander Aubrey Tillard, to return to harbour.

At the time of the accident *Firedrake* was about 1,200 yards off *E41*'s starboard bow. *E4* had been seen to dive, and on the last sighting of her periscope she had seemed in a favourable position for an attack on *E41*'s starboard bow. Nothing further was seen of *E4*. On receipt of the signal from *E41* stating that a collision had taken place, *Firedrake* moved in to rescue survivors. It took *Firedrake* less than two minutes to reach the point of collision. There was no trace of *E4* or *E41*. About twenty of *E41*'s crew had managed to clear the hatch before she had gone under. Commander Tillard was impressed by their composure: 'The behaviour of the survivors was all that could be desired and the entire absence of shouting or panic of any kind undoubtedly hastened the rescue work.' Of the survivors, fourteen were taken from the sea.

Hope of further survivors was on the wane when, after an hour and thirty minutes, Stoker Petty Officer William Brown came to the surface. Brown had escaped via the engine room hatch. Alone and in total darkness SPO Brown displayed exemplary coolness and courage, qualities which undoubtedly had saved his life.

A week after the collision *E41* was again on the surface. As already stated, *E41* became the first Royal Navy minelaying submarine. Regrettably there were no survivors from *E4*. She was located on the afternoon of the 17th. She was raised and put back into service.

There is always a risk of collision when submarines are exercising, especially when they endeavour to use their periscopes as little as possible. It was felt that for the sake of efficient training, all risks were acceptable. The two submarines were units of the 8th Flotilla. In the period the flotilla had been based at Harwich, over 1,600 exercising attacks had been made without serious accident. Both submarines were sold in 1922.

Lieutenant-Commander K.J. Duff-Dunbar was captain of *E16* when she was lost in the North Sea only a week after the accident off Harwich. One of the highlights of her patrols had been the sinking of *U6* off the Norwegian coast in September 1915. Although not rated as skilful as the sinking of *U6* the attack on a net-layer by *E16* some three months later was just as interesting.

The frequent sighting of British submarines off the Western Ems prompted the Germans to send out a 3,000-ton auxiliary to lay A/S nets. Accompanying this vessel was a torpedo boat, four trawlers, a small sloop, and several tugs and other small craft. The units were zigzagging around the net-layer. Lieutenant-Commander C.P. Talbot, captain of *E16* during this period, crossed the stern of one of the armed trawlers. This particular trawler was only 50 yards from the submarine, and as Talbot looked at her through his periscope he saw one of the crew at the stern pointing at him! But it was the net-layer that Talbot had singled out as target. The trawler blew her siren as a warning signal. The net-layer could not have been caught at a worse moment; she had a section of net on its way out over her stern and she was almost stopped. Talbot fired two torpedoes. The target sank in just over ten minutes.

How *E16* herself met her end is uncertain. On 18 August 1916, *E16* and *E38* (Lieutenant-Commander J. de B. Jessop) sailed harbour in the immediate prospect of a German movement. At seven o'clock that evening, John Jessop sighted *E16* seven miles ahead with they were some thirty-five miles due east of Yarmouth. This was the last sighting of *E16* by Jessop. At 0700 the smoke of five warships was seen off Terschelling by *E38*. Two splashes were observed close to one of the ships. As the squadron of ships appeared to be moving north *E38* shaped course west. Eventually losing sight of them, she resumed course for her station. The splashes? Possibly a depth-charge attack on *E23*, which was in the area at that time. Jessop began his return to harbour on the 20th.

Nothing was ever heard of *E16*. An attack by enemy gunfire on 22 August on a submarine's periscope might have been against *E16*. If so, then whether she was sunk, or damaged by the gunfire and later mined, is open to speculation. Lost with *E16* was Lieutenant-Commander Kenneth Duff-Dunbar, DSO, and thirty crew.

The Harwich submarines suffered two further losses in November. Lieutenant Geoffrey Biggs put to sea with *E30* on the 15th for a patrol between 54°N and 53°25'N, and between 3°30'E and 4°E. *E30* failed to return to Harwich when expected to do so and was not heard of again. Her loss was attributed to a mine in the Heligoland Bight. There is however a possibility that *E30* struck a mine off Orford Ness in a scattered minefield which was not located until 25 November. Two minefields, each of a dozen mines, were sown there during the month and claimed the sinking of the minesweeping trawlers *Burnley* and *Trevani* on 25 November and 3 December respectively.

This same minefield might also have been responsible for the loss of *E37* (Lieutenant-Commander R.F. Chisholm) with all hands, if a report by Lieutenant-Commander Robert Raikes, at the time captain of *E54*, is taken into consideration. At eleven o'clock on the night of 30 November Raikes and Robert Chisholm were outward bound from Harwich when Raikes felt a violent shock in latitude 52°5'N, near the war channel. Though at first he thought that he had struck wreckage, on later reflection he attributed the heavy shock to *E37* striking a mine.

# 1917

At 0730 on Friday 19 January the *E43* and *E36* sailed Harwich. Falling in astern of some minesweepers the two submarines proceeded at their ordered speed until 1126 when the minesweepers and submarines parted company. At this juncture Lieutenant Allan Poland (*E43*) ordered *E36*'s captain, Lieutenant T.B.S. MacGregor-Robertson, to proceed independently.

At 1142 Lieutenant Poland came to a stop. A British mine had broken free its anchorage and was adrift on the surface. The mine was sunk. Both submarines ploughed onwards against a strong north-east wind and a sea logged as moderate.

By 1500 Lieutenant Poland could no longer see *E36*. When last sighted she had been 4° slightly on the port quarter.

At 1850 *E43*'s bridge screen was carried away. Poland eased back to 5 knots until another screen had been fitted.

As the night wore on, weather conditions grew more turbulent. On the bridge with Poland was his OOW (Officer On Watch), Lieutenant Ingleby Jefferson, and Leading Signalman George Plowman. Leaving orders for the course and speed, and for a sharp lookout to be kept all round, Poland went below at 2140. A strong north-east wind was still blowing and the sea could have been described as heavy. Though the night was clear, it was very dark.

When Lieutenant Poland left the bridge, the lights of three trawlers had been visible: one about a mile off the port bow and the others two miles away off the starboard bow. The trawler to port was observed to alter course eastward. *E43* herself was still holding a northerly course.

In keeping with Poland's orders, Lieutenant Jefferson and George Plowman were maintaining a sharp lookout: Jefferson was displaying interest in the lights of the two trawlers off the starboard bow, whilst Plowman kept an eye on the lights of the trawler off to port.

'Submarine, sir!' Plowman indicated a shadowy figure some fifty yards away which was passing between *E43* and the lights of the trawler. For a second or two Jefferson could not make out anything. Then he too saw the black shape approaching on the crest of a wave.

'Hard a-starboard!' Jefferson yelled down the voice-pipe to Able Seaman Marsh, the helmsman. Within a second Charles Marsh was spinning the wheel in his hands for all he was worth. Jefferson grasped the handle of the telegraph and wrenched it to FULL ASTERN. For the moment no further action could be taken. He and Plowman stood with eyes firmly on the blacked-out submarine. Both men could hardly believe what was taking place. Unless a miracle happened *E43* would strike the unknown submarine at a point near her conning tower. Then *E43* swung away – but just a little too late. *E43* struck the submarine a hard glancing blow about ten feet from her stern. *E43* then appeared to rise over the submarine's stern. Less than fifteen seconds had elapsed between the moment of sighting and impact.

Although not actually on watch at the time, Acting Chief ERA Frederick Cowburn was in the after end of the engine room. He felt the shock of the collision and at once took charge. ERA William Newton, the watchkeeper, also felt the bump: 'I heard the telegraph gong ring, and almost immediately was thrown against the engine.' Recovering, Newton set about stopping the engines so as to throw the clutches out to go astern.

Not five minutes had passed since Poland had left the bridge when he heard 'a loud crash forward'. Giving orders for the foremost bulkhead door to be shut, and for both pumps to be put on the fore compartment, he dashed topside where Jefferson issued a brief explanation as to what had taken place. Poland continues: 'I was told the submarine had disappeared on the starboard quarter. I went full astern on both motors over where I judged to be the scene of the collision. The night was extremely dark and a heavy sea was running. I could see nothing. I then sighted a trawler steaming towards me. She was carrying trawler lights, arranged horizontally on her hull on the starboard side. I was forced to go ahead to clear the trawler, and thus lost my position. I remained in the vicinity about a quarter of an hour longer, but nothing was sighted. I then examined leaks in the fore compartment. I proceeded under engine and laid course for North Hinder Light Vessel.' *E43* arrived back at Harwich at 1127.

With hardly anything definite to go on, it was not known whether the unidentified submarine had been an Allied or hostile boat; and as no wreckage or anything else had been recovered, there was nothing to indicate with any certainty whether the submarine had been sunk or had escaped serious damage. But when no signal was received from *E36* at a time when she should have been in her patrol area, there were misgivings that she might have been the unknown submarine. And when Lieutenant MacGregor-Robertson failed to return to harbour by the morning of the 23rd, his date of arrival at Harwich, it was felt that *E36* was probably the unknown submarine.

At the time of the collision Lieutenant Poland believed *E36* to be several miles astern. Subsequent calculation indicated that at their estimated speeds *E36* would have been approximately two miles astern. Owing to the delay caused by Lieutenant Poland stopping to sink the mine and to fix another bridge screen, it required only a slight underestimation of *E36*'s speed to put her ahead. *E36* had been on an easterly heading when the accident occurred. A likely explanation for her being on an easterly course is that she did not want to be seen by the trawlers – which might have tried to ram – and was attempting to avoid them.

An inquiry into the incident found that (1) *E43* was being navigated with all proper care (2) that a careful lookout was being kept (3) that all possible steps were taken to avoid a collision.

Having joined the Submarine Service in August 1908, Lieutenant Thomas MacGregor-Robertson had been a submariner for eight years. He was described as being 'a likable and thoroughly efficient officer'.

Before January had run its course one of the revolutionary 'K' class submarines sank whilst undertaking acceptance trials in the sedate confines of Gareloch. The 'K' class was born out of a desire to produce a class of submarine capable of achieving a surface speed of 24 knots, the battle speed of the fleet, in the belief that submarines working in close co-operation with surface units would place an enemy at a marked disadvantage. The main difficulty in designing a fleet submarine was that the required speed of 24 knots was beyond the capabilities of diesel propulsion. The alternative power plant to diesel was the steam turbine. The use of steam in submarines presented designers with many problems, not the least of which were the stifling heat, the massive quantity of air required, and the length of time it took to dive. Despite these difficulties construction of the 'K's went ahead in the summer of 1915.

*K13* (Lieutenant-Commander G. Herbert) was the first of four of the class to be built on Clydeside. At eight o'clock on the morning of 29 January 1917, *K13* slipped her moorings and made her way down the Clyde towards Gareloch for the final part of her acceptance trials. By early afternoon Lieutenant-Commander Herbert had completed his first dive of the day. Apart from a small leak in the boiler room, the dive had been satisfactory. Leaving orders for the boiler room to be pumped dry, Herbert boarded the *Comet*, a small steamer doing duty as tender to *K13*, for lunch.

After an excellent meal Lieutenant-Commander Herbert returned to *K13* and set off to carry out the final dive before accepting *K13* as a worthy unit of the Royal Navy. *K13*'s normal complement of fifty-three had been swollen to eighty by the addition of civilian employees of the Fairfield Shipbuilding Company and several naval personnel, among whom numbered the captain and engineer officers of *K14* which was nearing completion at Fairfields.

At 1500 Herbert took *K13* under water for only the third time since her construction. The red light of an indicator was seen to be flickering but Engineer-Lieutenant Arthur Lane said that this was due to faulty wiring causing a bad contact. The indicator in question was of some importance as its function was to show whether the engine room ventilators were fully closed before diving. In the engine room Lane detailed an ERA to go into the boiler room and check if water had again leaked into it. It had. The ERA closed and fastened the watertight door before scurrying back to report that the boiler room was rapidly flooding. The captain was at once informed of the situation and urged to surface. Acting on this advice Herbert gave the commands for surfacing. The crew worked with speed and precision but the dive remained unchecked. The coxswain, Petty Officer Moth, called that the submarine was out of control. The false 10-ton keel was released but *K13*, seemingly with a will of her own, shrugged off all efforts to prevent her striking the bottom of Gareloch.

When the flurry of activity was over, the captain took stock of the situation. A roll-call produced grim figures: seven civilians and twenty-four naval personnel had perished. With about enough air to last an estimated eight hours, the situation for the forty-nine survivors looked unpromising.

*K13* was not the only submarine undertaking trials in Gareloch that day. *E50* was being put through her paces by Lieutenant-Commander Kenneth Michell, captain of *B10* when she had been bombed and sunk in Venice the previous August. Michell, only a mile from *K13* when she had dived, decided to remain in the vicinity to observe how the 'K' boat came to the surface.

As time progressed, and without sign that *K13* was about to surface, Lieutenant-Commander Michell felt the first pangs of uneasiness. He began to wonder if *K13* was in some kind of trouble. When four o'clock arrived and there was still no sign of *K13*, Michell became actively concerned for her safety. As darkness had now set in, Michell felt certain that had Godfrey Herbert been able to surface he would certainly have done so by then. Convinced that *E13* was in some kind of difficulty, Michell sent word to the Clyde that *K13* had in all probability encountered difficulties and that salvage equipment be made available.

Work had been in progress for several hours when rescue officers concluded that the men in the submarine might well die before *K13* could be raised to the surface. Divers managed to connect a high-pressure air-line to the submarine and to pump in live-saving air. Revived by the air the *K13* survivors blew the ballast tanks. The bow began to rise. Two rescue vessels hoved in on a 6½-inch wire that had been positioned beneath *K13*'s bow and raised it to within eight feet of the surface. A tube was connected to enable fresh air and food to be passed to the survivors. Later the bow was cleared of the surface and a hole burned in it with oxy-acetylene equipment. By nine o'clock on the evening of the 31st, fifty-four hours after she had dived, the first survivor was helped from the dark interior of *K13* into the glare of arc lamps and a huge cheer of welcome.

On 15 March, six weeks after the sinking, *K13* was brought to the surface. She returned to Fairfields and was eventually commissioned as *K22*.

It was in March 1917 that *E49* was sunk with the loss of all hands. On 3 March the minelayer *UC76* sailed Heligoland for Cromarty where she laid mines on the 9th before moving on to the Shetland Islands, where the following day she laid a minefield off Balta Sound – a small harbour in the northern-most of the larger islands which make up the group – which *G13* and *E49* had been using as a base since 8 March for patrolling off Muckle Flugga, the most northerly point of the British Isles.

At 1255 on the afternoon of 12 March, *E49* (Lieutenant B.A. Beal) was observed leaving Balta Sound by a coastal patrol. The submarine passed out of sight behind the small island of Huney, to the south of the entrance. Suddenly a loud explosion was heard. A column of smoke and water rose high behind the island. The submarine failed to make an appearance from behind Huney. An investigation revealed some sailors' caps and a grating afloat on the surface. The position was buoyed to aid divers in locating the submarine. Later an examination of the wreck disclosed that *E49*'s bows had been completely blown off. This suggested that she had been a victim of one of *UC76*'s mines.

\*

Less than a week after the loss of *E49* one of the old 'A' class sank. The *A10* sank at Eglinton Dock, Ardrossan, whilst moored alongside HMS *Pactolus* at the naval base.

Launched on 8 February 1905, *A10* had seen twelve years' service when she arrived at the west coast port in February 1917. At that time she was under the command of Lieutenant-Commander C.C. Dobson. Once she had paid off her crew, which she did on 16 February, Commander A.G. Wright (SNO Ardrossan) detailed Engineer-Lieutenant Robert Driscoll of *Pactolus* to inspect the vessel with the officer in charge to see that all was in order before assuming responsibility. Anxious to retain some of *A10*'s experienced crew to assist in looking after her, Commander Wright wrote to the Admiralty, receiving a reply on 13 March to the effect that no ratings were available. This disappointing news meant that Engineer-Lieutenant Driscoll would have to look after *A10* with ratings from *Pactolus*.

Over a month had passed when at 2030 on Friday 16 March Able Seaman William Honeywell boarded the silent *A10* to carry out his duties. Honeywell closed the fore hatch, switched on the submarine's stern lamp and ascertained that everything was correct for the night. As Honeywell stepped from *A10* to the submarine alongside her (*B4*), he noticed nothing amiss as regards to *A10*'s buoyancy, so it is reasonable to assume that at that time everything appeared to be in order. *A10* was observed by watchkeepers several times during the night and her trim gave no cause for concern.

*Saturday 17 March.* At 0630 crewmen scrubbing the forecastle of *Pactolus* heard a noise coming from the ship's starboard side. Curious as to what was going on, they took an inquisitive look over the side. They saw *A10* settling gradually lower and lower in the water until she disappeared from view. This took three minutes.

Apart from William Honeywell there were several ratings whose duty took them aboard *A10*. ERA Mathew Purvis had been detailed by Engineer-Lieutenant Driscoll to turn the submarine's engines every two days and to have a look round the submarine and then to report. Purvis had always found everything in order. Electrical Artificer Nicholas Pasco had been assigned the task of looking after *A10*'s batteries. To assist him Pasco had Leading Seaman George Weekes. Neither of these ratings had found anything amiss. As an investigation by Commander Wright into the possible cause of the sinking could shed no light on the matter, a court of inquiry was ordered. It was three weeks before the court was convened. In the intervening time the crew of *Pactolus*, with the use of two drifters, raised *A10* and beached her.

*Thursday 5 April.* The court assembled on board *Pactolus* for the inquiry. The evidence of Engineer-Lieutenant Robert Driscoll went some way to clearing up the mystery:

QUESTION: 'Did you ever find any indication of leakage in the boat?'

LT DRISCOLL: 'No.'

QUESTION: 'What steps did you take to ascertain whether she was sinking or not?'

LT DRISCOLL: 'I sent an ERA to test the tank by opening the top cock on the tank.'

QUESTION: 'As far as you knew, what was the state of water in the ballast tanks before she sank to the bottom?'

LT DRISCOLL: 'They were all blown on paying off.'

QUESTION: 'Do you consider they remained empty?'

LT DRISCOLL: 'I should say, yes. I had no evidence to say that they were otherwise.'

QUESTION: 'Had you any means of finding out whether there was any water in the ballast tanks?'

LT DRISCOLL: 'The only means would be to pump the tanks out by the motor on the boat, or by testing with the test cock; also, the inclinometer, if the ship was taking water, would show whether she was going down.'

QUESTION: 'Had you no signs of water coming in?'

LT DRISCOLL: 'I saw none at the time I went there.'

QUESTION: 'Did you ever get signs of water from the engines when turning engines?'

LT DRISCOLL: 'None.'

QUESTION: 'Do you say the ballast tanks were empty the night before the boat sank?'

LT DRISCOLL: 'As far as I know, yes.'

QUESTION: 'Can you account in any way for the boat sinking, and for the accumulation of water in the boat without signs of its coming in through the ballast tanks?'

LT DRISCOLL: 'There are no means of finding out the water in the ballast tanks on account of holes being found in the roof, which is the bottom of the battery tank.'

QUESTION: 'Did you know there were holes found in the bottom of the battery tank?'

LT DRISCOLL: 'I did not know there were holes there until I tested her. After raising the boat I found there were leaks from number one and number four ballast tanks to the battery tanks.'

QUESTION: 'How would you account for water entering the ballast tanks?'

LT DRISCOLL: 'By leak from the Kingston only, or by hull leakage.'

QUESTION: 'Granted that there had been a leakage in the ballast tanks and from ballast tanks to the battery tanks, how could you account for the sudden sinking of the vessel?'

LT DRISCOLL: 'If there was a leakage of water into the ballast tanks it would bring the vessel deeper into the water and submerge the vents from number one and number four auxiliary tanks, which cocks were all closed; but the master valve on the ship's side was open slightly, and cock to bilge inboard vent, which would also allow the water to run straight to the bilge.'

QUESTION: 'Should not all of those cocks have been closed?'

LT DRISCOLL: 'Yes.'

QUESTION: 'Did you take further steps to see that they were closed?'

LT DRISCOLL: 'On paying off the ship I went through the boat with the officer in charge and also the Chief ERA. The valves were all turned off for closed.'

QUESTION: 'Since then, have there been any work or using of the valves?'

LT DRISCOLL: 'Nothing had been done by me or my artificer.'

QUESTION: 'How do you account for the valves being opened?'

LT DRISCOLL: 'I could not say.'

QUESTION: 'What makes you say the valves were open when the boat sank?'

LT DRISCOLL: 'On putting air into the boat for raising I found a great leakage through this pipe, leaking from the vent box, which I plugged after beaching. On opening the boat I went to examine these valves and found that the master valve and inboard vent cock were open.'

QUESTION: 'You have no idea at all of anyone opening these valves?'

LT DRISCOLL: 'As a routine – no sir.'

QUESTION: 'Did you make it a practice at times to go through the boat and see that everything was closed, or send in anyone?'

LT DRISCOLL: 'I went in the boat on paying off, and also daily for about a week. Then I paid visits every three days and was satisfied that the boat was dry and all valves closed.'

The findings of the inquiry were that the sinking was caused by a leakage into the ballast tanks through the Kingston system. This leakage accumulated unnoticed owing to the ballast tanks venting through holes in the bottom of the battery tanks (which were the roof of the ballast tanks) until the vent hole to the master ventilation valve of the after main ballast vent and blow valve box was submerged. Water was then able to enter *A10* through a 1-inch pipe, the main vent valve and inboard vent cock being found open. The opening of the valves could not be explained as the evidence showed that they had been tested frequently and had never been found open. The last test had been made just two days prior to the sinking. The court could not attribute blame to any particular person. It was pointed out that except for ERA Mathew Purvis none of the officers or ratings responsible for *A10* had served in submarines and that the crew of *Pactolus* had some twenty-nine other vessels to maintain and keep running. *A10* remained naval property until April 1919 when she was sold to the Ardrossan Dockyard Company.

*

On the morning of Monday 16 April the *C25* and *C16* were exercising off Harwich with the destroyer *Melampus*. The day was clear with only a breeze to ruffle the surface of the sea. A run was made in which *C16* carried out a dummy attack and *C25* fired a torpedo. During a second run the roles would be reversed: *C25* to make the dummy run and *C16* to fire off a torpedo.

*C16* had already dived by the time *Melampus* commenced her run as target ship. As the destroyer made way at a steady 16 knots her OOW, Acting Sub-Lieutenant Harold Tingley, RCN, sighted *C25*'s periscope four points on the port bow. Tingley saw the periscope, which was about 500 yards off, rising as *C25* completed her run. Seven minutes later Tingley saw *C16*'s periscope protruding twelve inches above the surface. This second sighting was one point on the port bow and twenty-five yards distant. The captain of *Melampus*, Lieutenant-Commander Lawrence Bignell, also saw the tip of *C16*'s periscope; it was on a heading which would take her at right angles across the destroyer's bow.

Lieutenant Arthur Forbes, a submariner from *C7*, was on the bridge with Bignell. Forbes also saw *C16*'s periscope, which he thought was facing a direction away from *Melampus*, and gained the impression that the submarine might have been rising. Lieutenant

Forbes, later to lose his life when captain of *H5*, saw that there would be no time for *C16* to dive beneath *Melampus* – the only way to avoid a collision – and in any case *C16* almost certainly could not see *Melampus* as she would not have continued rising.

Lieutenant-Commander Bignell could see that collision was inevitable. Nevertheless, and in attempt to minimise the blow, he ordered *Melampus* full astern and the helm hard to starboard. *Melampus* was still making considerable headway when ten seconds later, at 0947, *C16* struck the destroyer near the stern.

From his vantage point on the bridge, Lieutenant Forbes made the following observation: 'A torpedo appeared immediately afterwards on the starboard quarter and a large quantity of air came up about five seconds after the collision and about 20 yards on the other side of the destroyer. The submarine appeared to continue along the bottom for about 50 yards, her progress being traced by disturbances on the water due to the escape of air. After this, bubbles continued to come up in the same spot for about half an hour.'

Bignell buoyed the position and radioed what had taken place. He then proceeded to recover the torpedo. A check revealed that damage to *Melampus* had been slight: apart from a fuel tank found to be leaking, a slight leak was also discovered in the warhead magazine. The hope that someone would escape from the submarine, which was at a depth of only 45 feet, was not fulfilled, and so there were no survivors. At 1610 that afternoon, a minesweeper located *C16* three-quarters of a mile north of the Rough Wreck Light Vessel, some seven miles east of Harwich. Diving operations were put in progress and continued, for an hour or so, until worsening weather brought things to a halt. *Melampus* returned to harbour.

The following day, by which time *Melampus* had been docked for examination, it was possible to deduce from marks on the destroyer's bottom that *C16*'s periscope, bridge rails, and the top of her conning tower had struck the ship. *Melampus* having way on at the time, *C16* then slid aft, scraping the keel and badly chipping one of each of the destroyer's centre and starboard propellers.

After *C16* had been raised and docked it was found that she had struck *Melampus*'s starboard bow with her conning tower, which had bent a little to port. Her periscope had also been bent to port from the top of its standard, but the standard itself was not bent. The fore hatch was found unclipped and the strongbacks removed; a lead pig of about 20 pounds was found under the rim and prevented the hatch from closing. Her forward hydroplanes were set at 15° rise, and those aft to 10° dive. Her periscope was discovered right down on the battery boards, but the wires were slack.

Further examination of *C16* gave some indication as to what might have taken place before the accident and after. It seems likely that owing to the shallow depth of the water *C16* had touched bottom and had been moved from a bow-up trim to a horizontal trim. Not wishing to chance upsetting the trim by pumping out or blowing, Lieutenant Boase, *C16*'s captain, had increased speed to force the boat back to her depth. The position of her hydroplanes and some of her instruments lend support to this theory. In opposition to this is that *C16*'s periscope was found lowered, whereas if the theory was correct the periscope could have been expected to have been raised to enable Lieutenant Boase to obtain a view at the earliest possible moment as *C16* got to her depth again.

The submarine's motors appear to have been only stopped at the impact, and not used again. The upper conning tower hatch lid had been wrenched half open; the flooding of the conning tower which resulted from this had sent *C16* to the bottom. The water then entered through a gap caused by a distortion of the lower conning tower hatch, closed at the time of the collision. An attempt was made to seal the leaking hatch with wedges, tallow, and articles of clothing. It is thought that although not tightly packed, the clothing, still in place on salvage, had to a large extent contained the water so that it was no great cause of concern.

An attempt to blow the main ballast tanks was not entirely successful. The reason for this was that the pipe leading to *C16*'s whistle (the whistle was attached to her conning tower) was broken in the collision; as the stop cock to the whistle valve had been left open, the air from the groups vented rapidly from the broken pipe.

The pumps had been used but it was believed that they had stopped through being shorted by water spraying from the lower conning tower hatch, which had been so badly distorted that it could not be opened by salvors and it had to be burned out. Hand pumps had been manned.

The water which had entered the boat ran aft. This, coupled with the blowing of No 1 main ballast, caused *C16*'s bows to rise until the forward depth-gauge indicated 16 feet. As the bows were so near to the surface, it was decided to blow the first lieutenant out through a torpedo tube in order to help with rescue operations.

When Samuel Anderson entered the torpedo tube he had tied to his wrist a note from Lieutenant Boase:

WE ARE IN 16 FEET OF WATER. THE WAY TO GET US OUT IS TO LIFT THE
BOWS BY THE SPECTACLE AND HAUL US OUT OF THE BOAT THROUGH
THE TUBES. H. BOASE.

The attempt to blow Anderson to the surface failed, possibly because
of the inclination of the tube and the fact that Anderson was a stock-
ily-built man. There was no further attempt to get a man to the surface by this method.

Some time around 1630 it was decided to abandon ship. Wearing
lifejackets the crew assembled in an orderly manner under the fore
hatch. An airlock was formed by 'cracking' the rear door of the starboard torpedo tube to partially flood the compartment. What then
took place might be considered the saddest part of the affair. When
the hatch lid was raised the fender above it jammed against the
super-structure casing, thus preventing the lid from opening perhaps
no more than ten inches. When the lid was dropped the pig of lead
attached to the fender swung in under the joint and held the lid open
about two inches. The airlock was lost. The compartment was
flooded. The occupants were drowned.

*C16* continued in service for another five years. When she was sold
in August 1922, she was then the only submarine of her class still in
service with the Royal Navy. Lieutenant Harold Boase had been in
the Submarine Service since March 1914.

Though not the most successful of U-boat captains Lieutenant-
Commander Walther Hans had a fair measure of success. One of his
victims was the light cruiser *Nottingham*. Another was the *C34*.

Arrangements were put in hand to keep two 'C' class submarines
on A/S patrol between the Orkneys and Shetlands. Consequently at
seven o'clock on the evening of 16 July, *C34* sailed from Scapa Flow
with the *Medea* and *C19* for the Fair Isle area, where she was to patrol
between the two groups of islands and as far east as 0°. *C34* had
orders to give special attention to convoys from and to Lerwick proceeding north and south.

At 1335 the following afternoon, *C34* (Lieutenant I.S. Jefferson)
was lying stopped on the surface, with tanks partially. flooded, in
about 59°30'N 0°5'W when she was sighted by Walther Hans (*U52*).
At 1446 the British submarine was hit by a torpedo. She sank at once
in a cloud of smoke and flame. When Hans closed the point where
*C34* had gone down, he found just one survivor: as Stoker Frank Sco-
ble, covered with oil, was hauled aboard *U52* he is alleged to have
uttered what the Germans described as a typically English expression: 'You have won the game.'

(*Top*) The black tug in this photograph alongside the lighter, covered ship is actually the camouflaged *E14*, the only ship in the history of the Royal Navy to win a VC on two different occasions. She was lost in the Dardanelles.

(*Centre*) *E4*, the outside submarine returns to Harwich with German prisoners. *E4* with *E16* and the *D3* were all destined to lose their crews, *E4* being raised after collision with *E41*, was put back into service and sold in 1922.

(*Bottom right*) *D3* picking up 48 survivors from the Q-ship *Warner*, sunk by the *U61* on 13th March 1917. Sadly, when survivors from the *D3* were in the water after being sunk by a French airship there was no one to aid them.

(*Below*) Lt-Cdr Saxton-White, later to win a posthumous VC when the *E14* was sunk in January 1918, prepares to go ashore shooting in Mudros.

(*Top*) To stop German troops reinforcing those at the end of the mole at Zeebrugge it was decided to blow a hole in the middle of it. Lt R. D. Sandford and his small crew put the ancient, petrol-driven *C3* in the exact spot despite being fired on at point-blank range by the Germans above him. Lt Sandford was awarded the VC. (*Centre*) The submarines at Killybegs, Ireland, based there for anti-submarine patrols, found the area ideal for giving boats a wash and brush up at low tide. On 26th June 1918, while on anti-submarine patrol, *D6* was sunk by the *UB73*.

 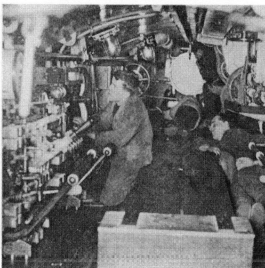

(*Bottom left*) Photographs taken in *E34*, a minelayer, two months before she was lost in the Heligoland Bight, July 1918. The boat is probably resting on the bottom as the three officers are in the wardroom which was a curtained off portion of the control room. The captain, Lt R.I. Pulleyne, seen here reading, held the DSO and DSC; the two others lost in the boat each held a DSC, submarine mine-laying being considered a hazardous occupation. (*Bottom right*) The watchkeeper in the motor room of *E34* keeps his eyes on the starboard switchboard while his five companions sleep. These conditions were luxurious compared with the sixty-two *A, B* and *C* boats.

After striking *C34* Hans had no further success on the patrol, which had been rewarded by the sinking of one submarine and four ships totalling 7,000 tons. By the 19th he was back at Heligoland being congratulated on his success.

Lieutenant Ingleby Jefferson, *C34*'s captain, was twenty-four years of age and the son of a doctor. Jefferson had been with the flotilla only since 24 June and was on his third patrol. Lieutenant Jefferson had been the Officer On Watch of *E43* in the North Sea collision with *E36*.

Lieutenant Edward Carre was captain of *E47* when she failed to return to harbour in August. *E47* had started life in Fairfield's yard, but had been completed by Beardmore. She was little more than twelve months old when she was lost in the North Sea, graveyard of so many submarines, by unknown causes some time round 20 August.

*

Between August 1915 and May 1917 fourteen 'G' class submarines were launched at four different yards. Similar in displacement to the 'E' class, the 'G's had a stern tube which fired the new 21-inch torpedo. Several of the 'G' class were sunk during the war. Foul weather and a case of mistaken identity contributed to the loss of *G9* in the early hours of Sunday 16 September.

Commander Charles Ramsey was having a none-to-easy-time of shepherding a convoy from Aspo Fiord, Norway, towards Lerwick. Appalling weather conditions had reduced the convoy's speed to 6 knots and Ramsey, controlling the convoy from HM Destroyer *Pasley*, was experiencing great difficulty in preventing the merchantmen from becoming detached during blinding rain squalls.

The *G9* (Lieutenant-Commander Hon B.P. Cary) had been at sea since sailing Scapa Flow at two o'clock on the afternoon of the 9th. By the 16th she was making way in heavy seas in the same area as the convoy. Lieutenant-Commander Cary – on the bridge peering through the darkness and rain with his navigator, a lookout, and a signalman – had information that a U-boat was somewhere in the area. Beneath his feet, his crew went quietly about their duties. One of the crew was Stoker W.A. Drake.

William Drake came off watch at midnight. Half an hour later he lay down to rest. On awakening Drake noticed that *G9*'s engines had stopped. The ringing of the telegraph for full speed ahead on main motors was followed by Cary's order, via the voice-pipe, calling for diving stations. Stoker Drake's account of *G9*'s loss states: 'We were still going ahead on main motors when I went midships and noticed we were getting the bow tubes ready. The captain then called down from the bridge and asked if the tubes were ready. The captain then called out for the director, but before he could get the director on the conning tower the order "Stand by . . . Fire!" was given. Both torpedoes were fired. The coxswain was then called from the control room to the bridge and the lookout was sent aft to get the stern tubes ready. Somebody then called down from the top and asked if the arc-flashing lamp switch was made. Then the navigator came down from the conning tower and went to the wardroom. The signalman started flashing. Then I felt a bump aft.'

*Pasley*'s stern lookout during the early hours of the 16th was Able Seaman Arthur Hodgson. Hodgson heard a 'buzzing noise' (this was a torpedo breaking surface as it neared the destroyer) and then saw a torpedo heading for, and then hit, *Pasley*.

From his station abaft the bridge, AB William Banforth also saw a torpedo. Banforth saw it leave the sea and hit the ship between the after torpedo tube and the stern.

In his account of the incident AB Horace Cann, on *Pasley*'s bridge, says: 'I heard the whirl of the propeller of a torpedo and then I saw a track coming towards the ship about two points before the starboard beam. I watched it hit the ship against the engine room. I also saw a single track pass the ship's stern. After that I saw a light flashing just on our starboard bow between 50 and 100 yards distant. We were then slewing to starboard. When the submarine was right ahead, we hit it, just before the conning tower.'

Of his part in the proceedings Leading Signalman R.H. Pattenden later recalled: 'At 0230 I sighted a torpedo coming from the starboard bow towards the after part of the ship and I cried out to the officer on watch "Torpedo approaching the ship!" The officer on watch immediately gave the order "Full speed ahead both . . . Hard a-port". Shortly after this I sighted another torpedo, the first having hit the ship but did not explode. The submarine started flashing. She was not known to be a submarine until she began flashing. She was apparently using a cruiser arc-lamp which lit up the whole of the submarine, and also lit up our bridge. I got hold of our lamp to make a reply and at the same time reported that she was one of our own. This I knew because she made the correct challenge. She was too close to prevent ramming.'

When the OOW, Midshipman Frank Wallace, saw the torpedo he

at once ordered the engines full ahead and the quarter-master, Able Seaman Colin MacIntosh, to helm hard to port. Wallace states: 'I saw the wash of a ship on our starboard side and put the helm midships, as we were turning too quickly to ram her with it hard over. When the captain arrived on the bridge, I informed him of what I had done. A light appeared flashing and I could dimly make out a submarine. The signalman called, "She's one of ours", and the captain gave the order, "Hard to port . . . .Stop both". But it was too late to miss her and she sank almost immediately.'

The force of the collision sent *G9* reeling. William Drake assembled under the conning tower with others of the crew. Drake continues: 'The boat heeled over to starboard and then there was a big rush of air up through the conning tower. I saw one man get up through the conning tower, and so I followed him. When I was half-way through the lower lid, somebody in the control room gave the order to close it and it caught me in the stomach. I got through the door and right onto the bridge.'

By this time *G9*'s stern had already settled very low in the water, hence the order to close the lower conning tower hatch. Stoker Drake made the bridge in record time. He saw two men only – one on the bridge and the other in the sea midway between the submarine and *Pasley*. Then *G9*'s stern dipped suddenly. She began to go under. At this point Drake was washed off the bridge. He began the struggle to reach the destroyer.

Commander Ramsey, *Pasley*'s CO, was in the charthouse when he felt the impact of the dud torpedo striking the ship. A moment later he received an emergency call from the bridge. Wondering what had happened, Ramsey hurried to the bridge. He arrived there just after Wallace had sighted *G9*'s wash and had put the helm to midships to ram.

'The state of affairs now', Ramsey was to report, 'was such that we would obviously ram our aggressor, as we were still swinging to starboard and she was steaming across our bow from starboard to port. Almost midships I saw a flash which lit up a submarine so I gave the order "Clear away depth-charges". The signalman then shouted "She's one of ours!", and at the same time I heard them shout in English. Immediately on striking, and seeing the submarine obviously sinking, which she did in about thirty seconds, I gave the orders "Out boats . . . Close down both". The officer on watch jumped down off the bridge and threw over all rope, etc., in the direction of the few shouts that were heard in the water. As the submarine

was apparently stationary I stopped the engines. I then jumped aft to
see that everything was being done. Lifebuoys and life-lines had been
thrown out and some of my men were down the side of the fenders;
another one tried to get hold of anybody; another man was getting
into a bowline with a view to getting overboard after a man in the
water. As everything possible was now being done I went on the
bridge.'

Lieutenant Robert Burger was lying full dressed, minus boots, on
his bunk when a dull thud awakened him. Curious as to what had
caused the noise he quickly made his way topside. For his trouble he
found that he could 'not see anything of note'. Returning below he
donned his lifejacket and, taking up his binoculars, made his way
back on deck. This time things were different. Moving to the port rail
he saw *G9* up-end and go down stern-first. He heard cries for help
coming from the sea, and then Ramsey calling for lines to be dropped
over the side. Drawing his knife Lieutenant Burger cut the after life-
lines which ran along the upper deck. He then went to where several
of the crew were assisting Able Seaman Henry Old to rescue Stoker
Drake. Following a brief word with Old, Burger went astern, where
not without difficulty he saw a submariner in the sea. The man was
in a lifebuoy and was no more than six or seven yards from the ship.
He cried out for help and another lifebuoy was thrown towards him.
When it was hauled in, it was found to be empty. The man was not
seen again.

Stoker Drake had to put up quite a struggle to reach the destroyer.
Battling against heavy seas he managed to gain a hold on one of the
life-lines hanging down the ship's side. How he achieved this he had
no idea as he was 'practically insensible' by the time he reached *Pasley*. With shouts of encouragement from *Pasley*'s crew, Drake tried to
maintain a hold on the line long enough to be hauled aboard; but his
strength was failing and the line kept slipping through his numbed
fingers. Seeing that Drake would be lost if not soon taken aboard,
Henry Old put a bowline round himself and went over the side to
assist Drake.

'They tried to haul us both up together,' Old was later to remark,
'and they could not manage it. They then sent me down a running
bowline and I passed this over the man's right arm and over his
head. I could not get it over his left arm. As soon as they took up the
strain on the running bowline, I shouted up to them to pull me
inboard. They pulled the other man afterwards,' William Drake, the
only *G9* survivor, was safely aboard *Pasley*.

Commander Ramsey remained in the vicinity for about thirty minutes without seeing or hearing further survivors. An engineer officer, Lieutenant-Commander J.A. White, carried out an inspection of *Pasley*'s collision damage. He found a lower store flooded and water coming through to an upper store. After further inspection he decided that the ship was in no immediate danger and informed Ramsey to this effect. White then pumped 71 tons of oil fuel into the sea from a forward tank. Using shores he was able to make *Pasley* more seaworthy. Commander Ramsey continued the escorting of the convoy to the Shetland Islands.

Lieutenant-Commander Byron Cary had been on the lookout for a U-boat expected from Muckle Flugga. It would seem that Cary had mistaken *Pasley* for the U-boat. That conditions were extremely bad does not in itself explain how Cary came to mistake a vessel with a light half-way up its mast (*Pasley* displayed such a light to assist the merchantmen) for a U-boat, which would be likely to show any lights at all. Was it possible that no one on *G9*'s bridge had seen the light? This seems very unlikely indeed, especially if one takes into consideration the reply of the stern-tube man who came from the bridge to the control room and, as he made his way aft, passed the remark that a U-boat with a light had been sighted. But why should *G9*'s bridge party believe that a U-boat would show a light? The only obvious explanation would appear to be that they thought the enemy had been forced to make a repair which entailed the use of a light to some degree, or that the U-boat was at a rendezvous point.

The length of time between the firing of the torpedoes and the ramming was about two minutes. There is evidence to suggest that soon after firing, Cary realised that a mistake had been made: he had asked for the cruiser arc-lamp and started signalling, which he would not have done had he no doubts that his target was a U-boat or an enemy destroyer.

*Pasley*'s bridge party was in no doubt that they had been attacked by an enemy submarine, and had acted accordingly. It should be noted that whereas Lieutenant-Commander Cary knew that an Allied convoy was somewhere in the area, Ramsey had no information as to the whereabouts of submarines.

Lieutenant-Commander Byron Cary was the second of three sons of the 12th Viscount Falkland. Cary was thirty at the time *G9* was sunk and had been in the Submarine Service since May 1909.

*

There were numerous occasions when units of the Grand Fleet made a sweep of the enemy coast looking for mischief. With the light cruiser *Blanche* at the head, the 12th Submarine Flotilla ventured forth as part of just such an operation.

*Blanche* was heading *K1*, *K3*, *K4*, and *K7*, in line ahead and in that order, when at 1730 on 18 November and at a point off the Danish coast, *Blanche* was forced to deviate sharply to port to avoid three unknown cruisers (probably of the 4th Light Cruiser Squadron) which without lights crossed her bows from starboard to port. Only prompt action by Lieutenant C.H. Luch in putting the helm over and switching on the navigation lights averted a collision. However, this abrupt change of course by *Blanche* took the submarines by surprise and in the resulting confusion two of them (*K1*, *K4*) collided.

*K1* had been keeping station some 500 yards astern of *Blanche* when Lieutenant John Philipson, the OOW, saw a red light suddenly appear two points off *K1*'s port bow. Gaining the impression that a vessel had passed through the line, Philipson ordered a course alteration to starboard. He had no sooner given the order than *Blanche*'s signal lamp flashed: ON NAVIGATION LIGHTS. The direction of the flashing lamp told Philipson that *Blanche* must have altered course; he at once changed course so as to bring *K1* back on station astern of *Blanche*.

Lieutenant-Commander Benning, *K1*'s captain, had left the bridge barely five minutes when he received a report of *Blanche*'s signal. Benning at once returned to the bridge: 'The searchlight was immediately put to full brilliancy and sidelights switched on,' reports Benning. 'I then realised that the boat had stopped without any orders from the bridge. It was reported that the turbines had stopped as salt-water was coming through the sprayers, therefore there was no steam. I told the signalman to report to *Blanche*. *K3* passed us close on the port side, not realising I was stopped. I then ordered the signal light to be flashed to port side. Immediately afterwards I saw a submarine closing on the port quarter, coming directly for *K1*. I could do nothing as I had no way on. In a few seconds *K4* struck us, on eighty-seven bulkhead beam tube-space and the control room.'

*K4*'s OOW, Lieutenant Clive Robinson, saw a red light appear on *K4*'s port bow. He correctly interpreted the light as being *Blanche*'s port bow light. As *Blanche* had apparently altered course to port without giving any 'ALTER COURSE' signal, Robinson called for the captain, Lieutenant-Commander David Stocks. 'I had been on the bridge a few minutes', says Stocks, 'and had kept *K4* on the same course as the stern of *K3*, intending to follow her round to the new course in succession, when between *K4* and *K3* I suddenly observed a red light very close to my starboard bow, about three points. Seeing a collision was inevitable I went hard to starboard to endeavour to minimise the blow; then full speed astern both. About twenty seconds after I had rung down full speed astern, *K4* struck *K1* a glancing blow abreast her conning tower and at the same time *K1*'s stern light became visible.'

After ordering *K1*'s watertight doors shut Charles Benning went below to inspect the damage. He saw that the beam tube-space was flooding rapidly and that water was pouring into the control room. The blowers were started and the foremost pump put on the control room bilge, but this made no impression on the amount of water coming in. It took only minutes for the batteries to begin releasing a large amount of chlorine gas. The collision had cut electric leads. When water had risen to the level of the severed leads *K1*'s lights went out and the blowers stopped. At this point Benning ordered the crew on deck. Two officers, Lieutenants Rendel and Lowther, remained in the control room shutting off valves and breaking switches until Herbert Rendel was overcome by gas and had to be taken topside by Lowther.

By this time *K1*'s upper deck was well under water and she had taken on a heavy list to port. Her conning tower and bridge-house were reeking with chlorine gas. *Blanche* was signalled that *K1* was sinking. The cruiser closed *K1*. Commanded by Lieutenants Boyd and Masson, two cutters were lowered and sent to the submarine. In the dark and in a difficult sea, the cutters made five trips to transfer all fifty-six of the submarine's crew to *Blanche*.

A discussion was held as to whether *K1* could be saved. For the reasons which follow, it was decided that she would have to be sunk: (1) *K1* had shipped a great deal of water and was considered to be slowly settling (2) the chlorine gas made it impossible for anyone to remain inside the boat (3) the possibility that anyone left on board to secure hawsers, etc., would not be saved if *K1* sank, as a rising sea would have made a rescue operation extremely hazardous (4) *K1*'s bollards and cables needed for towing were already under water. Another consideration was that *Blanche* and the other submarines had been stopped for more than an hour with navigation lights burn-

ing and searchlights directed on *K1* to facilitate crew rescue. As these
lights were visible quite some distance, and as the flotilla was in close
proximity to enemy waters, it was decided that the major duty of saving *K1*'s crew having been performed, to spend an hour or more in a
fruitless task was unjustifiable. The submarine was therefore sunk by
four direct hits from the 4-inch gun.

Within days of the return to harbour an inquiry into the incident
was opened. Of the circumstances which had led to the collision the
most glaring was the slowing down and stopping of *K1* at a critical
moment owing to water, in the place of oil fuel, passing through the
sprayers and extinguishing the boiler fires. It was revealed that this
had occurred soon after oil fuel to the sprayers was switched from one
group of tanks to another group.

The 'K' class were twin-hulled with the inner hull being the pressure hull and the outer hull a construction of light plating. Except for
the torpedo tubes, everything outside the pressure hull is open to the
sea and floods up when the submarine dives. In the 'K's the lower
half of the space between the two hulls was divided into twenty main
external ballast tanks, known as the 'Externals'. Situated along the
bottom of the submarine, and *within* the pressure hull, were further
tanks: main ballast, auxiliary ballast, and the fore and aft trimming
tanks. These were known as the 'Internals'. In the 'K' class the
under-sides of the oil fuel tanks were open to the sea, which meant
that the oil fuel rested on the water. As the oil fuel was used up, so it
was replaced in the fuel tank by more sea-water. This system helped
ease the problem of adjusting the ballast; but a flaw of the system was
that if the submarine rolled exessively in rough sea, the oil and water
were inclined to emulsify. If this happened the mixture could, and on
occasions did, put out the boiler fires and bring the submarine to a
halt through a loss of steam. Obviously the system required strict
supervision when oil fuel was being drawn from the external fuel
tanks, which begs the question: was enough care taken when *K1*'s oil
fuel to the sprayers was changed over to Nos 5 and 7 externals?

In his report of the collision Engineer-Lieutenant C.R. Hore of *K1*
states: 'At 1720 I was in the turbine room, at which time everything
was correct. We were using fuel from 'A' Group. The chief stoker
reported to me that 'A' Group contained 6 tons of oil fuel at this time.
I gave him orders to change over to No 7 starboard external and No
5 port external, both of which contained oil fuel. It was my intention
to use these two externals during the dark hours, when there would
be little chance of diving, and to change over to the remaining fuel
group, viz 'C' Group, at about daylight next morning when it was

estimated that the two externals would have been nearly emptied. At 1735 the aft suction valves, together with the inboard vents, were opened on these two externals and the fuel led to port settling tank from which fuel group took its suction. As soon as the external tanks had been put on I watched the gauge-glass in the port settling tank for signs of water, but it showed none. At 1740 the boiler room reported that water was coming through the sprayers. The steam rapidly went down. The turbines were stopped when steam had dropped to 50 pounds, this being at 1741. I immediately reported through to the control room. About a minute after this the noise of the collision was heard. Orders were passed through to close all watertight doors. All doors were closed, including funnels and boiler room vents . . .'

As might be expected, Engineer-Lieutenant Hore was a principal witness at the court of inquiry convened in HMS *Resolution* on 27 November.

QUESTION: 'Have you any means of telling when there is salt-water in an external?'

ENG-LT HORE: 'No.'

QUESTION: 'Is the glass water-gauge on the settling tank easily visible?'

ENG-LT HORE: 'Not easily.'

QUESTION: 'Did you take any precautions to see whether there was salt-water in the external?'

ENG-LT HORE: 'They are opened up every other day and examined. And always before going to sea we see them full up.'

QUESTION: 'It is a common occurrence to find salt-water in the externals?'

ENG-LT HORE: 'It has been noted before in submarines. We have had water before in *K1*, but nothing to stop the engines.'

QUESTION: 'How do you account for the fact that the gauge-glass in the port settling tank showed no sign of water, whereas at 1740 water was reported as coming in?'

ENG-LT HORE: 'It is very hard to account for. The gauge-glass is difficult to see. Looking at it personally, there was no sign of water at all.'

QUESTION: 'Considering the settling tank holds several tons of oil, how do you account for sufficient water getting through to put out all the fires in five minutes?'

ENG-LT HORE: 'I think the pipes from the external tanks to settling tanks were full of oil and it probably took a few minutes to consume this oil before the water followed it up from the external tank.'

QUESTION: 'You stated *K1* stopped within one minute of the time it was reported to you?'

ENG-LT HORE: 'Yes.'

QUESTION: 'Does that mean a large amount of water was coming through?'

ENG-LT HORE: 'Not necessarily a large amount, but that all sprayers were spraying water. A pocket of water came through and then we got oil again.'

QUESTION: 'It was quite a small amount of water?'

ENG-LT HORE: 'Yes. It must have been, for we had oil through in a few minutes.'

Also summoned to give evidence was Chief Stoker Frederick Cox. Cox had made the actual change over from 'A' Group to Nos 5 and 7 externals.

QUESTION: 'Is it possible to suck from external direct and deliver to boilers?'

CHIEF STO COX: 'Without going through the settling tanks – yes.'

QUESTION: 'Is it a different valve that has to be used?'

CHIEF STO COX: 'Yes.'

QUESTION: 'Is it close to it, or next to it?'

CHIEF STO COX: 'In the same compartment at a short distance.'

QUESTION: 'Were there any test cocks in external tanks?'

CHIEF STO COX: 'Yes.'

QUESTION: 'Did you try it?'

CHIEF STO COX: 'Yes.'

QUESTION: 'On which tank?'

CHIEF STO COX: 'Both of them.'

QUESTION: 'Does the pipe go right to the bottom of the tank?'

CHIEF STO COX: 'I could not say.'

QUESTION: 'When opened, did both show oil?'

CHIEF STO COX: 'Yes.'

QUESTION: 'How long did you keep them open?'

CHIEF STO COX: 'Some little time. Till I thought it was sufficient.'

With the conclusion of evidence both Lieutenant-Commander Benning and Engineer-Lieutenant Hore were censured for their part in the incident. The view was expressed that Nos 5 port and 7 starboard externals should have been tested *before* shifting over the fuel supply, and that Cecil Hore should have satisfied himself that this had been done. A puzzling aspect of the change over of fuel supply is that the settling tank contained sufficient oil fuel from 'A' Group of tanks to last about an hour at full speed after 'A' Group had been shut off; but as has been stated, water came through the sprayers about five minutes after Nos 5 and 7 tanks were connected up. There were two possible causes for this: either the settling tank, which held several tons of oil fuel, partially filled with water – and anyone who claimed to have tested the tank was mistaken – or the valve in the pipe which cuts out the settling tank was inadvertently opened, thus admitting water to the sprayers. It must be said, however, that both these possibilities were contrary to the stated evidence. It appears that the external tanks were tested for oil fuel, but owing to the test cock being at a higher level than the suction of the oil fuel supplying the tanks, the presence of a considerable quantity of water might not have been discovered.

After careful consideration of the event, it was thought that *K1* was some distance to starboard of *Blanche*'s track owing to the helm which was first applied when *Blanche*'s red light was observed. For this reason her stern light was not visible to the submarine astern of her. Also, it was considered that *K1* had forward motion up to the moment of impact and that Lieutenant-Commander David Stocks in *K4* (speed 16 knots) first sighted the port bow light of *K1* when both vessels were nearly abreast on courses converging at an angle of about 30°.

The court was of the opinion that Lieutenant-Commander Charles Benning contributed to the accident in that after *K1*'s engine had stopped he did not use her remaining speed to haul her out of line. It was also felt that Benning might have improved the situation had he not failed to give four blasts of his siren or 'R' (NOT UNDER CONTROL). The point was also made that Benning ordered his signalman, Leading Signalman John Lawson, to 'Flash a light on the port side', whereas a definite 'R' would have been of greater value.

Damage to *K4* had been limited to the bow (it had been pushed back about 3½ feet and bent to port) and a few leaky rivets in the pressure hull. Lieutenant-Commander Stocks, soon to be lost in *K4*, was judged to have taken all possible action to minimise the result of the collision when he realised that it was inevitable.

The cruiser *Blanche* did not escape criticism entirely: had *Blanche* given the sound signal I AM ALTERING COURSE TO PORT when taking action to avoid the unknown cruiser force, it would have assisted her following submarines in realising the situation.

*K1* was the last submarine loss of 1917. The year had been one of the most traumatic of the war. The huge losses in Flanders between June and December were in part responsible for the first signs of disillusionment among the civil population for the way in which the war up to then had been conducted. Also in 1917 came the first real shortage of food and goods. At a time when one out of every four ships leaving British ports fell victim to a mine or a U-boat attack, Prime Minister Lloyd George, against Admiralty advice, insisted that ships sailed in convoy. A dramatic falling off in sinkings followed this wise move.

# 1918

The first submarine loss of the year occurred when *G8* failed to return to harbour after a North Sea patrol. Captained at that time by Lieutenant John Tryon, she was lost through unknown causes some time around 14 January. Commanded by Lieutenant Martin Collier, *H10* also failed to return in January. She disappeared in the North Sea some time before the 20th. Tryon had joined the Submarine Service in June 1913, and Martin Collier in October of the same year.

In December 1917 the 12th and 13th Flotillas, both of which consisted of 'K' class submarines, moved from Scapa Flow to Rosyth in the Forth Estuary. Within weeks it was decided that the two flotillas would be units of a powerful Rosyth Force which was to take part in Operation EC1, an ambitious exercise which drew on the resources of almost the entire Grand Fleet.

In the evening of 31 January Sir Hugh Evan-Thomas, in command of the Rosyth Force, led his ships and submarines clear of harbour for the North Sea exercise with Admiral Beatty's Scapa Flow Force, which included a large number of battleships.

Captain Charles Little maintained a close eye on the 12th Flotilla (*K3, K4, K6, K7*) from the bridge of the cruiser *Fearless*. Little had commanded one of the Navy's first operational submarines. Another submarine veteran, Commander Ernest Leir, was responsible for *K11, K12, K14, K17* and *K22* of the 13th Flotilla. Leir, who had captained the very first 'K' boat in August 1916, led the flotilla from the destroyer *Ithuriel*. The submarines of both flotillas were in line astern.

Heading Sir Hugh's Rosyth Force was the cruiser *Courageous*. The rest of this formation was distributed as follows: Commander Leir's 13th Flotilla, then four battle-cruisers with escorting destroyers, then Little's 12th Flotilla, and bringing up the rear were the three battleships of the 5th Battle Squadron and their screening destroyers.

Darkness had fallen by the time the Rosyth Force arrived at the mouth of the estuary. A light mist had descended, making the task of maintaining station behind the shaded blue stern-light of the vessel ahead something of a problem.

May Island is about a mile in length and situated near the mouth of the Forth Estuary. As Sir Hugh's formation approached the island, two minesweeping trawlers (part of a group of eight that were sweeping for mines without any knowledge of Operation EC1) were sighted dead ahead. *K11* immediately reduced speed and swung to port; *K17* did likewise, but *K14*, although reducing her speed from 19 to 13 knots, held a straight course whilst at the same time wondering why the two submarines ahead had made a sudden change of course. The reason quickly became all too evident when the two trawlers were sighted a half mile ahead. As soon as Commander Harbottle (*K14*) realised that there was a possibility of collision with the trawlers, he too ordered a course alteration. The helmsman acknowledged the order and then cried that the helm had jammed. *K12*, next in line, passed clear. Harbottle's thoughts were now directed towards the battle-cruisers some four miles astern. If he was not careful, the big ships might easily slice him in two.

'The helm's freed itself, sir,' Able Seaman Curtis, the helmsman, informed Harbottle. Thankful that no serious incident had developed during the six minutes that the helm had apparently jammed, Harbottle resumed his course.

When *K12* had passed clear of Harbottle's submarine she had disappeared from the view of *K22*, following in *K12*'s wake. *K22*'s bridge party searched the darkness for a glimpse of *K12*'s rear light. Then 200 yards off the starboard bow they saw a light; but instead of this being the hoped-for blue rear light of *K12*, the light looming out of the darkness was red. The OOW, Lieutenant Laurence Dickinson, knew that this meant that the vessel ahead was lying directly across their course.

'Hard to starboard!' Even as Dickinson's order was being acted out it was already too late. At 19 knots *K22* struck the other vessel, which was *K14*, just behind the forward torpedo compartment. The reaction of both crews was immediate: all watertight doors were shut and secured. The forward compartments of both submarines were flooded but neither boat was in imminent danger of sinking.

The collision between the two submarines was bad enough, but if the approaching battle-cruisers and their escorting destroyers failed to notice the damaged submarines . . . The outcome did not bear thinking about. On sighting a red Very light fired by *K22*, the leading battle-cruiser passed safely to port at a speed of 21 knots. All the ships following her passed the two 'K' boats without mishap except for the last in line, the *Inflexible*. The big ship smashed into *K22* and ripped back thirty feet of the submarine's bows, so that they stuck out at right-angles to the rest of the hull. The *Inflexible* raced on and melted into the blackness.

*K22* had been involved in two accidents in twenty-five minutes. Below decks Petty Officer Oscar Moth, another Dardanelles veteran, recalled that it was one year to the day that he had been rescued from this same boat (she was then *K13*) in Gareloch.

When Commander Leir, by now some six miles away in *Ithuriel*, received word that two of his submarines had been involved in an accident he and his three remaining submarines (*K11, K12, K17*) turned about and made for the area of the accidents. *Ithuriel* and the submarines had not long completed the turn about when the battle-cruiser *Australia* made a sudden appearance out of the mist. A collision was narrowly avoided, as was another a few minutes later when the battle-cruiser's escorting destroyers caused a further need to take avoiding action. There was worse to come. Before Operation EC1 was fully underway, five submarines would be involved in accidents which would result in two of them being sunk.

Captain Little, in *Fearless*, was unaware that Ernest Leir had turned about and was heading towards *Fearless* and the 12th Flotilla. 'Lights!' An officer on *Fearless*'s bridge had seen the lights of two vessels, one astern of the other, off the port bow. Even as he peered into the darkness the lights of a third vessel, *K17*, was sighted about a half mile astern of the others. From *Fearless* a close watch was kept on the lights as the first two ships crossed their path before disappearing. Attention was then focused on *K17*, captained by Lieutenant-Commander Henry Hearn. Captain Little, expecting *K17* to pass down his port side in accordance with the rules of the sea, maintained his course and, surging ahead at 21 knots, quickly arrived at a point where a collision with *K17* was inevitable, even though Little called for a change of course and asked for full speed astern.

At 2030 the cruiser's bows struck *K17* a hard blow forward of the conning tower before sending her reeling along the port side. Water rushed into *K17* through a gaping hole in her pressure hull. Lieutenant Gerald Jackson, the first lieutenant, had been sitting on his bunk in the wardroom when a few seconds before the collision he heard the order to close all watertight doors. Jumping up he sprang at the door leading into the control room. Then *Fearless* struck. A violent lurch sent men sprawling. Jackson leaped through into the control room and with Leading Seaman Anthony Westbrook attempted to shut the door against a torrent of water. Then came the order to abandon ship. The crew left their duties and scrambled topside.

*K17*'s bow was soon under water, and going deeper by the second. As *K17* became increasingly awash, personnel on deck edged towards the stern. Some of the crew took to the water. *Fearless* busied herself with the search for survivors.

When *K17* had sailed harbour Signalman G.T.W. Kimbell had been ill with bronchitis in his bunk over the midship torpedo room. He had been ill for four days but, at last, his temperature was gradually returning to normal and his main concern was the frequency he was having to leave his bunk to visit the heads aft. Around eight o'clock, half an hour before the collision, Lieutenant Jackson paid him a visit.

'How are you feeling, Kimbell?'

'A bit better, sir.'

'Good. Let's just check your temperature.'

Jackson expressed satisfaction at Kimbell's temperature and said that after a night's rest he might be able to get up. Kimbell was brought a cup of chicken soup. After the soup he decided to visit the heads again and then try and settle down for the night.

'What again!' On his trips aft Kimbell had become used to the good-natured banter of the crew. Passing through the motor room on his way back to his bunk he was given a 'Goodnight, Bunting*. Hope you have a good night and are better in the morning.'

'I hope so too.'

Signalman Kimbell takes up the story: 'I had entered the passageway on my return to my bunk and I was about half-way along the passage when there was an almighty crash somewhere forward. The lights went out in the passage, leaving me in the dark. Immediately after hearing the order to close all watertight doors I heard the clips

* Bunting: slang for signalman. (Author).

being fastened in position on the doors at both ends of the passage. I was trapped. Knowing that a large spanner was handy I groped in the darkness until I found it. As I could hear water pouring into the forward compartment, I went to the after door and hit it with the spanner.

"'Who's there?" a voice said.

"'It's Kimbell. I'm trapped in the passage. Let me out." Against all regulations they opened the door very quickly to let me in.

"'What's happened?" they asked. I told them I didn't know, but that water was pouring into the boat forward. The engineer-officer was thoughtful for a moment or so before voicing his intentions. On the side of each compartment was stored HP air in large cylinders. The engineer-officer explained that he was going to release the HP air from the cylinders to help us escape from the engine room hatch. He ordered the chief engineer on to the ladder with his head inside the 9-inch-deep circular steel collar. "When I give the order, knock off the clips."'

The HP air was released. Pressure in the compartment increased. Signalman Kimbell was ordered onto the ladder so as to be the second man out of the compartment, which held about eighteen crew. When the order came to open the hatch, the chief engineer struck the clips. The pressure did the rest: the hatch flung open and out shot the men perched on the ladder.

As the engine room ratings made their way towards the surface the confusion of the night had still not played itself out. A quarter of a mile astern of *Fearless* was Lieutenant-Commander David Stocks with *K4*. On hearing the cruiser's siren sounding three short blasts for full astern, Stocks came to a halt. The next submarine in the line (*K3*) almost collided with the stationary *K4*. Herbert Shove, *K3*'s captain, came to a halt 500 yards farther on.

Elsewhere the *K6*, of the 12th Flotilla, and *K12* took avoiding action on catching sight of each other's lights. In the excitement the lieutenant on *K6*'s bridge lost sight of *K3*'s light, which he had been obediently following. Catching sight of another light ahead, and mistakingly thinking it was *K3*, he resumed station behind it. It was too late by the time he realised that the light was not *K3*'s, but that of another vessel which appeared to be stopped and lying broadside-on to his own submarine. Though both engines were put at full speed astern, there was no stopping *K6* from ramming *K4* with such force that Lieutenant-Commander Stocks' submarine was sliced almost in two halves. Locked together the two submarines began to sink. It seemed an eternity before *K6*'s thrashing propellers were able to draw her clear of *K4*. Her captain thought it prudent to switch on his after searchlight as a warning to the next submarine, Sam Gravener's *K7*.

Lieutenant-Commander Gravener was about half a mile behind *K6*. Gravener reduced speed on hearing a siren. When he found himself closing on *K6* he ordered full astern and swung to starboard. Gravener was congratulating himself on just missing *K6* when he saw the stricken *K4* across her bows. Gravener was horrified when he saw *K4*, sinking very fast, lying directly on his heading. Expecting to plough into her, Gravener was surprised and relieved when his keel lightly brushed the sinking *K4* as he passed over her. A little bewildered by the turn of events, he came to a halt. In the silence he could hear the cries for help coming from the survivors in the water. Then he saw the searchlight of *Fearless* singling out individuals. Moving slowly astern he began the search for survivors – not of *K4*, for there were none, but of *K17*.

The battleships of the 5th Battle Squadron had been warned of the collision by wireless but they were unaware that the two 'K' boat flotillas were still in the area and that Lieutenant-Commander Gravener was attempting to rescue from the sea survivors from *K17*'s accident with *Fearless*. What·happened next was one of the saddest moments of the whole calamitous chain of events: the three battleships passed by without striking any of the stationary submarines, but their escorting destroyers ploughed straight through survivors of *K17*. When the ships had passed, most of the men in the water were dead.

Signalman Kimbell, still weak from his days of illness, was making the best of things after his escape from *K17*'s engine room. George Kimbell relates what happened during his fight for survival: 'I came in touch with Stoker Petty Officer Savage. I did my best to keep his head above water but he went down, taking me with him. We came back up – and then went down again. By the time we came up the second time, Savage was ready to pass out. On going down for a third time I had enough strength left to free myself and surface.

'Cries from the others had ceased and I seemed to be on my own. I saw a small white light. I did not know how far away it was nor what it was. I set out floating and swimming towards it as well as my strength and confidence would permit. Then I saw the heavy white bow-waves of the battleships with their escorting destroyers on either side. Being a signalman of some experience I knew the dis-

tance between the big ships and the escorts, and the distance between the ships in line ahead. Putting all my remaining strength and
will power to the test I succeeded in getting between the ships. I
stayed in that area till they had passed me safely. Unfortunately during this time I had to stay in thick oil fuel for so long that, being in my
birthday suit, I was black all over, and had swallowed so much oil
that I was full up to my throat with it. But I was more concerned with
the white light. It was still there and seemed much nearer. I was
doing my best to swim, and float, on my back and was in that position when a light was shone on my face and I heard someone cry
"There's another one." A rope was thrown to me. I grasped it but
hadn't the strength to hold on to it for more than a second or two.
Another rope was thrown. This time it fell across my chest. As I held
it something came into my mind that I had learned in my training
ship: pass the rope round your body and under the arms and twist it
around its own part. This I did, and in this way I was hauled aboard
*K7*.' Signalman Kimbell was one of nine *K17* survivors. Now in his
nineties he is the only living survivor of *K17*'s crew of 31 January
1918.

A close examination of *K14*'s helm, the jamming of which had set
off the night of disaster, revealed nothing to indicate why it had jammed. She was scrapped in 1925.

*

The loss of Lieutenant Ralph Snook and *E50* (she was thought to ·
have been mined in the North Sea on or about 1 February) was followed by the loss of *H5* (Lieutenant A.W. Forbes) after a tragic
encounter with a British merchantman. *H5*'s crew numbered
twenty-five, of which no less than five held the DSM. She also had
aboard Ensign E.F.W. Childs, USN, for instructional purposes.

Lieutenant Forbes had put to sea from Bantry Bay for a patrol in
the Irish Sea. An American submariner, whom Ensign Childs had
had to replace for *H5*'s patrol, later stated: 'I saw *H5* sail, gall and
wormwood in my heart. The diminutive submarine stood past, her
tiny cross of St George whipping in the wind, her gallant little complement of officers and that prince of comrades, Earle Childs,
grouped around the conning tower. They saluted our colours and we
came to salute in return, then watched them slowly disappear into
the mist, outward bound, never to return.'

At 2030 on 2 March the steamer *Rutherglen* sighted a submarine in
position 53°4'N 4°40'W. *Rutherglen*'s master reported that the sub-

marine, which he thought was a U-boat, crossed his bows at considerable speed. *Rutherglen* rammed. Afterwards cries were heard and men seen in the water. There was also a strong smell of petrol. The position of the incident was almost identical to the area of *H5*'s patrol billet. It appears certain that the merchantman's victim had been *H5*.

As regards to *Rutherglen* having rammed a Royal Navy submarine it was decided that she should be left in ignorance of the submarine's true identity and that her crew should receive the usual reward for the sinking of a U-boat. The reason for this was that merchant vessels were encouraged to attack U-boats at every opportunity. Results depended largely on immediate action being taken by a merchant ship finding herself favourably positioned for ramming.

Lieutenant Arthur Forbes, DSO, was an excellent commanding officer and highly regarded by his superiors. Forbes had been aboard *Melampus* at the time of her collision with *C16*.

*H5* herself had had her moments: on 14 July 1916 she had torpedoed and sunk an outward bound *U51*.

HM submarine *D3* (Lieutenant W. Maitland-Dougall, RCN,) was victim of an error of identification. *D3* sailed Gosport on the afternoon of 7 March for an A/S patrol in the English Channel. Maitland-Dougall was under orders to make for St Helens, Isle of Wight. In company with the small patrol boat *Magnolia*, *D3* sailed St Helens round midnight 7/8 March to patrol the south-eastern area. She was to pick up an escort vessel off Brighton at three o'clock on the afternoon of the 14th, that is a week later, for the return to St Helens.

Not a great deal is known of *D3*'s movements during the week of her patrol. It is known that a Royal Naval Air Service airship sighted a submarine, believed to be *D3*, at 1655 on the 11th. The submarine fired the correct identification smoke signal.

The French airship AT-O became airborne at Le Havre at 1137, Tuesday 12th. By 1150 the Frenchman was making steady progress north on a course parallel to, and five miles from, the coast at an altitude of 810 feet and at a speed of 38 knots. At 1315 Lieutenant Sainte Rémy, the airship's commander, was over the roads of Dieppe. At this point the airship hovered for a short while in the vicinity of some minesweepers before steering north-west until 1330 when course was changed to make true west. The mist being low, the airship was taken to 1,600 feet in the hope of gaining a better view.

At 1420 one of the crew directed Sainte Rémy's attention towards a vessel to the north-east. Unable to make out what type of vessel it was, they headed towards it. As they approached *D3* she became recognizable as a submarine making route westwards at high speed. Lieutenant Sainte Rémy: 'Having the wind behind us and the sun on our backs I put the motors to full speed, keeping it in view and searching to identify it. The deck was entirely clear, no signal nor distinctive mark was visible. A few minutes before we came over her she sent up a certain number of rockets in our direction. The rockets seemed to come from the stern of the conning tower, flaming from the moment of being fired and terminating in a long tongue of fire. The rockets came nearer and nearer to the balloon and we were all under the firm impression that the submarine was trying to fire the balloon. The wireless operator, who was busy passing messages, on my order left his instruments and loaded the machine-gun. He shot short. Judging the distance too great I ordered firing to be stopped, to be resumed a little while after.

'The firing was very true. The luminous balls ricocheted on the hull. The rockets ceased to be fired and the submarine commenced to plunge at the moment when I dropped the first two bombs. They missed by about 20 metres. I came out immediately on the right and during the evolution the submarine disappeared rapidly. When the balloon came into position again for dropping bombs, a bluish-grey streak only was to be observed. This was not the submarine but its wake. At my direction the pilot passed a little in front of this streak and I dropped four bombs. The first two exploded exactly as regards range and position; the last two missed the object, falling a little distance away.

'Owing to the lightening of the airship in consequence of the discharge of bombs, she rose rapidly. The navigating pilot came head to wind. The wireless operator informed me that he could not be heard owing to the numerous messages being transmitted at the time and the weakness of his instrument. The mechanic, Beuveleg, was on watch and signalled to me a whitish streak about 200 metres to the south of the position of the explosion. It was an escape of air from the submarine, which was trying to come to the surface, but only the conning tower emerged. Supposing it to be too badly damaged to come to the surface again in such a short time, about three or four minutes, and having no further means of offensive, I gave the order to the navigating pilot to withdraw but to keep the position in view. To the wireless operator I gave the order to transmit the following message:

HAVE ENGAGED IN ACTION A SUBMARINE. DROPPED 6 BOMBS WITH SUC-
CESS.

The wireless operator replied that it was impossible for him to make himself heard.

'The airship rose still, stopping at a height of 1,200 metres. We then saw the submarine disappear again, leaving on the surface some things which we could not distinguish at first; but with the glass we saw that they were men swimming. We came over the position again and descended in spiral while the wireless operator on my order sent a distress signal to which no reply was received. I made him take in his aerial and came down to low altitude (20 metres). I tried in vain to speak to the men in the water. There were four men, some distance separating one from the other. My men and myself each dropped our Perrin lifebelts. One of the men shouted. To understand what he said I stopped the two motors. He spoke in English and I understood the phrase "You got us". I wanted then to save him with the cone anchor; it was calm but the balloon had still too much air, and also the large quantity of air contained in the ballonets caused the airship to pitch badly, an action which was impossible to check. I gave up this dangerous manoeuvre and, not being able to depend on the wireless, I came overland – taking into account, as carefully as possible in an airship, the speed and course to obtain a true bearing and exact distance; this enabled me to determine the position as 20 miles north of Fécamp. I then went in search of a ship to lead to the position.

'The first ship sighted was an escort trawler which could not leave the convoy. I shouted to her, therefore, "My wireless is out of action. There are some men in the water 20 miles north 10 west of Fécamp. Send a message."

'I next met a small isolated motor boat and gave her my message, but she made signs that she could not go. Knowing that I would find a torpedo boat between Cap D'Antifer and Le Havre, I proceeded along the coast and signalled the French destroyer *Typhone*, which was towing a fishing·smack. I shouted the same message. She immediately cast off the tow-rope and proceeded with me towards the position, trying at the same time to speak to me. I made her understand that (1) owing to the noise of the motors I could hear practically nothing (2) that the men to save were in the water with lifebelts on (3) that I would accompany her to help in the search. Even though my motors were running slow, my speed was greater than hers and I drew ahead at an altitude of 500 metres.

'With Fécamp bearing south, ten east, I started my search for the men, but without success. At 1810 it became foggy and I was afraid I would be unable to make Le Havre if I did not start before dark, as had happened before. I decided, therefore, to return. I went back to the *Typhone* and told her I was returning. I understood her to say that she would remain and patrol around the position. I arrived at Le Havre at 1925 after being seven hours and forty-eight minutes in the air.'

A major factor of the incident was signal identification. The French airship used none, whereas the British signals appear to have been quite unknown to the French. Apart from having signals for the period of her patrol, *D3* had painted on a wooden cover over her fore hatch the correct recognition mark (a white circle on a black background) for the period 1 to 15 March. As *D3*'s fore hatch recognition mark was observed by Lieutenant John Mansfield, captain of an 'E' class submarine which went on patrol the same day as *D3*, the idea that the Deck Recognition Mark might have been painted on canvas (as was occasionally done when submarines had to change the DRM during a patrol, whereby they incurred the risk of the canvas screen being washed away) can be dispensed with.

Lieutenant J.D.A. Musters (*C4*), patrolling to the north of *D3*, states that on the afternoon of the 12th he was keeping a periscope watch; the sea was calm and the weather hazy enough to deny him a clear view of the horizon. It was understood that in such weather conditions *D3* would lie or navigate on the surface trimmed down and ready for diving but keeping a lookout with glasses. It is assumed that Lieutenant Maitland-Dougall would probably see an approaching airship at a considerable distance, but as the airship had the sun behind her, not sooner than he would be sighted by her.

Weather conditions would have had a profound bearing on the course of action opened to Maitland-Dougall. If he dived on sighting the airship, in the calm sea his submarine would probably have been kept in sight and perhaps attacked. The possibility therefore was that he would decide to remain on the surface and make the recognition signal of the day, particularly as the procedure recommended to captains at that time was that if there was any doubt as to whether a submarine had been sighted or not, she should surface and use her identification signal.

The recognition signals for 12 March were known to Lieutenant Sainte Rémy and his crew. They were certain that *D3* had not given the inter-Allied recognition signal. Sainte Rémy's decision to attack may also have been influenced by his knowledge that at 1830 the previous evening an enemy submarine had been sighted south-west of Le Touquet. The use by *D3* of an unrecognized signal – the very form of which was unknown to Sainte Rémy, and which might have indicated that the submarine was opening an attack – provoked the use of the machine-gun, which was the actual cause of *D3* diving, and which, in turn, resulted in the use of bombs.

An inquiry into the incident found that responsibility for the error could not be attributed to Lieutenant Sainte Rémy who, in accordance with French and British instructions, should not have hesitated to attack a submarine not showing recognition signals and which was obviously preparing to dive. The short verbal exchange between Lieutenant Sainte Rémy and the four men in the water was the only reason for casting doubt that a German submarine had been sunk.

The bombs dropped were known as Type 'F'. Weighing 52 kilos and charged with 35 kilos of melinite, they were set to explode at a depth of 25 feet. Maitland-Dougall's decision to dive just as the first two bombs were dropped, and after having complied with the only instructions available for making recognition signals in such circumstances, was probably the only course open to him. The chances of him escaping fatal damage once underwater were very favourable. It must be considered sheer bad luck that *D3* was hit and mortally damaged by such small bombs.

At the outbreak of war William Maitland-Dougall was serving as Third Hand in *CC1* (*Canadian C1*). He has been described as being 'In the very front rank of the younger submarine captains and a most thorough, conscientious, and resourceful officer'. Lieutenant Maitland-Dougall was the first Royal Canadian Navy officer to command a British submarine.

\*

It was in April that the complex and brilliantly executed assault on the Belgian ports of Ostend and Zeebrugge took place. The assault was carried out with such dash and flair that eight Victoria Crosses were awarded, one of them to a submariner, for the night's work.

The St George's Day action at Zeebrugge had been 'on the books' for some time. By 1917 the sinking of Allied shipping by U-boats had been so great that concern for Britain's ability to continue the war began to be expressed. The base from which many U-boats put to sea was Bruges. This strongly defended port was eight miles from the open sea, to which access was gained by the use of two canals, one emerging at Ostend and the other at Zeebrugge. The plan to deny the use of these canals to U-boats entailed the sinking of blockships at their seaward ends. If this could be achieved the Germans would be obliged to frequent the more dangerous northerly routes to their Atlantic hunting grounds.

A vital aspect of the Zeebrugge assault was the partial destruction of a viaduct connecting the Zeebrugge Mole to the mainland to prevent reinforcements being rushed from Bruges during the action. As this part of the assault involved the use of submarines it is proposed to dwell on this part of the action only.

It was anticipated that one submarine would be sufficient to cause the required damage to the viaduct but as a precaution against breakdown, etc., two submarines were requisitioned from the 6th Flotilla at Portsmouth. The submarines selected were *C1* and *C3*. The plan was that a submarine, its bows packed with explosive, would be rammed under the viaduct. Once the crew was safely away (a motor skiff would be provided for this) a time-fuse would detonate the 5 tons of explosive. As the operation was extremely hazardous the submarine crews were to be unmarried volunteers. Furthermore, each submarine would be restricted in crew to two officers and four ratings. The captain of *C1*, Lieutenant Aubrey Newbold, was a bachelor. Newbold jumped at the chance to take his submarine on the Zeebrugge raid. The captain of *C3* was married and had to relinquish his command to a 26-year-old lieutenant, Richard Sandford.

The assault force put to sea on the evening of 22 April. The two submarines were towed by destroyers to a prearranged assembly point from which they were to make their own way to the viaduct. When *C3* cast off her tow Lieutenant Sandford set a course for the target. There was no sign of *C1*, nor any other vessel for that matter.

*C3* was still 1½ miles from the viaduct when the Germans identified positively advanced elements of the assault force as British. Shore batteries were at once brought into action. An adjustment to his course put Sandford nearer to his final position for the run up to the viaduct. Away to port a battle that would long be remembered was in progress.

Starshells bursting directly overhead tore away the darkness which up till then had lain a protective shield across *C3*. 'That's done it!' Sandford held *C3* steady on course and braced himself for the enemy gunfire that was certain to come.

A shell exploded close by. Further shells followed, each one thrusting a column of white water skyward. Then, just as suddenly as it had begun, the firing inexplicably came to a halt. In the hope of providing some cover Leading Seaman William Cleaver set off some smoke canisters. At full speed the submarine went racing towards the 300 yards long structure of steel girders. Unfavourable wind conditions caused the smoke to drift away, thus enabling searchlights sited atop the viaduct to take a hold of *C3* in their white grip. Surprisingly, no shots were fired. Puzzled at this lack of gunfire Lieutenant Sandford called a final course adjustment to the helmsman, Lieutenant John Howell-Price. They were now a hundred yards from the viaduct. This was the moment that Sandford should have brought into use the special gyroscopic steering gear to allow the crew to abandon the submarine, which would then find its own way to the target. He called the crew topside. The end was near and he did not want them below when it came.

At just over 9 knots *C3* went charging into the steel lattice work of the viaduct. There was an ear-piercing grinding and scraping noise as steel met steel. The old submarine rammed the viaduct with such force, her bows tore their way clean through the viaduct to finish several feet the other side of the structure. Her conning tower was held firmly by a tangled web of twisted steel. His Majesty's Submarine *C3* had been delivered to the enemy as instructed.

From high above came the sound of German voices, punctuated with bouts of sardonic laughter. The mystery as to why the Germans had withheld their fire became clear; they had mistakenly thought that the submarine was attempting to pass beneath the viaduct in ignorance that the area between the viaduct piers was too restricted for it to do so. Confident that the British were in for the shock of their lives, the Germans had stopped firing so as to take full advantage of the spectacle.

There remained one important task to perform before Sandford could take to the motor skiff which his comrades were launching for the escape: the igniting of the twelve-minute fuse to blow up the submarine. After lighting the fuse, Sandford scrambled with all speed down into the skiff. A bullet zipped passed his ear. The Germans, less than twenty feet away atop the viaduct, opened fire with rifles and machine-guns. The frail craft was quickly riddled with holes. Stoker Henry Bindall was hit. So was Sandford.

The skiff's propeller shaft had been broken in the haste of launching. As the engine was now useless, Petty Officer Coxswain Walter Harner and ERA Allan Roxburgh each took up one of the craft's small oars. At such short a range the Germans could hardly fail to hit someone. Harner twisted in pain as a bullet found its mark. Sandford, at the tiller, was hit for a second time. Howell-Price took charge of the tiller and Henry Cleaver took over the rowing from Harner. With searchlights maintaining a stranglehold on them, the flimsy skiff was inched, under murderous fire, away from the submarine. The water splashing in the bottom of the skiff was stained red with the blood of the wounded. How all six men had escaped death was little short of miraculous.

It took an all-out effort to put 200 yards between the skiff and *C3* before the submarine erupted in a mighty explosion and blasted a gap in the viaduct large enough to prevent German reinforcements joining the grim battles being fought along the length of the mole. For Sandford and his crew it was a moment of pure joy. The 5 tons of explosive had also put an end to the small-arms fire from atop the viaduct. The skiff's heroes were rescued by a picket boat and then transferred to the destroyer *Phoebe* for return home.

And what of *C1*? Several incidents had caused delay to her timing. She was within two miles of the objective when Lieutenant Newbold saw HMS *Vindictive* steering a homeward course. Aubrey Newbold took this to mean that the operation was either successfully concluded or a failure, and if the latter his submarine might be needed should a second attempt be made later on. With this in mind he put *C1* on a heading for Dover, arriving safely that afternoon.

After a spell in hospital Lieutenant Sandford was well enough to attend an investiture to receive his Victoria Cross. All of *C3*'s crew received recognition of their gallantry. On 23 November 1918, seven months after the action at Zeebrugge, Richard Sandford died of typhoid fever in a Yorkshire hospital.

Instances of submarines being sunk from an attack by an enemy submarine were comparatively few. The Royal Navy lost five submarines from such attacks, and the German Navy eighteen. HM Submarine *D6* featured in both totals.

Around midnight 11/12 May 1918, *D6* (Lieutenant C.B. Barry) was on patrol in the English Channel when she received a signal informing her that a U-boat had been sighted at dusk the previous evening. As a troop convoy was due in the U-boat's area some time after dawn on the 12th, *D6* was ordered to make speed to the area.

At about 0800 Claude Barry sighted the German on the surface and facing in the direction of the expected convoy. Barry closed to within 600 yards and fired two torpedoes. Lieutenant Barry, who later reached flag rank, was awarded the DSO and given command of one of the new 'R' class submarines.

Two months after the sinking of the German submarine, which had been the *UB72*, *D6*, now commanded by Lieutenant Samuel Brooks, was attacked and sunk off the Irish coast by *UB73*. This attack of 28 June left no survivors.

Of the twenty-eight 'E' class that were sunk in the war, the *E34* (Lieutenant R.I. Pulleyne) was the last. *E34* had sailed harbour for a patrol in the North Sea. She was lost with all hands some time round 20 July. Her captain's body was later washed ashore on one of the West Frisian Islands. Richard Pulleyne had been the only survivor of *B2*'s collision with *Amerika* in 1912.

Three submarines were sunk in October 1918. Shortly after midnight on 2/3 October, cruisers and destroyers of a Harwich force arrived at a position some twenty miles north of Terschelling. Sighting a northbound enemy convoy, the British ships turned their guns on it. It took only a few minutes of concentrated shelling for the convoy to be transformed into a collection of smoking hulks. The guns were silent and the survivors rescued by the time *L10* (Lieutenant-Commander A.E. Whitehouse) reached the area. At dawn, by which the British force had retired, *L10* remained in the vicinity in anticipation of further developments. It appears that Arthur Whitehouse had not long to wait. Later that day he reported that a number of German warships had arrived and were searching the location of the night attack. Whitehouse stated his intentions of attacking the enemy. After that signal nothing further was heard from *L10*.

The German squadron which had aroused Whitehouse's interest comprised four ships: the destroyers *S33* and *S34*, and the torpedo boats *V28* and *V29*. All four vessels were returning to Germany from their recently abandoned base at Zeebrugge. Only half of them would complete the passage.

There is no doubt that Lieutenant-Commander Whitehouse would have heard, if not actually seen, the explosions resulting from the destroyer *S34* touching off a mine. Damage to the German was so grave that the three other ships, ignoring the mine danger, were obliged to move in quickly to rescue the sinking destroyer's crew. Then came a second explosion. Whitehouse had attacked the *S33*. German thoughts that a second mine had been struck were soon discarded when a submarine's conning tower with a large *L10* painted on it was seen to break surface.

The reason for *L10* breaking surface is not known. The most obvious cause, and also the most likely, was her failure to compensate sufficiently, by shipping water, for the discharge of torpedoes. Another possibility is that a heavy swell might have brought her to the surface. And yet a third possibility, allied to the first, is that *L10* might have got out of control after firing her torpedoes: as she was more than 230 feet in length, it is possible that if her stern touched bottom, she was operating at a depth of 140 feet, she might have 'bounced' to the surface. Whatever the reason, rising in view of the enemy was to prove disastrous.

Though the *S33* had suffered major damage from the attack, she was still able to bring her guns into action against *L10*. The torpedo boats joined the assault. Under such an onslaught *L10* was hit and fatally holed. She sank with the loss of all hands. With *L10* disposed of, the *S33* radioed a report of the action, at the same time stating that she herself was seriously damaged. This signal was heard by a British listening post: thus the fate of *L10* became known to the Admiralty.

Lieutenant-Commander Whitehouse was probably aware that his attack had had some measure of success. What he could not have known was the extent of the damage he had inflicted on *S33*. The destroyer was in such a sorry state that she had to be sunk by the torpedo boats.

When Allied investigators examined German records after the war, all they could discover about the *L10* engagement was the radio message of *S33*. On the strength of this, prize bounty for *S33*'s loss was awarded to the dependents and relatives of *L10*'s crew. Nothing new was learned about the North Sea action. But this was not wholly unexpected. The engagement had taken place only a few weeks before the end of the war and it is almost certain that owing to the conditions that Germany was in at that time, no detailed report was made. With the inevitable confusion which followed Germany's defeat (many men left their ships and went straight to their homes) no one came forward to give evidence, and in time the action was forgotten.

Lieutenant-Commander Arthur Whitehouse was the son of a naval officer. Aged thirty at the time of *L10*'s loss, he had been a submariner since January 1910. He left a widow.

*L10* was the only 'L' class submarine to be lost during the war. Basically improved 'E's, the 'L' class were such fine submarines that some of them were still around after the Second World War.

The *J6* was also the only submarine of her class to be sunk during the war. The large 'J' class were ordered in January 1915. Seven 'J's were constructed and all served with the 11th Flotilla at Blyth from date of completion to 1918.

As there were few 'J' class in service the possibility of their unfamiliar outline being mistaken for that of a U-boat was always a greater hazard than usual. This, in part, is what happened on 15 October when *J6* was mistaken for a U-boat by one of the cloak-and-dagger Q-ships.

The *Cymric* was an old top-sail schooner which had been converted into a Q-ship. On the morning of Tuesday 15th she put to sea from the Firth of Forth and set a southerly course. Several U-boat sightings had been reported in the Blyth area. Perhaps a U-boat would be tempted to attack what would appear to be an easy victim. Weather-wise it was one of those days when sea and horizon seemed to merge. At about ten o'clock the schooner's crew was ordered to action stations. Less than 3,000 yards distant a submarine lay peacefully on the surface. While the gun crews waited tensely at their concealed armaments, the officers, glasses trained on the submarine, carefully noted details: first thing to strike the observers was that she was quite a large submarine. Also, her bow seemed unusual . . . Then she was recognized for what she was – a 'K' boat. Signals were exchanged. The crew was stood down. The two vessels parted company.

It was not long after this encounter that the Q-ship chanced on a second submarine. Again the call to action station. Once more a careful study was made of the submarine. Again she was 'one of ours'.

It was four o'clock and the watch was about to change when a third submarine was sighted. The sea was flat calm. Banks of mist made visibility a chance affair: at times it was reasonable but within moments it could reduce to a few hundred yards. The Q-ship slipped into her well-rehearsed drill.

The submarine was steering a course designed to take her close on the *Cymric*'s starboard beam. As the submarine drew closer, the eyes watching her every move became increasingly convinced that she was hostile and that she was taking a good look at the *Cymric* before sinking her at leisure.

The submarine was not a U-boat. She was the *J6* and was under the command of Lieutenant-Commander Geoffrey Warburton. The *Cymric*'s officers had been influenced in their asessment by what they thought was a large U6 painted on her conning tower. This misun-

derstanding arose because of something hanging down the side of the
conning tower and coincidentally completing the loop of the 'J', thus
transforming it into a 'U'. A flag hanging limply from the submarine's masthead was not readily distinguishable – and even if it
had been, *Cymric*'s captain might well have chosen to ignore it as he
had once lost the chance of sinking an enemy submarine when a U-
boat had tricked him into holding his fire by displaying a Royal Navy
ensign. Not wishing to be caught out again, and not realising that *U6*
had been sunk by *E16* three years earlier, he gave the order to break
the White Ensign and commence firing.

The moment the screens concealing the armaments were lowered,
the guns began firing independently from point-blank range. Two
men, one an officer, were seen on the bridge. The officer's companion
was in the act of raising a rifle to fire a recognition signal when the
first shell wounded him and killed the officer. A second shell
exploded in the control room, wrecking it completely.

*J6* was still making way and by this time was on the schooner's
starboard quarter, where the *Cymric*'s 4-inch gun could be brought to
bear. The very first shell from the 4-inch gun was on target. At this
stage a hatch on the submarine was seen to open and an officer rush
out on deck and begin waving with some vigour what looked like a
white tablecloth. The *Cymric* ceased fire. But the moment she did so,
the *J6* altered course and made directly for a bank of fog. *Cymric*
began firing again and continued to do so until *J6* was swallowed up
by the mist. Just before she disappeared her signalman was able to
work his lamp: H-E- L-P . . . H-E-L-P.

The schooner's auxiliary engine had been started. Making a
course alteration, she made for the point where *J6* had vanished. It
was thought that the submarine had sustained enough hits to sink
her, but that she might possibly be able to survive. *Cymric* wanted her
sunk and went after her. As expected the thick mist was something of
a problem. However, the problem solved itself when the mist lifted
suddenly and revealed the *J6* straight ahead. Her trim left no doubt
that she was sinking. The submarine's bows were well out of the
water and only a small part of her conning tower was still above the
surface. Some of her crew were in a small collapsible boat. Others
were floundering in the water. When the collapsible drew alongside
the schooner, it was noticed that a survivor's hatband was inscribed
HM SUBMARINES. It was a sad moment. The schooner's boat was lowered to help the men struggling in the sea. Some of the survivors were
in such desperate need of help that the rescuers had to dive in the sea

to support them. But for some rescue came too late and they drowned. Even though worked on for hours, others died aboard the schooner. Only about fifteen of *J6*'s crew survived the ordeal. *Cymric* signalled Blyth that she would enter harbour with survivors.

At an inquiry held the following day, the Q-ship was considered to have performed her duty correctly, and consequently was absolved of blame. That the *J6* – which had mistaken *Cymric* for a German Q-ship – had been wrongly identified was regarded as one of the unfortunate hazards of war. And this was how the survivors of *J6* viewed the incident. When the schooner's captain (an officer whose courage had in the part been rewarded with two DSOs, two DSCs, and an array of other awards) left the room in which the court had convened, the survivors arose, stood smartly to attention, and saluted.

Another of the October sinkings was *C12* (Lieutenant N. Manley). *C12* sank at Immingham when her main motors failed. Before the motors could be restarted, and before *C12* could be anchored, she was carried by the prevailing strong ebb tide against a destroyer moored at the eastern jetty at Immingham. The submarine was holed and began to sink. *C12*'s first lieutenant, Lieutenant G.H.S. Sulivan, remained below throughout, having at Manley's orders sent all hands topside. When *C12* was just about to submerge completely, Lieutenant Manley proceeded below, shutting the conning tower hatch behind him. The two officers inspected the boat until chlorine gas drove them into the conning tower. After securing the lower hatch cover they proceeded to flood the conning tower by slightly raising the lid of the upper hatch. Manley and Sulivan then made their way to the surface. Thanks to their efforts *C12* was raised and put back into service.

Lieutenant Manley retired from the Navy in 1920 owing to ill-health. It was Manley's ability and his capacity for hard work that permitted him to become only the second promotion from the lower-deck to command a submarine. Norman Manley died in July 1939.

The *G9* and *G8* were already at the bottom of the North Sea when *G7* (Lieutenant C.A.C. Russell) failed to return from a patrol in that area. Lost on or about 1 November, Charles Russell's *G7* was the last Royal Navy submarine to be sunk during the war. Ten days later what came to be known as The Great War came to an end.

## Between the Wars

(*Right*) *L55* arriving at Fort Blockhouse, on Christmas Eve 1918.

(*Centre*) HMS *Champion* bearing the dead of *L55* arrives alongside at Portsmouth.

(*Bottom*) Like all 'K' boats, *K5* was disliked and feared by her crew, and their misgivings were fully justified when *K5* went out of control and imploded on her way to the Atlantic seabed in January 1921.

*H47*, seen here in 1919 under the command of Lt 'Tommy' Thompson, later to be Winston Churchill's ADC during the Second World War. Only her commanding officer and one rating survived her collision with *L12* in July 1929.

(*Left*) PO R. Porch, seen here as a leading seaman, was the coxwain of the *H42* when she was rammed and sunk by the *Versatile* in March 1922. Typical of the dependable submarine rating, Porch had served on the steam-driven *K11* during the war (*Right*) *Versatile* in dock after ramming the *H42*. The damage to her keel shows that the impact must have been considerable and that the submarine had no chance of surviving.

# PART III

## BETWEEN THE WARS

# 1918

Within two weeks of the Great War coming to an end the *G11* became the first of more than a dozen Royal Navy submarines to be sunk between the two world wars.

Lieutenant Richard Sandford, VC, was captain of *G11* up until his fatal illness forced him to relinquish command. Temporary command of *G11* was given to Lieutenant-Commander G.F. Bradshaw whose own submarine (*L11*) was undergoing a refit. On 19 November Bradshaw sailed harbour for a short patrol. The guns of the Great War had been silent for just eight days.

*G11* arrived in her patrol area by 1700 the following day. At 2000 the next evening, a Friday, Bradshaw received a W/T signal ordering all Grand Fleet submarines to return to harbour. *G11*, in the vicinity of Dogger Bank, began the return passage with revolutions to give a steady speed of just under 11 knots. At this speed Bradshaw expected to sight Coquet Island Light, off the Northumbrian coast, at about or shortly after 1900 on the 22nd.

*Saturday 22nd.* It was 1830 when George Bradshaw noticed that the horizon appeared to be getting misty. He guessed that he would probably not sight Coquet Island until less than ten miles off. Ten minutes later he saw ahead what he took to be a rapidly thickening fog-bank. On entering thick fog shortly afterwards, he sensed something ahead. 'Do you see anything ahead?' Bradshaw questioned Petty Officer Coxswain William Palmer. Palmer had been on watch since 1645 and had so far sighted nothing in the blackness of the cold November night. 'No, sir.' The coxswain had no sooner replied when Bradshaw ordered the helm hard to starboard and both engines stopped. Even as Bradshaw was giving the order he sighted land close ahead. Just as the engines stopped, the submarine struck the rocky shore. At a speed of 9 knots *G11* ran up on a shelving rock until her bows were almost clear of the water. She at once began to bump heavily and soon after took on an 18° list to port. The list increased as each roller broke over her.

'On grounding,' Bradshaw was later to report, 'the keel was torn off and she was holed somewhere on the port quarter, either in the motor room or engine room. Subsequently port fore hydroplane shaft was snapped off and the shaft was forced into the boat, thus causing a leak. I imagine she was badly holed in the port engine room bilges, motor room, and possibly the after flat. Most of the keel was broken away from the pressure hull.'

Bradshaw saw that the submarine was fast aground and in imminent danger of capsizing. He ordered the crew up on deck. By now *G11* was over at an angle of 50° and bumping so heavily that she would soon be flooded. It appeared that the only course open to him was to get the crew to safety with all speed. On seeing low-lying land less than twenty yards off the bow, he ordered his first lieutenant, Lieutenant C.A. Smith, to get a line out forward and to get a hemp line over the bows to enable the crew to get down forward and onto the rocks.

Claude Smith had left the bridge at 1400 and had been resting on his bunk when *G11* struck. He saw several of the crew making for the conning tower. Telling them to stop where they were and await orders, he started to make his way forward to see if *G11* was making water. Just then he heard Bradshaw ordering the lower deck to be cleared as quickly as possible.

Another officer, Temporary Lieutenant Frederick MacLure, RNR, had this to say: 'I came up and saw we had struck but did not know what we had struck. I did not think we had hit the shore. The captain gave orders that everyone was to get on the fore-end of the boat. He said that there was land ahead of us and asked the second captain if it was possible to let the anchor go, and he said "No". Lieutenant Smith was right forward and I went to give a hand with the line. The locker was jammed and we could not get it open for some time. The captain told us to hurry up as the ship was going to capsize.'

Forcing the locker open and taking up a line, Smith dropped over the side. He had gone only a few yards when he fell into a hole. Scrambling out he continued to make for the shore, closely followed by Able Seaman George Birch.

*G11*'s crew were making their way topside and working their way forward when Bradshaw heard a call that a man, Telegraphist G.P. Back, had gone overboard. According to Petty Officer Palmer, the telegraphist had been thrown overboard from the port side of the bridge by a heavy bump of the submarine just as he (Back) had come up the conning tower hatch. The deck at this time was nearly vertical. Bradshaw switched on the Aldis lamp. After a few moments he saw George Back swimming towards the rocks about twenty yards on the port beam. Back was at that time some twenty yards from the rocks. The surf was so bad that Bradshaw felt that he could not risk letting anyone go into the water to help him. He ordered a heaving line to be thrown to Back but owing to the almost vertical position of the upper deck it was some time before the casing where the lines were stowed could be opened. By then George Back was unsighted.

When Lieutenant Smith called that he had made the shore with the line, Bradshaw ordered the crew shorewards while he directed the Aldis on the line held fast by Smith and George Birch. As the crew were making their way along the line, Stoker Pliny Foster was lost, though this was not known until later. Nothing was seen or heard of Foster after he had started along the line. Bradshaw considered it likely Foster was killed by being dashed against the rocks.

Bradshaw thought of entering *G11* to close the water-tight doors but realised that the angle of the submarine would make any attempt to close the doors futile. When all his crew were ashore he himself no longer had any reason to remain aboard. An hour after *G11* had struck the rocks, he made his way shorewards. Lieutenant-Commander Bradshaw continues: 'On getting ashore I took the crew up the cliffs to a shepherd's house about 200 yards south along the coast. They were all taken in by the lady of the house. I left Lieutenant Smith in charge and set out for the nearest telephone which was at Craster Coastguard Station, about 1¾ miles along the coast. On arrival there I reported the wreck of HM Submarine *G11* to the Senior Naval Officer (Blyth, Tyne, Tees) by telephone. I declined rocket apparatus but asked for wires to be sent down to secure the boat at low tide. I informed the chief officer of coastguard of the position of the wreck and discussed chances of salvage. He accompanied me to the wreck where he decided there was nothing to be done except to secure her with a wire on the shore to her bow. This was done at 2200. On arriving at the wreck I was informed that the crew had been mustered and that Stoker Foster also was missing, and that the coast had been searched by Lieutenant Smith and the crew but no sign of Back or Stoker Foster could be found. The crew were then billeted by Lt Smith at the shepherd's house in Howich village, and in Craster village. At about 0200, 23 November, Lieutenant-Commander A.M. Winser arrived with wires, etc., in a motor lorry. We inspected the wreck and again decided that nothing could be done. Later on Commander A. Somerville arrived and took command of the operation.'

Two days after the grounding *G11* shifted inshore about fifteen yards. The wreck was entered and the confidential books and papers recovered.

There were several reasons as to why *G11* ran aground on the rocks south of Craster Coastguard Station: one of them seems to have been an overestimation of the loss of speed due to the sea running at the time. As stated, George Bradshaw was temporarily in command of *G11* whilst his own submarine was undergoing a refit. The loss of speed in his own *L11* under similar conditions would have been greater owing to the proximity of the propellers to the surface. It was likely that this was a contributing factor in the grounding. It appears, also, that although it was a clear and very dark night at sea, a thick bank of fog was hanging over and just screening the coast from view. This made for an extremely dangerous situation for any vessel at all out in her dead reckoning. Another point which cannot entirely be ignored was that on the morning of the 22nd, the day of the grounding, Lieutenant MacLure reported that he did not consider the Forbes log accurate as it had stopped several times for a minute or so at a time. Sounding had not been taken prior to grounding owing to Lieutenant-Commander Bradshaw's belief that he was at least sixteen miles from land.

The loss of Telegraphist Back and Stoker Foster was to be regretted. Considering the circumstances it was fortunate that fatalities were so low; this in no small way was due to the combined efforts of Lieutenant Claude Smith and Able Seaman George Birch, the first to reach land, who took the line ashore under very difficult and dangerous conditions.

# 1919

The Russian Revolution and the signing by Russia and Germany of an armistice in November 1917 had brought an end to Royal Navy commitments in the Baltic. After a heated peace conference at Brest Litovsk on 3 March 1918, a treaty was signed ceding huge areas of Russia to the Central Powers. Over the next two years civil war took place in Russia. By the end of 1920 White resistance had ceased and the Armies of Intervention withdrawn.

During the period of unrest, the Allies had despatched military aid to the anti-Bolsheviks. It had been in November 1918, with Germany a beaten nation, that a Royal Navy Force had once again entered the Baltic. From its base at Revel this force set about assisting the new Baltic republics of Estonia, Latvia, and Lithuania against the savagery of the Bolsheviks who wished to take control. Soon after the surrender of the German High Seas Fleet the 3rd Light Cruiser Squadron, with destroyers of the 13th Flotilla, was *en route* for the Baltic Sea. The composition of this force was, after a time, changed: the 1st Light Cruiser Squadron was substituted and a flotilla of submarines added. The *E27* (Lieutenant-Commander A. Carrie) was a unit of this new force. It is to an officer of *E27* that thanks are extended for the account which follows:

'In April 1919 the flotilla was ordered to proceed to the Baltic. The Russian Revolution was in full swing and the Reds had not yet finished off the White Russians. There was a good deal of sporadic fighting in the area round Kronstadt. We were based at Revel in Estonia in the gulf of Finland. Some British cruisers and destroyers had preceded us to the Baltic and were based in a fiord to the east of Helsingfors to contain any Red warships that might come out of Kronstadt into the Baltic. We of the *Lucia*'s* flotilla provided the lookout for this force, patrolling in pairs off the western entrance of the Kronstadt Channel.

'Patrols in these waters were a very different matter to what we had become used to in the North Sea. The patrol area was very small and virtually landlocked; so the two submarines on patrol were stationed thus: one in the advanced position and the other as a back-up some miles to the rear. The water in the Gulf was fairly fresh and very calm and clear. The smell from the Pinewoods surrounding the patrol area was very strong and pleasant, and in the still air one could hear the noises of the dogs barking ashore and occasional bursts of gunfire. We were warned not to approach too close to the entrance of the Kronstadt Channel as there were a lot of Russian mines about whose position was uncertain; not a very comforting thought. Consequently, when on patrol we spent most of our time on the surface. We felt very exposed and obvious lying thus, but fortunately there was a small island called Seskar some miles to the west of the entrance to the Channel which we stopped off, using it as a background. From this position we could see up the Kronstadt Channel, the top of the lighthouse on Kronstadt being clearly visible.

'Our first patrol was abortive. We sat on the surface close to the

* Submarine depot ship (Author).

island of Seskar, bathed in the lovely warm water and found it all rather enjoyable. Our second patrol was more lively.' On her second patrol *E27* attacked but failed to register a hit on a cruiser. She next fired two torpedoes at a destroyer but again failed to score a hit (it was thought that the fresh water had upset the torpedoes' balance). Disappointed at the lack of success, *E27* set off on 4 June for a noon rendezvous with Lieutenant Charles Chapman's *L55*, due to take over the patrol from *E27*. The narrative continues: 'In due course *L55* turned up: Commander Chapman and Lieutenant Southwell, the latter a friend of mine. We had to transfer a confidential book so we went alongside. We told them about our attack on the destroyers an hour or so earlier, and whose smoke could still be seen up the Channel. As we moved off to return to base we heard Commander Chapman giving orders down the voice-pipe about torpedoes and diving.

'Some four or five hours later while we were still on route for Revel, we intercepted a signal from the rear submarine on patrol with *L55*: it was to the effect that *L55* appeared to have been sunk as a heavy explosion and firing from destroyers had been seen in the area where *L55* had been seen to dive. From what we learnt later, it transpired that, shortly after we had left, the two destroyers had returned down the Channel again and had carried out some high speed manoeuvres in the area where *L55* had dived, and in the course of which the heavy explosion and firing had taken place. Whether *L55* had been caught in a sweep and blown to the surface was not known. There were no survivors. . . . . .'

Though more than half a century has passed since the loss of *L55*, very little has emerged concerning the actual sinking. However, it is known that *L55* had been patrolling between Caporski Bay and Bjorka Bay, where the British Naval Force had an advanced base. The report of the back-up submarine states that Soviet ships were observed approaching this submarine, which then dived. Shortly afterwards *L55* was seen to be enveloped in a cloud of black smoke just as an explosion was heard, from which it was wrongly inferred that *L55* had struck a mine.

On 6 June, two days after the sinking, a Bolshevist communiqué announced that a submarine which had attacked their ships as they were leaving the Gulf of Caporski had been sunk. The ships concerned were the destroyers *Gavril* and *Azard*.

'An excellent officer and a charming messmate who is and will continue to do very well,' thus commented Martin Nasmith of Lieutenant Chapman just five months prior to *L55*'s loss. The son of a naval officer, Charles Chapman had been no stranger to the Baltic. In October 1914 he had been Lieutenant-Commander Max Horton's first lieutenant when *E9* had foxed German defences in her breakthrough into the Baltic. Lieutenant Chapman, awarded a DSC for his service in submarines, was thirty years of age. He left a widow.

During the course of the next nine years the fate of *L55* and her crew was forgotten. Then came August 1928 and a Soviet announcement that *L55* had been raised and docked. This news prompted the Admiralty to request the return of the remains of *L55*'s officers and crew. In agreeing to this the Soviet authorities insisted that no British warship would be allowed to enter a Soviet port to receive the coffins containing the remains. Unwilling to make use of a man-of-war of a foreign Navy the British decided that one of their own merchant ships would take on the coffins at Kronstadt for transference to a Royal Navy ship once outside Soviet waters. Consequently the Admiralty announced: 'Negotiations with the Soviet Government are still proceeding. It is intended that HMS *Champion* shall meet the merchant vessel in the Baltic and take over from her the remains of the officers and men of *L55*.' *Champion* was a 1915 *Calliope* class cruiser. The merchantman would be the Ellerman-Wilson Line steamer *Truro*.

*August 29.* It was 2110 when the *Truro* arrived at Kronstadt and came to anchor in the roads. Officials of the Soviet Navy, customs, and police boarded her to clear ship and offer permits for any of the crew who wished to go ashore. *Truro*'s main hold was prepared for the reception of the coffins.

*August 30.* At 1330 a large lighter with the coffins arrived alongside *Truro*. The lighter was decorated with evergreens. Mounting guard over the coffins were twenty Soviet sailors with fixed bayonets. A naval band on the lighter played several funeral marches. *Truro*'s master, Captain W. Dearing, relates what happened next: 'We started immediately to put the coffins on board with our own gear. Except for very brief intervals the band played during the loading, which occupied about an hour. All ships in the harbour were flying flags at half-mast, and the crew of Russian warships manned ship. The whole of the proceedings were carried out in a most respectful manner. When the loadings were completed I witnessed and received an official document, also a list of coffins and contents, and a list of three baskets of personal effects, which I eventually handed to the captain of HMS *Champion* at Revel. I expressed my appreciation to the USSR representative of the courteous and kind reception which had been extended to the *Truro*, and of the respectful manner in which the whole of the proceedings were carried out. The Norwegian Consul kindly interpreted. At 1440 I sailed from Kronstadt, passing several men-of-war, each of which saluted the *Truro* as she passed out to sea.'

HMS *Champion* had sailed Portsmouth at 1315 on Saturday 25th. She arrived at Revel on the morning of the 30th. At eleven o'clock the following morning *Truro* was sighted approaching the harbour. All shipping at once lowered their flags, as did official buildings ashore. As *Truro* secured alongside *Champion* she was received by a guard of thirty sailors and four Royal Marine buglers.

As the first of the coffins arrived aboard the cruiser, four seaman sentries were posted at the four corners of the quarter-deck with arms reversed, and four Royal Marine sentries were similarly posted on the after superstructure. Pouring rain and a strong wind lashed the seamen during the transferring of the coffins, begun at 1300, from *Truro*'s hold to the deck of the cruiser. Aboard *Champion* the coffins were arranged on both sides of the quarter-deck and each draped with a Union Flag. The coffins said to contain the remains of *L55*'s officers were placed right aft; they were distinguished by a small white cross. All the coffins had been numbered but the documents accompanying them gave no clue as to identification. The coffins themselves were made of inch-thick deal boards and painted black. Crudely constructed they were already showing signs of warping and it was strongly recommended that coffins should be prepared in England and the remains transferred to them for burial.

When all the coffins were safely aboard *Champion*, *Truro* was given permission to sail. By 1350 she was on her way to London.

At 1545 an Estonian naval and military guard of two hundred marched on to the jetty. They saluted the coffins as they passed and halted in line, and in three ranks, opposite *Champion*. The reception of floral tributes then began. One tribute drew particular attention: a poorly clad elderly peasant woman made her way quietly to the quarter-deck where she placed a bunch of wild flowers on a coffin before moving away sobbing. In spite of the adverse weather conditions, a large crowd gathered for the official ceremony. Government, military, naval and other dignitaries passed along the rows of coffins saluting the dead and depositing wreaths. When this part of the ceremony had been completed the visitors left *Champion* and stood on the jetty whilst an Estonian military band played 'Nearer My God to Thee'. *Champion*'s crew stood smartly to attention and those on the jetty bared their heads. The Estonian naval and military guard then fired three volleys. Royal Marine buglers sounded The Last Post to complete the ceremony.

'*Champion* proceeded at 1630 and as she left the jetty the Royal Marine band played Chopin's Funeral March', *Champion*'s captain was to record. 'Meanwhile those who had laid wreaths stood on the jetty astern of the ship to watch her leave. A gale was blowing, making the exit from the entrance to the harbour a difficult manoeuvre as it was only a quarter cable* broad and a heavy sea was running. Two tugs assisted but owing to the sea they had to cast off and seek shelter before the ship was in deep water. Fortunately an extra boiler had been connected on account of the weather and the ship turned into the sea at full power. Considerable quantities of black mud was churned up by the propellers and the situation for a few moments was unpleasant. On arrival in the roads, seven-minute guns were fired by the Estonian destroyer division and the ship then anchored in order to strike the coffins below.

'The weather continued to get worse and visibility became bad from very heavy rain storms. I therefore decided to remain at anchor until the visibility improved, and eventually sailed at 1800 on the Saturday morning, September 1, when a gale was still blowing but the sky was clear.' *Champion* arrived alongside at Portsmouth at 1730 on the 5th.

On 7 September, *L55*'s crew were buried in a single thirty feet square grave at the Royal Navy Cemetery, Haslar. Today a visitor to the grave will see a large headstone inscribed with the names of all forty-two of *L55*'s crew.

*

A second Royal Navy submarine sunk in 1919, though in nothing like such dramatic circumstances as *L55*, was the *H41* (Lieutenant-Commander N.R. Peploe). The slow-speed main engine basin trials of HMS *Vulcan* had been arranged to take place at Blyth on the morning of 18 October, preparatory to her leaving for Portsmouth the following week. Through an oversight the trial was started at 0925 with three 'H' class submarines at *Vulcan*'s after trot. Immediately the trial had begun *H41*, the inside submarine, was drawn in sufficiently to foul *Vulcan*'s port propeller. Before *Vulcan*'s engines could be stopped the submarine was holed abreast the starboard main motor and she began to sink quite rapidly by the stern. The crew made all effort to close bulkhead doors and ventilators but as the submarine con-

* 150 feet (Author).

tinued to sink by the stern, the order was given to abandon ship. However, suspended from *Vulcan* by three wires to her foremost bits and by a wire-sling right round her forward, *H41* was prevented from sinking completely. It was hoped to maintain her in that position until salvage operations could be got under way. But this was not to be. *H41* continued to ship water and eventually parted the wire-sling round her forepart. She then submerged. The bow wires were eased out to permit her to rest on the bottom in an upright position. Soon after high water *Vulcan* was successfully withdrawn from between *H41* and the jetty. Three blades of her port propeller had sustained damage.

So, the situation when divers went down to inspect the damage was thus: the submarine had a slight inclination up by the bow and a very heavy list to port. Damage was reported as being a V-shaped hole 3 feet long by 4 inches at its widest part. The hole was about 3 feet below the centre line of the hull. Though at low water *H41* lay at a depth of only 24 feet the soft mud made it extremely difficult to place wires beneath her. The hope was that once wires were in position she could be lifted off the bottom at maximum high water for movement farther up river into shallow water, where the hole could be patched and the submarine pumped out prior to docking for more complete repairs.

On the morning of 23 October she was transported ahead about 150 feet. Over the next few days the operation was repeated and on the afternoon of the 25th, *H41* had reached the desired position at the head of the south harbour.

This new position did not come up to expectations. The place had been selected on local information, which soundings had borne out. A gain in depth of 11 feet, would have been all that was required, had been indicated. Unfortunately the bottom, though of harder mud than before, was not as hard as was expected. Also, instead of being less in depth, the mud was considerably greater, it being as much as eight feet deep. *H41* settled into this and consequently the conning tower hatch was just awash at low water.

Diving operations were continued: the fore hatch was shored down, blanks with internal suctions were fitted to both the conning tower and engine room hatches, a collision mat was secured over the damaged hull, and such valves and bulkhead doors opened or closed as appeared necessary for pumping operations. Because the muddy bottom restricted diving to daylight hours only, progress was slow and it was not until Wednesday 28th that the pumps could be started.

After pumping out as much water as possible, efforts were made to right *H41* with a direct pull by tug on the conning tower but the mud in which she was embedded made it impossible to shift her – as it did, also, for the placing beneath her of more wire for the purpose of par-buckling upright with a hopper, it being considered desirable not to try to do it with the big wires already round her in case they might foul and be of no further use if required for lifting her.

By 1 November it had become clear that *H41* would have to be lifted and taken farther up river. This was successfully accomplished on the 6th. The next day hoses were being placed down the conning tower when *H41* slid bodily down stream a few feet. With a strong ebb running at the time, she settled with a slightly bigger angle to port; thereby it was decided to pick her up again and turn her up-stream, and if possible to put her in shallow water. Owing to her awkward position a bad lift was obtained. But on the afternoon of Saturday 8th she was grounded in the new position, where at low water she was found to be lying at an inclination of $11\frac{1}{2}°$ up by the bow and 14° to port. Her bow-up angle made her conning tower hatch accessible for four hours' tide each way, and her fore hatch two hours each way. Pumping operations were delayed while the pump suction to the engine room hatch, carried away in the last slip, was repaired, so it was not until the 13th that pumping operations started in earnest. Compartments were cleared one at a time with motor and hand-pumps and then closed off, the engine room becoming accessi-ble on the 14th. As soon as extra suction could be fitted from inside, the submarine was completely pumped out and on the afternoon of the following day she floated on an even keel.

*H41* was towed in to shallower water where the mat over the dam-aged area was reinforced. On Tuesday 18th, *H41* was successfully refloated and towed to the Tyne where a patch was fitted over the damaged area. On the morning of 21 November, thirty-three days after the accident, *H41* was taken to Armstrong's High Walker yard pending sale.

Just over three months later *H41* was sold off.

On 19 January the Atlantic Fleet left harbour for a spring cruise to the Mediterranean. On its way south the fleet divided into two separate forces for an exercise which included five 'K' boats (*K5, K8, K9, K15, K22*), led by the cruiser *Inconstant*. For the remainder of the 19th, and throughout the night, the two opposing forces steamed towards their respective battle areas. By mid-morning (20th) the exercise was underway at a point 120 miles south- west of the Isles of Scilly. Sighting the enemy on the horizon, *Inconstant* signalled her submarines to prepare for an attack, whilst she herself swung about as if to retreat.

*K5* (Lieutenant-Commander J.A. Gaimes) was the first to slip beneath the surface. *K9* had a frustrating time trying to dive, her bow vents having inadvertently been left shut, thereby making her bows light; the matter was eventually sorted out and she joined her sisters under water. In *K22* Lieutenant-Commander Allan Poland (CO of *E43* when she collided with *E36* in January 1917) was also experiencing difficulty in diving, though in Poland's case it was not trying to dive that was the problem – but of trying not to! *K22* refused to halt her downwards progress until Poland ordered full astern on both motors and all tanks blown. *K22* went back to the surface and was out of the exercise.

By early afternoon the part of the 'K's in the exercise was over. They began surfacing at their respective locations to radio their positions to *Inconstant*. From *K5* there was no such call. At 1409 the cruiser asked *K5* to report her position. There was no answer. *Inconstant* then asked the four submarines if they could see *K5*. Each gave a negative reply. The rest of the fleet was asked if they were in contact with *K5*. Again a negative reply.

After returning to the position where each submarine had been at the time of diving, a judgement on the likely course of *K5* was made. At 1742 a large patch of oil and some wreckage was discovered. The position (48°53'N 8°52'W) was approximately 1½ miles from where the submarines had dived. *K9* recovered several pieces of wood, identifiable as belonging to a 'K' boat. Evidently *K5* had gone down deep, about 600 feet, and had broken up. The following morning the lid of a ditty box was seen floating on the surface. There was no further trace that a submarine and her crew had ever existed.

It was established that *K5* had dived at 1130 at a normal angle and without difficulty. Almost fifteen minutes later, at 1144, she was seen on the surface. She dived again at once and was never seen again.

Lieutenant-Commander John Gaimes, DSO, captain of *K5*, was thirty-four and had been in the Submarine Service since January 1904. A successful wartime 'E' boat captain, he had served in *Inconstant* for six months prior to relieving Commander John Hutchings as captain of *K5*.

*

On the night of 25 June the *K15* (Commander G.F. Bradshaw) sank as she lay alongside the cruiser *Canterbury* in the tidal basin at Portsmouth.

*K15*'s watchkeeper was making his rounds when to his astonishment he saw that the submarine's stern was under water. The startled man went rushing below to awaken the sleeping crew. Fortunately the majority of *K15*'s crew were on leave so the few submariners aboard were able to make a dash to the safety of *Canterbury*. Nothing could be done to save the submarine and she sank.

Daylight and a low tide revealed *K15*'s funnels and part of her conning tower above the surface. Salvage operations were at once put in hand. With most of the watertight doors having been left open, plus a manhole door on the cable locker, the submarine had been extensively flooded. The situation was such that although the salvage crew worked very hard over long hours, it still took almost two weeks to raise the submarine.

The reason for *K15*'s sinking was almost certainly due to the hot weather which had persisted throughout the day: the oil in the hydraulic system which closed the vents of the external ballast tanks had expanded and overflowed. In the coolness of evening the remaining oil in the system had contracted, causing a drop in oil pressure. This loss of pressure had loosened the vents and allowed air to escape. An increase in sea-water in the ballast tanks, caused by the escaping air, took the submarine to the bottom.

Commander George Bradshaw, on leave at the time of *K15*'s sinking, had entered the Navy in 1903. Awarded a DSO in 1917, he had been captain of *G11* at the time she ran aground in November 1918. After retirement he became well-known as a marine artist. Commander Bradshaw died in October 1960, aged seventy-two.


# 1922


HM submarine *H42* (Lieutenant D.C. Sealy) was a unit of the 3rd Flotilla. A Vickers-built submarine, *H42* was a comparatively new submarine when she was accidentally sunk on the morning of 23 March. The submarine had spent Christmas at Portsmouth before leaving in January with elements of the Atlantic Fleet for a spring cruise and exercise in the Mediterranean.

'Stand by to surface.' Lieutenant Sealy was giving the order for the last time. James Price, his first lieutenant, stood close at hand. 'Surface!' High pressure air hissed into *H42*'s tanks. The submarine moved towards the surface in the vicinity of Europa Point, an area at the southernmost extremity of Gibraltar.

Under the command of Commander Victor Campbell, HM destroyer *Versatile* was making way at 20 knots when *H42* made a sudden appearance some 120 feet ahead and in a direct line to the destroyer's track. Unable to take effective avoiding action *Versatile*, homeward bound for England, struck the submarine just abaft her conning tower and almost cut her in two. *H42* went quickly to the bottom and gave up no survivors. *Versatile* returned to Gibraltar.

The loss of *H42* cast a gloom over the Rock. Lieutenant Sealy had been a popular officer and had had many friends at Gibraltar. Sealy, a West Countryman, his home was at Matheaston in Somerset, had served in submarines for many years. In October 1916 he had been awarded a DSC in recognition of his war service. A further honour was bestowed on him in April 1918 when he received a Bar to his DSC for submarine operations in the Baltic, where Douglas Sealy had commanded *C27*.

Lieutenant James Price, from Clarbeston in South Wales, was the son of a solicitor. Educated at Osborne and Dartmouth, Price had twice been mentioned in despatches and had been awarded a DSC for war service. Twenty-four years of age, Price had transferred from *K5* only weeks before her loss.

*H42*'s third officer, Lieutenant Thomas Oswell, hailed from the Surrey village of Holmbury St Mary.

# 1923

The crown colony of Hong Kong – the name means fragrant harbour – became a British possession in 1841. Strictly speaking, the 23 square miles expanse of water known as Hong Kong Harbour is not really a harbour at all, but a strait which separates the island from the Kowloon Peninsula, which with the island forms the two halves of the city. Unlike other major seaports Hong Kong has few berths. Most of the ships that visit the harbour moor at off-shore buoys, from which they load and discharge their cargoes by lighter. The reason that such an ancient system persists is because the typhoons which rage across the China Sea from July to October are too severe for ships to withstand if moored to a pier.

During the twenties when Hong Kong was in much greater use as a naval base than today, the problem of where to site submarines to afford them the greatest security during a typhoon was of some concern. The Senior Submarine Officer of the Reserve Submarine Flotilla at Hong Kong was Lieutenant J. Cresswell. Once the likelihood of a typhoon striking the island had been established it was part of Cresswell's duties to assist and advise Commander C.E. Brooke, commander of the dockyard, on the disposition of the submarines in his (Cresswell's) charge. Cresswell's reserve flotilla consisted of the submarines *L1, L2, L3, L8, L9*, and *L20*. Of these *L1, L3*, and *L9* were without motive power; the *L2, L8*, and *L20* all had motive power, though only *L2* could put hers to use as the two other submarines were in dry-dock.

For an expected typhoon of 18 August 1923, *L1*'s bow was secured to a buoy in the dockyard basin and her stern secured to the corner of the basin with wires. *L3* and *L9* were secured to buoys in the harbour. The typhoon arrangements for *L2* were that she would be positioned alongside a wall and made ready to proceed to a buoy in the harbour if necessary. Though the disposition of submarines was by no means ideal, it was based on the result of experience gained during previous typhoons.

The six submarines of the Reserve Submarine Flotilla were divided into two groups, 'A' and 'B'. In command of 'A' Group (*L1, L9, L20*) was Lieutenant T.D.K. Williams. The first lieutenant of 'A' Group, Lieutenant D.E.G. Wemyss, was instructed by Lieutenant Williams to ensure that, with the help of dockyard personnel, *L9* was secured to No 13 Buoy in the harbour. David Wemyss completed this order and then returned to the shore after giving the four ratings aboard *L9* instructions that in case of difficulty they were to fire off two Very lights; also, a watchkeeper was to remain on the bridge with orders that if *L9* broke adrift, the starboard anchor was to be released. By six o'clock on the evening of the 17th, fifteen hours before the full force of a typhoon would hit the colony, preparations for the coming storm were completed.

The typhoon had formed to the south of the Pacific island of Guam, 2,000 miles south-east of Hong Kong, on the 11th. Its track was lost for a while on the 15th, but it was picked up again around six o'clock on the morning of the 16th. Over the next twenty-four hours (that is up to 0600 on the day the typhoon struck Hong Kong) its movement was a little short of this.

*Saturday 18th.* At 0920 a black cross was hoisted and bombs fired to indicate that the typhoon was about to strike Hong Kong. Twenty minutes later east-to-west winds of 123 miles an hour were battering the Colony.

In rapidly deteriorating conditions Petty Officer Coxswain W. Gordon, in charge of *L9*, instructed Stoker William Roach to check that the engine room hatches were watertight and to close the aftermost bulkhead door. As the winds and seas grew in strength, the cable securing *L9* to the buoy came under increasing strain. Petty Officer Gordon was making his way up the conning tower to the bridge when the storm-ravaged *L9* broke free of No 13 Buoy. Mindful of his orders to fire off Very lights and to release the starboard anchor, Gordon set about trying to put them into effect under the most difficult of conditions. Taking hold of the wayward *L9* the seas sent her crashing into the harbour wall. First her fore-end struck. Then her bows swung out and her stern crashed hard against the wall.

'I tried again to let go the anchor,' Willi Gordon was later to recall, 'but owing to the bumping I could not keep my feet on the deck. I then climbed back to the bridge. The stoker came up from below and reported that he could not close the watertight doors as he could not keep his feet and had only candle-light to work with.'

Stoker Roach confirms that he could not close the watertight doors: 'When the cable broke I was told to go and close the bulkhead door between the motor room and the engine room. I went down the conning tower and got a candle from the wardroom forward. I went back into the engine room and tried to close the bulkhead door but owing to the electric leads and the pitching of the boat I could not get the leads away. Then the boat hit two or three times. I heard a rush of water and the boat seemed to be breaking up. I went back to the coxswain on the bridge and told him I could not close the bulkhead door.' The leads mentioned by William Roach were dockyard temporary lighting leads.

The *L9* was crashing into the harbour wall with considerable force. Petty Officer Gordon: 'I could not get any assistance from the shore. I think that if at that time a wire had been passed to me I would have managed to get it over the bollard; but getting no assistance I used my own discretion and, thinking that the boat was in a sinking condition and being broken up against the dockyard wall, and not knowing what she would do next. To save life I gave orders to jump the boat.' Though one of the ratings was injured during the scramble to abandon ship, Gordon, Roach, Leading Seaman Horswell, and Able Seaman Marrage all successfully cleared ship.

*L9* was now completely at the mercy of the elements. It was at this stage of the proceedings that Lieutenant T.H. Dickson caught sight of her. Lieutenant Dickson: 'I was in charge of the submarines in the basin and dock under the orders of Lt Williams. At about 0900 I went down to the submarine *L8* and secured her as far as possible in case the dock was flooded. Shortly after this I assisted the *Ginyo Maru* to get a wire out to secure her stern. Whilst doing this *L9* appeared alongside the wall. Observing no one on board, I thought possibly the crew were inside the boat, I jumped on to her casing and hailed down her conning tower. As there was no answer I went forward and attempted to get the towing pendant out to the jetty. I secured the life-line from a dockyard lifebuoy round it, and the men on the jetty manned this. Unfortunately this lifeline parted twice. Meanwhile *L9* had been bumping very heavily forward, causing considerable damage to her starboard hydroplane. As soon as her stern got alongside the *Ginyo Maru*, heavy bumping took place and in my opinion this is where she sustained the vital damage. When her stern was abreast the bows of the *Ginyo Maru*, *L9*'s propellers must have got entangled with the *Ginyo Maru*'s cable, which was still attached to her buoy. This held her, and her bows started to swing round. Just about this time I felt a quiver in the boat, which appeared to be caused by the collapse of the after engine room bulkhead. *L9* started to sink rapidly after this and I attempted to climb up a wire which ran over her from the *Ginyo Maru*'s forecastle to the buoy the latter had been secured to. Unfortunately this parted.' Soon after, the submarine turned up her nose and sank.

On 23 August an inquiry into the sinking of *L9* took place. At its conclusion the following was expressed:

We are of the opinion that taking into consideration the conditions of uncertainty which obtained during the approach of a typhoon as to the prospective main force and direction of the wind, every care was taken, based on previous experience, to dispose the six submarines in position of as much safety as available conditions allowed and that therefore no blame is attributable to any officer concerned for securing *L9* to No 13 Buoy from which she broke adrift and was sunk.

We are of the opinion that Petty Officer Willi Gordon, and the three men under his charge, acted hastily in abandoning *L9* at the north wall, where she first struck, and if they had remained in *L9* when Lt Thomas Hugh Dickson boarded her at the west wall it may have been possible to secure *L9* by a wire from the west wall and thereby to have saved her. Taking into consideration the absolutely abnormal conditions, with the wind registering 130 miles an hour and low visibility existing, together with the fact that Petty Officer Gordon considered that *L9* had been holed by contact with the north wall, we are of the opinion that no blame be attributed to him for what was possibly an error of judgment in acting too hastily.

We are of the opinion that orders should have been given to Petty Officer Gordon to close all doors before and abaft the control room whilst lying at the buoy with increasingly bad weather and that in the absence of such instructions he should have ordered the watertight doors closed. For this lack of precaution we consider that Lt John Cresswell and Lt Thomas Dudley Kenneth Williams are to blame – the former officer as Senior Submarine Officer for not having included in his other instructions definite orders as to the closing of watertight doors in submarines without motive power lying at buoys under typhoon conditions, and the latter officer as senior officer of 'A' Group in that he did not take these steps as regards *L9*, being a submarine in the group under his command. Also that Petty Officer Gordon is to blame in a lesser degree in that he did not close the watertight doors on his own initiative.

The arrangements for the disposition of submarines were probably as good as could be devised. It seems unlikely that any good purpose would have been served if Petty Officer Gordon and his three companions had remained aboard *L9* in the prevailing circumstances. Perhaps orders of a more definite nature should have been given to Gordon as regards the shutting of watertight doors, and that as commanding officer of 'A' Group Lieutenant Williams should have been the one to ensure that such orders were given. However, it must be said that Williams had been given permission early on the Friday afternoon to proceed on ordinary recreation leave as it was thought that the movement of submarines would not take place until the Saturday afternoon. Williams was therefore absent when *L9* was moved and so was not able to take any steps that he might have considered necessary on the movements ordered. Although Petty Officer Gordon was obliged to keep open the watertight doors leading forward so as to ensure access to the bow compartments for anchor work (he had also received verbal orders regarding constant inspection of the motor room), he might possibly have taken the precaution of ensuring that all watertight doors could be cleared ready for instant closing.

The typhoon raged from 0900 to 1100. One hundred people lost their lives and much damaged occurred. At the point where *L9* went down, there now stands a Shrine of Remembrance in the city hall. Three weeks after her sinking, *L9* was raised and placed in shallow water. She was refitted and served for another four years before being scrapped at Hong Kong in June 1927.

# 1924

It was during Exercise GA that the *L24* (Lieutenant-Commander P.L. Eddis) was struck by the battleship *Resolution* and sank with the loss of all hands. The objective of Exercise GA was threefold: (1) to provide submarines with experience in receiving aircraft reports of enemy movements (2) to give submarines experience in attacking a battle fleet (3) to exercise aerial reconnaissance. The two forces involved in the exercise were identified as Red and Blue. Red Force consisted of battleships, destroyers, and submarines. Blue Force comprised submarines from flotillas attached to HMS *Dolphin* and

*Maidstone*. Aircraft from 10th Group RAF were assigned a role with Blue Force.

Exercise GA dictated that Red Force was to sail from Portland early on 10 January and proceed down Channel. It was hoped that the use of aircraft by Blue Force would enable groups of Blue Force submarines to obtain positions for an attack. To make life a bit more difficult for Blue Force, it was deemed that its submarines could not approach close to Portland Bill on account of strong Red anti-submarine patrols. The exercise was to take place on 10 January and begin when Red Force passed westward of Portland Bill; it would end when Red's battle fleet crossed the line Eddystone Light-Les Hanois (Guernsey), or at 1530 on the 10th.

At 0345 on the morning of the exercise Blue Force submarines, which had spent the night anchored off the minesweeper *Ross* in Weymouth Bay, weighed and proceeded to a position on their charts. By 0810 they had reached the position. The submarines, hitherto on the the surface, dived to adjust trim. At 0920 contact was made with the opposing Red Force.

The 29,000-ton battleship *Resolution* (Captain J.E.T. Harber) sailed Portland astern of the 1st Division of the 1st Battle Squadron. At about 0845 the battleship *Revenge* assumed station immediately ahead of *Resolution*. Shortly after passing Portland Bill the fleet formed divisions in line ahead disposed abeam to starboard, *Resolution* being the rear ship, that is the fourth ship of the 1st Division. The fleet had been at sea several hours when *Resolution*'s second officer on watch, Lieutenant Charles Crawshay, pointed to a disturbance on the surface of the sea off the port bow: 'That looks like a torpedo track, sir.'

Captain Harber, standing by the compass, disagreed. 'No, it's not a torpedo. No torpedoes are being fired today.'

The disturbance continued to hold Crawshay's attention. As *Resolution* grew closer to the disturbance Crawshay saw that it was not the track of a torpedo but froth on the surface which appeared to look, if viewed from above, the same sort of shape as a submarine would make: an oval froth mark in the middle of a fore-and-aft streak. 'Look, sir! It looks as if a submarine has broken surface there, and gone down again.'

Captain Harber took a good look at the small patch of disturbed water, situated 50 yards abreast the stem of *Resolution*, before replying: 'It might have been caused by the propellers of the ships ahead, as there are similar patches on the starboard bow.' Captain Harber had no sooner finished speaking than he and Crawshay felt a slight bump, apparently under the bridge. The clock showed 1113.

'It feels as if we have struck a submarine, sir,' ventured Crawshay.

'I think a collision with a submarine would cause a heavier bump than that,' retorted Harber, believing the bump had been caused by something inboard; nevertheless he gave an order for a careful look-out to be kept on both bow quarters.

Captain G.O. Stephenson, the commanding officer of *Revenge*, the ship directly ahead of *Resolution*, relates what he saw from *Revenge*. 'Shortly after 1100 I heard the chief yeoman report a submarine on the port beam. I observed a large swirl of discoloured water about 300 yards distant, Red 100. I imagined this was a submarine about to break surface after a dummy attack. Almost immediately afterwards I observed a periscope in the patch coming towards the battleship line. The periscope was well out of the water, about 4 feet, and the submarine seemed to be travelling fast and was endeavouring to pass between *Revenge* and *Resolution*. I followed the movement of the periscope closely and feared that the submarine must be rammed. As the periscope moved across *Revenge*'s wake and arrived at a certain distance across the starboard bow of *Resolution*, I had a feeling of great relief as I then believed that she had just cleared the *Resolution*. I estimated that the periscope was in sight about fifty seconds. A minute or two after this, *Resolution*'s signal was received reporting a heavy bump felt and my attention was called to *Resolution*'s starboard paravane chain* having apparently been carried away. *Resolution* was informed of this by signal.'

Commander Frank Elliott also witnessed a periscope: 'I was on the fore-bridge (compass platform) of *Revenge* when, at about 1110, I heard the report of a submarine on the port beam. In order to get a clear view, I climbed onto the port 6-inch director tower. I saw a periscope, showing about 6 to 8 feet above water, on *Revenge*'s port quarter and moving in such a direction as to pass at right angles across the bows of *Resolution* from port to starboard. My first impression was that *Resolution* would ram her. My next impression was that there was so much periscope showing, *Resolution* must see her. I watched the periscope pass between the *Revenge* and *Resolution*, close across the bows of *Resolution*, and I then jumped off the director tower and crossed to the starboard side of the bridge to see if she would

* A fish-shaped device with fins or vanes, towed from the bow for deflecting mines along a wire and severing their moorings (Author).

break the surface – exclaiming at the same time "My God! That was a close shave!", or something to that effect – as I had at the time the certain impression that she had cleared the bows of *Resolution* in safety. I am also pretty certain that I saw the periscope cross the bows of *Resolution* because it was with a feeling of immense relief that I crossed to the other side expecting it to come out any moment. It was some minutes after this incident that I heard a report that *Resolution*'s starboard paravane chain had carried away.'

Gunner S.H. Vennard (*Revenge*) had also observed the track of *L24*'s periscope: 'My attention was called to a submarine which had appeared on the port beam. I at first observed the feather and almost immediately about a foot of the periscope above the water, distance approximately 800 yards. A submarine appeared to be steaming a course to cross our stern at an angle of about 45° to our track. The periscope began rising until about 3 feet was showing above the water. It ceased to rise and then began to disappear rapidly, finally disappearing close to *Resolution*'s port bow. I thought there was a great danger of the submarine being wrecked and watched to see if *Resolution* showed any sign of shock or of the engines going astern. I thought I saw the *Resolution*'s bow lifted to the sea at the moment I would have expected her to hit the submarine. There was nothing unusual about the motion and I did not think it was caused by striking the submarine. I then watched for the submarine to appear on the starboard side of *Resolution*, but during a space of five minutes nothing appeared.'

Another interested observer in *Revenge* was Leading Seaman Horace Sansom: 'I was on the admiral's bridge and sighted one periscope, brown in colour, endeavouring to get between the two ships, speed about 10 knots. I watched the periscope until it got nearly ahead of *Resolution* and 50 yards distant, when the periscope suddenly dipped as though to do a crash dive. At this moment I turned to the Flag Lieutenant and said "By God, sir, she'll ram her!" I did not see anything of the periscope on the starboard side of *Resolution* at all.'

Yeoman of Signals Alfred Foltard, of *Resolution*, saw two submarines, *H23* and *H48*. At about 1110 he saw a surfaced *H23* pass down between the lines off the starboard side of *Resolution*. A minute or so later *H48* surfaced 300 to 400 yards off the port beam. Of *L24* he saw nothing. So unlike *H23* and *H48*, *L24* had not surfaced after attacking. The tremor felt by *Resolution* now assumed a somwhat sinister aspect. This, and the reports of a periscope so near to *Resolu-*

*tion*'s bow, made it almost certain that the submarine had encountered difficulties. Salvage vessels were dispatched to the area and a search for the missing *L24* got underway. Meanwhile *Resolution* returned to harbour and at 1640 dropped anchor. Her divers then went down to examine her stem. As darkness was approaching, the inspection was short and, because the water had been clouded by the ship's propellers during anchoring, was of little value.

By the afternoon of the next day the weather in the vicinity where *L24* was thought to have come to rest took a turn for the worse and eventually became too rough for divers to descend. By the 12th, all hope of saving life having long been abandoned, hostile weather conditions were still much in evidence. Leaving just one vessel to maintain a solitary vigil near the buoyed position, the remaining ships returned to harbour.

For the wife of Chief ERA Andrew Wallace – the chief had perished in *L24* – the accident was a time of great sadness as she had lost a former husband in the February 1912 collision of *A3* and *Hazard*. Two other submariners lost with *L24* were Telegraphist Thomas Backhurst and his friend Leading Seaman William Dempsey. Both had been taken prisoner by the Turks when Lieutenant-Commander Cochrane's *E7* had been scuttled at the A/S net in the Dardanelles during the war.

The depth of water and the treacherous currents in the vicinity where *L24* had gone down made it certain that any attempt to raise her would be extremely hazardous. It was therefore decided to leave the submarine where she lay.

Although at first there was an element of doubt as to whether a collision had actually taken place, subsequent inquiries soon dispelled them: it was noted that *H23* and *H48* had surfaced on completion of their attack, whereas *L24*, third member and leader of the group, had failed to do so. Further evidence in favour of a collision was revealed after an examination of *Resolution*'s port paravane chain indicated that a link which would have been at the very bottom of the keel was fractured, and the link connected to it had been severely scored and appeared to have been pressed quite hard by a heavy weight sliding down it. As the damaged links were at a depth of 32 feet it seems unlikely that any submerged wreckage would be at that depth. Another point was that the swirl seen close on *Resolution*'s port bow immediately before the collision could have been caused by the wash from the propellers of a submarine attempting a rapid dive. Also to be considered was that a patch of discoloured water was seen on

*Resolution*'s port side immediately following the collision. One last point: a piece of electric cable was discovered attached to the port side of *Resolution*'s bilge keel. There was no evidence to connect the fragment with *L24*, but some waste attached to it was heavily impregnated with oil fuel.

The reason as to how *L24* found herself in such dangerous circumstances must naturally be supposition. A possible cause of the accident was that Lieutenant-Commander Eddis had attacked the *Revenge* and was unaware of the close proximity of *Resolution*. It seems likely that Paul Eddis thought that he had attacked the last ship of the line and was surfacing in the normal manner when he became aware of the danger, either by catching a glimpse of *Resolution* through his periscope or by the use of hydrophones. Eddis's reaction would have been instantaneous: a rapid dive underneath the approaching battleship would have seemed to offer the best chance of avoiding a collision. Depending on the steepness of the angle of dive, *L24*'s stern would have been 20 to 30 feet higher than her bow. It would appear, should the supposition be correct, that the submarine just failed to clear the base of *Resolution*'s stem, thereby causing the breakage of the paravane chain. This impact was probably slight and passed unnoticed aboard *Resolution*. The natural tendency of this action would be to force *L24* down, listing her to port. She would have then most likely passed aft of the ship's bottom and, owing to movement of *Resolution* caused by the swell, and possibly to action taken by Lieutenant-Commander Eddis to bring *L24* to the surface after the first impact, the battleship might have come down on the submarine, causing the slight bump which had been felt aboard the ship.

Lieutenant-Commander Paul Eddis was a highly experienced officer. Apart from his normal duties Eddis also assisted in the passing out of officers qualifying for the Submarine Service. It will be recalled that Eddis had been Geoffrey Layton's first lieutenant during *E13*'s abortive attempt to enter the Baltic in August 1915.

# 1925

It was in April 1918 that the Royal Navy took delivery of a new class of submarine. Only four of the class were ever launched. They were designated the 'M' class and were of an approximate displacement to the 'K's. At war's end the largest guns in use by submarines were 4-inch. *M1, M2,* and *M3* had a gun of battleship proportions. And that was precisely where their guns came from – a battleship that had seen better days and was ready for the breakers' yard.

*M1* had been in existence for six years when during an exercise in November 1925 she met with a tragic end. Part of the exercise, which took place off the south coast of Devon, entailed the minesweepers *Burslem, Newark, Sherborne,* and *Truro* acting out the role of cruisers coming down-Channel to engage a supposed troop convoy enacted by the depot ships *Alecto* and *Maidstone* and the minesweeper *Ross.* The troop convoy would be steaming a reciprocal course and following the normal up-Channel track of merchantmen. The convoy would have as escort five submarines: *L17* was to scout five miles ahead of the convoy, whilst *L22* and *L23* would screen the convoy's starboard side and *M1* and *M3* the port side.

*Thursday 12 November.* At 0303 the *M1* (Lieutenant-Commander A.M. Carrie) and *M3* (Lieutenant-Commander C. Mayers) sailed Plymouth Sound in company to take part in the exercise. The submarines proceeded on the surface and in line ahead, *M1* being 400 yards astern of *M3*, and by 0645 had arrived at their stations. By this time the ENE wind was fresh with a moderate sea. Visibility was six or more miles.

*0652*: Several ships were sighted by the submarines. At first they were thought to be merchantmen but by 0700 they had been identified as the four minesweepers representing enemy cruisers. Lieutenant-Commander Mayers signalled Carrie to alter course together and for *M1* to take station a half-mile astern of *M3*.

*0707.* Mayers signalled *M1* to dive.

*0722.* Both submarines were now submerged. Mayers called *M1* and made the signal: STAND BY FOR GUN ACTION. A minute later fessenden was heard asking *M3* to repeat the message. Mayers did as asked and then signalled: RISE IMMEDIATELY.

*0726.* Colin Mayers, captain of *M3* for more than two years, surfaced. Whilst engaged in 'gun action' with the enemy, he sighted *M1* about three miles off the beam and heading in a westerly direction. During the next three minutes Mayers sighted *M1* at frequent intervals. Then *M1* disappeared.

*0730.* The minesweeper *Newark* sighted *M1* on the surface. Between 0730 and 0736 the *M1* and *Newark* exchanged signals, both ves-

* Fessenden was underwater signalling apparatus.

sels claiming each other. The two vessels were about a half-mile apart. The nearest surface ship was the Swedish collier *Vidar\**, a mile to the north-west.

*0737. M1*, about a half-mile from Lieutenant-Commander Hugh Curry's *Newark*, was seen to dive. She was not seen again for forty-two years.

No one concerned with the exercise had any idea of what had happened to *M1*. In the days following her loss, theories as to the cause of her disappearance were aired, but without any survivors or recovery of the submarine the actual cause of her loss would remain, so it seemed, a mystery for some time to come. Then came a report from the captain of the collier *Vidar*.

The *Vidar*, owned by Svea of the Stockholm Steamship Company, had sailed from the Queen Alexandria Dock in Cardiff on the morning of 11 November, the day before *M1*'s loss, with 2,900 tons of Welsh coal. Her destination was Stockholm. At 1300 the ship's pilot disembarked. *Vidar* then made way for Land's End. There was a high following sea, but it did not at that time cause much inconvenience.

After rounding Land's End and entering the English Channel the sea became rougher and waves began to break over the collier. At about 0700 on the 12th, *Vidar* was to the south of Start Point. It was noted that British warships appeared to be carrying out some kind of manoeuvres.

The *M1* had been seen to dive for the last time at 0737. It was eight minutes after this that *Vidar* was shaken by a heavy blow forward. The helmsman thought a preliminary slight shock which he had felt was due to pitching, the ship being thrown slightly off course. *Vidar* resumed her course, but with the next pitch came the heavy blow already mentioned. This blow was so strong that for a time it seemed that *Vidar* would fail to answer the helm. An entry in the ship's log noted the incident:

*0745.* Heavy breaking sea. Shipping water over. Two severe shakings were felt as if vessel had struck something hard below water. As some English men-of-war were seen to be exercising in the vicinity, it was supposed that they had fired some submarine bombs, as our own ship after sounding was found perfectly tight.

So, Captain Anell, *Vidar*'s master, and his first officer, Einar

* A 2,159 tons vessel built at Port Glasgow in 1907 by Murdock & Murray.

Lundberg, thought that an underwater explosion, possibly depth-charges, had occurred nearby. Both of these officers were members of the Swedish Naval Reserve and in their service with that organization had had ample opportunity of observing the result of underwater explosions on ships. With their not inconsiderable experience to draw on, these officers found nothing to modify their opinion that some underwater detonation had taken place. Having arrived at this decision they saw no reason why they should not continue their way home without communicating with the British warships, which showed no concern as to the possible danger to any submarines in the area.

At this point attention should be drawn to the Notices For Mariners for April 1925. These make special reference to the area where *M1* disappeared by referring to underwater explosions for the removal of the wreckage of the 11,000 tons cruiser HMS *Ariadne*, torpedoed in July 1917. Mariners were asked to note that underwater explosions could cause shocks to vessels in the vicinity. Shocks had on occasions been reported by vessels as encounters with submerged objects.

Over the days it took to arrive at the Kiel Canal, Captain Anell made the passage in total ignorance that a search for a missing submarine was taking place in the English Channel. An entry in his ship's log for the afternoon of 16 November reads:

> During the passage through the Kiel Canal it was said that an English submarine had been sunk in the English Channel last Thursday. This was confirmed after reading German papers.

This German press report put a different light on the incident of the previous Thursday morning. Captain Anell had second thoughts about the suspected underwater explosion when it was realised that it had occurred in the same position and at the same time as the reported submarine loss. A coincidence? Perhaps. Anell at once radioed a report of his experience to his company in Stockholm. The company notified the Swedish Defence Department, which in turn forwarded the report to the Admiralty in London.

The *Vidar* arrived at Värta harbour at eight o'clock on the morning of the 19th, but was unable to berth until later in the day. The following morning a diver went down to examine *Vidar*'s hull; he found her stem bent to port just by the forefoot, probably the strongest part of the hull. Several rivets were missing and some plates damaged. After the discharge of *Vidar*'s cargo, the damage to her stem could clearly be seen on the waterline. It was evident that *Vidar* had struck a submerged object. Time and place suggested that it could have been *M1*. Later a dry-dock inspection revealed that traces of paint on *Vidar*'s stem was identical to that of *M1*.

*Vidar*'s contribution towards the accident had been negligible. Her first officer had been in charge of the bridge at the time of the collision. Neither he nor any of the crew saw any indication that submarines were in the area. A large Japanese steamer, the *Aden Maru*, was close astern of *Vidar* when the accident took place. Soon after the incident the Japanese vessel had put on a turn of speed and passed *Vidar*, giving no indication that she had noticed anything amiss.

Lieutenant-Commander Carrie had been captain of *M1* since July 1925. After Osborne and Dartmouth, and a spell in destroyers, Carrie had joined the Submarine Service. After two years on the China Station, Carrie returned home to serve in the Big Ship Navy. Appointed to HMS *Hood* he served in her during a world cruise, after which he returned to submarines. Aged thirty at the time of his loss, Alec Carrie had been married only eleven months. He left a five-week-old son.

The search for the lost submarine went on for a month. On 2 December the Admiralty announced:

> Diving operations in connection with the submarine *M1* have been discontinued as no positive results have been obtained. It is not considered necessary to prolong the search as the cause of her loss has been fully established.

And there the curtain on the *M1* descended. Once in a while her name would crop up but except for the close-knit community of submariners the *M1* and the fate of the sixty-nine officers and men who had perished were largely forgotten.

*September 1967.* The salvage vessel *Comrades* was out searching for the wreck of a torpedoed ship. The *Comrades* stopped at a likely position. The first of four divers to go down was Frank Charles. Through the gloom Charles saw the long shape of a submarine. The *M1* had been found at last.

When the *H29* sank to the bottom of No 2 Basin at HM Dockyard, Devonport, on Monday 9 August, more civilian than naval lives were lost.

On the morning of the 9th, Mr Henry Hill, a fitter at Devonport, crossed the gangway to *H29*. 'So you'll be off when these trials are done with,' Hill's companion said with a smile.

'I will.' Hill's reply touched a cheery note. 'And to tell the truth, I'm quite looking forward to it.' Henry Hill was referring to his annual holiday. He should have travelled to St Ives the previous Saturday with his wife and child but the basin trials of *H29* had forced him to remain behind. Before the day was over, Hill and five other men working on *H29* would be dead.

The *H29* (Lieutenant F.H.E. Skyrme) lay secured fore and aft alongside the south wall in No 2 Basin. She had recently completed a refit and the basin trials scheduled for the 9th entailed the firing of dummy torpedoes to test the mechanism of the torpedo tubes, and engine trials. At eight o'clock on the morning of the trials, the submarine had been lightened by the pumping out of the auxiliary ballast tanks. To enable the tubes' mechanism to be tested it was necessary to take *H29* down to her normal trim. It was decided that this would be done after one o'clock when the crew and dockyard personnel would have returned from lunch. In the meantime the engine trials were got underway.

At 1145 *H29*'s captain went ashore, but not before giving orders to his first lieutenant, Lieutenant M.E. Wevell, that the tube tests were to be carried out at the first opportunity. Most of the work on *H29* was suspended during the lunch hour. Lieutenant Wevell, who had left the submarine for a while, returned at about 1330. After first going to the engine room hatch to check that the engine trials had restarted, he went below to supervise the tube tests. Wavell explained to Chief ERA Robert Dalton that he wished to trim the submarine forward for the test firing. He declined the suggestion to trim the forward tanks as this would have brought the propellers too close to the surface and interfered with the engine trials; instead, he decided that Nos 2 and 3 main ballast should be used, as a small amount of water let into these tanks would bring *H29* down on an even keel. Leaving Dalton he went to the control room, where the Kingston valves are operated, and instructed Stoker Petty Officer

George Aske that he was 'going to put a drop of water into two and three main ballast' and that he was going on deck to check when the submarine was trimmed for firing.

Arriving on deck Malcolm Wevell went to the bow. He heard No 2 main ballast venting. When satisfied that *H29* was low enough in the water, he gave the order to stop flooding. On returning below he told the torpedo gunner's mate that the test firing could begin.

The firing tests were in progress when several dockyard hands came hurrying from aft. 'What's the matter?' The scurrying men made no reply to Wevell's query in their dash to the forward hatch. Rightly concerned by their action, Lieutenant Wevell went on deck. He at once saw the reason for their haste to get topside: *H29*'s after end was low in the water. Wevell also saw Lieutenant Skyrme and heard him ordering the watertight doors to be shut. Wevell repeated this order down the fore hatch and called for No 3 ballast tank to be blown.

On his return to *H29* Frank Skyrme went below through the fore hatch and proceeded aft to the engine room to ensure that work, in general, was in progress. He then went forward, stopping at intervals to chat to men at work. Via the fore hatch he then went up on deck where on arrival he noticed that *H29* was low in the water at her after end. Knowing that all the hatches were open he hurried to the after hatch, which would be the first hatch to submerge, with the intention of closing it. To his dismay he discovered that a 4-inch pipe had been lowered through the hatch for ventilation purposes. Water was just starting to trickle over the rim of the hatch. Leaving an ERA to try and shut the hatch, Skyrme ran to the fore hatch and dashed below. Ordering the shutting of watertight doors he rushed aft to try and cut the offending ventilation pipe. By the time he had cut halfway through the pipe, the water had become too deep for him to continue. Abandoning the task he made his way to the bridge.

Water entered *H29* at a fast rate and eventually forced her under water. As *H29* sank she listed to starboard, the side nearest the wall to which she was secured. As she went down, Lieutenant Skyrme managed to grab a hold of a chain hanging from the side of the dock and scramble ashore. *H29* sank by the stern until the fore hatch reached the water-line: she then levelled out on an even keel.

It took some time to establish beyond doubt that six men, five civilians and one naval, had been trapped inside *H29*, which had taken about two minutes to sink. Three of the civilians were married. The only naval fatality had been Chief ERA Robert Dalton. Dalton, who

(*Top left*) A survivor from the *E13*, and after escaping from internment in Denmark, Lt Paul Eddis returned to England to take command of the *E38*. An exceptionally cheerful man, he was popular with officers and men alike. He went down on the *L24*. (*Top right*) 23-year-old Percy Farley, now the only living survivor of HM Submarine *Poseidon*, aboard the depot ship *Medway* at Wei Hai Wei two days before *Poseidon*'s loss in June 1931.

The dazzle painted *M1* at speed. Despite her bulk, *M1* could dive in 90 seconds and was very easy to handle underwater.

*M2* getting ready to fly off her Parnell Peto seaplane, an operation which may have later contributed to her loss in January 1932.

(*Left*) 'God bless this ship and all who sail in her.' The traditional toast, given by Mrs A. J. Power when she launched *Thetis*, brought no good fortune. A total of 161 men were lost in her in peace and war.

(*Below*) The picture that shocked the nation! The imprisoned crew of *Thetis* slowly die as helpless crews vainly try to cut a hole in the stern.

lived with his widowed mother at Southsea, was aged forty and had served in submarines around twenty years. It was expected that he would shortly have transferred to General Service.

*H29* was resurfaced the following Thursday. Five bodies were found huddled together at the foot of the fore hatch. Another body was discovered in the control room.

In August an inquiry as to the cause of death was held at Devonport Guildhall. When asked by the coroner, Mr J. Pearce, why *H29* had sunk, Lieutenant Skyrme replied that the after hatch had come under water owing to the flooding of No 3 main ballast tank.

Lieutenant Malcolm Wevell said in evidence that after calling down the fore hatch for the watertight doors to be shut he called, also, for No 3 ballast tank to be blown. How he came to leave *H29* he did not know. He recalled ordering the fore hatch to be shut, but that that could not be done owing to the rush of water. After that he remembered nothing very clearly except that he was carried by a torrent of water to a position beneath the fore hatch. He had made a successful grab at the hatchway ladder. His left foot had then become held fast by something on the starboard side. He subsequently became unconscious and did not know how he had cleared the submarine. On regaining his senses he had found himself floating in the water. When Wevell was asked by the coroner if, when he told George Aske that he intended putting a drop of water into No 2 and No 3 main ballast, he intended to convey to Petty Officer Aske that that was an order for him (Aske) to put water into the tanks, Wevell replied that it was not. The coroner then said: 'So it really comes to this, the statement which you made to the stoker petty officer was misconstrued by him to be an order.' Lieutenant Wevell agreed that that was so.

Stoker Petty Officer George Aske then took the stand. He stated that when in harbour his chief duty was to carry out the orders of the first lieutenant as to the trim of the submarine. He controlled the Kingston valves and the vents, unless someone else was either detailed for the duty or to assist him. Aske went on to say that before Lieutenant Wevell had gone up on deck Wevell had said to him, 'I want to trim down the boat a little. Put some water in two and three tanks.' Petty Officer Aske had taken that to be an order and had started on No 2 by first seeing that the vent was closed. He then opened the Kingstons and proceeded to the vent and opened it. The next order he received from Lieutenant Wevell was to 'shut off' but this he was already doing as he knew the tank was full. 'I then proceeded to put some water into No 3 tank,' stated Aske. 'I slightly opened the vent valve of No 3 and stood by for two or three seconds. I then saw a splash of water come over the engine room hatch. On seeing this I immediately shut the vent, ran back to the control room, put on the "blow" to No 3, and then stood by until the majority of the men below had got up either through the conning tower hatch or the fore hatch. The water was coming in from both fore and aft. From the control room I went up through the conning tower and was the last person to leave the bridge. It all happened in about two minutes.' George Aske went on to say that as a rule the first lieutenant told him why they were trimming, but on this occasion he did not do so and it was not until after the accident that he learned that they were to do water shots. When the coroner asked him if he had been surprised at having to submerge without being told the reason, Aske replied that he had not.

'If you had known you were to submerge for the purpose of firing torpedo tubes only, how much water would you have let into the tanks?' questioned the coroner.

'Not a great deal.'

'Not as much as was let in?'

'No.'

In his summing up, the coroner said that it was a case as to whether or not a definite order had been given to submerge the submarine by filling the tanks. He was convinced that George Aske thought that Lieutenant Wevell had told him to put water in the tanks. If the order had been made clearer, and more clearly understood, the accident would not have happened. The coroner went on to say that he did not see how blame could be attributed to any particular person. It was a mistake to which all were liable: to misconstrue what had been said.

At a court martial held in September at the Royal Navy Barracks, Devonport, Lieutenant Wevell pleaded not guilty to negligently or by default hazarding *H29*. The court found the charges proved because Lieutenant Wevell had failed (1) to give orders for trimming the submarine in a definite manner (2) to investigate immediately the flooding of No 2 main ballast tank (3) to ensure that the engine room hatch and the fore hatch were shut before the main ballast tanks were flooded. Lieutenant Wevell was sentenced to be dismissed *Maidstone* and to be severely reprimanded. Malcolm Wevell had an excellent service record. His character and ability were judged high.

Lieutenant Skyrme, later to command *M2*, was found guilty of negligence for omitting to take charge of the submarine and of not having a clear understanding with his first lieutenant as to what that officer's intentions were as regards to trim.

Stoker Petty Officer Aske had also to face court martial proceedings. He was charged that he had negligently performed the duty imposed on him in that he flooded Nos 2 and 3 main ballast tanks of *H29* without waiting for definite and specific orders for opening the valves and vents. Stoker Petty Officer Aske successfully pleaded that he had been given a definite order to flood the tanks, and that he had acted upon it. He was found not guilty.

It was decided that *H29* would cost more than her value to put in order. Within a year she was scrapped.

# 1929

It was January when a dredger struck the periscope of *L5*. The submarine surfaced without difficulty and was able to return to Portsmouth with her periscope bent over but otherwise none the worse for the encounter. In March the *L26* was damaged in the Mediterranean. She was able to make Gibraltar for repairs. Two months later an 'H' class (*H28*) received slight damage when she collided with a steamer in the Bruges Canal. Then in July the *H47* (Lieutenant R.J. Gardner) sank in collision with Lieutenant-Commander H.P.K. Oram's *L12*. A crewman of *L12* recalls what took place on the morning of Tuesday 9 July:

'I had been in submarines for seven or eight years when I was drafted as steward to the *L12*. Normally 'L' boats do not carry stewards, but this was a training-class trip and there were a lot of officers on board doing their final training before passing out for the Submarine Service.

'We took an ordinary training route – a cruise round the British Isles. There was one other submarine with us, the *L14*. Our captain, Lieutenant-Commander Harry Oram, was in command of the flotilla. We left Portsmouth about the end of June, 1929, and on 8 July we went into Lamlash and tied up alongside the *Iron Duke*. We were due to sail again early the next morning, and we did not get any shore leave.

'Soon after we had tied up, a third submarine came alongside. She was the *H47*, on independent exercises in the Irish Sea. Several of us had friends among her crew. During the evening our leading signal-man, John Bull, went down to see his chums. John was a pal of mine, and I shall always remember two things about him. One was that he believed in reincarnation. He did not talk about it much – indeed, I only found out about it by chance when we were together in Malta. There John told me that he firmly believed that he had lived before and that he would live again. The other thing I remember about John is that he always wore cycle clips round his ankles, to stop his bell-bottomed trousers from flapping about when he was running up and down the conning tower; for as leading signalman he had to do a lot of chasing up and down. John was wearing his cycle clips when he came back from the *H47* that evening at about ten o'clock; but there was not much else that was familiar about him. I got a shock when I saw him. He looked as if he had seen a ghost.

"'What's the matter, John?" I asked.

"'Let's have a yarn," he said. His voice was shaky.

'I said he needed a tot of rum, and took him down to the pantry. We had a tot each, but it did not seem to do much good. He was as jumpy and nervy as a kitten. I had never seen him like this before. After a bit he told me the reason. It was the *H47*. The crew, John said, were uneasy and restless. They seemed to have a premonition that some-thing was going to happen to them. It was as if a hoodoo was on the boat. That sort of thing was bad enough on any ship, but probably worst of all in a submarine. It worried me to see John affected like this, and I tried to talk him out of it. We yarned for about an hour, but I could not cheer him up. Indeed, he had more influence on me than I had on him, and when I turned in, although I tried not to show it, I was properly on edge.

'We got underway in the early hours of the morning, heading for St Ives Bay. I turned out at about five, and had enough work to stop me from brooding any more. The usual routine was advanced because of the training, which started at eight. The training-class officers had their mess in the fore-ends, and I served their breakfast at seven. The regular ship's officers messed in the wardroom, and most of them had had breakfast when the captain came down from the bridge at about 0755. I was there with the officers' cook, Tom Fulcher. Tom was on his first submarine trip.'

At about the same time as Lieutenant-Commander Oram was leaving the bridge of *L12*, Lieutenant Gardner was arriving on *H47*'s bridge to relieve the OOW. The submarines, which had the depot ship *Alecto* in company, were at that moment about 15 miles west of Strumble Head and twelve miles north of St David's Head on the Pembrokeshire coast. At 0803 Gardner observed that *L12*, which was then before the beam of *H47*, was altering course to starboard. He judged that the alteration was slight.

The *L12* continued to swing to starboard. Considering a collision was likely if *L12* maintained her swing, Lieutenant Gardner ordered full speed astern and collision stations. Several blasts were sounded on *H47*'s whistle and at the same time she altered course in a vain effort to avoid collision. *H47* was going astern, but had not gathered sternway, when at 0810 *L12* struck her at right angles on the port side and just abaft the foremost control room bulkhead, *L12*'s bow penetrating about two feet. It took only fifteen seconds for *H47* to start to sink bow-first towards the bottom.

Lieutenant-Commander Oram states that he was on his way to the bridge when he heard two blasts on *L12*'s whistle. Alarmed he hastened his steps, feeling the motors running astern as he did so. On reaching the bridge he saw that *L12* was approaching *H47* from a distance of about 40 yards. 'The *H47*'s bow was overlapping the *L12*'s bow and a collision was inevitable,' says Oram. 'It occurred twenty seconds after I arrived on the bridge.' Oram's first thought was towards the rescue of survivors, and to this end he called for anything floatable to be brought topside ready for use if necessary. Able Seaman A.E.R. Sampson was at his station at the foot of the conning tower. Gathering some lifebelts he rushed topside.

*L12* had begun to go down by the bow. Oram and the rest of the bridge party were swept into the sea. For a few dreadful moments it looked as if *L12* would also be lost as the sea surged in through the open conning tower hatch. As a torrent of water cascaded into the control room, Sid Reynolds leaped onto the ladder and reached up to release the pin which held the hatch cover open. The cover slammed shut. *L12*'s steward again takes up the story: 'A few minutes after eight a messenger came into the wardroom. He was Able Seaman Sampson. We learned afterwards that he had been sent to tell the captain that the *L14* had signalled that she had a hot bearing and had had to reduce speed, and the bridge wanted permission to do the same. The captain nodded and said a few words to Sampson, and followed him out of the wardroom.

'Within a matter of seconds I heard a few blasts on the submarine whistle. That meant something was wrong. We were cruising on the surface, and I guessed that probably we were making a quick turn to avoid another vessel. Then I felt that we were going full speed astern. I say I *felt* it, because there was no indicator in the wardroom to show me. But I was as sure as if I had been standing on the bridge watching the waves go by.

'"Shut the fore-end door, Tom," I shouted.

'Tom dashed to shut the door, and I went to help him shove the clips on. In those days watertight doors were fastened by clips – now it is done with a wheel. Shutting that door cut off any water that might get into the fore-ends if our bows were holed. I had no reason to think this would happen, but the whistle and the fact that we were going full speed astern made me take this precaution. For the same reason Tom and I went through the wardroom into the next compartment, the crew space, and shut the dividing watertight door. We were just shoving the clips on when we felt the boat shiver and tremble. If we had not been holding the clips at that moment we should probably have landed on the deck. That told me for certain that either we had hit something, or something had hit us. And I knew it was on the bows. I cannot say quite how I knew that. Perhaps it was intuition – a sixth sense. But I had a feeling amounting almost to certainty that at that very moment our fore-ends were filling with water.

'We ran through the crew space into the control room. What happened while I was there took only seconds, although it will take much longer to tell. Somehow – I never learned quite how – I lost sight of Tom, and found myself with Sid Reynolds in the control room. Sid was the "tankie" – the coxswain's right-hand man, who looked after food and other stores. He was a sailor of the old school, and I cannot think of anyone I would sooner have had with me in that emergency. It was a real emergency now, for by the time I reached the control room there was a distinct angle on the boat. Our bows were going down – and that, I reckoned, could only mean that I was right, and our fore-ends had been holed and we were flooding. Sid and I dashed across to the middle of the control room, to the bottom of the ladder leading up the conning tower to the bridge. We looked up the conning tower – and saw a pair of legs, about half-way up. Above, I could see a blue sky.

'"We'd better stop down here," said Sid.

'"I think you're right, Sid," I said – but I was thinking longingly of that patch of blue sky. Of course Sid was right. It was a split-second decision, as it had to be. It was born of long training – for we had not had orders to abandon ship, and until they came it was our job to remain below. As it happened, that decision saved our lives.

'The angle was steeper now, and Sid ran across to one of the bulk-heads, pulling out his jack-knife as he crawled under machinery to get to the drop keel. This was a release wheel holding 5 tons of ballast, in the form of two large lumps of steel fitted to the keel. It was always kept locked, but the padlock was secured with a leather thong that could be cut in the case of emergency. Sid cut the leather and gave the wheel a turn and the keel dropped.

'The angle of the submarine was something like 45° now, and while Sid was wriggling out again, water suddenly started sloshing down the conning tower. It came in masses, drenching us and throwing us in a heap against the bulkhead. I looked at Sid, and Sid looked at me, opened his mouth, and – I shall never forget it – said: "What about our fortnight's pay?" He meant the pay that had accumulated since we had left Portsmouth, where we had had our last shore leave. If I had been another Sid I might have been able to give him an answer in the same vein – but all I thought of at that moment was getting out alive.

'Sid reached the conning tower again, and managed to take out the pin that held up the lower lid. The weight of the water at once pressed the lid shut – but not completely. In those days the leads to the Sperry compass went up through the conning tower – afterwards special holes were made in the bulkheads of submarines for this purpose. The presence of these leads meant that a small amount of water could still get through from the conning tower. Still, we had stopped the flood.

'The angle of the boat stayed at about 45° and then, suddenly, she righted herself. Almost before we realised it we were on a completely even keel.

'"We're on the bottom now," said Sid. "We'll have to do something – quick!"

'We looked at the depth-gauge, expecting to see that we were down a hundred feet or more – and got the shock of our lives. The gauge showed a depth of 7 feet! Thinking the needle had stuck, we tapped the glass. The needle remained steady – at 7 feet. Bewildered, I looked at the periscope. Then I almost let out a cheer as I saw the sun shining above. The gauge was telling the truth. We were nowhere near the bottom. The boat was still on the surface. There could not have been water in the fore-ends – we had not been holed at all. The difference between zero and 7 feet on the gauge could probably be accounted for by the water we had shipped through the conning tower. There was still water in the conning tower, and it was still coming through. But now we had another worry. Sid was wrinkling his nose and sniffing.

'"Chlorine," he said. "'I smelt it at the same time, and realised at once what had happened. The water we had taken had gone down under the boards and got into the batteries, and the gas was seeping up.

'"Try the gun trunk," said Sid. The gun trunk, or gun hatch, was in the crew space. It was like a smaller edition of the conning tower, with a ladder inside and lids above and below. The bottom lid was closed when we reached it, but Sid soon got it open. He did not go up at once; nor did I. There were others of the crew with us now, who had come from the after end of the boat. I did not see who was the first to go up the gun hatch, because I was looking at Sid. He seemed to be covered with blood. Sid was looking at me, and did not show any signs of pain or distress. Indeed, I got the impression that he was more concerned about me than himself. He gave me a comforting grin, and patted me lightly on the shoulder. "Never mind, we'll get out of this," he said, in a sort of tone a man might use when trying to reassure a dying comrade.

'I was about the third or fourth to go up the gun hatch, and it was a wonderful relief to get out into the sunlight and gulp in fresh clean air. We were safe now, I was sure; but I was no nearer to knowing what had happened. For some peculiar reason our bows must have taken a dip of 40 feet or more, and then come up again. I could not imagine why.

'There was soon quite a crowd round the gun, including Sid and Tom Fulcher. But there was no sign of the captain, and at first I thought there was no one at all on the bridge. Then I saw the figure of a man – a small man, soaked and dripping water – on the bridge.

'*I had never seen him in my life before!*

'I knew all the crew of the *L12* by sight – and this man was not one of them. I went over to him. He looked as if he had been washed up by the sea.

'"Where the hell have you come from?" I asked.

'"You've just sunk us," he said.

'"Us?" I stared at him. "Who's us?"

'"The *H47*."

'"The *H47*?" He must have thought me stupid, the way I repeated everything he said. "Then where's everybody?" I was looking over the side for survivors.

'The man from *H47* pointed. "Over there," he said.

'I looked – and could just make out little blobs in the water, about half a mile away.

'"You had a lot of sternway on," he added.

'Then I began to understand. We had hit the *H47* almost amidships – later I learned we had struck her abaft control room foremost bulkhead. Our bows had penetrated about two feet, and she had sunk in a few seconds. And she had taken us down with her! She had dragged our bows down 40 feet or more – until her weight released us, and we came up again. Or rather until our bows came up – for our stern must have been sticking up in the air. Because we had a lot of sternway on, we had evened off about half a mile away from the scene of the collision. You can get the idea of what happened if you throw a wooden pole obliquely into the water. It jerks back as it comes to the surface. A similar thing had happened to us.

'Our captain had reached the bridge only a few seconds before the collision. He had been swept overboard, together with everyone else on the bridge, including several of our training-class officers. They were the blobs in the water that I could see, swimming for their lives – they, with any other survivors from the *H47*.

'This still did not explain how this one man had managed to change boats. In a few breathless, graphic sentences he told me. He was Stoker Petty Officer Hicks, and he had been relieved just before the collision. He had gone on the bridge for a breather before breakfast. The only other person up top was the captain of *H47*, Lieutenant Gardner. Hicks had seen the *L12* approaching, and had actually looked over the side and watched our bows go right into the *H47*. He was a non-swimmer – and, with great presence of mind, he jumped over the side and on to our bows, and clung to the jackstay. The next moment he was submerged, but he clung on. He clung on to that jackstay while he was pulled down 40 feet – and he was still clinging when our bows surfaced, bringing him up half a mile away from the scene of the collision. "I was just hanging there, like a piece of washing on the line," he told me. It was the most remarkable escape I had ever heard of.

'The *L12* was not badly damaged, but we were too far away to be able to help the men in the water. We just screwed up our eyes and stared, wondering how many of them were from our own crew and how many from the *H47*, while the *L14* went to the rescue.

'It was then that I noticed that my white shirt had dark patches on it – big red stains that looked like blood. I felt myself for a cut, but could not find one. One of the crew saw what I was doing – and let out a yell. "My red lead powder!" he exclaimed – and then explained. He had left a packet of red lead powder stored in the control room, on the pipes overhead. The packet must have fallen off when the boat had angled and shot through the stream of water coming down the conning tower, which had given Sid and me a soaking. That explained why Sid had been so solicitous about me, just before I had come up the gun hatch. Each of us had thought the other was badly wounded!

'He and I cleaned ourselves up and we had a tot of rum. Afterwards we wished we hadn't, because chlorine and alcohol do not mix, and we were violently sick. One or two of the gas victims had a touch of hysteria and had to be held down.'

Several of the men who had been swept off *L12*'s bridge with Lieutenant-Commander Oram did not survive. Recovering from his unexpected ducking, Oram saw to his relief that he was not alone. Although Petty Officer Wheeler and Leading Signalman Bull were nowhere to be seen, and would not survive, Oram did see Able Seaman Arthur Sampson struggling close by and an officer swimming to Sampson's aid. The officer managed to push a lifebelt into the AB's hands. Oram was later to recall that at this stage: 'Sampson appeared to me to take hold of the lifebelt and place it round his chest. It was one of the sausage-shaped lifebelts one blows up with one's mouth. There were several in the water. I got one myself eventually.'

The third submarine of the group (*L14*) put about to assist. On hearing that one of the submarines had been sunk, ERA Herbert Billings went topside. Recognizing at once that Arthur Sampson was in acute distress Billings went to help him out of the sea. He noted that Able Seaman Sampson was frothing at the mouth. Herbert Billings applied artificial respiration but Sampson was beyond all help.

Only three men (Lieutenant Gardner, Stoker Petty Officer Hicks, Petty Officer Telegraphist Sydney Cleburne) of *H47* survived the sinking. Petty Officer Cleburne had a remarkable escape. He had been in his wireless cabinet, which was part of the control room compartment. He had opened the door of his cabinet just as the bows of *L12* came crashing through into the control room. The onrush of water threw the control room's occupants hard against the bulkheads, but Telegraphist Cleburne was simply swept off his feet and flung up the ladder, from which he shot straight up through the conning tower and into the air. Telegraphist Cleburne splashed into the sea to become the only crewman from inside *H47* to survive the collision. For Sydney Cleburne this fearful experience was the second time he had been near to losing his life in a submarine accident: he had transferred from *M1* only forty-eight hours prior to her tragic encounter with the *Vidar* in November 1915.

*Portsmouth, 26 July.* The first of three courts martial resulting from the collision opened under the presidency of Captain F.A. Sommerville. *L12*'s navigating officer stood tight-lipped as the charge against him was read out: 'Lieutenant Claude Stanley Griffiths Keen, RNR, HMS *Dolphin*, of 'D' Group of submarines in reserve, then being a person subject to the Naval Discipline Act, did negligently or by default hazard HM Submarine *L12*, for that he did handle the said ship in such a manner as to cause a collision between the said ship and *H47* on 9 July 1929.'

'Not guilty, sir,' Keen replied firmly.

Lieutenant Claude Keen had been an officer of the Royal Naval Reserve for four years and at the time of the accident was on leave from his employers for the purpose of naval service. In giving evidence Keen stated that he went to the bridge to take over OOW duties from Sub-Lieutenant Wise. Wise had drawn his attention to *H47* and had remarked that if the present course and speed of *H47* was maintained *L12* would have to alter course. Keen decided that a course alteration was necessary and passed the message to the control room: 'Tell the captain *H47* is trying to cross our bows.' For reasons unknown, this message was not received by Lieutenant-Commander Oram.

When *H47* was 800 yards from *L12* Lieutenant Keen altered course to starboard without considering it necessary to repeat the message to the captain, nor to confirm that it had reached him when a collision seemed inevitable.

After considering the evidence the court gave a verdict of guilty on both charges. Lieutenant Keen was ordered to be dismissed his ship, HMS *Dolphin*, and to be severely reprimanded. Perhaps a little sympathy towards Lieutenant Keen would not be entirely misplaced. After giving the order to alter course he fully expected to clear *H47* by 400 to 600 yards. Keen believed that had *H47* continued to hold her course, instead of stopping, the collision would have been avoided.

As commanding officer of *L12* Lieutenant-Commander Oram had also to face a court martial. The charge against him was that he did negligently or by default suffer the *L12* to be hazarded. Oram pleaded not guilty.

A circumstantial letter, read by the Deputy Judge-Advocate, set out the circumstances of the collision. It submitted that Lieutenant-Commander Oram was to blame in that (1) as captain of *L12* he left the bridge in charge of a sub-lieutenant under training in submarines when the situation was such as to require his personal attention on the bridge on account of *H47* being on a converging course, which might require an alteration of course by *L12* or some such action to be taken (2) omitting to make a proper turn-over to Lieutenant Keen, who was required to take OOW from the officer under instruction, Sub-Lieutenant Wise, in a case of emergency, especially observing that *H47* was steering a converging course.

In giving evidence Sub-Lieutenant Wise said that he took over as OOW from Lieutenant-Commander Oram at 0750. The captain then went below. Wise further stated: '*H47* was at this time about 2 miles distant. I made repeated bearings on *H47* and drew the conclusion that if *L12* held her course there was risk of a collision. I was on the point of sending down to the commander when Lieutenant Keen arrived. I told him the situation and said that by rule of the road he would have to give way to *H47*.' Lieutenant Keen then passed a message to Lieutenant-Commander Oram, informing him that *H47* was attempting to cross their bows. Wise did not hear any reply to the message, though for him to have heard a reply Lieutenant Keen would have had to repeat the reply back. It was three minutes after Keen decided to alter course that the collision occurred. Wise, who had never been granted a watch-keeping certificate, said that he had frequently kept watch during the hours of daylight and at night, and that when he took over the watch from Lieutenant-Commander Oram he had not regarded the situation as at all awkward, but as it developed it became decidedly so.

Another witness, Able Seaman G.J. Rogers, reported that he received from Lieutenant Keen the message: 'Ask the captain if we can ease down, as *H47* is crossing our bows.' Rogers repeated the message to Oram, who had nodded his head in consent. A message that the captain had given his consent was sent to the bridge.

In his defence of the charge of negligently or by default suffering *L12* to be hazarded Lieutenant-Commander Oram stated that when he turned over the watch to Sub-Lieutenant Wise there were no navigational or other difficulties. The only message from the bridge he received whilst in the wardroom was from Able Seaman Sampson (who had died after rescue) stating that *L14* had a warm bearing and had had to ease down and that 'The bridge wishes to know if they could ease down too'. To this he had replied: 'Yes, certainly.' Oram stated that he had heard nothing at all about *H47*.

Lieutenant F.W. Lipscombe, who had been in the wardroom when Oram received a message, said in evidence that he had heard Sampson's message to the captain. Lipscombe stated that that message was the only one received by Oram, who had then left for the bridge.

Also called to give evidence was Signalman A.W. Simpson. Simpson stated that he had heard Lieutenant Keen pass down to Lieutenant-Commander Oram: 'Ask permission if we can ease down, as *H47* is crossing our bows.' And afterwards: 'Ask the captain to come to the bridge as *H47* is getting very close.'

The court found the charge against Lieutenant-Commander Oram not proved, and he was acquitted.

The court martial of Lieutenant Robert Gardner, the captain of *H47*, was held at Portsmouth on 2 August. Gardner faced four charges (1) negligently or by default losing submarine *H47* (2) negligently or by default hazarding submarine *H47* (3) not handling submarine *H47* in such a manner as to avoid consequences of the negligent navigation of submarine *L12* (4) not handling submarine *H47* in such a manner as to minimize the negligent navigation of submarine *L12*.

The Judge-Advocate read out a circumstantial letter which concluded:

> ... From the evidence it appears that the accused is to blame in that he did not take adequate steps to avoid a collision with *L12*. By maintaining a course and speed that brought his ship unduly close to the *L12* and the *L14* (two ships in the line ahead), and without clearly ascertaining that he would pass astern of the line, Lt Gardner hazarded *H47*.

It was also submitted that Lieutenant Gardner negligently performed his duty in that by putting the engines full speed astern at the same time as the helm was put hard to port, he failed to avoid or minimize the consequences of the negligent navigation of *L12*.

In reply to the charges, Robert Gardner replied: 'I plead not guilty, sir.'

The court, after considering in private for over an hour, acquitted Gardner on the first and second charges – negligently or by default losing *H47*, and negligently or by default hazarding *H47*. The third and fourth charges were found proved, and on these charges the sentence of the court was that Lieutenant Gardner be reprimanded.

For the Royal Navy Submarine Service the inter-war years were a time for absorbing the lessons learned in four years of combat. These were years of experiment and the adoption of new ideas and techniques. The first of the fully post- war designs were the 'O' class submarines. Based on the successful 'L's, a batch of three 'O' class submarines (*Otway, Oberon, Oxley*) was launched in 1926. Two years later a second batch consisting of *Odin, Osiris, Oswald, Otus, Olympus,* and *Orpheus* was launched in the space of ten months. Similar to the 'O' class were the ten submarines of the 'P' and 'R' classes. Commissioned between 1929 and 1930, all but two (*Proteus* and *Rover*) of these submarines were lost in the Second World War. One of the 'P' class, the *Poseidon*, was sunk in the Far East in June 1931.

*Poseidon* had been one of four submarines, the others being *Perseus, Proteus,* and *Pandora*, which had set out for the China Station in December 1930. The British naval base in China at the beginning of the thirties was at Wei Hai Wei on the north-east coast of the Chinese Province of Shantung. Wei Hai Wei had been leased to Britain under a Convention of July 1898 for as long a period as Port Arthur, a hundred miles north in Manchuria, was in the possession of Russia. In October 1930 Wei Hai Wei was officially handed back to China. In view of this, an arrangement between Britain and China stated that until China was in a position to establish a naval base on an extensive scale, the British would still have full access to facilities at Wei Hai Wei, which under British influence had received extensive development.

The captain of *Poseidon* was Lieutenant-Commander B.W. Galpin, an officer of outstanding ability. In a report of December 1922 by the captain of *L9*, in which Bernard Galpin was first lieutenant, he was thus described:

> Ability above average. A very keen, hard working and efficient First Lieutenant of a submarine. Has a good command of men and a very thorough knowledge of his submarine. Is musical and plays Rugby football well. Should make a good CO of a submarine.

By December 1924 Galpin was in command of *H31*. A report of this period, by none other than Max Horton, states:

I have a high opinion of this officer in every respect. Smart, quiet and efficient. Good on paper. Another lecturer. Thinks for himself, and initiative well developed. Maintains his submarine to a high standard.

Another report by Admiral Horton is even more glowing:

An excellent leader who exercises a strong influence for good of the flotilla. Tactful. Personality – quiet and determined. Spends much of his time investigating ideas for improvement in submarines. Would make a good staff officer.

Lieutenant-Commander Galpin was already in command of *Poseidon* when in December 1930 she joined the 4th Flotilla. Lest there be any doubts as to the high esteem in which Bernard Galpin was held, another report concerning this gifted officer really shows his value:

Reliability and zeal exceptional. Remainder above average. This officer has commanded *Poseidon* with marked ability. Previous to his appointment he was employed as instructional officer to the submarine commanding officers qualifying course, where he showed exceptional ability and zeal. He encouraged great keenness and promoted a high standard among the officers under his instruction. He recently showed marked energy and administrative ability in connection with the combined operation in the Isle of Wight. Lt-Cdr Galpin, apart from being a very able officer has plenty of personality and character, combined with a charming manner. I am confident he will do well in the higher ranks of the Service and strongly recommend him for special promotion. Ability in handling ship above average. Fit in all respects for really important command in due course.

Clearly, *Poseidon*'s captain was a man of very exceptional qualities and character.

On the morning of 9 June 1931 *Poseidon* was exercising twenty miles north of Wei Hai Wei when the Chinese steamer *Yuta* made an appearance on the scene. Lieutenant-Commander Galpin, on the bridge with his signalman, takes up the story: 'At 1145 the *Poseidon* came to the surface and remained stationary on a course of 235°. At 1204 the *Yuta* was off the port beam about 1,500 yards away and steering approximately north-west. The submarine was about three points on the starboard bow of the *Yuta*. The submarine went ahead at 4 knots. At 1215 I ordered hard to starboard helm and blew the whistle twice. The *Yuta* was about 1,200 yards away, slightly before the port beam. At 1209 I saw the *Yuta* alter her course to starboard, and blew the siren twice again. The *Poseidon*'s course was then about 70°. At 1212 came the collision. The *Yuta* struck at right angles, steering about north. Sea calm. Sky blue with clouds. Visibility 6 miles.'

*Yuta*, a British-built ship, was making passage between Shanghai and Newchwang with a cargo of 27,000 bags of flour but no passengers. A report of the collision from Tadashi Iyeishi, *Yuta*'s captain, was precise and to the point:

> At noon sighted the submarine on the starboard side about 4 miles off. Steered north forty-two west, speed 10 knots. At 1208 sighted the submarine on the starboard side 3 miles off. The submarine commenced to go ahead. At 1210 helm hard to port. At 1211 full speed astern. At 1212 collided with submarine.

The 42-year-old steamer cut a large V-shaped hole about three feet below the top of *Poseidon*'s saddle tank and a few feet forward of her fore gun-tower. The order was given to abandon ship.

Percy Farley, a survivor of the collision, has this to say of the collision: 'During the day's exercise with the submarine tender and target ship HMS *Marazion*, the *Poseidon* had heaved to for dinner-break. At about 1212 she was just about to get underway on the order of stand by for diving stations when the main telegraph from the bridge went to full speed astern. At the same time the verbal order "Stand by for collision. Shut watertight doors" came from the bridge. The engine room watertight door was being shut against the control room at the same time as the collision – which occurred at the fore-end of the control room's starboard side – fractured the pressure hull. The order was given from the bridge: "Blow all tanks. Abandon ship."

'Personnel on station between the shut watertight door of the engine room and the shut watertight door of the forward torpedo space made their escape by way of the conning tower. As the compartment was flooding, and knowing that one of the battery spaces had been fractured and gases were blowing and smoke issuing, no time was wasted in collecting DSEA* as they would have hampered the speed and efficiency of the personnel escaping up the ladder of the conning tower. (The time given at the inquiry states that *Poseidon* sank in under two minutes after the collision, leaving all personnel

---

* Davis Submerged Escape Apparatus (Author).

except one in the water without any survival gear.)

'An able seaman on the bridge at the time of the collision made a jump on to the anchor cable of the *Yuta* and climbed inboard while the steamer's bows were locked into the *Poseidon*. He put several lines over the side, receiving no help from the Chinese crew. Several of us managed to climb inboard. Stoker Albert Winter, who had been in extreme difficulties, was the first man to be hauled up. Being in a drowned condition he was resuscitated but died of oil fuel poisoning shortly after being taken aboard *Marazion*, Stoker Winter was the only casualty of the personnel who had escaped from the control room. HMS *Marazion*, lying about two miles off at the time of the accident, attended the area. *Marazion* came alongside the steamer to transfer the survivors and to leave a guard on board to assist the captain of the *Yuta*. She also laid a marker buoy at the area of the wreck.' Percy Farley, now the only living survivor of the disaster, says of Lieutenant-Commander Galpin: 'He was admired by all his crew as a disciplinarian, and for his courage in the water.'

*Poseidon* had sunk too fast for many of her crew to escape, consequently twenty-six men had gone down with her. Of these, eighteen were aft and eight were forward. The most senior rank in the fore-end was Petty Officer P.W. Willis, the torpedo gunner's mate. When the order had come to shut watertight doors, Willis called for the compartment door to be shut. This took a united effort as the bulkhead had buckled. *Poseidon* had then lurched to starboard and had sunk with a heavy inclination by the bows. At the moment of the collision the electric light leads were cut. During preparations to escape, the survivors had to contend with the occasional use of a torch only.

*Poseidon* lay on the muddy bottom of the Yellow Sea. Realising that they would need all the help they could get, Petty Officer Willis said the Lord's Prayer as other survivors stood with bowed heads. Willis then ordered his companions to put on DSEA. When this had been done a wire hawser was rigged across the hatchway to form a support for the men to stand on whilst the compartment was flooding.

The period spent waiting for the compartment to flood was used by Willis to keep the men in good spirits. Able Seaman Vincent Nagle also used the time to good effect by instructing officers' steward Ah Hai, one of two Chinese stewards, in the use of his DSEA and was undoubtedly instrumental in saving the steward's life. During this period of waiting the oxygen in some of the DSEA ran low. One AB told Willis that his oxygen flask was exhausted, as he could no longer hear it bubbling. Willis then tested his own and, finding it empty, comforted the worried man by saying, 'You can't hear anything in mine – yet there's plenty left.' This reassured the anxious man and helped maintain an atmosphere of calm, which could make all the difference between success or failure.

After about two hours Willis considered that pressure inside the submarine was high enough for an attempt to be made at opening the hatch. It was discovered that considerable effort was required before the hatch cover opened sufficiently for Able Seamen Arthur Lovock and Edmond Holt to shoot upwards to the surface. No sooner had Lovock and Holt passed through the hatch than the loss of pressure within the submarine reclosed the hatch cover, thereby making it necessary to await further flooding before another escape could be attempted. On reaching the surface Lovock and Holt were in such poor condition that Lovock died almost immediately. Edmond Holt, though himself in a state of complete exhaustion, supported Lovock until they were taken aboard a waiting rescue boat.

It was an hour before conditions were ideal for the remaining six men to attempt an escape. The hatch cover opened a little easier and the survivors made their bid for freedom. As only four of the six reached the surface, it seems likely that an able seaman and a Chinese steward fouled something and were prevented from rescue.

Of the eighteen crew in the after end, none was able to escape. A *Poseidon* Relief Fund was set up on the China Station for the relatives of the twenty-two lost submariners. From this fund, which totalled some £8,000, a portion was made available to the grandfather of officers' steward Ho Shung who had failed to surface with Petty officer Willis's party. Ho Shung had lived on the island of Liukungtao. He had been an orphan and was unmarried, but he helped to support his blind grandfather.

In July the *Poseidon* survivors boarded the liner *Rawalpindi* for their return to Britain. They arrived in London to a rousing welcome. A number of the survivors received awards. Petty Officer Willis received the Albert Medal. The *Poseidon* ordeal seems to have left its mark on the gallant Willis as he later suffered from neurasthenia, a nervous complaint, and he died at the comparatively young age of fifty-five.

Lieutenant-Commander Bernard Galpin was tried by court martial for the loss of his command. He was charged with (1) negligently or by default losing HMS *Poseidon* (2) negligently or by default hazarding HMS *Poseidon* (3) negligently performing the duty

imposed on him as commanding officer of HMS *Poseidon* in not handling HMS *Poseidon* in such a way as to minimize the consequences of
the negligent navigation of the SS *Yuta*. The finding of the court was
that charges one and three were not proved. Charge two was found
proved. The sentence imposed was that Lieutenant-Commander
Galpin be dismissed from HMS *Medway* and severely reprimanded.

Percy Farley continued to serve in submarines for several years.
He then transferred to surface ships. During the Second World War
he was attached to the Royal Marines Special Service (Commandos)
as chief petty officer. He left the Navy in 1949 after twenty-two years'
service. He joined Vauxhall Motors, remaining with that firm until
1972. Percy Farley lives not far from HMS *Dolphin*.

It was recognized that the raising of *Poseidon* would be a difficult
and hazardous operation with the possibility of success unlikely.
Divers reported that after only four days on the seabed the *Poseidon*
had settled six feet in the mud. In view of all the difficulties a salvage
team would have to face, and the likelihood that *Poseidon* would eventually sink in the soft mud, the decision was made to leave her undisturbed.

# 1932

The first Admiralty announcement concerning the loss of the *M2*
(Lieutenant-Commander J.D. de M. Leathes) came on the night of
26 January:

> News has been received this evening that submarine *M2* dived at about
> 1030 this morning off Portland, and since then no further communica-
> tion has been received from her. Destroyers and submarines from Port-
> land are searching the area in which she was last known to be, and every
> endeavour is being made to establish communication with her.

The *M2*'s complement of sixty included two RAF personnel.

HM Submarine *M2* was unusual in that she was able to accommo-
date a small seaplane, a Parnall Peto. As with her sister ship *M1*, she
had originally been fitted with a 12-inch gun. In 1927 the gun was
removed and in its place was installed a watertight hangar for the
Peto. When the pilot needed to take off from the submarine, a
catapult would launch the little aeroplane into the air from a specially constructed ramp. On its return the plane would alight close to

the submarine to be hoisted back aboard by a small crane.

It was just after nine o'clock on the morning of the 26th when *M2* sailed Portland for a routine exercise. *M2* headed for West Bay, fifteen miles west of Portland Bill, where she intended to link up with submarines from Portsmouth and other units of the 6th Flotilla at Portland. At 1011 Lieutenant-Commander Leathes signalled the depot ship *Titania* that he intended to dive at about 1030. This was the last communication with *M2*.

There was no real cause for anxiety when *Titania*'s busy wireless operators reported that radio communication with *M2* had been lost. It was assumed that the loss of contact was merely a communication problem and that it would rectify itself in due course. But the mood changed when *M2*, due to arrive back at Portland at 1615, failed to make an appearance. Search vessels were sent out in the hope of locating the submarine. *M2* carried DSEA so there was a chance that if she could not surface, some of the crew might escape. The search craft were to be disappointed.

In the early hours of the following morning the Admiralty announced that:

> An object presumed to be *M2* has been located 3 miles west of Portland in 17 fathoms* and on a sandy bottom. Salvage craft and divers have been sent from Portsmouth to this position with the utmost dispatch.

Unfortunately the object turned out to be an old wreck. The official telegrams informing relatives of *M2*'s loss followed shortly after the Admiralty announcement. A recipient of one of the buff-coloured envelopes was the wife of 27-year-old Thomas Morris. Able Seaman Morris was only a month away from his naval discharge after completing twelve years service. Tom Morris, father of three, had been a survivor of the *Poseidon* disaster.

The precise location of *M2* was made all the more difficult to ascertain owing to the large number of wrecks in the vicinity of West Bay, well known as 'The Bay Of A Thousand Wrecks'. Unfortunately there was no way of telling whether a sweep wire had taken a hold on the missing submarine or an old wreck until divers had made an examination.

It was whilst these preliminary sweeps were in progress that the Admiralty received information that Captain A.E. Howard of the

* 102 feet (Author).

Newcastle coaster *Tynesider* had sighted what was thought to be the *M2*. Captain Howard reported that between 1115 and 1130 on the morning of *M2*'s disappearance, his ship was outward bound from Charlestown with a cargo of china clay. As he approached Portland for bunkers, Captain Howard sighted a submarine with a letter 'M' on its conning tower, and not more than a half-mile from his ship. As *Tynesider* closed the submarine, Howard saw it dive suddenly, her stern being first beneath the surface. Howard continued passage to Portland, arriving at 1430 that afternoon. Having refuelled *Tynesider*, Captain Howard was clearing harbour just as a submarine was entering. Howard took this submarine to be the same one as he had sighted earlier; therefore a submarine diving stern-first, a detail which had intrigued him and had caused him a little anxiety, was not an uncommon occurrence, and so everything was in order. Later that evening Captain Howard heard on the radio that *M2* was missing. He had become concerned when the assumed position of her disappearance differed from that where he had seen the submarine dive.

The master of another vessel also volunteered information. Captain Hunt's *Crown of Denmark* was within a half-mile of the position given by Howard when at 1840 he saw on the port beam a bright flash of light. The light dimmed, then reappeared very briefly before disappearing completely. Ten minutes later two loud explosions were heard. All this was quite puzzling, as Captain Hunt could see nothing on the surface to account for it. Hunt then realised that a submarine might be in the area.

A week passed and still the exact position of *M2* remained a mystery. Then, on 3 February, the destroyer *Torrid*'s sonar picked up sounds 'of a nature which indicated the presence of a sunken submarine'. The minesweepers *Dunoon* and *Pangborne* confirmed the finding with sweep wires. Divers from HMS *Albury*, fighting against strong tides and poor visibility, were by ten o'clock that night able to report that *M2* had been found in position 50°34'N 02°33'W.

*M2* lay at a depth of about 90 feet and 3 miles from where *Tynesider*'s captain had stated that he had seen a submarine dive. She was not far from the position reported by Captain Hunt of the *Crown of Denmark*. The divers found *M2* lying with her stern in the sand and her bow raised sufficiently off the seabed for them to walk beneath.

On 5 February a memorial service was held over the point where *M2* had foundered. On the same day it was announced:

Diving operations on *M2* up to date have revealed that the hangar door and the upper conning tower hatch are open, and that the forward hatch and engine room hatch are closed. It has not yet been ascertained whether the lower conning tower hatch and the hatch inside the hangar giving access to the interior of the submarine are closed or open. It has been decided that the salvage of *M2* is to continue, weather permitting.

The statement seemed to imply that Lieutenant-Commander Leathes had been practising the launching of *M2*'s aeroplane. If, as suspected, the accident had occurred during a practice launch of the Peto, the most likely cause would appear to be that the hangar door had been opened too soon. If this was in fact the case, and if the small access hatch* from the pressure hull into the hangar was also open, a torrent of water would have cascaded speedily through the submarine. However, had this been the case the water would have entered compartments forward of the control room, causing *M2* to sink bow-first. But Captain Howard had clearly witnessed *M2* submerge stern-first, and grooves on the seabed and damage to *M2*'s propellers seemed to agree with this.

Another theory as to the sinking is that the vent valves to the ballast tanks aft had inadvertently been left open. If this was so, the after ballast tanks would start refilling as soon as *M2* had surfaced. On arriving on the bridge, Leathes would at once have realised what was happening and would have returned below and ordered the vents shut. But by that time the stern had probably dropped so far beneath the surface that the open hangar would have also been shipping water which, because the stern was well down, would cause the water to pass through the open access door and run sternwards, sinking *M2* stern-first as witnessed by Captain Howard.

A third possible cause of the sinking lay in the customary system for surfacing *M2* for an aeroplane launching. It was usual to get the hangar door clear of the surface by driving *M2* upwards and forwards on her propellers with her hydroplanes set to rise and whilst her ballast tanks were still being blown. Clearly, a hydroplane or engine failure, or some other unknown reason, when the after ballast tanks still contained water would result in fearful complications.

From the outset it was anticipated that the raising of *M2* would be very difficult. The submarine was at a depth of about a hundred feet so her accessibility was not beyond divers. What was beyond them was the changeable, usually for the worse, British weather which at

* 24-inch x 18-inch.

times not only made diving a thoroughly unpleasant and dangerous affair, but made it a total impossibility.

On 18 March a diver brought to the surface the body of Leading Seaman Albert Jacobs. Leading Seaman Jacobs had joined the Navy as a boy and had spent half his life in the Service. He left a widow and young daughter. It appears likely that Jacobs had been a member of the aeroplane's launching party. Via the small access hatch, the launching party would have passed from the submarine's interior and into the hangar whilst *M2* was still submerged. Once she had broken surface the hangar door would have been hydraulically lowered to form a platform over which rails connected the hangar with the launching catapult. Once the Peto was airborne, the hangar door was closed and the submarine dived, the whole operation having taken about five minutes.

Salvage work had been in progress five months when on 1 July a second body, that of Leading Aircraftman Leslie Gregory, was discovered in complete flying outfit, which supports the theory that a flight was about to be made.

The plan for raising *M2* involved the sealing of all openings prior to pumping in air under high pressure. Several hatches were discovered open and work, even when the weather permitted it, in closing and sealing the hatches was a long and arduous task.

During the weekend of 9/11 July an attempt at raising *M2* was made. Her bows were raised 15 feet with little difficulty, but a leak from the bow torpedo tubes was serious enough to call a halt to the work. On 27 September another attempt was made. With four lifting pontoons, positioned one on each side of both bow and stern, supplying additional buoyancy the lift went quite well until a wire on one of the forward pontoons gave way. Another attempt on the following day almost brought success but a hawser to HMS *Moordale* parted when *M2* was within 18 feet of the surface.

The final attempt to raise *M2* began on the night of 6 December. At 1520 the following day, the two stern pontoons broke surface. The rising of the stern pontoons at a faster rate than those at the bow gave cause for some anxious moments. HMS *Tedworth*'s compressors screamed with the effort to increase lifting power at the bow. For some time the weather had been deteriorating. By late afternoon the wind had increased sufficiently to warrant the stern being lowered back to the seabed. On 8 December, more than ten months after *M2* had sailed Portland, the Admiralty announced: 'It has been decided to abandon finally all salvage operations on *M2* . . .'

Over the years since the sinking of *M2*, experienced amateur skin-divers have made dives on the wreck. They have reported that *M2* lies on an even keel and appears in such good condition that she looks capable of bursting into action at any moment. Nowadays *M2* is used as a known target for the training of sonar operators.

# 1939

The water slapping against the side of the tug *Grebecock* went unnoticed by Lieutenant Coltart. The young officer was beginning to feel anxious; the submarine *Thetis* was not carrying out the prearranged programme. Several hours had passed since *Thetis* had dived. As part of her itinerary she should have surfaced, and then dived again. As Coltart focused his attention in the vicinity where he hoped *Thetis* would emerge, his thoughts returned to her dive, which on reflection now seemed rather odd. Coltart's anxiety was growing by the minute.

The *Thetis* (Lieutenant-Commander G.H. Bolus) had sailed Birkenhead at 0940 on 1 June. The new submarine had made for Liverpool Bay to undertake diving trials. *Thetis*, third of the new 'T' class, had never dived in the open sea. By 1330 *Thetis* was 38 miles from Birkenhead and some fifteen miles north of Great Ormes Head on the Welsh coast. Now was the moment for the civilians not wishing to make the dive to transfer to the *Grebecock*, doing duty as a tender. Up to thirty of those aboard *Thetis* had been expected to transfer, so it was a surprise to Lieutenant-Commander Bolus when all who were eligible to transfer elected to remain for the dive. So *Thetis*, in addition to her normal complement of fifty-three, had an extra fifty personnel aboard, employees of the builders (Cammell Laird) and Royal Navy observers.

At 1340 Bolus dispatched a signal stating his diving position and intended duration of dive, which was to be three hours. At 1400 precisely, Bolus gave the order to dive. The submarine's main vents were opened and the ballast tanks flooded. This would ensure that *Thetis*, moving forward at a steady 5 knots and with hydroplanes at 10° of dive would start to submerge, but despite all these actions she would not dive. With all main ballast tanks full, Bolus gave the order to flood the auxiliary tanks, normally used only to balance a submarine in the sea. Even this failed to put the submarine under water.

*Thetis* now had all her tanks flooded and fifty extra personnel on board, yet the top of her deck guard-rails were still not awash. With an increase in speed and with hydroplanes set at hard to dive, *Thetis* went deeper – but not deep enough to cover her conning tower. Difficulty in getting a submarine to make its first dive was not an uncommon occurrence. In calculating a submarine's trim it was considered a wise move to make her on the light side for her first dive at sea. In the case of *Thetis* the trim had been calculated far too light. A check was ordered as to why *Thetis* was resisting attempts to put her beneath the surface.

The first thing to do was to check that *Thetis* had taken on board all the water she was supposed to have in order to make her dive. Part of the check entailed an examination of the bow torpedo tubes. The six bow tubes were divided into two vertical rows of three and numbered from the top downwards, with even numbers to port and odd numbers to starboard. Tubes five and six, the bottom tubes of each row, should each contain a hundred gallons of water. The 1,600 pounds of water in these tubes could be the crucial factor in deciding whether *Thetis* dived or remained stubbornly on the surface. Lieutenant Frederick Woods, the torpedo officer, decided to make a check of all six torpedo tubes.

Beginning with number one tube Woods opened a small test-cock leading into the tube. Movement of a lever brought into alignment two adjacent holes from which water would spurt if present in the tube. A puff of air came out, suggesting that the torpedo tube was empty or partially empty. The rear door of the tube was then opened and Woods directed his torch to the inside. The tube was clean and dry. Woods then went on to give tubes two, three, and four the same inspection, omitting the additional step of opening the drain-valve fitted to each tube as a further method of determining whether water was present in the tube. Then came the check of the bottom tube on the starboard side, tube number five. Woods opened the test-cock, just as he had done twice before on this tube. The result was the same as before – there was no hiss of air or spray of water. Under Woods' direction Leading Seaman Hambrook began to move the lever to open the door of the tube.

Unlike the other four levers, the lever of five tube moved only with difficulty. Hambrook applied more pressure. The lever moved towards its fully open position but just before it got there water sprayed out from the bottom of the door. Moments later the pressure of water in the tube flung open the door with a loud crash. A torrent of water cascaded into the compartment. The force of the water was so great that there was not the slightest hope of closing the torpedo tube door. 'Tell the control room to blow!' Woods yelled to Petty Officer Mitchell, one of the five crewmen at the scene.

In the control room Guy Bolus did not need telling that he had a problem on his hands. Bolus had heard the distant *whooosh* followed by the clang of the tube's rear door crashing open. Then came the sudden increase of pressure on his ears. He at once gave the command that would have sent *Thetis* upwards had the situation then developing not been so grim.

Water was entering the torpedo stowage compartment at such speed that in a minute or so it had risen to the level of the coaming of the watertight door. There was a desperate struggle to shut the watertight door. To secure the compartment's forward watertight door eighteen individual butterfly nuts had to be turned. One of these nuts fell out of a spring clip and was hanging down between the door and the coaming. This made it impossible to fasten the door tight. Precious seconds were lost whilst the nut was being pushed back in to its clip. Then the two forward compartments were plunged into darkness.

The flood of water through five tube served only to increase the angle of dive, and thus greater effort was required by those struggling to shut the forward watertight door as they had to pull 'up hill'. Acting as a spur was the knowledge that *Thetis* could surface with one compartment flooded – with two she could not. In the control room Bolus was trying to make the best of a situation growing infinitely worse by the second. If the water rushing into the torpedo space managed to gain a hold in the torpedo stowage compartment, that could prove fatal; should it then overflow into the next compartment, under which was housed the batteries, the problem of chlorine gas would add considerably to their plight.

'Leave the forward watertight door.' Guy Bolus had made up his mind. His order was passed to Lieutenant Woods. He and his party did as ordered and scrambled through the darkened torpedo stowage compartment, by then knee-deep in water. After passing through the compartment's aft watertight door, which had a single control wheel at its centre, the door was slammed shut. A few rapid turns of the central wheel ensured that the batteries would remain dry. The submarine's bow then struck the seabed at a 45° angle.

*Thetis* levelled off and settled at 150 feet. Calling a halt to the blowing of tanks, Bolus ordered half astern on both motors in the hope of freeing *Thetis* from the mud. All that happened was that her stern lifted off the bottom. After this failure an indicator buoy was released and a smoke-candle fired.

An evaluation of the circumstances showed that the odds were very much against them: *Thetis* was out of sight of land and away from normal shipping lanes; the tug *Grebenock* had no underwater communications apparatus and had a short-range radio telephone that was inadequate for the job at hand; with two compartments flooded *Thetis* had less air than usual and had double her normal complement. As twenty-four hours was thought to be the limit of their endurance, their best hope appeared to lie in taking *Thetis* back to the surface. In theory this would not be too difficult. In practice it was very near impossible. Their regaining the surface hinged on whether the flooded compartments could be drained. In order to accomplish this vital operation it was proposed that a volunteer wearing DSEA should enter the flooded torpedo stowage compartment through the forward escape chamber. The escape chamber had three exits: one upwards, one into the mess compartment, and one into the flooded area. The volunteer would have to make his way forward to the torpedo space and close the door of five tube. He would then open two drain-valves before returning to the escape chamber. The pumps would drain the flooded area to enable *Thetis* to surface as normal. The drawback to this happening was that the volunteer would have to withstand a pressure of 70 pounds for about fifteen minutes. There was also the matter of him having to do the task in total darkness, except for the feeble light of a small torch. The likelihood of the volunteer completing the assignment did not look promising.

By 1600 Lieutenant Harold Chapman, the first lieutenant, was in the chamber with cold sea-water rising about him. Chapman could not take the pressure and had to be released from the chamber. Next, Lieutenant Woods and Petty Officer Mitchell made an attempt together. The pressure also proved too much for Mitchell and the chamber had to be drained. When a third attempt failed, the idea was abandoned.

Lieutenant Coltart, reflecting on the manner in which *Thetis* had dived, began to feel a little uneasy. After an hour of trying to dive she had gone down much too quickly to his way of thinking. Yet it seemed almost impossible for a brand-new submarine to meet with serious difficulty. Not wishing to cause any unnecessary alarm Coltart decided to wait a little longer before notifying anyone that he was becoming concerned with developments.

*Thetis* had been submerged for two hours when Coltart sent a message to Fort Blockhouse, the submarine base at Gosport, inquiring as to the expected duration of *Thetis*'s dive. He hoped that this carefully worded message would alert Fort Blockhouse that something was amiss, but not seriously so. For various reasons it was well over an hour before Coltart's message arrived at its intended source. Fortunately Fort Blockhouse was already concerned about *Thetis* as they had not received her surfacing report, due at 1640. The Fort Blockhouse radio, along with several other stations, had been trying to contact *Thetis* since 1645. Coltart's message had been enough to prompt further action. Five minutes after its receipt, a search of the area by ships and aircraft was ordered. Darkness was less than three hours away.

The destroyer *Brazen* (Lieutenant-Commander R.H. Mills), on a southerly course from the Clyde to Plymouth, was fifty-five miles from the search area when she received a signal to proceed with haste and establish contact with *Thetis*. It had just turned 2100 when *Brazen*, first ship to arrive on the scene, sighted *Grebecock*. Because of currents the tug had drifted some distance from where *Thetis* had been seen to dive some six hours previous. The drift made it difficult for Coltart to give Mills anything other than an estimate of *Thetis*'s last known position.

At about the same time as *Brazen* had made contact with *Grebecock* a flight of four Scottish-based Ansons flew over the search area looking for signs of *Thetis*. In the fading light their leader caught sight of the submarine's indicator buoy. Though the buoy's position proved to be only about a mile from the submarine's true position, on rechecking his figures the Anson's navigator made an error which put *Thetis* about seven miles from where she actually was. This new position sent *Brazen* on a hopeless all-night search with searchlight and asdic.

Dawn 2 June found *Brazen* still on her fruitless search. After a further two hours Lieutenant-Commander Mills committed himself to a new search area. Fifty minutes later he sighted the stern of *Thetis* high out of the water. Close by was the red indicator buoy. Mills closed and dropped small explosive charges alongside *Thetis* to announce his arrival.

Lieutenant Commander Bolus had intended to send men to the

surface as soon as he was assured that a vessel would be there to rescue them. *Brazen* had not yet arrived when deteriorating circumstances forced Bolus to proceed with escapes in the hope that a fishing boat or some other craft would rescue them. Captain H.P.K. Oram, commanding officer of *L12* when she collided with *H47* ten years earlier, was in command of the flotilla in which *Thetis* was to serve for a while after completion of her trials and her acceptance by her captain. Captain Oram had joined *Thetis* for the day to familiarize himself with her officers and to see them at work. The decision to include Oram in the first escape bid seemed a wise choice as being an ex-submariner himself he would have the knowledge and be of sufficiently high rank to get quick action – and with only six hours of air remaining, speed of action was vital. From several volunteers Guy Bolus selected Lieutenant Woods to escape with Captain Oram, his reason being that Woods' intimate knowledge of *Thetis* would be of considerable value.

The submarine had been brought to a 50° angle to bring her aft escape chamber within 25 feet of the surface. Captain Oram and Woods were actually in the escape chamber when *Brazen*'s exploding charges indicated her arrival. When the chamber was flooded completely, Woods opened the hatch and made towards the surface with Captain Oram. Soon after, they were aboard *Brazen* sipping hot drinks.

Encouraged by the arrival of ships and by the escape of Oram and Woods, the chamber was prepared for a second attempt. Conditions in *Thetis* were now critical. Even the most minor exertion required considerable effort. At 1000 Leading Stoker Walter Arnold and Mr Frank Shaw arrived on the surface. They revealed that unless the crew received practical assistance very soon, they would be beyond help.

As there was no guarantee that the 18 feet of *Thetis'* stern showing above water would remain thus, a light wire from the salvage vessel *Vigilant* was looped around the stern to forestall any sudden loss. Aided by tugs the *Vigilant* slowly heaved the submarine's stern farther out of the sea. From *Vigilant* a man was ferried to the exposed stern with instructions to remove two cover plates from a manhole. The top cover plate came off with no problem. As he loosened the bolts on the inner cover plate he heard air, under pressure, escaping. Not being a submariner he called for advice to the men who had ferried him to the stern. They in turn asked *Vigilant* for advice. Back came word that he was to continue. By this time he had been an hour on the stern, and it was starting to make ominous movements. Before he could open the covers again, he was ordered back to the boat.

A tug arrived from Birkenhead with oxy-acetylene equipment. At 1500 an effort was made to raise the stern sufficiently to permit a hole large enough for entry into the hull to be cut. This move caused the 3½-inch wire of *Vigilant* to part. *Thetis* slipped gently beneath the surface. The fate of ninety-nine men was now sealed.

*Thetis* was the last submarine to be sunk between the two world wars. Of the fourteen sinkings no less than six had taken place with the loss of all hands.

Submarine construction during the Second World War was confined almost exclusively to the 'S', 'U', and 'T' class. The popular 'S' class were constructed over a period of fourteen years. The first of the class, *Swordfish,* was launched at Chatham on 10 November 1931, and the last, *Sentinel,* on 27 July 1945. Smaller than the 'L's of World War One, the 'S' boats were of excellent design and gave years of outstanding service. Sixty-two of the class were constructed, mostly by Cammell Laird, a figure not rivalled by any class of submarine either before or since.

Built to replace the handy 'H' boats, the 'U' class were intended to be a coastal patrol submarine which would be economical, particularly in manpower, and also able to serve as a training submarine. The 'U's proved to be ideally suited for the Mediterranean, and it was in that area that they achieved undying fame. All but two of the class were built by Vickers at Barrow and at their yard at High Walker in Newcastle.

*Triton* was the first of the 'T's. She was launched at Barrow in October 1937. Armed with ten 21-inch torpedo tubes the fifty-two 'T' class were the most potent of the British submarines. They had almost twice the displacement of the 'U' class.

Throughout the war years the design of the 'S', 'U', and 'T' class was constantly under review in order to incorporate the experience of war service. As fighting ships all three classes performed to a very high standard. These, in the main, were the submarines with which the Royal Navy was pledged to fight the undersea battles of the Second World War.

# PART IV

## THE SECOND WORLD WAR

# 1939

Ships of His Majesty's Navy were already at war stations when on 3 September the Admiralty dispatched the signal: 1100 COMMENCE HOSTILITIES AT ONCE AGAINST GERMANY.

The war had been in progress for little more than a week when the Royal Navy lost not only its first submarine of the war, but its first vessel of any description. The victim was the ageing *Oxley* (Lieutenant-Commander H.G. Bowerman). The assailant was HM submarine *Triton* (Lieutenant-Commander H.P. de C. Steel).

In company with three other submarines, *Oxley* and *Triton* were on reconnaissance patrol off Norway when the incident that caused the loss of *Oxley* took place. The five submarines were positioned twelve miles apart. *Oxley*'s billet was in what had been termed Sector 4, whilst *Triton* had a patrol area in Sector 5. All five submarines appear to have experienced much difficulty in maintaining their positions. This seems to have been mainly due to irregular sets and, because of the possibility of detection by aircraft, the disinclination of the commanding officers to surface for sights.

*September 10.* Though at times communications had been poor, *Oxley* and *Triton* had been in contact by supersonic transmission several times during the day. At 2004 *Triton* surfaced. A fix was obtained which gave her position: Oberstad Light 067°, Kvasseim Light 110°. This position put *Triton* slightly west and south of her patrol billet. The night was dark and overcast, with a slight drizzle. It was Lieutenant-Commander Steel's intention to patrol to the southward on a mean course of 190°. In order to get on that line he steered 170° – zigzagging 30°, 15° each side of the mean course – at 3 to 4 knots. *Triton* proceeded trimmed down and charging on her port engine. Land was about eight miles distant on her port beam. Before leaving the bridge to go below, Steel left orders with his OOW, Lieutenant H.A. Stacey, to keep clear of a merchant ship (on *Triton*'s port quarter was a merchantman, visible only with binoculars, on a southerly heading), and in any case to get end-on. Steel agreed with the OOW that he should alter course to starboard on sighting with the glasses the merchant ship's navigation lights.

Shortly before Stacey anticipated sighting the merchant ship's lights, there suddenly appeared a light directly ahead. Stacey at once altered course to starboard, sending a message to Steel accordingly. It was 2055. No sooner had *Triton* begun her swing to starboard than Stacey with binoculars saw a submarine to starboard. 'Captain to the bridge immediately.' Stacey began to steady *Triton* with the sighting fine on the starboard bow. He estimated the range at one mile but was prepared to find that it was much less as the light looked very close.

Lieutenant Stacey's urgent call sent Steel hurrying from the wardroom. At first he could make out nothing in the blackness. Then with binoculars he distinguished an object very fine on the port bow. He ordered the bow external torpedo tubes (7 and 8 tubes) to stand by. The crew went quickly to diving stations. Steel broke the charge and stopped the starboard engine. *Triton* proceeded on main motors. It was soon after this that Steel recognized the object as a submarine. Lieutenant-Commander Steel: 'I took the ship and kept *Triton* bows-on. From what I could see I appeared to be on a broad track, I should say about 130°, and the object was steering in a north-westerly direction. It occurred to me that it might be *Oxley*. I dismissed the thought almost as soon as it had crossed my mind because earlier in the afternoon* I had been in communication with *Oxley* and I had given her my position accurately, which was two miles south of my billet (No 5) and *Oxley* had acknowledged this. I had also given her my course which was at that time 154°.'

When *Triton* was on the surface it was the practice of Leading Signalman Eric Cavanaugh to remain in the control room with a telegraphist to relieve him to go forward for meals. Cavanaugh had just gone forward when he was called to the bridge. He arrived immediately after Steel. A lookout seized the signal lamp from its stowage and handed it to him. 'Stand by to make the challenge,' said Steel. And then, 'Don't flash that lamp until I tell you. Do you know the challenge?'

'Yes, sir. FO, and the reply DY.'

As soon as the sights were on and Steel knew that the armament was ready, he ordered Cavanaugh to slowly flash the challenge. When after twenty seconds there was no answering DY signal from

---

* At 1600 (Author).

the other submarine, Steel ordered the challenge repeated. Again there was no reply. Steel then ordered: 'Stand by the grenàde.' The port lookout, Able Seaman John Day, took up the rifle-grenade. Steel had been closely studying the submarine. As she was trimmed down very low, he could see nothing of her bow or shape. He thought the conning tower did not look like *Oxley*'s. Try as he might, he could see no outstanding points of identification, such as periscope standards. He ordered a third challenge to be made. Cavanaugh again worked the lamp. There was no response. Steel ordered the rifle-grenade fired. John Day released the pin and fired a grenade. It rose well and burst. Three green lights were seen. With the other submarine having made no response throughout, Steel was certain that the submarine was hostile.

Fifteen seconds after the grenade had burst, Steel ordered the torpedoes fired. Tubes 7 and 8 were emptied at three second intervals. About thirty seconds after firing, what was described as 'indeterminate flashing' was observed coming from the submarine. The flashing lasted two seconds and was unreadable. It was not morse code. Then came an explosion, indicating a hit. A fix by Harry Stacey placed *Triton* 035° Obrestad Light, 105° Egero Light, which placed her 4¼ miles inside her sector. By the time *Triton* had closed the vicinity of the sinking, the submarine had disappeared completely. From the sea came cries for help. Three men were seen swimming.

Lieutenant Guy Watkins was in *Triton*'s control room when the order came from the bridge to send topside three men with lines. Watkins complied as ordered and then quickly went topside himself. To help the survivors swimming in the water, he and Stacey attached a line round themselves and took to the oil-covered sea. Between them they were able to rescue *Oxley*'s captain and an able seaman who had just taken on lookout duties when *Oxley* was hit and sunk. The third survivor, Lieutenant F.K. Manley, RNR, was seen by Telegraphist Williamson, who directed an Aldis lamp on him, to be swimming quite well when he suddenly sank from view. He was not seen again. *Triton* continued to search for survivors, but none was found.

The sinking of *Oxley* in such circumstances was naturally a cause for concern. It was puzzling as to how the two submarines had managed to arrive at the same location. Also a puzzle was the reason for *Oxley*'s failure to reply to *Triton*'s challenge, and the reason why *Oxley* herself had not flashed a challenge or fired a grenade. An investigation revealed that the circumstances leading to the confrontation were a combination of error and misfortune.

As has already been stated, *Oxley* and *Triton* had been assigned billets in adjacent sectors. From 1400 onwards on Sunday 10th, *Oxley* was at periscope depth. Her speed varied between 2 and 3 knots and her course was roughly 158°. From 1500, supersonic transmission with *Triton* having been extensive and definite, and knowing that *Triton* could clearly see land, *Oxley* assumed her position to be 1½ miles inside the eastern limit of her own sector, and about 8 miles to the south-east of her patrol position. She was thought to be just over 7 miles and 240° from *Triton*. *Oxley* had then headed northwards, course about 240°, for about two hours before returning to 158° and maintaining that course until surfacing at 2030. Lieutenant-Commander Bowerman: 'At about 1900 it was reported to me that communication with *Triton* had been established but was lost immediately after the following information had been obtained: the bearing, range, and course of *Triton* being 010°, 4,900 yards, 334° respectively. I questioned closely my HTD [Higher Telegraphist Detector] with regard to the bearing and range as I considered both very improbable. He appeared quite certain of the information which he had stated and told me that the repeated fading of communication precluded any possibility of further communication but could give me no reason for this. I did not consider the second range and bearing could be correct in view of the earlier definite information, and as these ships were on opposite courses I considered the safest course was to proceed in the direction I was going, in view of the fact I should be surfacing about one and a half hours later. I was very surprised that I was as near the edge of my area as my fix gave me, although I had discovered earlier during my patrol the strong sets and the time interval in this case being so short.'

On surfacing at 2030, Bowerman observed the glare of Obrestad and Egero Lights but was uncertain as to whether it was only the glare or the actual lights as there was apparently misty rain over the land. He thought that he was two miles inside the eastern limit of his sector, when in fact he was about four miles inside the western area of *Triton*'s sector. Bowerman had set a course of 330° and was proceeding towards his patrol position at 5 knots when Lieutenant F.K. Manley, RNR, arrived at the bridge to assume duty as OOW. It was then about 2045. Bowerman warned Manley of the possibility of sighting *Triton*. He then left the bridge. After checking *Oxley*'s position and course on the chart, he went to the wardroom. A few minutes later he was called to the bridge. Lieutenant-Commander

Bowerman: 'On emerging from the upper conning tower hatch the Officer On Watch told me that a submarine was just abaft the starboard beam and had fired a grenade. He told me that we had fired a grenade in answer but that it had failed to function. I asked him if he had made the private signal reply. His answer was "Yes", but it must have been hesitant or doubtful because I remember telling him to make it again to be certain. He had just commenced making it; I had by this time got out of the conning tower and was looking to starboard. Although my eyes were not by that time accustomed to the light, I saw a flash immediately beneath me and heard a dull explosion. The ship shook and she seemed to list to port and break in two from the centre.'

By plotting the known courses and bearings of *Triton*, and such courses and bearings which could be recalled by Bowerman, it was possible to approximate the positions of both submarines from 1500 on the 10th, until the sinking at nine o'clock that night. By this method it became clear that *Oxley* was considerably to the eastward of her estimated position, and that *Triton* was well within her own sector. Bowerman had been misled by his HTD giving him a range of 7¼ miles from *Triton*. The fact that he could see the glare of the lights of Obrestad and Egero should have warned him of his easterly drift. From what is known of the incident, it would appear that *Oxley* had sighted *Triton* only after she herself had been under observation for some time, and that Bowerman had been called to the bridge too late to have had much influence on subsequent events. There is some evidence to suggest that *Oxley*'s lookouts were slack. The failure of *Oxley*'s rifle-grenade to burst must be considered sheer bad luck. *Triton*'s part in the incident was considered praiseworthy. Steel had realised the possibility of *Oxley* being in the vicinity. He had challenged three times with the lamp and had fired a grenade. Thus, he was considered to be completely free of blame. The loss of *Oxley* and so many of her fine crew under such circumstances and so early in the war was a very sad blow.

Command of *Triton* passed to Lieutenant-Commander E.F. Pizey, eminently suited to take command of the submarine after the *Oxley* incident. Lieutenant-Commander Harold Bowerman went on to command a destroyer with success. Lieutenant-Commander Pat Steel took the post of instructor at Fort Blockhouse. It was Steel's task to put aspirant commanding officers through their COQC (Commanding Officers Qualifying Course), known to all as the 'Perisher'.

# 1940

'HM Submarine *Undine* sailed from Blyth on 31 December 1939', reports *Undine*'s captain, Lieutenant-Commander A.S. Jackson, in his account of her loss. 'When well clear of the convoy routes I submerged to adjust trim and to carry out routine tests. The asdic* did not function correctly and shortly afterwards the asdic dome was found to be flooded. *Undine* had been docked at Blyth earlier in December and the asdic dome and oscillator had been overhauled and refitted by depot ship's staff. The cause of the flooding, and consequent putting out of action of the asdic installation, was considered to be due to a faulty rubber joint, or to a fault in the fitting of the joint. The hydrophone installation had been in a most unsatisfactory condition for many months, but there had been no opportunity to carry out the extensive repairs and renewals which were required. No blame is attached to Petty Officer Cryer, telegraphist detector rating, for the condition of the asdic and hydrophone installation as he only joined on the day of sailing.

'Nothing worthy of report occurred whilst in areas 'E' and 'B' until 7 January 1940, when the weather conditions were flat calm and visibility varying between a few hundred yards and maximum, owing to fog. At about 0940, when in position very approximately 20 miles WSW of Heligoland, on a course of 275°, an eastbound trawler was sighted on the starboard bow. I turned to starboard to attack, but could not get round quickly enough and the trawler disappeared in the fog.

'About ten minutes later, approximately 0950, two trawlers

---

* An acronym of Allied Submarine Detection Investigation Committee. Asdic was a device for underwater searching. It consisted of ultrasonic pulses and an electronic circuit to measure the time taken for the pulse to reach a target and for its echo, or 'ping', to return. As it also produced echoes from shoals of fish, wrecks and whirlpools its operator had to be highly trained to tell the difference. (Author).

(minesweepers) were sighted to the southward, steering to the east-ward, at a range of approximately 2,000 yards. I turned and carried out an attack, firing one torpedo on a 90° track at the leading trawler, estimating her speed as 12 knots. The torpedo missed, passing 1 to 2 metres astern, according to the German coxswain who was on the bridge at the time and who informed me that their speed had been 14 knots. The sea was so calm that I considered it inadvisable to show the periscope again for some time, so I turned to a westerly course with all auxiliary machinery stopped.

'About four minutes after firing there was a moderately loud exp-losion. I endeavoured to explain this as being the torpedo hitting the bottom, but it was followed by a second explosion which was obvi-ously a depth-charge. A short time later there occurred three more explosions, apparently nearer. The asdic being completely out of action, and the hydrophones almost useless, I was unable to form any picture of what was happening on the surface. The depth of water was about 12-14 fathoms. Bearing in mind the experience of HM Submarine *Spearfish*, I proceeded at a depth of 40 to 50 feet as slowly as possible, and turning to the northward.

'A period of complete quiet followed for about five minutes. Thinking there might be a possibility of attacking again and that the enemy had broken off the hunt, I returned to periscope depth and raised the low-powered periscope – only to look directly at a trawler on the starboard beam and so close that I could only see her port side from the bridge to the after end of the engine room casing. I immediately ordered "Down periscope. Sixty feet", but before the submarine had really started to go down there were three violent explosions: one aft, one forward, and another. I was informed later by Leading Telegraphist Monsarrat that he had heard a noise on the port side of the control room which sounded like a depth-charge scraping the pressure hull, but I have no personal recollection of this.

'The submarine was blown upwards. Some lights and glass were broken. There was a steady leak in the engine room from near the hatch, and a leak in the galley. I was later informed that the fore-end had flooded and had had to be abandoned. Both sets of hydroplanes were reported out of action, the fore-hydroplanes at hard to rise, but the after hydroplanes appeared to be working. I ordered "Take her down. Flood Q",* but the submarine continued to rise until the periscope standards broke surface (giving many of the crew the

* The Q tank is flooded for quick diving.

impression that the drop keel had fallen off); I therefore raised the low-powered periscope and saw a trawler, bows-on the starboard beam and at a range of approximately a half-mile. Considering that it was impossible to get the submarine down again to a safe depth before being rammed, I ordered, "Surface. Burn the CBs*. Prepare the charge". I then went on the bridge, followed by the leading signalman who acting on my orders waved the negative flag, which was the best substitute for a white flag available. (Note: *Undine* was not fitted with a gun.)

'I saw two German trawlers with 3-pounder (?) guns and machine-guns, the nearer one having turned parallel to *Undine* on the starboard beam and the other on the starboard bow. They continued firing for a short time after the negative flag had been down, but I learned later that this was contrary to the orders given on the bridge of one of the trawlers and was due to the guns' crews getting excited at their first real target. No damage was caused by the gunfire, but the starboard fore-hydroplane was seen to be hard to rise and the spindle bent upwards due to depth-charging.

'Abandon ship was ordered. The crew started to come up on the bridge. When about a dozen men were on the bridge the submarine started to go down, but the Kingstons had been opened by this time and main ballast was blown. This fact is mentioned as it convinced me that the drop keel had not fallen off. As the crew mustered on the casing I went below to see if the destruction of confidential books and signalling publications were nearly completed and the scuttling charges prepared. Before leaving the bridge I gave orders that I was to be informed if any boat approached, as I had seen one being lowered by one of the trawlers. The confidential books and signal publications, of which only essential copies were carried, were almost burnt, but the charge had not been set owing to the detonators being stowed in the fore-ends, which was flooded. At this time a signal was broadcast in plain language on the submarine-wave frequency: NEGATIVE ZONE B.

'I returned to the bridge and ordered the crew into the water. Lieutenant Stewart reported that all CB books and signal publications had been burnt and that the first lieutenant was standing by the main vents. I ordered Lieutenant Stewart and Chief Petty Officer Telegraphist Jordan onto the bridge, and the first lieutenant to open the main vents. All main vents appeared to open and the submarine began to sink.

---

* Confidential Books (Author).

'The officers and CPO Telegraphist Jordan swam towards the German trawlers. When about 50 yards from the submarine I looked back to watch her dive, but the upper part of the conning tower was still showing. The water was very cold, just above freezing point. As I could see no reason why she should not sink I continued swimming towards the nearest German trawler, which picked me up. The upper part of the conning tower was still showing when I was taken below, but I have since heard the following accounts. A German officer boarded the submarine and went down to the control room but was driven out by gas, having found out nothing. I was told this by the officer himself, who asked me what gas we had been using. I replied that it was either chlorine from the battery, or smoke from the burning books. Secondly, Leading Telegraphist Monsarrat informed me later that he had seen a column of flame and smoke shoot up from the conning tower hatch, after which the submarine sank.

'My own personal experience was that after about three quarters of an hour to an hour in the crew's quarters of the trawler, I was taken aft by a German sub-lieutenant. There was no sign of *Undine*. When I asked him if she had sunk, he shrugged his shoulders and had pointed to a buoy. I am of the opinion that one of the depth-charges which exploded near the bows jammed number one main vent shut. Number one main ballast was blown with the remainder of the main ballast, but the vent probably did not open when the main vents were opened from the control room. The weight of the water in the fore-end, combined with the water leaking through the galley and engine room, would eventually overcome the buoyance caused by number one main ballast being empty and I consider there was no doubt that *Undine* sank.

'All officers and men were picked up by the two German trawlers, which were joined by a third either during or just after the picking up of the crew. About fifty per cent of the crew were picked up by each of the trawlers, three officers by one and myself by the other. The behaviour of all officers and men throughout was in accordance with the highest traditions of the Royal Navy.'

A German report of *Undine*'s loss adds further interest to Lieutenant-Commander Allan Jackson's account:

*12th Minesweeper Flotilla. Bight of Heligoland.*
Minesweepers *M1207*, *M1204*, and *M1201* were grouped for A/S pursuit. The boats *M1207* and *M1201* were the only ones fitted with revolving

hydrophones. At 0945 *M1204* reported a submarine in sight, while at the same time explosions were heard. Gunfire was also heard. The conning tower of a submarine was distinctly seen. The submarine turned to starboard and appeared to be making an attack on *M1201*. *M1204* manoeuvred towards the submarine which was proceeding at 6 knots, helm to starboard. It was later reported that *M1204* had sunk the submarine and had saved most of her crew. *M1201* placed a towing hawser to the submarine after it had been searched but, as she towed, the submarine began to slip. The minesweeper crew boarded her with gas-masks, lanterns, and tools in an effort to stop the engines and close the conning tower hatch so as to make the towing possible. The submarine, however, sank shortly afterwards, taking with her some of the crew of *M1201*. She lay on an even keel in 37 metres of water. The position was marked by three buoys.

The prisoners were brought to Wilhelmshaven. Three officers (Lt Spencer, Lt Harvey*, Lt Stewart) were saved with thirty petty officers and crew. The commanding officer of the submarine, Lt-Cdr Allan Spencer Jackson, and thirteen men were rescued by *M1201*. The submarine was the English *Undine*. The commanding officer was questioned, but did not impart any particular information.

The submarine had been observing DN-S Group for several days. On 7th January a torpedo had been fired because the leader boat had been seen without escort. The first two depth-charges had not done any damage to the submarine. After firing the torpedo the commanding officer had run on a reciprocal course and thought the first depth-charge explosion was that of his own torpedo. He used the periscope to see the result of the hit and observed that the vessel attacked was quite close on his starboard side. He submerged at once but the fourth and fifth depth-charges had such a devastating effect that the forward torpedo room filled with water and the helm stuck fast in the starboard position. Four depth-charges struck the stern, and a fifth forward. The submarine surfaced without the commanding officer being able to prevent it. He burned the secret papers. His position by day had been west of Heligoland, out of visibility from the island, at about 20 miles distant. At night he had regularly surfaced north of Heligoland.

Launched at Barrow in October 1937, *Undine* had been the first of the 'U' class.

It was only a matter of hours after the loss of *Undine* that *Seahorse* met her end. *Seahorse* was one of the four original 'S' class. She had narrowly escaped being destroyed when on the third day of the war

---

* *Undine*'s first lieutenant (Author).

she was attacked by friendly aircraft. When *Seahorse* (Lieutenant D.S. Massey Dawson) failed to return from patrol it was thought that she had been mined in the Heligoland Bight. But this assumption was later to prove doubtful. An examination of German records shows that on the afternoon of 7 January a submarine, possibly *Seahorse*, was attacked by vessels of the 1st Minesweeper Flotilla in position 54°19'N 7°30'E. A brief report of the incident by the 1st Minesweeper Flotilla states:

> At 1318 a submarine was sighted and the alarm was given. The submarine's location was obtained and nine depth-charges dropped. Success not observed. Submarine noises were heard through the echo ranger and revolving directional hydrophones. A buoy was dropped. After the attack a further clear echo was obtained and three depth-charges dropped. UJ anchored near position, but heavy fog prevented further attack. Six depth-charges each of double throws had been dropped on the located position of the submarine, but no proof of success was obtained.

There seems every likelihood that the submarine had been *Seahorse* and that she had been damaged sufficiently to prevent her regaining the surface. *Seahorse* had sailed Blyth on 26 December for patrol off western Denmark. Transferring to an area off the entrance to the Elbe on 30 December, she was due to return to Blyth on 9 January. German radio announced her loss on 16 January 1940.

Lieutenant Dennis Massey Dawson, *Seahorse*'s captain, had joined HMS *Erebus* as a cadet in September 1928. He had reported at HMS *Dolphin* in May 1932, and thereafter all his service had been in submarines. In January 1939 he took his COQC and on 15 April was appointed captain of *Seahorse*. Lieutenant Massey Dawson had been married six months.

The loss of *Starfish* on 9 January meant that three submarines had been sunk in three days. *Starfish* sailed Blyth on the evening of 5 January. The events of the 9th are, in the main, related here by her captain, Lieutenant T.A. Turner:

'Nothing worthy of note took place during the first days of the patrol. At 0100 on the 9th *Starfish* entered the southernmost part of the patrol area. Course 190°. Speed 6 knots. *Starfish* dived at 0540 and at 0800 course was altered to approximately 140°. This course should have taken us to a position some five miles south-west of Heligoland, which, as far as I could recall, it was hoped would be sighted at dusk on the 9th. Weather was overcast with moderate to good visibility. Wind south-east, force 3 to 4.

'At about 0930 Lieutenant Wardle (Torpedo Officer), who was on watch, reported an enemy destroyer in sight fine on the starboard bow. I proceeded to the control room and confirmed this report. The enemy craft appeared to be a destroyer – although, from the silhouette carried, her crows-nest seemed to be slightly higher than most German destroyers. On sighting, *Starfish* was ½° on the enemy's port bow, her course being 330°. I cannot now remember the sighting range, but I consider it to have been between four and five miles. I decided to attack. The order for diving stations was given, while all tubes were ordered to be brought to the ready. Course and speed were altered as necessary to carry out an advancing attack on the enemy's port bow, the initial alteration of course being a large one to starboard to increase the distance off track.

'Some moments after the beginning of the attack, Electrical Artificer Yates, whose duty it was to transmit orders from the control room to the tubes, asked whether he should pass the orders by order-instrument or by word of mouth. Being intent on the attack I paid little attention to this request, but told him to carry on passing the orders by word of mouth, imagining that the reliability of the order-instrument was in doubt, when in point of fact the latter was in perfect order and his query was both unnecessary and misleading. I then carried on with the attack, altering course as necesarry to port to get on a broad firing track. On Electrical Artificer Yates' reporting that all the tubes were "blown up" I told him that he was to fire numbers one, two, three, and four tubes only (torpedoes were staggered at 8 and 12 feet), and in that order, at three-second intervals on the order "Fire". I also told him to report as soon as the tubes were ready. I was now reaching the final stages of the attack and, as the distance off track was still rather small, I fired up the track-angle and steadied on a course of 190°. Electrical Artificer Yates reported: "One, two, three, and four tubes ready". At 0951, having grouped-up and the sights being on, I gave the order, "Fire".

'It was not possible to make use of the asdic set during the attack as it had developed a minor fault, which was in the process of being repaired, shortly before the attack started. However, the hydrophones were employed and from the enemy's revolutions the speed was estimated at 19 knots and the range of firing at 500 yards. The final ME-YOU was thus: ME 190°, 500 yards – YOU 330°, 19 knots.

'Immediately after I had given the order to fire, I ordered 60 feet and started altering course through 180° to 270°. I was somewhat surprised that the trim of the boat was so little upset on firing. A few moments later Petty Officer Clark, the TGM, reported that no torpedoes had been fired. He had received no orders after the one to "blow up" all tubes, and had never made any report to the control room that they were in the "ready" position. I do not consider that this petty officer was in any way to blame for the misfiring of the torpedoes.

'After this report I decided to make further observations of the enemy's movements in the hope of making an attack later. After listening on the hydrophones I ordered periscope depth. At 0956, having steadied on course 270° and reduced speed to group down one, slow, I raised the periscope on a bearing of approximately 135°, the bearing on which I hoped to sight the enemy; it was not till I trained the periscope right aft that I did this. The enemy was lying stopped and beam-on at a range of something less than one cable. This was the first sighting I had had of the enemy on a broad bearing and I now identified her as a minesweeper, and not a destroyer.

'Considering it possible that the periscope had been sighted, I ordered 60 feet and increased speed to group down two. As the submarine was levelling off at 60 feet, two depth-charges were dropped in the vicinity, the time then being 0945. No damage was sustained, but both hydroplanes were reported inoperative in power. At this moment the angle on the boat was 4° blow-up, with 15° rise helm on the fore-planes. The boat started to come up and, in view of the shallowness, it was considered best to bottom. Both motors were stopped. The boat settled on an even keel, showing 85 feet on the forward gauge and 90 feet on the after one. All motors were stopped and complete silence kept.

'I decided to remain bottomed for a short time only. I knew, particularly after the experience of *Spearfish*, that it was best to remain underway if successful evasion was to be carried out. Accordingly, when at 1050 Electrical Artificer Yates asked permission to restart one of the Sperry motors to prevent gyro wandering, I granted it. No sooner had he done this than four depth-charges were dropped fairly close to the submarine. A large number of lights were broken and a large number of air leaks were started on the high pressure air-line, but these defects were soon remedied. It was impossible even at the time to determine whether or not the dropping of these four depth-charges came as a result of the starting of the Sperry motor or was purely coincidental; but it was difficult, particularly after the enemy's inactivity up to that moment, to feel that it was not a case of cause and effect. I therefore decided to remain stopped until the dark (sunset was 1630) when the chances of successful evasion and further offensive action seemed greater. *Starfish* had been fitted with a special unit (A/S 4, for listening to German A/S impulses) prior to this patrol. This proved most efficient, although an alternative power supply had to be arranged. It was possible to listen throughout to the enemy's procedure, etc., and to form rough estimations of the range at which they were working.

'One depth-charge was dropped at noon, causing no damage. At 1440 the enemy obtained contact. Two heavy attacks were made in close succession and some twenty depth-charges were dropped very close to the submarine, the enemy passing right overhead on both occasions. In the pressure hull the rivets had sheered and the shell-plating had sprung at the first frame abaft 'A' bulkhead, starboard side, causing a very heavy leak. The after bulkhead of 'A' had also been badly buckled and water was pouring through both the starboard side and the bottom. The compartment was shut off immediately. The after bulkhead remained watertight except for the starboard trench door, which owing to distortion leaked slightly. Both the conning tower and the gun tower had been severely damaged and water started to weep through the lower hatches. Numbers of rivets throughout the boat had been rendered partially defective and there were numerous air leaks on the HP airline. Serious damage had been caused to the pressure hull beneath or near the drain oil tanks in the engine room, although it was impossible to assess the extent of this. Such repairs were made as was possible under the conditions.

'At 1600 tea and soup were issued, and in view of the uncertainty of the situation all patrol orders were destroyed by tearing them up and placing them in oil fuel. All confidential books and signal publications were collected and locked in the CB chest.

'At 1645 a small high-speed engine, which had been stopped for some minutes, was heard very distinctly overhead, while between 1700 and 1715 the enemy passed overhead on two occasions. No depth-charges were dropped. It had now become apparent from the enemy's A/S impulses that the minesweeper had been joined by an additional unit.

'By 1800 the situation in the submarine was serious. Both the torpedo trenches and all the bilges were nearly full. The engine room crankcases and starboard main motor bearing were flooded, while water was present in the lubricating oil drain-tanks. Water was pouring through the starboard engine clutch and was lapping the starboard main motor casing. Mr Dodsworth, the engineer-officer, considered that it would still be possible to carry out repairs, given sufficient time, on the main engines to enable at least one of them to be used. It was thought likely that if the submarine remained dived much longer the main motors would be out of action.

'By this time I had formed the opinion that there was no likelihood of the enemy leaving the vicinity in the near future. After weighing up the situation, and having received full reports from the first lieutenant and engineer-officer on the state of their departments, I decided that the best hope, although a slight one, of successful evasion lay in surfacing and attempting to slip away in the darkness. It was estimated that the enemy craft were lying at a distance of 7 to 8 cables. Under the circumstances, offensive action was impossible.

'At 1815 lifebelts were issued and the after escape hatch rigged as a precautionary measure. At 1820 the order to surface was given. The submarine came up stern-first at a very heavy angle, and appeared to hang there as I passed the word aft to open the after escape hatch. A few moments later, however, the bows broke out and the boat assumed a normal angle. I proceeded on deck through the engine room hatch. On each side of the boat at a distance of some 50 yards was a lit buoy. I went up to the bridge and at this moment the enemy, who were lying on each bow at a range of about 1,200 yards, illuminated us with searchlights. A few minutes later they opened fire with a machine gun, firing a short burst wide of the bridge.

'I ordered Mr Dodsworth to go below and flood main ballast one side only, and Lieutenant Wardle to throw the CB chest over the side. The latter was soon done and Mr Dodsworth, working under great difficulties, managed to open number four starboard main vent, and also the 4-inch flood valve on the main line. The boat listed very heavily and water started lapping through the engine room hatch. As the boat listed I had given the order to abandon ship, considering it was wise for the crew to be clear. As the submarine did not sink immediately, some of the men climbed back on board, while others were picked up by the minesweeper.'

There is no doubt that with her forward compartments flooded, *Starfish*'s crew were fortunate to escape with their lives. That she was in only 90 feet of water, and that Lieutenant Wardle had released the drop keel, were instrumental in there being any survivors. Wardle recalls: 'After dropping the drop keel the stern gradually came up with the bow still on the bottom. When we were at a bow-down angle of about 45° we reckoned that we had a sporting chance of getting out of the stern hatch, and amazingly this was so.'

Of the events of 9 January Chief Engine Room Artificer G.H. Jagger recalls: 'The captain sent me aft to try and organize an escape. I climbed up the main engine valve-rockers and managed to get into the after ends. After considerable blowing of the main ballast tanks, and attempting to use the propellers, the vessel gave a shudder and eventually rose stern-first to the surface. We started to remove the clips from the hatch. As the last clip came off, the hatch cover shot open owing to the pressure within, and I was propelled through the hatch and into the sea. I swam towards the nearest vessel, which had lowered a boat similar to a Royal Navy whaler, and with many others was picked up. One of the vessels nosed towards *Starfish* and put her bows alongside. Some of the crew took advantage of this and climbed on board, and so did not even get their feet wet.'

Lieutenant Wardle had managed to clear the after escape hatch only to find that he had forgotten about the confidential books. 'I had to scramble down to the control room again to lug up the safe with all the books in it and chuck it over the side. To this day I cannot think how I managed to do it.' Ten months later Geoffrey Wardle was a prisoner in Colditz.

Lieutenant Turner continues his narrative: 'The Germans appeared to have little idea as to how to deal with the submarine, which was gradually settling. They informed me later that no one had been below and suggested that we had taken precautions to ensure the sinking of the submarine. After a few minutes on the upper deck of the minesweeper we were put below and at 1910, the time at which I was told *Starfish* had sunk, both minesweepers got underway. Our treatment by the Germans was correct and humane. They informed me that they knew the exact position of the submarine owing to the appearance of a large air-bubble after one of their heavy attacks. Also, I was informed that they intended to stay in the vicinity for two days if the need arose.'

Chief ERA George Jagger concludes: 'Once aboard the minesweeper we were taken to the engine room to dry out and to thaw out. Some time round dawn the following morning, we were landed at Wilhelmshaven. It was bitterly cold with deep snow. We were marched to a large barrack-type building, which turned out to be a German naval school. We were separated into officers, non-commissioned officers, and ratings. We were billeted in classrooms (which we later realised had been well bugged and that all our conversation had been recorded) equipped with double tier bunks and left under strong guard and with a minimum of food for ten to fourteen days.'

With others of the crew, Chief ERA Jagger was sent to Spandenburg Prisoner of War Camp – Oflag IXA. George Jagger had entered the Navy direct from school, in December 1927, and had 'served in *Starfish* for two years at the time of her sinking.

*

On 8 April 1940 the township of Lillesand, on the south-east tip of Norway, was startled by an explosion from the direction of the Skagerrak. Nothing further was heard until the engines of three fishing boats were heard chugging towards harbour through the fog. When the boats had secured alongside, the anxious townspeople were surprised to see German soldiers, some injured and others obviously dead, sprawled about the boats' decks. The soldiers had been a part of an invading army when their troop-ship *Rio de Janeiro* had been torpedoed by the Polish submarine *Orzel*. It was a signal from *Orzel* which alerted the British that an invasion of Norway was actually in progress.

On the day following *Orzel*'s opening shot in the battle for Norway, the *Thistle* (Lieutenant-Commander W.F. Haselfoot) became the first of four submarines to be sunk in April. Haselfoot's orders were to enter Stavanger at his discretion and attack German shipping reported as having arrived in the harbour. Haselfoot signalled his intention of complying with orders on 10 April. At the same time he reported having two torpedoes left after having unsuccessfully attacked a U-boat off Skudesnes. At the news of this attack Haselfoot's orders to enter Stavanger Harbour were cancelled and replaced with instructions to patrol off Skudesnes, with the obvious intention of surprising the U- boat again. After this exchange of signals nothing further was heard from *Thistle*. The cause of her loss was later revealed as resulting from an attack by the *U4*, which Wilfred Haselfoot had reported as having unsuccessfully attacked on the 9th. Sighting a surfaced *Thistle* off Utsira, *U4* had torpedoed her at 0113 on the morning of the 10th. *Thistle* had not given up survivors. The *U4* was one of the few U- boats to fight the war from start to finish. She surrendered in May 1945.

Less than nine hours after the sinking of *Thistle*, the *Tarpon* (Lieutenant-Commander H.J. Caldwell) was lost with all hands. At 2330 on 5 April *Tarpon* sailed Portsmouth for Rosyth in company with HM Submarine *Severn*. The two submarines were to take passage north with convoy FN39. Both *Tarpon* and *Severn* were advised to be prepared to leave FN39 and proceed on patrol; the reason for the warning was that VAS (Vice-Admiral Submarines) was convinced that a German invasion of Norway was imminent. Consequently on 7 April VAS redisposed his submarines at sea and ordered others to sail. At 2007 *Tarpon* and *Severn* were ordered to leave FN39 and proceed north-east.

*Monday 8th.* *Orzel* signalled that the invasion of Norway was in progress. At 1810 *Tarpon* reported her course and position.

*Tuesday 9th.* At 1756 *Tarpon* was ordered to 56°30'N 06°20'E.

*Wednesday 10th.* At 1656 *Tarpon* was ordered to 57°N 06°E. Unknown to VAS *Tarpon* had been sunk earlier that day.

At 0724 on the day of *Tarpon*'s loss, and in position 56°43'N 06°33.5'E, the German Q-ship *Schiff 40* sighted a torpedo passing astern. Three minutes later the track of a second torpedo was seen to run parallel to that of the first. At 0728 an explosion, to be followed by a second at 0730, was heard. These explosions were assumed by the Germans to be the torpedoes striking the seabed. A periscope was then sighted. Sonar and HE* contact was quickly established and at 0730 depth-charges were dropped over the contact. The appearance of two RAF Hudsons forced *Schiff 40* to suspend the attack and to conceal her depth-charges. Whilst a Hudson circled above the ship, contact with the submarine was maintained. The Hudsons remained in the vicinity until observing a Dornier flying-boat, to which they immediately gave chase.

At 0905 Lieutenant Kircheiss, *Schiff 40*'s captain, dropped a pattern of sixteen depth-charges. For *Tarpon*, and it is almost certain that the submarine was *Tarpon*, this attack was devastating: large quantities of oil and air-bubbles were observed in three places. As a distinct echo was still in evidence, a further eight depth-charges were dropped. By this time *Tarpon* may have already been beyond help. When a firm echo was registered over the same position, a further three depth-charges were dropped. Oil and air-bubbles continued to rise. Having pin-pointed *Tarpon* at 120 feet, Lieutenant Kircheiss began to drop small patterns of depth-charges on the wreck. At 1252 depth-charges tore the submarine open. To the surface came wreckage and items from within the submarine: mittens, gloves, a cigarette packet with the words 'HM Ships only', fragments of clothing, a copy of Royal Navy regulations for the maintenance and firing of torpedo tubes, and a crushed Nestle's cocoa tin. Kircheiss con-

---

* Hydrophone Effect.

tinued to drop depth-charges from time to time until darkness. *Schiff 40* remained in the area until about five o'clock the following morning.

*Saturday 20th.* At 1124 *Tarpon* was signalled to leave patrol at sunset and proceed to Rosyth. She was expected to arrive in harbour on the morning of the 23rd.

Lieutenant-Commander Herbert Caldwell, *Tarpon*'s captain, had served in the Navy for twenty years. Caldwell's exceptional qualities had gained him a commission from the lower deck. Herbert Caldwell left a widow.

Tragedy again struck, when an attack by German vessels on 18 April possibly accounted for the loss of Lieutenant-Commander G.H.S. Haward's *Sterlet*. A Chatham-built submarine, *Sterlet* was serving with the 2nd Flotilla at Harwich at the outbreak of war, but at the time of her loss, during her seventh patrol, she was a unit of the 3rd Flotilla, also based at Harwich.

*April 8. Sterlet* sailed harbour for a patrol in the Skagerrak. At 1656 on 10 April she was instructed to proceed to a billet in position 58°28'N 11°06'E. She was routed along 57°50'N between 8°30'E and 10°30'E. In a 2130 signal of 12 April *Sterlet* reported having unsuccessfully attacked a convoy of three merchantmen and a destroyer steaming a westward course at 12 knots in position 57°47'N 9°30'E. No further signals were received from her.

*Sterlet* is believed to have arrived in her billet off Sote Fiord at about noon on 13 April. The following day Vice Admiral Submarines created eight 10-mile-wide patrol zones (C6 to C13) and ordered submarines in the Skagerrak to proceed to patrol their allotted zones. *Sterlet*'s zone, C10, extended from 58°20'N to 58°30'N and, as with the other zones, from 9°30'E to the limit of Swedish territorial waters.

At 1751 on 22 April, *Sterlet* was ordered to leave zone C10 after sunset that day. She was routed along 57°50'N between 9°E and 7°30'E with instructions to report the situation when west of 10°E. Nothing was heard from her and she failed to arrive back at Harwich.

Although no signals had been received from *Sterlet* after 12 April, it is accepted that she was still in operation and that at about 2307 on 15 April she torpedoed the 2,500 tons German gunnery ship *Brummer* two miles inside C12, *Triad*'s zone. Escorted by the torpedo boats *Jaguar* and *Falke* and the escort vessel *F5*, *Brummer* was attacked in position 58°42'N 10°00'E. On a torpedo track being sighted off the port quarter, *Brummer* successfully took avoiding action; as she turned to starboard, a further two torpedoes were seen to pass ahead.

Zones C6 to C9 were to the south of *Sterlet*, and zones C11 to C13 to her north. The attack on *Brummer* had taken place twelve miles outside *Sterlet*'s zone and, as already stated, two miles inside *Triad*'s zone. It is known that several submarines did at times briefly leave their zones either through encountering an unexpected northern or southerly set, seeking out or pursuing targets, or because of an error of navigation; but even though submarines do appear to have left their zones and the attack on *Brummer* had occurred twelve miles outside *Sterlet*'s zone, there still can be little doubt that *Sterlet* had attacked the *Brummer*. The fact that no submarine reported having attacked *Brummer*, and because *Sterlet* was the only submarine which failed to return from patrol, makes it almost certain that *Sterlet* had been the aggressor, and therefore was still in operation by that date. It seems likely that *Sterlet*, having made no sightings in her zone, had ventured to cover C11 zone, knowing it to be vacant, and had strayed a further two miles into C12 zone.

*Sterlet*'s torpedo hit had seriously damaged *Brummer*, the torpedo having also caused an ammunition explosion. While the *Jaguar* stood by the stricken ship, *Falke* and *F5* made for the vicinity of the firing. Both units dropped depth-charges. It is possible that sonar contact was established, though not on *Sterlet*: barely a mile away was the *Triad*. At 2312 *Triad* observed two airborne flares, probably rockets fired by *Brummer* to give warning of *Sterlet*'s attack. Believing that she had been sighted, *Triad* called diving stations, which might explain why the two explosions were not heard by *Triad*. Depth-charges were dropped fairly close to *Triad* but no damage resulted.

Attempts to take the *Brummer* in tow were unsuccessful. Out of control, she drifted towards the Norwegian coast. The more serious of her wounded were transferred to *F5*, which shortly after midnight departed for Frederikshavn. Just before 0700, 16 April, the *Brummer* sank in position 052° Tvesten Light 0.8 mile.

Apart from the A/S attacks by *Brummer*'s escorts during the early hours of 16 April, there was one other A/S attack that day: at 1510 the minesweeper *M8*, of the 1st MF Flotilla, registered a good sonar contact off Horten in Oslo Fiord. *M8* carried out five depth-charge attacks on a moving contact. After the first attack a slight trace of oil was noted; also, following each attack there was observed a trail of bubbles in the vicinity of the explosions. When *M8* was joined by *M7*, both units conducted attacks on what had by then become a stationary target. No evidence of damage came to the surface. With the onset of darkness *M8* and *M7* cleared the area. Over the course of the next two days *M8* returned to the location. The contact was easily found and had not moved.

Subsequent investigation revealed that none of the submarines which returned from patrol in the Skagerrak was in Oslo Fiord on 16 April. It is very unlikely that *Sterlet*, after sinking *Brummer*, would have made for Oslo Fiord rather than set a course for her billet in C12. It should be noted that a few days previous to this incident the *Triad* had been patrolling off the entrance to Oslo Fiord, which was in her zone. *Triad*'s captain believed that the strong A/S patrols in the fiord – plus the short moonlit nights and the capacity of his battery – made it impracticable to venture into the fiord as far as Horten. This, and the fact that the seabed in Oslo Fiord was rocky and would thus be prone to false echoes from A/S vessels sonar, make it fairly certain that the depth-charge attacks had not been against a submarine; but of course the over-riding factor against the attack having been made on a submarine was that the heavy depth-charging of a stationary contact had produced no oil or surface wreckage of, any kind when one could have reasonably expected at least some small objects (paper, rags, pencils, etc.,) to have risen to the surface.

For quite some time after the war there was a belief that *Sterlet* had been sunk by depth-charge attacks of 18 April. A German report of April 1940 provides the reason for this line of thought:

12TH UJ FLOTILLA. 50°03'N 11°07'E.
*UJ123, UJ126, UJ128* on patrol. At 1300 oil traces were seen and location obtained. *UJ128* dropped eight depth-charges. The submarine was located on a south-easterly course. Depth of water 90-100 metres. Submarine zigzagged and frequently stopped her motors, so that the support of the echo ranger by the revolving directional hydrophones was insufficient. *UJ126* began her attack with a salvo of ten depth-charges, six depth-charges astern with a setting of 60 metres. Neither oil nor air-bubbles seen. *UJ125* dropped six depth-charges without result.

After renewed location of submarine on an easterly course, *UJ126* dropped eight depth-charges without result. Further location was lost in Karingoe Fiord, where the submarine probably sought shelter. Hydrophone sweep in fiord until the early hours of the morning. Location obtained at 0400 and eight depth-charges. After the attack, two barrels of benzine were found floating in the water, and also a deck-plank and a bucket marked F3. The alarm was given again. A clear location was obtained south-west of Haroe. Two deterrent depth-charges were dropped. The submarine attempted to escape on a zigzag course in a south-easterly direction, but *UJ126* attacked with six depth-charges. Another attack was made by *UJ128*, which had obtained location on revolving hydrophones and six depth-charges were dropped. No results observed. Noises and location led to the Hjertoe Fiord but the rocky ground prevented the location being held, and the noises were lost.

To have been in the vicinity of this action, *Sterlet* would have had to have crossed C9 zone and much of C8, the zone in which the attack took place. At that point she would have been seventeen miles south of her position. It does not seem likely that *Sterlet* would have deliberately moved so far southwards, and as the position was in close proximity to the Swedish coast the likelihood of her unintentionally straying there through an error of navigation, the possible cause of her entering *Triad*'s zone, seems unlikely. And yet the 12th UJ Flotilla's report states clearly that the 'Submarine zigzagged and frequently stopped her motors'. This does appear to indicate that a submarine was in the area; however, the items observed after the depth-charging in the early hours of the 19th are more likely to have come from an old wreck rather than from a submarine. Furthermore, events elsewhere do not favour the attacks by the UJ craft on the afternoon of the 18th as being the cause of *Sterlet*'s loss, as the following accounts will show.

At 1516 on 17 April a vessel of the German Anti-Submarine Warfare School sighted in position 58°57'N 10°12'E a surfaced submarine. The A/S craft made for the point of sighting and dropped one depth-charge where the presumed submarine had dived. As no visible signs of success were observed, and as a submarine would not normally surface in daylight, the sighting thought of as a submarine must be considered suspect. But nevertheless, after darkness the following day, and in the same area, a submarine was definitely sighted. At 2142 the escorts *T190* and *M75* of a southbound convoy sighted in the bright moonlight the tracks of two torpedoes. The torpedoes came from the direction of the starboard beam and passed ahead of the convoy's leading ship. *M75* then sighted a submarine, estimated at a distance of just under sixty yards. The escort at once attacked with five depth-charges. The submarine, which more than likely would have been in the process of gaining depth, then briefly broke surface. *T190* also attacked but the three depth-charges released by her failed to explode owing to an error in drill. As a detailed report of the encounter cannot now be found, what eventu ally happened to the submarine is not known with any certainty.

At this stage it might be helpful to review one or two points. *Sterlet* had sailed Harwich on 8 April. On 12 April she signalled the result of her unsuccessful attack on a convoy. On 15 April she sank the *Brummer* – yet of this attack she made no signal. This might suggest that she was sunk in the counter-attacks by *Brummer*'s escorts; but the Germans made no claim to have sunk or damaged a submarine. *Sterlet*'s failure to transmit a report of *Brummer*'s sinking might indicate nothing more than her transmitter had been damaged in the counter-attack, though such happenings were infrequent. The submarine seen by *M75* on 19 April was almost certainly *Sterlet*, though she was patrolling quite some way from her zone. Unless her receiver had been rendered unserviceable, she would have known that the whole area north of her zone was free of submarines, the *Triad* having departed during the early hours of 17 April to patrol off Arendal. If after having sunk *Brummer* the *Sterlet* experienced a dearth of targets, and all indications point towards this being so, her captain could have approached Oslo Fiord in hopes of shipping in that area being more prolific than farther south. The attack by *M75* could have destroyed the submarine. On the other hand the submarine appears to have been blown momentarily to the surface, which suggests that the depth-charges had been regulated to explode too deep. If damage to the submarine had been such that she had looked to be in danger of sinking, Lieutenant-Commander Haward would have surfaced, and there is no evidence that the submarine had reappeared on the surface. So there is a possibility that she had survived *M75*'s attack.

If the submarine attacked by *M75* had been *Sterlet* and if *Sterlet* had survived the encounter, then she perhaps had been sunk elsewhere and by other means. An attack by aircraft can be excluded as it has been possible to identify submarines attacked by this method during the period in question. Mining must invariably be taken into consideration. German mining of the Skagerrak began on 8 April. Prior to *Sterlet*'s order to return to harbour, four minefields were laid between Kristiansand and Hantsholm. One of the minefields extended from 58°02'N 7°57.7'E to 57°49.2'N 7°51.2'E. This field, consisting of more than 320 contact mines moored at a depth of between 6½ and 16½ feet, lay athwart *Sterlet*'s return route. *Sterlet* would have taken surface passage through the mined area on the night of 22-23 April. For *Sterlet* to have encountered this minefield it must be assumed that she had survived until 22 April, as in the 1751 signal of 22 April she had been instructed to report when west of 10°E, and this she had not done. The position 10°E was some distance before *Sterlet* would have arrived in the mined area, so it must be assumed that she had either been sunk before the 22nd, or that her transmitter was inoperative and that she had in fact proceeded as ordered, striking a mine in the process.

There is insufficient evidence to say beyond doubt as to how *Sterlet* was sunk. The attack by *M75* appears to offer the most reliable explanation as a submarine was identified and speedily attacked with apparently some success.

Lieutenant-Commander Gerard Haward had entered the Navy as a cadet in 1927. He had joined the Submarine Service after his promotion to lieutenant in April 1932. On successfully completing his COQC he was appointed captain of *H43* in April 1939. His appointment to *H43* was for four months: on 1 August Haward took command of *Sterlet*.

Day after day, by sea and by air, the German build up of men and material in Norway continued unabated. To help Norway in her struggle against the Nazi war machine, Allied troops had by 15 April made landings in northern Norway. With British and Norwegians fighting side by side, it was ironic that it should have been a Norwegian freighter that sank HM Submarine *Unity* in a collision which claimed the lives of four submariners.

At 1730 on the evening of Monday 29 April the *Unity* (Lieutenant F.J. Brooks) put to sea from Blyth. Visibility on leaving harbour was 300 yards. By the time *Unity* entered the main swept channel, which she did at 1830, visibility had reduced to a hundred yards owing to the heavy mist closing in further. At 1900 Lieutenant G.E. Hunt made an appearance on the bridge to relieve the officer on watch, Lieutenant J.F. Trickey; however, as the OOW was hoping to sight a war channel buoy, Hunt did not take over the watch at once but assisted as a lookout in the search for the buoy.

Earlier that day the Norwegian freighter *Atle Jarl* had sailed the Scottish port of Methil, which lies snugly on the north shore of the Firth of Forth, with a cargo of coal and coke. In convoy the *Atle Jarl* headed south for the Tyne and for her chance encounter with *Unity*.

At the time Lieutenant Hunt arrived on *Unity*'s bridge to take over the watch, the submarine and *Atle Jarl* (sixth ship of the convoy) were in close proximity to each other, though neither vessel was aware of this as darkness and the fog had successfully shielded all movement. At 1907 a prolonged blast of a ship's siren was heard on *Unity*'s bridge. Ordering a long blast in reply, Lieutenant Brooks put the wheel hard to starboard. The submarine was still swinging to starboard when the blast of another siren was heard fine on the starboard bow. On hearing this second siren, Brooks ordered the wheel midships and the engines to full speed astern. Leading Telegraphist Peter Birnie immediately operated the bridge telegraph to FULL SPEED ASTERN, hearing at the same time Lieutenant Brooks order the watertight doors to be shut. At that moment the *Atle Jarl*, steering a course that would take her into collision with *Unity*, was sighted less than 50 yards away as she emerged from the fog. *Unity* sounded three blasts on her siren, to which the Norwegian replied likewise. It was apparent to Brooks that a collision was likely. Realizing the danger Brooks gave the order: 'Collision stations. Prepare to abandon ship.' At 1910 the *Atle Jarl* struck the submarine at a speed of 4 knots, and at an angle of 90°, in the vicinity of the port forward hydroplane. From reports it appears that the force of the collision was not heavy. *Unity*, going astern at 2 knots, listed very little on impact. When the two vessels drew apart it was evident to Brooks that *Unity* was not about to remain on the surface for long. The engines had been left working at full astern for as long as possible to assist *Unity* in staying afloat, but as the *Atle Jarl* vanished into the fog Brooks ordered them stopped.

Leading Seaman William Hill, on duty in *Unity*'s engine room, states: 'We were going astern for some time when I observed that Able Seaman Hare was attempting to shut the engine room bulkhead door. By motions to him and the engine room staff this was prevented till both engines were stopped. It was then carried out. We were still going astern when the first lieutenant opened the door and gave the order to abandon ship. Both of us, myself and Able Seaman Miller, made to move forward to obey that order. Miller had preceded me slightly when I received the order: "Stop starboard." I went back and stopped starboard. Then I picked up two lifebelts and, throwing one lifebelt to Miller, left the boat.'

Chief ERA Alfred Potter was in his mess when he felt the motors go full astern. He went to the control room: 'Hearing the order "Shut watertight doors" I went to the engine room door to prevent it being shut before the engines were stopped,' says Potter. 'Able Seaman Hare was trying to shut it. When the engines were stopped I shut the engine room door, thinking it was a precautionary measure. I returned to the control room and found the first lieutenant by the ladder and the crew beginning to go up to the bridge. The first lieutenant said: "No hurry. There is only 3 feet showing on the diving gauges." I did not hear "abandon ship" given. I then realized something was happening and went to my bunk to get my lifebelt. While I was putting this on, DSEA were being got out by the crew. When I left the control there were about six people left. There seemed to be no hurry. I did not feel any bump. When I got onto the bridge the bow of the submarine was awash.'

Most of the crew had made their way topside and were crowded on the bridge. Because *Unity* had taken a bow-down angle, some of the crew were ordered off the bridge and towards the stern. Now to the experience of ERA Rob Roy McCurrach: 'There was no panic, indeed, such a thing would be unforgivable. Personally I thought the whole thing another exercise. As far as I can recall, I was the last but one up the ladder. Miller followed me. As I stepped out onto the packed conning tower I heard the captain say: "I must have the main motors stopped". As I went to go back down and do this, I almost trod on Miller's head. "I'll go, Bob. I'm better placed", said Miller. He returned below. Then the captain wanted the bridge cleared a bit. I climbed down on to the casing and stood in my stocking-feet on the hull. I felt the vibration stop. As I slid into the water I wondered if I'd catch cold. Momentarily I thought I could do with a piece of my mother's blackberry-and-apple pie. I then swam away from the boat. Turning, I waited to see if there would be some suction as she went down. There was none. When the motors stopped, she went down. Her stern rose high, water streaming from props, hydroplanes, rudder. I stripped of a great deal of my clothing. I had no lifebelt. The crew were well spread out. Leading Seaman Hill was nearest to me, so I swam to him. Just as we reached the top of a swell, we spotted a lifeboat. We made towards it, but they failed to see us and altered course. Most demoralizing that. When Hill and I finally managed to get to a lifeboat, the men aboard were like zombies. Helped by Hill, I managed to get in. I then helped Bill. Between us we then pulled the captain in. I took an oar as we rowed about looking for survivors. I guess we were all in shock. When we went alongside the *Atle Jarl* I grabbed the rope ladder at the top of a swell and made my way inboard and down to the boiler room, where I stripped and hung up my sodden clothes.'

*Unity* had taken an angle of 25°. When she sank four to five minutes after the collision, she took two of the crew with her, Lieutenant John Low, the first lieutenant, and Able Seaman Henry Miller.

The submariners, who minutes earlier had been going quietly about their duties, had found themselves floundering in the cold

North Sea with a convoy scattered around in the mist. The *Atle Jarl* had not strayed far from the scene. In half an hour all but two of the survivors had been rescued and transferred to *Atle Jarl*. At the request of Lieutenant Brooks, the freighter's master agreed to remain in the vicinity for an hour and thirty minutes in the hope of rescuing the two missing crew, Able Seaman Hare and Stoker Shelton. Neither was recovered.

The conduct of his ship's company in such trying circumstances gave Brooks cause for much satisfaction. In his report of the incident he singled out several of the company for special mention: Lieutenant J.F. Trickey for his assistance and encouragement of ratings in difficulties in the sea, particularly as Trickey was unable to swim more than a few yards; Lieutenant G.E. Hunt for his cheerfulness and efficiency during rescue, and later aboard *Atle Jarl*; Stoker Alfred Burvill for risking his life in attempting to rescue a drowning shipmate. Brooks was also generously disposed to mention the Norwegians for their promptness in dispatching two rescue boats, and for their kindness over the hours that followed.

The exemplary conduct of Lieutenant John Low and Able Seaman Henry Miller did not go unrecognized. The calm demeanour of Lieutenant Low had done much to assist in a speedy and orderly escape. His concern for the safety of the crew and the manner in which he had fulfilled his duty was in keeping with the high standard expected of submarine officers. Both Low and Miller could not have been unaware of the fearful risk of remaining below decks to assist and to give the crew every opportunity of clearing the submarine. For their courage both Lieutenant Low and Able Seaman Miller were awarded the Empire Gallantry Medal, later exchanged for the George Cross.

After survivors' leave, *Unity*'s crew was divided among *Upright* and *Utmost*, both nearing completion at Vickers.

It transpired that Lieutenant Brooks had been unaware that the Methil-Tyne convoy was at sea. This should not have been the case. Before sailing Blyth, Lieutenant Brooks should have received signal 1428/29/4 (2.28 p.m./29th/April), which among other things would have informed him that the Methil-Tyne convoy was due off Blyth at about 1930. Brooks was certain that he had not been shown or told of this signal. Lieutenant Trickey, Lieutenant Hunt, and Leading Signalman Moon, *Unity*'s signalman, all denied knowledge of signal 1428/29/4. On the afternoon of 23 May a court of inquiry convened at Blyth to investigate the collision. *Unity*'s captain was summoned to give evidence.

QUESTION: 'Were you sending the usual signals for the prevention of collision at sea whilst you were underway?'

LT BROOKS: 'No.'

QUESTION: 'I take it, then, that the first sound signal you made was after hearing one long blast from the direction right ahead?'

LT BROOKS: 'Yes.'

QUESTION: 'Did you anticipate that the war channel would be clear of shipping?'

LT BROOKS: 'Yes, except for small craft.'

QUESTION: 'Have you got any listening devices by which you can hear under water?'

LT BROOKS: 'Yes.'

QUESTION: 'Were these manned?'

LT BROOKS: 'No, sir.'

QUESTION: 'Would you tell the board, briefly, what these devices are?'

LT BROOKS: 'An A/S receiving set.'

QUESTION: 'Was it in working order?'

LT BROOKS: 'Yes.'

QUESTION: 'Is it a set of any use, when you are running on the surface, for detecting the presence of any ship at reasonable distance?'

LT BROOKS: 'No, not with both engines running as the sound made by the engines muffles the reception of outside noise.'

QUESTION: 'In view of the very low visibility, what were your objections to running on the motors only, so that you could have made use of your A/S set?'

LT BROOKS: 'In view of the fact that the run up the swept channel was of five hours' duration I would not have been justified in exhausting my batteries at this time.'

QUESTION: 'What was the state of the watertight doors on leaving Blyth?'

LT BROOKS: 'Fore-end doors shut. Remainder open.'

QUESTION: 'Were you in patrol routine?'

LT BROOKS: 'Yes.'

QUESTION: 'According to Captain S6's report, you had no knowledge of Commander-In-Chief's, Rosyth, signal timed 1428/29/4 indicating, among other things, that convoy Methil-Tyne was due off Blyth at about 1930?'

LT BROOKS: 'No. I had no knowledge of this.'

QUESTION: 'Is there any statement you would like to make regarding your ignorance of the contents of this signal?'

LT BROOKS: 'Had I known a southbound convoy was due I should have taken steps to keep out of its way.'

QUESTION: 'What steps would you have taken to avoid the convoy?'

LT BROOKS: 'I could have delayed my time of sailing, or proceeded outside the swept channel where practicable.'

QUESTION: 'Can you explain why this signal 1428/29/4 was not shown to you?'

LT BROOKS: 'My signalman, who should have collected the signal, and my navigating officer, who checked all signals shortly before sailing, both say they had not seen this signal.'

QUESTION: 'With regard to the signal concerning the movements of the Methil-Tyne convoy: it seems clear that there must inevitably be a certain space of time between the typing of your sailing orders and the moment of sailing – and during this time movement signals might be received. Therefore, what steps did you take to find out the latest information?'

LT BROOKS: 'The movement of ships likely to affect *Unity* on passage and patrol were contained in an appendix to the patrol orders. This appendix was completed shortly before sailing. I took this appendix into the staff office and went through it with the Staff Officer Operations. After this, as a normal routine, I should have gone through any signals affecting me with the staff officer, and discussed it with him. As it was now practically time to sail, our discussion consisted of little more than going through the appendix and the question of convoy Methil-Tyne did not come up.'

QUESTION: 'As the signal 1428/29/4 arrived before you sailed at 1730, can you give any reason for it not being shown to you?'

LT BROOKS: 'No. It should have been collected by my signalman from the distributing office and shown to me. Had it arrived at the last moment, it should have been brought to the submarine by messenger just before sailing.'

In an attempt to discover why signal 1428/29/4 had not been brought to the attention of Lieutenant Brooks, Chief Yeoman of Signals Christopher Reading, in charge of the SDO (Signal Distribution Office) of HMS *Elfin*, was called and asked if he could recall distributing to *Unity* signal 1428/29/4 from the C-in-C, Rosyth. The chief yeoman replied that the signalman on watch had distributed that signal and that he himself had no explanation as to why *Unity* had seemingly not received it. In answer to a question as to whether the signal had been received in the SDO in sufficient time to have been collected by Leading Signalman Moon, the chief yeoman stated that the signal had been received in ample time and there was no question of having to send it to *Unity* by special messenger. When asked if he remembered if anyone else had taken any signals for *Unity* that day, Reading answered that a Wren messenger had, and that she had taken them after Leading Signalman Moon had visited the SDO.

Signalman Walter Warren performed his duties at the Signal Distribution Office. He had been summoned to the inquiry.

QUESTION: 'Which watch were you keeping on 29 April, the day *Unity* sailed for patrol?'

SIG WARREN: 'I had the afternoon watch.'

QUESTION: 'Do you remember a signal 1428/29/4 being received from Commander-in-Chief, Rosyth, concerning the movements of certain ships and the Methil-Tyne convoy which was due off Blyth about 1930?'

SIG WARREN: 'Yes.'

QUESTION: 'Can you remember what the distribution of that signal was?'

SIG WARREN: 'Captain S, Commander S, Staff Officer Operations, *Unity*, and *Seal*.'

QUESTION: 'How was it distributed to HMS *Unity*?'

SIG WARREN: '*Unity* has a distribution pigeon-hole, and *Unity*'s signalman collects them at regular intervals.'

QUESTION: 'Can you remember whether this signal was collected from *Unity*'s pigeon-hole, and if so, when?'

SIG WARREN: 'Not during the afternoon watch.'

QUESTION: 'Can you remember whether it was still in *Unity*'s pigeon-hole when you went off watch at four o'clock?'

SIG WARREN: 'Yes. It was in the pigeon-hole.'

When Signalman Warren came off watch at the SDO, Telegraphist Percy Marks took Warren's post at the office. Marks was asked if he could recall, on commencing his watch at four o'clock, whether there were any signals in *Unity*'s pigeon-hole. To this Marks replied that he was not sure.

QUESTION: 'Did any arrive whilst you were on watch?'

TEL MARKS: 'Yes. The first one was the one addressed to the *Seal* and *Unity*, and I delivered that by hand to the leading signalman of *Unity*.'

AB Campbell of the *Undine* (centre) distributes Red Cross parcels in Oflag IXA, which they shared for a time with the RAF and French prisoners. In keeping with the traditions and high morale of the Submarine Service CPO 'Tubby' Lister and CPO F. W. Hammond made a 'home run' from Colditz!

*Thistle* at speed on builder's trials. Armed with ten torpedo tubes, she was torpedoed in 1940 by the *U4*, a small training submarine with three torpedo tubes.

The *Shark*, with her casing and bridge crowded with dead, wounded and exhausted men is lashed to a German anti-submarine vessel. Like the *Shark* at Jutland, the submarine went down after fighting against superior forces yet the name *Shark*, like those of *Salmon, Unbeaten, Thunderbolt* and other distinguished submarines has been ignored by the Naming Committee in favour of names which have no submarine history.

(*Left*) AB Miller who was awarded a posthumous George Cross after he and the first lieutenant, Lieutenant John Low, went below to stop the motors of the *Unity* after she had been rammed by a Norwegian ship. Miller was the second of the family to die in submarines, his brother having been killed in them. (*Right*) Lt-Cdr Ener Bettica, who sank *Grampus* in June 1940, was himself killed in action when in December 1942 his destroyer, *Folgore*, encountered a British naval force. (*Below*) The first of the forty-five British submarines to be lost in the Mediterranean in June 1940, the *Odin* was large, elderly and unsuitable for service there. Coming from the easy-going life in Hong Kong to the cauldron of the Mediterranean the China boats may have found the violent transition from peace to war difficult.

(*Left*) The gallant captain of *Shark*, Rear-Admiral Peter Buckley in 1953. (*Right*) Lt-Cdr E. O. Bickford at the periscope of the *Salmon*. In the space of nine days *Salmon* sank the *U36* and torpedoed and damaged the cruisers *Leipzig* and *Nürnberg*.

(*Below*) *Oswald* in pre-war days. Of the fifteen 'O', 'P' and 'R' class sent to the Mediterranean from the China station only four survived. They were too unwieldy for the type of patrols carried out by British and Allied submarines there, close inshore and rarely out of sight of the coast. *Oswald* was caught on the surface at night and paid the price.

The *Enrico Toti* and *Rainbow* do battle in October 1940. The action, illustrated by the Italian artist Claudus, is from a detailed description by Lt-Cdr Bandino Bandini. *Rainbow* is in the background. (*Inset*) Lt-Cdr Bandino Bandini aboard the Italian submarine *Enrico Toti* around the time that he sank *Rainbow*.

*Triad* on trials before being signed for by her captain on behalf of the Admiralty. She took part in the Norwegian campaign, but disappeared in October 1940 after leaving Malta for her second patrol.

QUESTION: 'What were the others?'

TEL MARKS: 'There were five or six QZHs.* The leading signalman went into the message room and came and said that they were coming through on the teleprinter. He said he could not wait, so I said I would get them off. Then I went into the message room and asked the teleprinter operator if she would hurry up with them because *Seal* and *Unity* were both under sailing orders. Then as soon as these signals came out, I sent the Wren messenger down to *Seal* and *Unity* with them.'

QUESTION: 'Do you remember handling message 1428/29/4 from Commander-in-Chief, Rosyth, concerning movements of certain ships?'

TEL MARKS: 'I cannot remember handling that one, sir.'

It would appear that there was no one who could state beyond any doubt that Leading Signalman Moon, or anyone else from *Unity*, had actually collected or had been handed signal 1428/29/4. Obviously, what Thomas Moon had to say to the court in connection with the signal was of the greatest importance.

QUESTION: 'Can you explain how it was that the signal 1428/29/4 from the Commander-in-Chief, Rosyth, was not delivered either to the captain of *Unity* nor to any of *Unity*'s officers?'

LDG SIG MOON: 'No.'

QUESTION: 'Did you collect any signals from the Signal Distribution Office shortly before sailing?'

LDG SIG MOON: 'Just before she sailed.'

QUESTION: 'Have you any recollection as to whether the signal 1428/29/4 was among those you collected?'

LDG SIG MOON: 'No.'

QUESTION: 'What did you do with the signals you collected from the SDO on the afternoon of 29 April?'

LDG SIG MOON: 'The only signals I remember collecting from the SDO were, I think, two QZHs. Four more QZHs were sent down by special messenger just before we sailed. These had been handed to the first lieutenant, who gave them to me. No other signals were received by me.'

As John Low, the first lieutenant, was dead, and as all of *Unity*'s con-

---

* A QZH signal relates to mines (Author).

fidential books, signals publications, and other confidential papers
had gone down with the submarine, the question of whether the signal had been received by *Unity* could not be fully substantiated. And
there the matter was laid to rest. Perhaps it was only to be expected
that Lieutenant Brooks and Leading Signalman Moon should come
in for a certain amount of criticism from the court. *Unity*'s patrol
orders had stated that she was to proceed with 'dispatch'. This
expression was regarded by submarine officers as implying that a
submarine is to proceed on the surface by day, unless compelled to
dive, and did not necessarily have the same meaning applicable to
surface ships to proceed at three-fifths power. *Unity* had been proceeding at 8 knots – too fast in the limited visibility thought the court,
particularly in view of the fact that information contained in the
appendix to *Unity*'s patrol orders indicated that the enemy were
unlikely to be in the vicinity, thus the need for speed was not pressing. The court also felt that Lieutenant Brooks's failure to use sound
signals until the siren of another vessel was heard was a mistake.
Very much in Brooks's favour was his rapid realization that nothing
was going to save *Unity* from sinking, and sinking quickly. If Brooks
had hesitated in the hope that something could be done to save the
submarine, then many of the crew might have perished. The decision
of the court as regards Lieutenant Brooks was that sufficient blame
could not be attributed to him to justify any disciplinary action
against him.

The court was of the opinion that Leading Signalman Moon had
collected signal 1428/29/4 (and also Captain S6's signal 1552/29/4
which referred to the former) from the Signal Distribution Office of
HMS *Elfin* at some time before *Unity* sailed. In giving evidence,
Moon had clearly denied all knowledge of the signals. The failure of
the signals' contents to be made known to Brooks had without doubt
been a contributing factor of the collision with *Atle Jarl*. Although
much of the blame for *Unity*'s loss was directed towards Thomas
Moon, a certain degree of responsibility must rest with Lieutenant
Brooks and Captain Submarine's Staff Officer, since they failed to
discuss the latest information concerning movements in the war
channel, one of the very things for which last-minute meetings at a
signal office had been designed.

Though Leading Signalman Moon had been considered neglect-
ful in his duty, the probability of obtaining sufficient evidence to secure a conviction for the offence was deemed remote, and so the
assembly of a court martial was not considered justified. It was also

considered undesirable that the offence should be dealt with summarily, as the powers of punishment of Captain S would not be compatible with the offence and its consequences. Moon later joined *Utmost* (Lieutenant-Commander R.D. Cayley). When Cayley moved on to command *P311* he took with him Leading Signalman Moon. Moon lost his life when *P311* was sunk with all hands. As Cayley appears to have thought highly of Thomas Moon, Moon must have been a very competent Signalman.

*Unity* had been commissioned in August 1938. Her first captain had been Lieutenant-Commander S.H. Pinchin. After ten months with *Unity*, Pinchin relinquished command to Lieutenant J.F.B. Brown. Brown had been in command for two months when war broke out. He did eight patrols before being relieved by Brooks on 20 April 1940, so Brooks had been *Unity*'s captain for only nine days when she was sunk.

Lieutenant Brooks had taken his COQC in April 1939. The following July he had been appointed captain of *L23*. Brooks had been Spare CO at Blyth for three weeks when appointed to *Unity*. After survivors' leave he took command of *Upright* at Barrow on 5 July 1940. Brooks did two patrols from Portsmouth prior to taking *Upright* to the Mediterranean, where she became the first 'U' class to do a patrol. In December 1940 he was relieved of his command. In February 1942 Brooks joined the staff at HMS *Dolphin*, the submarine base. After five months he transferred to the Admiralty's Operations Division Staff. On 3 June 1943 Lieutenant-Commander Brooks took to the air in a Beaufighter of W/236 Squadron, probably as an observer. Shortly after becoming airborne the Beaufighter was attacked by eight Ju88s. The navigator, acting as rear-gunner, was severely wounded. With Francis Brooks having taken over as rear-gunner, the pilot dived to sea-level. The Ju88s remained in pursuit, scoring several hits on the Beaufighter. During one of these attacks Brooks was mortally wounded. Though further damaged, the Beaufighter managed to shake off the enemy and reach Predannack, where she crash-landed. Thus did *Unity*'s captain fail to survive the war.

\*

April turned to May, a month during which the minelaying submarine *Seal* reluctantly changed her allegiance. Built at Chatham, *Seal* was commissioned in February 1939 as the sixth and last of the

*Porpoise* class. Designed to lay up to fifty mines from the stern, her eight 21-inch torpedo tubes made her a danger to an enemy unfortunate enough to cross her bows. Command of the new minelayer was given to Lieutenant-Commander R.P. Lonsdale, a widower of some two years with a young son. Lonsdale, far removed in appearance and manner from the usual public image of how a submarine commander should look and behave, was a quiet and likable officer who ran his submarine with efficiency and a minimum of fuss.

*Seal* was in Aden, *en route* for the China Station, when hostilities in Europe broke out. Cancellation of her orders was immediate and she was ordered to return home. *Seal* was quickly thrust into battle and had completed several patrols when she sailed Immingham on 29 April for a mine-lay in the Kattegat. During the early hours of 4 May *Seal* rounded the Skaw and entered the Kattegat. Soon after this she encountered the minelayer *Narwahl* returning from a similar expedition. *Seal*'s next encounter was anything but friendly. Lonsdale had trimmed down so that only the conning tower was visible; even so, just before dawn a German aircraft sighted her and swooped to attack. There was a scramble down the hatch as *Seal* hurriedly dived.

The submarine shook at the force of the exploding bombs. Some lights went out. Luckily, the damage was not serious; but of course *Seal*'s presence was now known to the enemy. It did not take long for the Germans to act on the sighting: *Seal* soon met up with a group of A/S trawlers, the behaviour of which led Lonsdale to believe that they were expecting him. This was of no real surprise. What was disturbing was that the trawlers were directly in the path of Lonsdale's priority area for the lay. As the water was not deep enough for him to pass beneath them without detection, he set off to lay his mines in an alternative area.

At 0900 the lay began, even though A/S trawlers were nearby. By 0945 Lonsdale was ready to clear the area. This was easier said than done. The Germans were taking stringent measures to prevent *Seal* ever leaving the Kattegat. At about three o'clock in the afternoon another group of A/S vessels joined the hunt. Between them the two groups began to narrow the area available to *Seal* for escape. As the hours slipped by, Lonsdale manoeuvred *Seal* skilfully away from the enemy. Then the whole operation came to an abrupt end. Around seven o'clock a fierce explosion shook the submarine. *Seal* had wandered into a minefield and had touched off a mine with her stern. With ears ringing from the deafening explosion, the crew hastened to perform emergency drill as *Seal* went to the bottom and buried her stern firmly in the mud of the Kattegat. When the Germans, who had been in the vicinity all day, failed to put in an appearance Lonsdale became puzzled as to how they could have strayed far enough from the area not to have heard an explosion.

*Seal* had been dived since the bomb attack had forced her under at 0230. Lonsdale proposed to attempt a surfacing at 2230. As the hours to nightfall slipped by, the air in the submarine became increasingly foul. Such was the crew's confidence in Lonsdale, that at no time did they not believe that 'The skipper will see us through.'

'Stand by to surface.' High pressure air forced the water out of the main ballast tanks.

'Half ahead.' *Seal*'s bows began to move upwards.

'Full ahead.' Her bows moved higher – but her stern remained firmly implanted in the mud.

'Stop blowing.' Though he must have felt it, Lonsdale showed no disappointment at *Seal*'s failure to respond more positively.

'Stop main motors.' *Seal*'s bows slowly settled. With the air growing fouler by the minute, Lonsdale knew that he could not delay too long in making a second attempt to surface; the crew were showing a marked effect from breathing oxygen-starved air.

In addition to her main ballast tanks *Seal* had, as have all submarine, several trimming tanks. Almost all of these tanks had been pumped out. Work on clearing every last drop of water out of the trimming system was put in progress. Some oil fuel tanks and some fresh water tanks were also emptied. As a final step in the grim life-or-death struggle, Lonsdale ordered *Seal*'s 11-ton drop keel to be released. This last measure was taken only in moments of acute desperation as without its drop keel it was almost impossible for a submarine to dive.

'Stand by to surface.' The procedure for surfacing was re-enacted. If *Seal* failed to reach the surface this time – then in all probability she would never do so. The attempt was a repetition of the previous failure, except that the effort had left them worse off than before, as now there was very little HP air available. In addition, *Seal*'s batteries had been considerably weakened. It looked very much like the end. Then the engineer-officer remembered that there were two very small reserve tanks still in a flooded condition. These tanks were so small that, under normal circumstances, they were kept flooded as they were too minute to affect *Seal*'s buoyancy one way or the other. Both tanks were then blown, but as expected their emptying made no difference at all. Everything that they could think of which might have helped the situation had been done. There was now nothing to do but pray.

Lieutenant-Commander Lonsdale was a man of strong religious convictions. His religion was a source of much comfort and strength for him. Now in his moment of great need Lonsdale turned to his religion for help. He expressed his wish to say a prayer. Those in the control room made an effort to rise to their feet, but even this was beyond the strength of some.

Lonsdale decided on a final attempt to free *Seal* from the mud of the Kattegat. For this attempt he asked that anyone with strength enough should move as far forward in the submarine as possible. The hope, a rather forlorn one, was that the extra weight forward, small though it would be, might just be sufficient literally to tip the scales in their favour and prise *Seal*'s stern from the mud. The move up the steep incline towards the bow took the greatest effort of physical strength and will power by those able to comply with Lonsdale's bidding. When all was ready, Lonsdale ordered the boat surfaced.

*Seal* broke surface at 0130, twenty-three hours after having dived. With her motors screaming and smoking, the submarine, shaking so violently that it was feared she would break apart, tore herself free of the seabed. After slowly levelling out, *Seal* had floated gently to the surface. First through the hatch was Lonsdale. There were signs of an approaching dawn. In the far distance the lights of neutral Sweden could just be made out. Lonsdale had in mind to make for Sweden, though whether the submarine would reach Sweden even if undisturbed by the enemy was by no means certain. *Seal*'s after end was well flooded. Her refusal to answer the helm, possibly due to a damaged rudder, was also a cause of concern. As *Seal* was facing towards German-held Denmark, the proposed attempt to reach Sweden was to be made stern-first.

One of the engines breaking down put an end to all thoughts of escape. The failure of the engine meant that *Seal*, with the use of a single propeller only, could do no more than move in a circle. Sweden was out of the question. There was nowhere else to go. It was then that they heard the aircraft.

It was Leutnant Mehrens, observer and captain of a small Arado seaplane, who first sighted *Seal*. The Arado circled and then attacked with gunfire. Lonsdale ordered his signalman to flash something, he did not care what, with the lamp. The delight of Mehrens in having found a surfaced enemy took a bit of a knock when he saw the flashing light. For a moment he wondered if he had made the mistake of attacking a Swedish submarine. Then, evidently having made up his mind that the submarine was not Swedish or German, he dropped a bomb. The bomb missed its target, as did another bomb of a follow-up attack. Having expended all his bombs and ammunition, Mehrens radioed a report of the sighting. He had just resigned himself to keeping *Seal* under observation until the arrival of surface craft, when a second Arado appeared. In a series of attacks the new arrival strafed and bombed *Seal*. Fire from *Seal*'s two Lewis guns, one manned by Lonsdale, continued to show defiance until both guns jammed permanently. Hits by cannon-shells had punctured a port ballast tank. *Seal* took on a heavy list to port. Then her one remaining engine stopped.

*Seal* was now in dire trouble: unable to move even in circles, she also lacked fire power; deep in hostile territory, she was under attack and unable to dive; enemy surface craft were undoubtedly on their way; she was slowly sinking. Certain that there was no way out for *Seal*, all confidential books and other material were destroyed. Top secret asdic equipment was smashed and dropped overboard.

Lieutenant-Commander Lonsdale had given serious thought to surrendering the submarine. In the early months of the war not all British submarines were equipped with scuttling charges for rapid sinking. Fitted in *Seal*'s bilges were two depth-charges set to explode at 50 feet on the submarine being flooded. Lonsdale's worry was that if *Seal* was sunk before his crew could be rescued, she would blow up and kill the crew in the water. On the other hand, if *Seal* was left to be taken in tow she would sink, of that there could be no doubt, long before she could be docked or beached. Lonsdale decided that he could not risk the lives of his crew. He would have to permit the Germans temporary custody of *Seal*.

Karl Schmidt, observer and captain of the second Arado, was surprised to see the white flag, actually a table-cloth, of surrender fluttering from *Seal*'s conning tower. The flyers were aware that had the submarine been able to dive she would certainly have done so long ago. It looked very much as if the submarine really was going to surrender. Schmidt ordered his pilot to set down close to *Seal*.

'Where is the captain?' Schmidt called to the crowd on *Seal*'s bridge. On identifying himself as CO, Lonsdale was told to swim to the Arado. The young airman grasped Lonsdale's hand and pulled him from the water. 'Good morning,' gasped Lonsdale in what from his point of view must have been the understatement of the year. He then went into a charade about *Seal* being in Swedish territorial waters. Understandably, Karl Schmidt was having none of it. Lonsdale was bundled into the Arado's cockpit and carried off to captivity.

At 0630 an ex-fishing trawler, a unit of the German Navy, arrived on the scene. Its first lieutenant, Heinz Nolte, boarded *Seal* with a party of ratings. Accompanied by Lieutenant (E) Clarke, the German went on an inspection of *Seal* whilst her crew were transferred to the trawler. A line was then passed to *Seal* and in perfect towing weather the journey to the Danish port of Frederikshavn began. *Seal* was so far down at the stern and had taken such a pronounced list to port that her crew believed that she could not possibly stay afloat long enough to reach harbour. But by late afternoon *Seal* had confounded the odds and was safely in harbour to be worked on for the trip to the Fatherland. By 11 May *Seal* was in Germany. In early 1941 she was commissioned into the German Navy. The Germans considered *Seal* inferior to their own submarines and were it not for her propaganda value she would have been unceremoniously scrapped. Great effort was made to make *Seal* operational but this was never achieved. By mid-1943 she was regarded as worthless. Stripped of anything of value, *Seal* was left to rust at Kiel Dockyard.

*Portsmouth, April 1946.* Lieutenant-Commander Rupert Lonsdale faced a court martial in respect of the loss of his command. At its conclusion Lonsdale left the proceedings having been honourably acquitted of all charges. Shortly after, he resigned his commission and entered the Church to become the Reverend R.P. Lonsdale.

Towards the end of May the gallant Polish submarine *Orzel* failed to return from patrol. She had sailed Rosyth 23 May and was due to return 6 June. Nothing was heard from her after leaving harbour.

The battle for Norway was still much in evidence when the Germans launched their 10 May western offensive by invading Holland, Belgium, and Luxembourg. On the same day Winston Churchill accepted the office of Prime Minister. By June France was a beaten nation and henceforth was unable to provide much constructive assistance to the Allies. On 21 June a Franco-German armistice was signed. Ten days later the French Government was exiled to Vichy where on 5 July it broke off relations with Britain. Although the French had given up the fight, the British had no such intentions. In northern waters, as elsewhere, Royal Navy submarines were giving a good account of themselves, and none more so than *Shark*.

The keel of HM Submarine *Shark* was laid down on 12 June 1933. Launched at Chatham in June 1934, at the time of her loss she was under the command of Lieutenant-Commander Peter Buckley, a resourceful thirty-year-old who was to put up a spirited fight before circumstances forces him to scuttle his command.

In September 1939 Buckley was serving in Malta with *Shark*. At the outbreak of war he was ordered home along with *Salmon, Sealion,* and *Snapper*. Operating from Harwich up until the French surrender, he then moved north to continue patrols from the Firth of Forth. It was during this period (early July) that Winston Churchill feared a possible assault on Britain via the enemy's Norwegian bases. To give early warning of any such move, submarines were ordered to keep watch for barge concentrations and to report if any such happenings were noted.

At the beginning of July the *Sealion* (Lieutenant-Commander B. Bryant) was on patrol off southern Norway. After a harrowing period in the Skagerrak, *Sealion* took up a position off Stavanger, where it was believed an invasion fleet was being assembled. German A/S patrols (sea and air) at this time were almost continuous in that area, so submarines were not expected to patrol off Stavanger for more than four days, after which they should be relieved by another submarine to enable the crew to rest and for the batteries to be charged. Bryant had not long arrived at his billet when he sighted, and afterwards attacked, a heavily escorted convoy. But Bryant's luck was out and retribution was swift: A/S measures became even more intense and it was only with the greatest difficulty that *Sealion* was able to put amps in the batteries. Air activity had become particularly fierce; in fact it became so fierce that Bryant felt that he had to warn Buckley, due to relieve him the next day, to stay away. Raising *Sealion* so that only her conning tower showed above water, Bryant opened the upper hatch. He was half-way through the hatch when the sudden appearance of an aircraft from behind low clouds forced *Sealion* under. Soon after midnight on 4 July, Bryant again tried to surface to use the radio, but again he was sighted from the air and forced to dive. The air inside the submarine was already foul; it would be many hours before clean air would again surge through *Sealion*.

*Friday 5th.* It was approaching midnight when Ben Bryant scrambled through the hatch and onto the bridge. Towards the horizon he saw lines of tracer and some flashes. *Shark* was fighting for her very existence.

An A/S patrol had surprised *Shark* on the surface. Lieutenant-Commander Buckley had been at the periscope having a good 'look-see'. In his mind he was enumerating the reasons why he would shortly have to surface. (1) the batteries were low after a long day's

diving in rough sea (2) he had been ordered to patrol off the entrance
to a fiord on the 6th and 7th of July (it was now the 5th), so it would
be impossible to charge for any length of time on the following night
(3) although there was no real darkness in these northern latitudes at
this time of the year, the night would be at its darkest at 2230, and it
was now 2200.

'Right, Number One, let's take her up.' Buckley had made up his
mind. *Shark* was about thirty miles from Skudesnes and, so it seemed,
in a comparatively safe position – at least, nothing had been seen all
day.

'Twenty-five feet, sir . . . 20 feet, sir . . . 15 feet, sir.' The upper
hatch lid was flung open and Buckley and the lookouts dashed onto
the bridge. No enemy were in sight. The starboard engine was
started and Buckley ordered 60° zigs every five minutes, and a 180°
turn after ten minutes at a speed of 8 knots. He had intended to
charge the batteries with the port engine but, owing to a leaky blast
air connection in a piston, the charge never got underway.

*Shark* had been surfaced some fifteen minutes when a cry from the
aft lookout reported a seaplane right astern. The bridge was cleared
with all haste and *Shark* was dived, though not as fast as Buckley
would have wished as she was head-on to a heavy swell. The depth-
gauge in the control room had not registered 20 feet when two or
three bombs fell very close to the stern. These were speedily followed
by at least two more bombs. Lieutenant-Commander Buckley takes
up the narrative:

'Considerable damage was caused by the explosions: lights were
put out, Sperry went off the board, and both hydroplanes and steering failed. The starboard main motor was out of action and an electric fire was started behind it. The HP air-lines aft of the engine room
bulkhead "started", so the line was isolated at the bulkhead. There
was a leak behind the port main motor switchboard and water was
coming in in this place. The after hydroplanes were jammed hard to
rise and could not be moved either with power or by hand. The boat
now took up an angle on the bow of about 35° bow-up. The bow
broke surface in spite of having filled all possible tanks and attempting to lighten the boat aft. The (available) port main motor was
worked full speed. As soon as the bow broke surface a hail of
machine-gun bullets was heard on the hull, and bombs were dropped around us. After what seemed an incredibly long period, it was
probably not more than a minute or two, the boat at last began to
gain depth, although at the same angle by the stern. As soon as we

were reasonably deep I commenced to trim on main ballast, but with no result; whenever the speed of the port main motor was altered, the boat took up a greater angle and it was impossible to run at a slower speed than full ahead group up. The after main ballast tanks were competely emptied with no apparent effect on the angle. The boat continued to gain depth rapidly in spite of all efforts to frustrate it. It was then reported that the HP air was very low and that water was coming in aft. The battery I knew to be very low, so that when the control room gauge showed 210 feet I decided to use all the remaining HP air in an attempt to bring the boat to the surface and try to get away under cover of what night there might be. By blowing all main tanks she started to rise at 256 feet by the control room gauge, 320 feet aft. The boat surfaced at an incredible angle and most of the gear, which had not already done so during the initial dive, took charge.

'On reaching the surface there was only 750 pounds per square inch of HP air remaining. We got underway on the starboard engine immediately, the time then being 2245, and, using the port main motor half ahead group up until the port engine could be made ready, I attempted to set a westerly course in order to take us clear from the land with the object of carrying out a detailed inspection of the damage, although I was satisfied that a further dive would be impossible.

'The main aerial abaft the bridge had been carried away, but the petty officer telegraphist eventually rigged a jury aerial and a signal was sent asking for assistance. Further, the port engine was very stiff to blow over and it appeared as though the bearings aft of the engine room were considerably out of line. Eventually she started, but it was found impossible to obtain more than 260 revs.

'It was now that we discovered for certain the real damage that finally sealed our fate: the rudder was jammed hard to port. Attempts were made to steer by main engines. Unfortunately all efforts failed as the port engine would not go fast enough to counteract the effects of the rudder, in spite of slowing down and, on one occasion, stopping the starboard engine. The situation at approximately 2315 was therefore as follows:

(1) We were on the surface and unable to dive.
(2) A signal had been sent asking for assistance.
(3) It was to all intents and purpose broad daylight, with no chance of visibility decreasing.

(4) The port shaft was apparently out of line.

(5) Most of the propeller guards were shattered.

(6) There was a leak behind the port main motor panel.

(7) The after ends were flooded to over the level of the shaft.

(8) All lubricating oil had been washed from Plummer and Thrust bearings.

(9) The ballast pump was running at full speed and not keeping the leak in hand.

(10) The stern was twisted to starboard for about 20 feet aft, and opened back from the after escape chamber.

(11) There was a very large dent in the pressure hull over the after ends.

(12) A split jacket on the starboard group exhaust valve wedging was employed, thus the flow of water circulating into the engine room was restricted.

(13) No 1 Battery was showing signs of overheating and was giving off dense fumes and smoke. No 1 Battery fuses were therefore dopped but this had little effect on reducing smoke.

(14) Most electrical circuits, including Sperry, were out of action. The circulating pump starters failed from time to time and were eventually held on by judicious use of string.

(15) With the steering gear out of action we had no alternative but to steer to port in circles of varying diameter. This was made possible by altering the revs of the starboard engine as much as possible, although it was deemed inadvisable to stop the engine more than absolutely necessary on account of the shortage of air.

'The 3-inch gun was manned and all HE* ammunition was brought up on deck. The Lewis gun and all rifles were manned on the bridge, as we were determined to use all available means of having a crack at the enemy, and if possible to hold them off until help arrived. Below, demolition charges were rigged in the torpedo compartment and AS office. All CBs and secret charts were prepared for destruction. Weighted books were thrown over the side (depth of water 130 fathoms) and then the bulk of the books and charts were torn into minute fragments and burned in the conning tower.

'About midnight we were spotted. We were then subjected to continuous bombing attacks. The first attack was very low. One bomb which exploded on the starboard side holed number four starboard

---

* High Explosive (Author).

main ballast tank, as well as washing two men over the side. The boat was by now listing heavily to starboard. We kept fairly upright by running the blower and admitting water to the port tanks, although I was reluctant to do this as we were losing buoyancy the whole time owing to the leaks aft in the engine room. During the action a Heinkel seaplane was used as a marker. She flew round us the whole time, keeping up a steady fire with her cannon; but this appeared to be ineffective, though many rounds hit the pressure hull. We set the HE ammunition at the lowest fuse setting and concentrated on keeping the Heinkel at a reasonable range with the 3-inch gun, whilst the Lewis gun and rifles were used against the planes making the bomb attacks.

'At some time or other, I'm afraid times throughout are only very approximate, shouts were heard coming from the water close to us and we soon recognized the voices of Leading Signalman Eric Eaton and Leading Seaman Gerald Pain, the two who had fallen overboard during the first attack. Although I was doubtful as to whether we could start the engines again, I decided to stop and pick them up as there appeared to be a slight lull in the bombing attacks, though the Heinkel continued her steady stream of fire. This evolution was completed without incident and Eaton and Pain were rescued. They were still in wonderful spirits, although obviously tired. Later on they helped in the excellent work which was done by the crew.

'At about 0120 I realized that I had made a mistake in giving a course and speed in my signal, as it would mislead the authorities into thinking we had made good our escape. As the attacks were now getting more frequent and the seaplane was obviously not going to allow us to get out of sight, I ordered a signal in plain language to be sent; despite all efforts of the petty officer telegraphist the WT office breakers would not 'hold on' and so the attempt to transmit the signal was defeated.

'The wardroom and engine room were by now full of smoke and fumes from the batteries (the torpedo room and after ends had been isolated by the bulkhead doors). The water-level in the engine room was rising, so it was necessary to change over the pump suction from the after ends to the engine room, and vice versa in order to get the best results. It became necessary to clear the magazines of all ammunition as the wardroom was rapidly becoming untenable. This was done personally by the first lieutenant using DSEA as a gasmask. Working in the magazines under these conditions was extremely unpleasant but the task was completed successfully, although workers had to take several 'breathers' under the conning tower hatch before they could continue. Great work was also being done by the engine room staff in keeping the engines working and altering the revs of the starboard engine. It was deemed inadvisable to touch the port engine at all after she had once been started. The engine room was choking with fumes and the conditions were very bad; however, the engineer-officer and two of his ERAs managed successfully to deal with the situations as they arose, spending any spare time under the conning tower getting breathers of fresh air until either an engine movement was necessary or some fresh contingency had to be met or overcome.

'On deck the 3-inch gun, the Lewis gun, and the rifles were manned and the remainder of the crew employed as supply parties, for which the most essential job was the filling of the Lewis gun's pans as they became empty. This latter was a wholetime job as, on practically every occasion of a bombing attack being carried out, the contents of a small pan would be exhausted. During an attack an HE shell exploded close under the stern of a Dornier. The plane made off towards Stavanger with sparks coming from it, amid loud cheers from *Shark*'s crew who naturally assumed that it had been hit. It is quite possible that this might have been the case.

'At about 0245 Petty Officer James Gibson fell over the side and was never seen again. This was a sad blow to everyone as he was a very competent petty officer who had shown his real merits under active service conditions. I cannot say what caused him to fall overboard, but it is probable that he was killed outright by one of the bullets that were flying round at this time.

'At some time round 0300 four Messerschmitt Me109s appeared from the direction of Stavanger, and from then on they continued to rake the bridge and guns' crews with machine-gun and cannon fire. Their fire was devastating and it was obvious to me that the end was now in sight, although everyone stuck to their posts in a magnificent manner until wounded or killed.

'One of the seaplanes signalled us by light: STOP OR STEER TOWARDS STAVANGER. No notice was taken of this signal but about fifteen minutes later – after continuous attacks from the 109s and our ammunition being expended, and having many wounded or dead, I could not tell which – I reluctantly decided to capitulate. Nearly all of our casualties had been sustained during the attacks of the Messerschmitts, and at the finish the bridge was a shambles of wounded men, blood, and empty cartridge cases. Stoker James Walsh had been killed outright.

'After we had been stopped for about thirty minutes, one of the small seaplanes landed close astern of us. Its two airmen eventually came aboard. Shortly after this their plane broke adrift and heeled over and sank. They explained that they had been hit in one of the floats during the action, but I think it more probable that they had damaged their float when landing but did not like to admit it. The pilot and observer appeared very nervous and the former was particularly loath to remove his finger from the trigger of his Luger. These two were quite content to remain on the bridge, so there was ample opportunity for the first lieutenant and officers to go below for the purpose of destroying everything which might have been of interest to the Germans. Wounded men were attended to as well as possible. They were laid out on the gun platform as the atmosphere inside the boat had by now become almost impossible.

'Everything was now ready for blowing up. The exact moment at which to take this step was a question that had exercised my mind, in view of the large number of wounded on board. To my mind there was no point in doing it until there was any likelihood of the boat being taken in tow, and this would not be possible until such craft had arrived. I therefore decided not to take any action until such craft had arrived fairly close to the boat, when there would be a reasonable chance of the wounded being picked up.

'About 0500 one of the large seaplanes landed and two officers came aboard from a rubber boat. After a great deal of manoeuvring I was eventually got on board the seaplane where my wounded leg and head were made as comfortable as possible. About thirty minutes later I was joined by Sub-Lieutenant Robert Barnes and we took off for Stavanger at about 0615. When we left *Shark* she was lying very low in the water, stern-down, and I was certain she would sink very shortly. Overhead, seaplanes, bombers, and fighters were flying round and, when we left, the gallant *Shark* was at the mercy of at least ten hostile aircraft.'

As Lieutenant-Commander Buckley and Robert Barnes were flown off for medical treatment the crew settled down to await developments. Those of the wounded who were fit to move were wrapped up and positioned on the gun platform. Their dressings were renewed for as long as supplies lasted. Rum and cigarettes were issued to men without head wounds. DSEA were fitted to the helpless. The WT and AS cabins were broken up. By the time this had been done the engine room was well flooded and *Shark* was appreciably low in the water and rolling very sluggishly in the westerly swell.

At about 0730 smoke was seen in the direction of Stavanger. An hour later four trawlers arrived. One of the trawlers secured alongside *Shark*'s starboard side whilst two of the other trawlers performed the same act to port. The wounded were then transferred to the trawlers where they were looked after by a naval doctor sent out for that purpose.

It was 0900 before the trawlers were ready to return to Stavanger. Two of them attempted to take *Shark* in tow. Almost immediately *Shark* began to sink. The tow was hastily cut. For those in a position to see, the sight of *Shark* going down was a memorable one: first her stern became completely awash; then increasingly more of her after end disappeared beneath the surface. The end came suddenly. *Shark*'s bows rose up out of the water as her stern sank vertically. Even as she sank, *Shark* had not completely given up the fight: her last action was to strike and damage the propellers of a trawler, so it was an enemy vessel that was towed to Stavanger and not *Shark*. Although it was sad to see her go, it was very satisfying, and a great relief, to know that she would not fall into enemy hands. *Shark* sank in 700 feet of water at a point 30 miles south-west of Stavanger.

Lieutenant-Commander Buckley had been badly wounded in his head and leg. Following three weeks' hospitalization at Stavanger, Buckley was taken by ambulance to Oslo to spend a further three weeks in hospital. A move to a hospital in Poland followed. Thereafter came POW camps until war's end. In due course Peter Buckley, a submariner since 1931, returned to active service. After more than forty distinguished years in the Royal Navy, Rear-Admiral Buckley, CB, DSO, retired in 1965. From his home in Hampshire the admiral comments: 'Throughout the action all the men displayed great courage, and their spirit remained excellent to the end.'

The loss of *Shark* on the Saturday was followed on the Sunday with the loss of *Salmon* (Commander E.O. Bickford). To Edward Bickford and *Salmon* had gone the distinction of sinking *U36*, the first U-boat to fall to a Royal Navy submarine.

For her last patrol *Salmon* sailed Rosyth on 4 July for position 57°20'N 05°00'E. On 9 July *Salmon* was ordered to 58°40'N 04°30'E, off Skudesnes. On the 11th she was signalled to move twenty miles north. The next day *Salmon* was ordered to return to harbour. No signals had been received from her during the patrol. She failed to return to harbour.

It was thought that *Salmon* had been sunk by enemy aircraft. This assessment was made following a German communique of 5 July which reported that one submarine had been sunk and another damaged at the time of the loss of *Shark*. It was felt that the submarine claimed as sunk could have been *Salmon*, as she was due to arrive at her patrol position on that date. When positions of German minefields became known, it was realized that *Salmon* had been routed across a minefield that had been laid in July 1940. *Salmon* is thought to have been mined in position 57°22'N 05°00'E on 9 July.

The loss of the submarine minelayer *Narwhal* also came in July. *Narwhal* (Lieutenant-Commander R.J. Burch) sailed Blyth at 1500 on the 22nd. Twenty-four hours later, almost to the minute, she was lying at the bottom of the North Sea as a useless wreck.

*Narwhal*'s mission was to lay a minefield (FD22) in position 63°16'N 07°13'E. Her orders were to proceed on the surface, except within thirty miles of 59°29'N 02°34'E. Burch was expected to report the lay completed by the 28th, but no such signal was received. By 30 July – nothing had been heard from *Narwhal* since her departure from Blyth – Lieutenant-Commander Burch was ordered to report. There was no reply.

An attack on a submarine by a Dornier aircraft at 1455 on the 23rd was assessed by the Germans as 'Very probably destroyed' and thought by them to have been *Porpoise*. The submarine had in fact been *Narwhal*. Flag Officer Submarines gave *Narwhal*'s estimated position at six o'clock on the 23rd at 55°30'N 01°10'E and at six o'clock on the morning of the 24th as 58°50'N 02°20'E. This meant that on the afternoon of the 23rd *Narwhal* would have been at the exact position where the Dornier made the attack.

Lieutenant-Commander Ronald Burch had entered the Navy as a cadet in 1925. He joined submarines in May 1930. Burch had been awarded a DSO in June for 'Daring, endurance, and resource in the conduct of hazardous and successful operations in submarines.'

\*

There is more than one theory as to how the big River class submarine *Thames* (Lieutenant-Commander W.D. Dunkerley) met her end. Having undergone a long refit, *Thames* was on her first war patrol when she went missing in July.

*Monday 22nd.* *Thames* sailed Dundee, passing Bell Rock at 1000, routed through 57°46'N 02°32'E and 58°12'N 03°48'E to patrol position 57°30'N 05°30'E. Her speed was 13½ knots, though east of 02°30'E she would have been dived by day.

*Tuesday 23rd.* At 1939 *Thames* was ordered to leave her patrol position 57°30'N 05°30'E and proceed to patrol in the vicinity of 57°15'N

04°00'E. Shortly afterwards, at 2336, she was directed to proceed to 57°20'N 04°40'E, the reason being an interception of a German force suspected of minelaying.

*Wednesday 24th*. *Thames* was ordered, at 1412, to proceed and patrol in the vicinity of 57°35'N 06°00'E.

*Thursday 25th*. At 1157 *Thames* was ordered to proceed through 58°40'N 03°30'E and 58°00'N 02°00'E so as to arrive in the vicinity of 56°45'N 03°50'E by six o'clock on the evening of the 28th. She would patrol at that position until the afternoon of 4 August, and then return to Dundee. However, as the threat of invasion was not considered imminent, on the afternoon of 2 August submarines in the North Sea were ordered to return to harbour, *Thames* being ordered to leave patrol at ten o'clock that night and proceed with dispatch to Dundee to arrive the following day.

*Friday 26th*. The narrative returns to 26 July as on this day it is almost certain that *Thames* attacked an enemy warship. The German torpedo boat *Luchs* (Lieutenant-Commander K.F. Kassbaum) was just west of the Skagerrak when she encountered *Thames*. *Luchs* was part of a screen for the battle-cruiser *Gneisenau* and the cruiser *Nürnberg*. *Luchs* was positioned about 900 yards off *Gneisenau*'s port beam. It was about 1550 when a cry was heard that a torpedo track had been sighted off *Luchs*'s port beam. Lieutenant-Commander Kassbaum, on the starboard side of the bridge, called to the helmsman; 'Hard to port.' Before he could take a step towards the port side of the bridge, the torpedo hit the ship. Lieutenant-Commander Kassbaum: 'The force of the explosion was fierce. Smoke and steam obscured any sight. Debris was flying all around us. Something hot hit my left cheek. Seconds later, when the smoke had cleared a bit, I saw the after part of the ship, with the propellers high in the air, disappearing under water with incredible speed. It was gone within thirty seconds. The explosion had ripped *Luchs* apart. The rest of my ship was turning to starboard with the bow high in the air and steadily sinking.' After an hour in the sea only fifty, out of a complement of 155, out of those who survived the explosion were rescued.

There is a theory that *Thames* might have been damaged by the explosion. Lieutenant-Commander 'Dunks' Dunkerley was probably attacking the battle-cruiser *Gneisenau*. Concentrating on his target, he may not have seen *Luchs*, steaming at 25 knots, approaching from astern of *Gneisenau*. *Luchs* cut across Dunkerley's firing track, thereby shortening the range and exploding the torpedo, probably the first of a salvo, between 40 and 50 yards from *Thames*. The torpedo had hit between the two funnels and under the forward set of three torpedo tubes. All the boilers had exploded and possibly torpedoes as well. Also, *Thames* being on a converging course with *Luchs*, whose course was that of *Gneisenau*, there might be a very slight possibility that *Thames* was in collision with the sinking fore part of *Luchs*, which had begun to turn to port just as the torpedo struck. It must be said that the loss of *Thames* as a result of the explosion or a collision is extremely unlikely.

The possibility of *Luchs* having been sunk by a submarine other than *Thames* can be quickly dispensed with. Only *Snapper* was close enough to the area to have encountered the German force. On her return to harbour, *Snapper* reported no such encounter. Although there is no concrete evidence to point to *Thames* as having been the aggressor, and hence keeping alive the remote possibility of having been sunk by the explosion of *Luchs*, there seems little doubt that she had made the attack. *Thames*'s position at six o'clock on the morning of the attack was estimated by Flag Officer Submarines as 58°20'N 04°30'E. If this estimate is accurate, then *Thames* would have passed close to the position 58°26'N 04°10'E, where *Luchs* was sunk, at about 0800 and would have missed the enemy by about eight hours. Having said this, it is by no means inconceivable that *Thames* departed her patrol area in 57°35'N 06°00'E up to eight hours later than estimated by Flag Officer Submarines, as this would still have left her ample time to arrive in 56°45'N 03°50' by six o'clock on the evening of the 28th as ordered. *Thames*'s initial course on leaving her patrol area would have been almost reciprocal to that of the enemy force, so she may well have sunk the *Luchs*.

If *Thames* is unlikely to have been sunk during her attack on the *Luchs*, then she must have met her end some other way. The question of minefields looms large in an analysis of the loss of *Thames* as she is known to have passed through several during the course of her patrol. The order at 1939 of the 23rd to proceed to 57°15'N 04°00'E would have entailed crossing German Minefield No 17, which extended for almost nineteen miles from 57°20.5'N 05°03.5'E to 57°38.3'N 04°54'E and comprised 501 EMDs. The order at 1412 on the 24th to proceed to 57°35'N 06°00'E would have brought *Thames* back through the same minefield. Notwithstanding this, there were two further occasions on which she would have passed through minefields. In response to the order of Thursday 25th to proceed through 58°40'N 03°30'E and 58°00'N 02°00'E, *Thames* would have crossed German Minefield No 19, consisting of 660 EMCs extending from 57°56.5'N 02°36'E to 58°16.8'N 02°24.5'E, and in carrying out the instruction to return with dispatch to Dundee from her position in 56°45'N 03°50'E she would have crossed German Minefield No 16A, comprising some 200 EMDs extending from 56°37'N 03°33'E to 56°51'N 03°24.5'E.

The EMC and EMD are general-purpose moored contact mines. Of the two types, the EMC was much the larger. In the minefields in question the mines were moored at a relatively shallow depth of 10 feet below mean low water springs. A reconstruction of *Thames*'s track chart show that both crossings of Minefield 17 would have been made during daylight, and therefore *Thames* would have been dived. If Flag Officer Submarine's estimated positions for 0600 the 26th and 0600 the 27th are correct, then *Thames* would have crossed Minefield 19 at night and on the surface. However, if *Thames* torpedoed the *Luchs*, as appears likely, she would have been several hours astern of her estimated position and would have crossed Minefield 19 in daylight on the morning of 27 July and would therefore have been dived. Her crossing of Minefield 16A would have been made surfaced since, apart from its being made at night, the order to proceed 'with dispatch' implied a requirement to proceed on the surface by day also. The mines were laid too shallow to be effective against a dived submarine, though there was always the possibility of fouling a mooring wire and dragging a mine down onto the submarine. The possibility, however, of a large submarine like *Thames*, with a draught of 13½ feet at standard displacement, striking a shallow-moored mine whilst proceeding at night would appear to be greater. As Lieutenant-Commander Dunkerley made no WT transmissions whatsoever, it is that much harder to assess *Thames*'s loss. The favoured opinion would appear to be that *Thames* struck a mine on the night of 2/3 August when near position 56°45'N 03°26'E and was sunk.

Lieutenant-Commander William Dunkerley had entered Dartmouth in September 1921. He had joined the Submarine Service in 1929. Prior to his appointment to *Thames* he had been captain of *H43*. Dunkerly, thirty-two at the time of his loss, had been married only a few months.

*

HM Submarine *Spearfish* was under the command of Lieutenant J.H. Eaden and serving with the 2nd Flotilla at Harwich when war broke out. During her second patrol *Spearfish* was so badly damaged from depth-charge attacks that she had to spend almost six months under repair at Newcastle. By the completion of her refit, Lieutenant-Commander J.H. Forbes had been appointed as captain. *Spearfish* then moved north to operate with the 6th Flotilla at Blyth. But for her last patrol she put to sea from Rosyth on 31 July for an area off the Norwegian coast.

On 1 August – and at a point 145 miles east by south of Cape Nose Head and 180 miles WSW of Stavanger – *Spearfish* was sighted through the periscope of *U34*. (Lieutenant-Commander Wilhelm Rollmann). *U34* was nearing the end of a very successful patrol. With his one remaining torpedo Rollman sent *Spearfish* to the bottom. From the sea was rescued the only survivor, Able Seaman William Pester. A newcomer to submarines, Pester had been drafted to *Spearfish* just prior to her sailing Rosyth.

When *U34* returned to harbour a few days later, her ship's company were greeted as heroes. A radio broadcast of her arrival, intended for German consumption, was picked up by British naval intelligence. Details of the occasion were noted thus:

Now a U-boat returns which has surpassed all figures so far achieved. Lt-Cdr Rollmann was able to report to his superiors the sinking of 76,000 tons of merchant shipping and two war vessels* . . . Rear-Admiral Dönitz, commander of the U-boat fleet, stands on the pier. Orders, march music (We're off to Fight England), and cheers are heard. A speech, probably by Dönitz, can be heard indistinctly. Rollmann is congratulated on sinking a destroyer and a submarine and so many merchant ships. The Führer has conferred the Knight's Insignia of the Iron Cross on him . . . Asked about the sinking of the submarine, Rollmann says that it is an odd and by no means pleasant feeling for a U-boat commander to sink an enemy submarine. It is also very difficult. The only thing to be seen is the ship's conning tower. When the submarine was sighted he saw that it was one of the smaller, very modern craft. It was, however, very far away and he did not tell his crew against what sort of vessel his torpedo was directed. When the explosion was heard and he told the crew that an enemy submarine had been sunk, a wave of joy swept through the ship. He immediately surfaced and went to the spot where the English submarine had been sunk. He arrived after four minutes and picked up the sole survivor, a sailor, who was taken on board. He was well treated and after his slight injuries were dressed, he was put into a bunk.

* *Spearfish* and the destroyer *Whirlwind* (Author).

Lieutenant-Commander John Forbes, DSO, had entered Osborne in
May 1920 and the Submarine Service in 1928. As for *U34*, she was
sunk off Memel in August 1943 in collision with the German depot
ship *Lech*.

*

In September 1939 Britain and Germany had roughly fifty-five submarines apiece. Included among the British total were nine of the old
'H' class and three of the 'L's. Although the older submarines were
later used for training purposes only, in 1939-40 some of them were
selected for operational patrols. From May to August 1940, some of
the 'H' class maintained a surveillance of the Dutch coast to give
early warning of an impending invasion force. After the danger of
invasion had receded, the 'H's continued to patrol the Dutch coast
as, apart from other important considerations, these patrols were
useful in that they allowed commanding officers and crews to gain
experience of operating in enemy waters.

When Lieutenant Michael Langley was appointed to command
*Swordfish* his position as captain of *H49* was taken by 28-year-old
Lieutenant R.E. Coltart, DSC. In the early hours of 17 October Coltart put to sea from Harwich for what was to be his only patrol as
*H49*'s captain. During the night of the 17th/18th, the submarine was
at her billet off the Dutch coast. After charging batteries, Coltart
dived at dawn and began a dived patrol. By afternoon the mist which
had been in evidence for much of the day was quite dense. It would
appear that the poor visibility had some influence on Lieutenant Coltart's decision to surface in daylight; also, the heavy mist offered an
opportunity to ventilate the submarine. For whatever the reason,
after hydrophones failed to detect any vessels in the vicinity, Coltart
brought *H49* to the surface at about 1510.

A group of five trawlers comprised the German 11th A/S Flotilla.
With Lieutenant-Commander Wolfgang Kaden in overall command, the flotilla was very close to where *H49* had surfaced on that
misty October afternoon. Why this A/S force should have escaped
*H49*'s attention is not clear; what is clear is that the trawlers were
sighted almost immediately on *H49* surfacing. She was at once
ordered to be dived. Richard Coltart's hopes that his presence had
been concealed by the mist were to be quickly dashed.

It was the helmsman of Kaden's own trawler (*UJ116*) who sighted
the 'black spot' 40° off the starboard bow. The helmsman thought
that he had sighted a 'sail or something similar' and informed the

OOW, who with binoculars recognized the conning tower of a submarine between 2,000 and 3,000 yards' distance. Kaden ordered maximum revolutions. A German report of what next took place states:

> Location was difficult but at 1620 the echo ranger obtained a bearing at 305° and about 1,800 metres distance. The submarine had apparently laid itself on the sea bottom. A buoy was dropped and an attack made on course 296°. Two depth-charge groups of three charges each were dropped. Echo ranger became damaged and *UJ118* received orders to report at the location with her set. Meanwhile *UJ116* worked with revolving hydrophones. Noises were heard. However, these soon ceased and a run was made with three groups of depth-charges on course 22°. A large oil track appeared, which had a strong odour. An attack was made in this oil track for the third time, with seven depth-charges. More oil appeared and a large air-bubble stretched along the surface. A fourth run was made without location. Three depth-charges were dropped in the air-bubble patch.

On sighting the enemy Coltart had ordered 60 feet. For an hour he tried to escape the trawlers, of which the effort to seek him out could clearly be recognized. Then the chilling note of *UJ116*'s echo ranger was heard to echo off the submarine. The first pattern of depth-charges, at 1638, had been devastating: all the lights had gone out and the main motors had stopped. *H49*, out of control, went to the bottom where she remained with a heavy list. The silence from the surface which had followed this attack had led the crew to hope that the trawlers had lost contact. The restoration of lighting helped ease tension. Damage reports were not encouraging: air was escaping through the high- pressure line, several glands were leaking, water was entering through the engine room hatch, and the forward torpedo space had been flooded.

By 1700 *UJ116*'s echo ranger was again in working order. At 1731 Lieutenant-Commander Kaden made a second attack. An hour later he had again attacked. This third attack had resulted in a large column of oil and water erupting from the sea. Eight minutes passed. Another three charges were dropped. Following violent explosions, large quantities of oil were seen to come to the surface. Three oranges were also observed. The German report notes that an attack at 1850 was not completed:

> A fifth run followed, but as there appeared to be a man swimming among

the oil, the attack was broken off to permit *UJ116* to rescue the man and take him on board. After waiting all night on the position in which the sinking had occurred, and after locating the wreck again on the following morning, *UJ116* returned to Den Helder with the prisoner.

The prisoner was Leading Stoker G.W. Oliver. Throughout the attacks Oliver had been at his station in the engine room. To Oliver the second attack seemed far worse than the first. The lights had gone out for a second time and Oliver and his companions had found it almost impossible to stand. When DSEA were issued Oliver found himself without a DSEA as there were insufficient to go round. He then heard the hissing of air as Richard Coltart made a fruitless attempt to surface. Leaking HP air cylinders had increased pressure inside *H49* to such an extent that to breathe out demanded a concentrated effort. Oliver felt only half aware of what was taking place elsewhere in the submarine. Recovering from a brief period of unconsciousness he made out a 'circular light of pale green' immediately above him. He then felt himself being lifted towards the light by the great air pressure within *H49*. He found himself hurtling through the engine room hatch, which had probably been blown open by the last pattern of depth-charges. Striking the jumping wire above the hatch, he kicked himself free and struggled towards the fading daylight.

With binoculars Lieutenant-Commander Kaden observed what he had first taken to be a baulk of wood from the submarine. When he saw the 'wood' move he realized it was a man. Apart from the foul-smelling oil the first thing George Oliver had noticed on reaching the surface was a red indicator buoy with German markings. The buoy was no more than twenty yards away. Farther afield he saw the A/S trawlers. 'When I got to the surface a German trawler steamed towards me,' says Oliver. 'Two Germans in a Carley raft yanked me aboard and then took me to the trawler.'

Though the German report states that Leading Stoker Oliver was taken to Den Helder, Oliver thinks that he was put ashore at Harlegan. He was held at Harlegan for a day and then transferred to Wilhelmshaven, where he spent the next eight days. From Wilhelmshaven he was taken to the Polish POW camp at Thorn. During his confinement at Thorn he met Able Seaman William Pester, the lone survivor of *Spearfish*. After two years in Poland George Oliver was transferred to a POW camp in Germany. Now in his eighties, George Oliver lives in Hartlepool.

*H49* was not Wolfgang Kaden's only submarine success. After transferring to Arctic duties Kaden sank the Russian submarine *K23* off North Cape in May 1942. Soon after this he lost his life when a ship he was aboard struck a mine.

In early 1984 a Dutch diver, Hans Eelman, was diving west of Texel Island when he discovered the wreck of *H49* at a depth of 30 feet. *H49* is of course considered to be a war grave.

When the *Swordfish* (Lieutenant M.A. Langley) fell victim to a mine in November 1940 there were no survivors at all to relate the experience. She had sailed Fort Blockhouse on 7 November with the intention of relieving *Usk* in the vicinity of Brest. The duty of these submarines was to report any concentration of enemy shipping on a cross-Channel heading, and then to attack. Nothing was heard of *Swordfish* after her having sailed harbour, even though on the 15th and 16th she was ordered to report her position. Lieutenant Michael Langley had left *H49* the previous month, so he had survived *H49*'s loss by only three weeks.

The fate of *Swordfish*, on her twelfth patrol when lost, remained a matter for speculation for more than forty years. The possibility that she had been sunk off Brest by German destroyers was not without credence. However, in July 1983 the speculation came to an end when Martin Woodward, a director of the Bembridge Maritime Museum, was diving on a wreck a few miles south of St Catherine's Point, Isle of Wight. Woodward was searching for a wreck of the Great War when by chance he discovered the wreck of *Swordfish*, 200 miles or more from where she was thought to be. 'She is in very good condition and there are still traces of paint on her,' reports Woodward. 'It was quite spectacular because the visibility was so clear and it was virtually as though she had gone down a short time before.'

*Swordfish* is lying at a depth of 150 feet and is in two halves, with the break just forward of her gun mounting. The stern section is upright but the bow section is lying on its port side. The forward hydroplanes are set to dive and the bridge telegraphs are at 'SLOW AHEAD'. She was steering due west when sunk. As her after escape hatch was open, it seems very probable that some of the crew attempted to escape. If any did reach the surface on that night, their chances of surviving the cold without the prompt assistance of a passing vessel had proved hopeless. To sum up: *Swordfish* had been mined shortly after sailing Portsmouth Harbour. She had probably struck the mine soon after diving to catch a trim before surfacing to make her run towards Ushant at best speed during the hours of darkness.

\*

The war in the Mediterranean was a hard-fought contest. As the history of the Royal Navy's wartime submarine losses dwells almost exclusively on the Mediterranean theatre of operations from this point onwards, it will be as well to say a few words as regards Britain's interests in this area.

Since the time of Nelson the might of the Royal Navy had kept the Mediterranean Sea a British lake. Care of the western end had for many years been entrusted to Gibraltar. The island of Malta was ideally situated as a base for Central Mediterranean activity, whilst Cyprus and Suez were able to maintain a watchful eye on the eastern sector. For much of the Second World War British submarines operated from Gibraltar (8th Flotilla), Alexandria (1st Flotilla), and Malta (10th Flotilla), with the latter being the centre of focus for uncomfortably long periods – periods during which the Allies waited with great apprehension to see if the battered island could hold out against starvation and savage air attacks.

Malta had been occupied successively by Phoenicians, Greeks, Carthaginians, Romans and Arabs. From 1530 until 1798 the island was ruled by the Knights of St John. The capture of Malta from Napoleon in 1800 brought the island under British domination. With an area of 120 square miles and a population of 300,000 it is half the size of the Isle of Man, with a population six times as great. The superb natural harbours of Malta had long been one of its main attractions. The strategic value of Malta as a base and the advantages offered by its harbours were soon recognized by the British. With commendable foresight they invested a considerable amount of capital and expertise in developing the island as a naval base. Malta's famous Grand Harbour is two miles in length and eighty feet deep with several large inlets, some of which offered extensive dockyard facilities. Separated from the Grand Harbour by a three-mile-wide finger of land is Marsamxett Harbour. In this 1½ miles long strength of water is situated the rocky outcrop known as Manoel Island, on which was sited the submarine base.

In the early stages of the war the Mediterranean appeared to be securely under Allied control: Britain had her bases, and the French had naval strongholds in Tunisia, Algeria, and southern France. With the French surrender of June 1940 the situation altered significantly. Gone went the use of the French bases, and with them any assistance which the French fleet may have been able to provide. Italy's entry into the war in June 1940 in support of Nazi Germany was a grave but not unforeseen blow to British interests in the Mediterranean. Of all the Royal Navy bases, Malta was the most vulnerable. With Sicily only fifty miles away, Malta was an easy prey for enemy bombers.

Over half the Royal Navy's wartime submarine losses took place in the Mediterranean and adjoining seas. First of a long and distinguished line of HM Submarines to be lost in the Mediterranean was the *Odin*. At Singapore when hostilities flared in Europe, *Odin* was ordered to Colombo to patrol vital supply routes in the Indian Ocean. In April 1940 she sailed Ceylon (now Sri Lanka) for the Mediterranean. Passing through the Suez Canal, she arrived at Port Said on 21 April. By the 26th she was tied up at Malta.

When Italy declared war on the Allies on 10 June, *Odin* (Lieutenant-Commander K.M. Woods) was on an observation patrol twelve miles north-east of St. Elmo Light, Malta. At 0035 on 11 June *Odin* acknowledged Captain S Malta's signal ordering her to proceed in execution of previous orders to patrol in the Gulf of Taranto. *Odin* was routed about fifteen miles clear of, and parallel to, the coast of Calabria until due south of Capo Colonna, when she was in turn north and enter the Gulf of Taranto. *Odin* was due to leave her patrol area at 1930 on 17 June and was expected to arrive in the submarine sanctuary off Malta at one o'clock on the afternoon of 20 June. *Odin* signalled no ETA. At 1930 on the 18th she was ordered to proceed to Alexandria and to acknowledge the signal at 0001 on the 19th. This signal to *Odin* was made seven times in all, six times on the night of the 18th/19th and again at 1007 on the 19th. By this time *Odin* had been sunk for five days.

The Italian naval base of Taranto was a natural target for observation by submarine, so it was not long before the Royal Italian Navy quickly put into operation a system of A/S sweeps of the Gulf of Taranto. On the night of 13 June three torpedo boat squadrons (7th, 8th, 15th), numbering some twelve vessels, set out from Taranto on just such a mission. Dispersal of the squadrons for the sweep was as follows: the 7th to patrol the western area, the 8th the eastern sector, and the 15th the area between Capo San Maria di Leuca and Capo Colonna.

The 7th Squadron, comprising the destroyers *Dardo, Saetta, Freccia*, and *Strale*, sailed harbour at 2100. After passing the mine barrage the squadron headed south at 15 knots. The report of Lieutenant-Commander Andrea Fê d'Ostiani, *Strale*'s captain, tells of the beginning of the end for *Odin*:

At 2321 on the 13th at 39°42'N 17°21'E when on route, with course at 150°, to the search zone allocated to me I sighted in the luminous wake of the moon and 100° from the starboard bow, and at a distance of 2,700 metres, a large submarine on the surface and apparently armed with two guns. Putting the engines to full speed (27 knots with the two boilers operating) and all helm to starboard, I made for the enemy. On reaching a point a thousand metres from the submarine I ascertained that, after putting her motors to full speed, the submarine manoeuvred in a manner to make a rapid dive. Afraid of losing her I approached from port at 35° and launched one torpedo from the bow. The speed of the manoeuvre, the noise of the boiler ventilators, and the motion of the ship all combined to prevent me from following the torpedo's course. The first lieutenant and other officers present on the bridge stated that the torpedo was aimed on target. Personnel of the WT room and numerous persons on deck stated that they heard a dull detonation. A couple of minutes later the submarine, of which we could see only the top of the two periscopes, began rising until its turret was above the surface. I gave the order to open fire. Four shots were fired and all hit the target.

I again decided to ram the submarine, which by now was not more than 400-500 metres away. Turning to starboard I put the bow on the enemy. While executing the turn I saw at the submarine's stern the characteristic air-bubbles of a torpedo launching. A few moments later the wake of a torpedo passed within a few metres of *Strale*'s stern. In her *very fast* attempt to escape, the submarine, instead of diving, persisted in showing her conning tower, and at moments even the top of her stern. Under such conditions I chased the submarine and got to within 200-250 metres of her. Whilst I was telling the personnel on deck to prepare themselves for a collision, the submarine suddenly disappeared. Passing over her vertical, I launched seven depth-charges regulated from 25 to 50 metres. I then returned to the point of launching and fired a further two depth-charges, one regulated to 75 metres and the other to 100 metres. Reducing speed I completed another turn on the zone. I then interrupted the hunt and resumed the search course assigned to me.

At 0157, two hours thirty-six minutes after *Strale*'s attack, *Odin* was sighted by the torpedo boat *Baleno* of the 8th Squadron. *Odin* was then nine miles from where she had been attacked by *Strale*. Though by this time the moonlight was fading, Lieutenant-Commander Carlo Maffei-Faccioli, *Baleno*'s captain, sighted *Odin* breaking surface at a distance of just over a thousand yards. Calling for maximum revolutions Maffei-Faccioli went racing towards *Odin* with intent to ram. *Odin* began to submerge, finally disappearing altogether. Passing over the area *Baleno* dropped two depth-charges. Making a rapid turn, *Baleno* released three more charges at the same point.

Later that morning, and again in the afternoon, the Italians sent aloft an aircraft to survey the area of the attacks. An oilpatch was observed at the location of *Strale*'s attack. This suggested that *Odin* had suffered damage from the attack, though possibly not serious damage as she would have begun a return to harbour. In the area of *Baleno*'s attack an oil spread of 500 x 400 yards was sighted. The next morning further observation of the area revealed an oil slick of roughly ten miles square. The Italians believed that the attacks of *Strale* and *Baleno* had been made on two individual submarines, and that one of them had been sunk.

The *Baleno* had been completed in 1932. On 16 April 1941 she was attacked by British destroyers and severely damaged. The next day she capsized and sank. Carlo Maffei-Faccioli served with distinction until his retirement from the Navy on 1 September 1953 with the rank of captain.

*Strale*'s captain, Andrea Fê d'Ostiani, had entered the Naval Academy of Livorno in 1918. He had commanded *Strale* for two years when he left her to become first lieutenant of the cruiser *Bolzano*. At the time of the Italian armistice he was in overall command of a group of torpedo boats. Captain Fê d'Ostiani retired from the Navy in June 1946 and now lives in Rome.

*Odin*'s captain, Lieutenant-Commander Kenneth Woods, was the son of Lieutenant-Colonel C.R.S. Woods. In May 1921 Woods entered Dartmouth. He joined the Submarine Service in 1929. He had served in *Odin*, *Thames*, and *Starfish* prior to his appointment as captain of *Swordfish*, his first command. Woods was aged thirty-two and left a widow.

The *Odin* was not forgotten by the Navy. On 4 November 1960 another HM Submarine *Odin* was launched by Cammell Laird at Birkenhead.

The second victim of Italian A/S measures was the minelayer *Grampus* (Lieutenant-Commander C.A. Rowe). *Grampus* sailed Malta on 10 June. After a preliminary reconnaissance of her area she laid mines in the swept channel between Augusta and Syracuse. On

13 June she reported having made a successful lay. Nothing further was heard from *Grampus* and by 24 June she was reported as overdue. By that time *Grampus* had been at the bottom of the Mediterranean for more than a week.

Charles Rowe had remained in the area of his minelaying activities. On the morning of the 14th he attacked with torpedoes the Italian torpedo boat *Polluce*, a unit of the 13th Torpedo Boat Squadron which was on an A/S sweep in an area off Syracuse. *Polluce* sighted a torpedo wake in time to take evasive action.

At 1830 on 16 June, the 13th Torpedo Boat Squadron, under the overall command of Commander Aldo Rossi, sailed Syracuse for an A/S sweep. Once free of harbour the squadron (*Circe, Clio, Calliope, Polluce*) increased speed to 25 knots. The evening was clear and the sea calm. After half an hour's steaming due east, the squadron had neared a prearranged point from which it was to begin the night's A/S sweep.

At 1902 *Circe*'s captain, Commander Rossi, was informed of a periscope sighting 60 yards to port. This was *Grampus*. *Circe* at once turned to port and went racing back along the squadron's track. Commander Rossi:

> At 1904 I judged we were in range and started to launch the depth-charges. At 1904.40 Sub-Lt Crucian sighted to port a torpedo leaping out of the water. Soon after, another officer, Midshipman Lambelet, sighted the wake of a torpedo.

The order was given to launch depth-charges. By 1909 all the charges on deck had been expended.

Lieutenant Agretti, captain of *Clio*, saw *Circe* swing about and guessed her intentions. Moving away to port Agretti turned about and followed *Circe*, dropping depth-charges in the process.

The third ship of the formation was Lieutenant Bettica's *Polluce*. At 1903 a Lieutenant Radovani saw the wakes of two torpedoes heading towards *Polluce*. Bettica ordered full speed ahead and put the helm hard to starboard. One of the torpedoes passed close to *Polluce*'s bow and the other astern. Continuing with starboard helm Bettica began launching depth-charges. On completing the turn, a mass of air-bubbles was observed on the surface. *Grampus* appeared to be in difficulties. Bettica followed the trail of bubbles, dropping depth-charges as he did so. It was the ninth charge, one of 50 kg regulated for 165 feet, which destroyed *Grampus* completely. A column of water with black foam and mixed with wreckage was flung up. When the water had settled, a patch of oil was visible on the surface. *Polluce* approached and dropped more depth-charges. The oil patch expanded to reach a diameter of between 150 and 200 yards. A mass of small air-bubbles came to the surface along with further wreckage. *Polluce* remained near the wreckage until 2015. Lieutenant Bettica informed *Circe* of his observations and at 2025 set course to rejoin the squadron.

On having identified the presence of a submarine the Italians had acted with speed. The manoeuvring of the squadron, which had taken place in a circular area of just over 800 yards, had been carried out with skill and confidence. The submarine had been sunk in just fifteen minutes after the reported sighting. Sixty-one depth-charges had been launched.

*Polluce* also failed to survive the war, being sunk by aircraft in September 1942. Lieutenant Bettica was commanding the destroyer *Folgore* when he was killed in an action with British destroyers and cruisers on 2 December 1942. The officer commanding the 13th Torpedo Boat Squadron, Commander Aldo Rossi, retired from the Navy on 27 January 1963 with the rank of vice-admiral. He died in Rome on 28 February 1981.

Between 1956 and 1959 the new *Porpoise* class submarines entered service. These submarines numbered eight. One of them took the name of *Grampus*.

\*

When the *Orpheus* (Lieutenant-Commander J.A.S. Wise) was lost with all hands on or about 19 June it meant that in the space of one week no less than three submarines and 170 highly trained and experienced crewmen had been lost with very little to show for their efforts.

Wise was patrolling to the south-west of Malta when on the night of 10 June a signal from Captain S10 (Malta) ordered him to proceed in execution of previous orders to a prearranged area off Corfu. After acknowledging the signal at 2354, Wise shaped course for his billet.

*Tuesday 11th. 2115.* As there was a possibility of Greek submarine activity close to his area, Lieutenant-Commander Wise was recalled. Wise acknowledged the signal and took up a patrol south-west of Sicily.

*Tuesday 18th. 1930. Orpheus* was ordered by Captain S10 to proceed to Alexandria.

*Wednesday 19th. 1211.* Captain S1 (Alexandria) ordered *Orpheus* to establish a patrol off Benghazi in an area designated 'H', which at that time was an area within 40 miles of Benghazi. Captain S1's signal was acknowledged by *Orpheus* at 1416, and again at 2115.

*Thursday 20th.* During the early evening *Orpheus* was ordered to leave patrol after 1600 on the 22nd, and to arrive Alexandria 0230, 26 June. She was not told to acknowledge this signal.

*Saturday 22nd.* Captain S1 amended *Orpheus*'s route to Alexandria. Again *Orpheus* was not required to acknowledge receipt of the signal.

So, after acknowledging receipt of a signal at 2115 on 19 June – at which time it was estimated that she was about a hundred miles north-west of Benghazi – nothing further was heard from *Orpheus*. There are several theories as to why *Orpheus* failed to return to harbour, but the most likely is that she was lost through mining.

*Orpheus* had been the last of the 'O' class to be launched. She had arrived in the Mediterranean from the East Indies with *Odin, Olympus*, and *Otus*, the latter being the only one of the quartet to survive the war.

Lieutenant-Commander James Wise had entered Dartmouth in May 1921. He had served as a cadet and midshipman in the *Royal Oak* and *Repulse*. He joined submarines in April 1929. Wise was twenty-nine. He left a widow.

*Phoenix* and *Rorqual* sailed Alexandria on 3 July for the Central Mediterranean, arriving in their respective areas on the 8th. The Mediterranean Fleet had been carrying out an operation to cover a convoy from Alexandria to Malta. Owing to heavy air attacks it was deduced that an Italian fleet was also at sea. The decision was thus taken to operate the fleet off the Sicilian coast during the night of 9/10 July. Lieutenant-Commander Ronald Dewhurst (*Rorqual*) was ordered to keep north and west of a position south of Capo Spartivento, Sardinia, whilst Lieutenant-Commander Hugh Nowell patrolled the south-east corner of Sicily with *Phoenix*. On the 9th Hugh Nowell reported having sighted the Italian battleships *Giulio Cesare* and *Conte Di Cavour* with an escort of four destroyers. *Phoenix*, still *en route* to her billet south-east of Sicily, had sighted the force in the area of Agrigento. In an amplifying report she stated having attacked the enemy at long range and claimed one unconfirmed hit. *Phoenix* had then continued toward her billet off Sicily. Although nothing was heard from *Phoenix* after she acknowledged a signal at 2350 on 14 July, she was still in action.

The Italian torpedo boat *Albatros* (Lieutenant-Commander Ales-

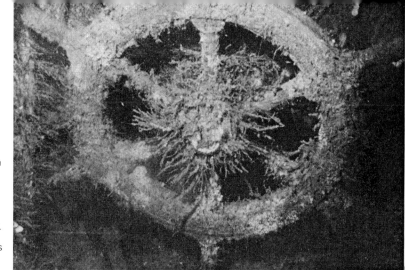

The wooden, upper deck steering wheel of the *Swordfish* thought to be lost off the French coast in November 1940 but discovered by accident by Mr Martin Woodward of the Bembridge Maritime Museum in 1983, just south of St Catherine's Point, Isle of Wight. Ironically, *Swordfish* was lost in a minefield only a few hours after leaving her base, HMS *Dolphin* in Gosport. To guard against souvenir-hunters Mr Woodward refuses to divulge the position to anyone.

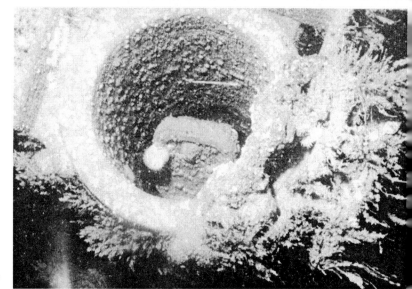

The Barr and Stroud search periscope of the *Swordfish* in the housed position inside the periscope standard.

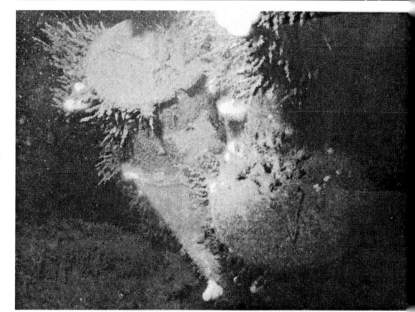

The upper deck telegraphs showing 'Slow Ahead' possibly an indication that the boat was dived when the accident happened or they would have been at 'Half Ahead' for surface running.

(*Top left*) *Cachalot* after a peacetime ramming by the Italian merchant ship *Beppo*. In July 1941 the submarine made a rash gun attack at night on a ship which could barely be seen. The target, thought to be a merchant ship, turned out to be the Italian destroyer *Papa* and *Cachalot* did not survive a second ramming by an Italian ship!

(*Bottom left*) ERA (Engine Room Artificer) Whyte, lost in *Perseus*

(*Right*) Johannes Ploch, the only survivor from the *U374*, sunk by the *Unbeaten* (Lt-Cdr E. A. Woodward) which surfaced four miles off the Italian coast to pick him up. There was also a sole survivor from the *U301*, a midshipman, sunk by the *Sahib*. In their turn, both *Unbeaten* and *Sahib* were sunk.

*Tempest* on the surface after a seven hour battering from the Italian torpedo boat *Circe* which reduced the boat internally to shambles. As with her other three victims, once *Circe* gained contact she never let go until she had sunk the target.

Lt R. J. Hemingway takes a visiting Russian delegation out for a day trip from Holy Loch in his new 'U' class submarine *P38*. On her first working up patrol in the Bay of Biscay, the Officer of the Watch was washed overboard in heavy weather and lost.

The captain of the destroyer escort *Pegaso*, Lt-Cdr Francesco Acton, in 1942, the year he sank *Upholder*.

P36 on the surface at Malta after sixteen years on the bottom at the submarine base in Malta.

British crews rarely paraded on the casing to receive their commanding officers, as was customary in the German U-boats, but on this occasion the crew of *Upholder* are waiting to give three cheers to their revered captain, Lt-Cdr M. D. Wanklyn, on the occasion of his winning the VC.

The two top scoring British submarines, *Urge* and the bulbous-nosed *Upholder*, alongside the submarine base on Manoel Island, Malta. British and Allied submarines played a decisive part in the defeat of the Axis powers in North Africa and the 200,000 tons of shipping sunk by these two submarines contributed towards that defeat.

sandro Mazzetti) put to sea from Messina at 0545 on 10 July to provide escort for the tanker *Dora C.* At 0630 *Albatros* and the tanker
began the journey, via the swept channel, to Augusta. At 1252, by
which time the little convoy was off the lighthouse of San Croce,
Augusta, *Albatros* sighted the wakes of two torpedoes. The torpedoes,
fired from a seawards direction from a range of 1,500 yards, passed
one forward and one close to the stern of *Albatros.* The torpedo boat
went quickly into action. At full speed, 24 knots, she raced down the
torpedo wakes. Ten depth-charges were launched. While the tanker
made her way into Augusta without further incident, the *Albatros,*
aided by two MAS boats*, remained in the vicinity of *Phoenix*'s
attack to conduct an A/S search which continued until the following
morning. There was no further contact with *Phoenix.*

It seems probable that Mazzetti's rapid counter-attack had
brought Hugh Nowell's war to an end. The speed at which he had
arrived at the origin of the attack had possibly caught *Phoenix* before
she had moved perhaps a hundred yards beyond her point of attack.
The depth-charges had probably damaged *Phoenix* sufficiently to
prevent her surfacing at some later stage. The fact that there were no
reports of mine explosions in the Augusta area at the time of *Phoenix*'s
activities would seem to add weight to the premise that Mazzetti had
sunk *Phoenix.*

Lieutenant-Commander Alessandro Mazzetti retired from the
Navy on 27 January 1945. He died in Rome on 10 November 1948.

Aged thirty-four at the time of his loss, Lieutenant-Commander
Gilbert Hugh Nowell had entered Osborne in May 1919. Except for
brief periods of General Service, Nowell was in submarines for ten
years. In 1938 he qualified at the Staff College, and in January 1939
was appointed Staff Officer (Operations) with the 4th Flotilla in
China. Hugh Nowell was devoted to the Navy and died in the way he
would have wished, in command of his ship on active service. He left
a widow.

What *Phoenix* had failed to do was accomplished by Lieutenant
John Wraith's *Upright. Upright* sailed Malta at 1600 on 22 September
1941. Of the sinking of *Albatros* her log states:

*27 September 1941.*
0820. Sighted a torpedo boat on an A/S search in position 8 miles NW of
Cape Rasocolmo.

* Similar to British Motor Torpedo Boats.

0855. Launched one Mark IV torpedo against the torpedo boat, which stayed on a constant course at 4½ knots.

0855.5. Launched second Mark IV torpedo by 'aiming'.

0858. One explosion after a torpedo had completed its 3,000 yards course.

*Albatros* broke in two. The forward half sank at once and the stern five minutes later. Thirty-five of the eighty-three crew were lost.

August 1940 opened with the loss of *Oswald* (Lieutenant-Commander D.A. Fraser). *Oswald* left the comparative comfort of the depot ship *Medway* at Alexandria on 19 July for a patrol east of Sicily. David Fraser had been captain of *Oswald* for less than five months, having relieved Commander G.M. Sladen as CO the previous March.

*Oswald* had been in contact with the enemy several times during the patrol when at 0730 on 30 July Fraser sighted an Italian cruiser of the *Condotti* class making way north towards the Straits of Messina. No action could be taken and no signals reporting the sighting were made. At 1230 four cruisers and some destroyers were sighted, also on a northerly course. Not long after this an escorted convoy was observed heading out of the Straits. David Fraser decided to attack.

The convoy comprised three merchantmen and several destroyers. It was bound for Tripoli at a speed of 7 knots. It was two o'clock when a torpedo of *Oswald*'s was sighted off to port by a machine-gunner of the destroyer *Grecale*. The destroyer turned to port and increased speed for an attack. When a further two torpedoes were sighted close to *Grecale*'s stern, the Italians became doubtful as to *Oswald*'s position, which had been to the destroyer's stern. By the time they realized the general direction of the submarine, the possibility of effective action had passed. *Grecale* joined the convoy. *Grecale*'s captain signalled the presence of a submarine twenty miles to the south of Cape dell'Armi.

The High Command at Sicily had at that time gathered the major part of its modern destroyers and torpedo boats for escort duties to three convoys to North African ports, thus the only vessel immediately available to search for *Oswald* was an old torpedo boat. This vessel remained at sea throughout the night but had no success. However, as the 14th and 16th Destroyer Squadrons were to leave Augusta on 1 August for Taranto, it was arranged that whilst *en route* the ships would conduct an anti-submarine sweep to the south of Capo Spartivento, Italy, and afterwards in the Gulf of Taranto. Taking part in the sweep were the destroyers *Antonio Da Noli, Ugolino Vivaldi, Nicoloso Da Recco, Antoniotto Usodimare,* and *Emanuele Pessagno.* The destroyers sailed Augusta at 1900 and by 2025 were able to begin the sweep on a 55° bearing, speed 19 knots. The night was dark with a calm sea. The sweep proceeded with the destroyers beam-on to each other and with a distance of four miles between each ship. Nearest to Capo Spartivento, which was to port, was the *Da Noli* and farthest was the *Pessagno* at twenty miles.

It was approaching 2350 when the *Vivaldi* (Captain Giovanni Galati) made visual contact with *Oswald.* Captain Galati: 'I sighted to port at a range of approximately 2,500 metres, and at approximately 70° on the bow, a large submarine, completely surfaced, which I judged to be stationary, lying almost parallel to my course. I made an enemy report, ordered forthwith the maximum speed (27 knots) obtainable when using all three boilers, and altered course by more than 100° using full helm in order to get the bows on to the submarine and ram her. When I was 1,000 to 1,500 metres off I saw the submarine, in her turn, alter course to port and present herself to me end-on, and therefore in a good position for firing.'

*Oswald* had surfaced at 2100. The bridge party at the time *Vivaldi* sighted *Oswald* consisted of Lieutenant M.S. Hodson, who was OOW, Able Seaman E.R. Burbridge, the starboard lookout, and Able Seaman Frank Seaton, port lookout. Able Seaman Burbridge had arrived on watch at 2340: 'I had been up there about twelve minutes and had become accustomed to the night. I had just done a good sweep forward. I rested my eyes a second, and swept back again. On Green 160 I saw an object. It was a destroyer. I reported it on sighting. I assumed at that moment that she had either been in a haze astern, or to port. It was impossible for her to have gotten so close. She was only 1½ miles away. I estimated that there was 2½ miles visibility. I reported to the officer on watch. Lieutenant Hodson, who shouted down the voice pipe to the control tower: "Enemy ship in sight".'

Lieutenant-Commander Fraser was in the wardroom deciphering a signal with the first lieutenant, Lieutenant G.R. Marsh, when the bridge sighted *Vivaldi.* Fraser dashed to the bridge. Able Seaman Burbridge: 'The captain arrived after a minute. He had no glasses. He appeared to be blinded coming from the lights within. As it was more important for the captain to have glasses, I handed him mine. He still could not see the destroyer, which by then was Green 110 a half-mile distant. It was slightly sheering away. By then tube-ready orders were shouted up to the bridge, three and four tubes first and then one and two stern tubes. In about four and a half to five minutes after sighting the enemy, all the tubes had been reported ready to the bridge. When the captain sighted the destroyer he told the navigating officer to order port 15. The destroyer still conformed and kept herself in a relative position on our beam, remaining there for about four minutes. Suddenly she apparently flashed up another boiler. I could tell by the dense smoke. Our inclination lessened. The navigating officer, captain, and port lookout were watching with glasses. The navigating officer said to the captain: "She is turning away". The captain remarked: 'Thank Christ for that." I could see a plume of water on her bow and said: "She is turning towards us." This was immediately confirmed by the captain and navigating officer. The captain gave the order hard to port. As the boat turned away, it was inevitable as we turned round that the destroyer would catch and ram as we turned under port helm, as she was closing in on us. We could see we would be stern to her. When she was 100 yards astern to us, at my estimated speed of 15 knots, the captain gave the order to abandon ship.' It was then approximately 2358.

*Vivaldi*'s captain continues: 'I tried as far as I could to increase the angle of incidence with the enemy hull, now very close to *Vivaldi*. The submarine appeared to have already begun to submerge. When I judged myself to be 400 to 500 metres away I ordered a reduction in speed with a view to minimizing the damage which in all probability would be sustained by the bows of the destroyer.

'The collision, not very violent, occurred on the starboard side of the submarine, somewhere abaft the conning tower and at an angle of 15°-20°. The enemy boat, listing heavily to port, dropped astern along the port side of *Vivaldi*, who in her turn also listed. The superstructure of the submarine grazed the destroyer, which merely sustained a graze 4 to 5 metres long on the upper part of the forecastle. The graze was made by the conning tower. I immediately ordered all the depth-charges in the chutes to be dropped (four of 100kg and six of 50g set to depths from 25 to 100 metres). Continuing on my course, at high speed I withdrew to approximately 1,000 to 1,500 metres. I could see the submarine, though very indistinctly, still awash. I led round and, whilst manoeuvering round the position of the enemy ship in order to avoid becoming the target for probable torpedoes, I fired a torpedo to starboard. Simultaneously, I opened fire with the forward 120 (two rounds of starshell and three pairs of HE shell).'

*Vivaldi* had struck *Oswald* a hard glancing blow abreast the after hatch, severely damaging the ballast tanks as she passed along the side of the submarine. Lieutenant Michael Pope was detailed by Fraser to check for damage. Pope reported that the engineers' space aft was flooded, and that *Oswald* was making water in the forward tube space. The after hatch was distorted and Pope could not close it.

Within a few minutes of the order to abandon ship most of the crew had made their way topside. Warrant Engineer George Mitchell: 'Whilst going up the conning tower there were further explosions and flashes coming down the conning tower hatch. On arriving on the bridge I asked the captain what had happened. He pointed off our starboard and said the ship lying there had just struck us. He said that as she passed, she had dropped depth-charges. I asked what he intended to do. He said that he thought then that it would be impossible for the ship to dive again, and if necessary he was going to sink the ship. By this time the majority of the crew were on the bridge. I said to him: 'Shall I take the crew away?" He told me to do so.' The crew made their way forward and took to the water.

Chief Petty Officer John Kirk: 'I had no DSEA, so I hung on to Leading Stoker Able for about ten minutes; then I found I was getting cold, so I went on swimming. After about three-quarters of an hour in the water, there was the first of three explosions. About an hour and a half after the boat had gone down, we were swimming in oil fuel.'

Stoker Petty Officer Charles Collier: 'A minute or two after I had swum away from the boat, Stoker Young was shouting for assistance. I swam over and kept him afloat for quite a few minutes. I got cramp and stitch. He started struggling, so I let go of him. I submerged to put pressure on my foot and get rid of the cramp. When I surfaced he was screaming for me. That was the last I heard of him.' Neither Collier nor George Young had DSEA.

Leading Seaman Harry Moore: 'I remained for'ard on the casing. The boat was still underway and circling to port as I had left the wheel hard over, and the main motors were running. When the main vents were opened I swam away from the boat. I remained with the main party in the water. When the destroyer approached for the third time, it stopped. They yelled from the quarter-deck asking what nationality we were. We yelled out, "English".'

The light from a small hand torch used by Lieutenant-Commander Fraser was seen by *Vivaldi*. Captain Galati: 'A faint, alternating flash from a luminous source led me to believe that the submarine was still afloat. I therefore made straight for the light in order to repeat the ramming action, this time at a speed not exceeding 12 knots in order not to expose the stem of the destroyer to further damage. I found, however, that the submarine had disappeared and the water was full of men calling out insistently for help. I lowered the motor launch and proceeded to rescue the victims in two batches. Fifty-two of the fifty-five members of the *Oswald* were saved. Among them were the captain and officers. None of them were wounded. Many of the survivors arrived on board naked or almost naked. I arranged for them to be supplied with blankets and refreshments, and had cigarettes distributed to them. I then saw that they were clothed with regulation capes supplied by the ship's personnel. From the moment they arrived on board the *Vivaldi*, the officers were separated from the crew and assembled in the officers' mess. At 0120 (2 August), the motor launch having been hoisted in, I proceeded on my way to Taranto.' As stated by Captain Galati, three of the crew had not survived: George Young, Leonard Woodfield, and ERA William Chaff.

The submariners remained at Taranto for about nine days. They were then sent to prisoner of war camps. Later, some of the crew escaped captivity and joined the Allies.

On 9 September 1943 the *Vivaldi* was sunk by gunfire when in action against German forces. Rear-Admiral Giovanni Galati retired from the Navy on 19 February 1950. He died in Rome on 15 October 1971.

*

*Triad* was launched at Barrow just prior to the outbreak of war. After serving through the Norwegian campaign *Triad* was ordered to the Mediterranean. How she came to be sunk is not known for certain. Newly arrived at Malta, and under the command of Lieutenant-Commander G.S. Salt, *Triad* sailed harbour on 9 October under orders to patrol the Libyan coast whilst *en route* to join the 1st Flotilla at Alexandria. Due to arrive in harbour on the 20th, she failed to make an appearance. The most likely cause of *Triad*'s loss was mining.

The younger son of Colonel Sir Thomas Salt, DSO, George Salt was a very popular officer. A Dartmouth entrant of September 1921, Salt joined the Submarine Service in 1929. By 1931 he was serving in China with *Oswald*. It was towards the end of his service on the China Station that he and four other young naval officers had the *Tai Mo Shan*, a small ketch, built to their own design. In 1933 they decided to sail *Tai Mo Shan* from Hong Kong to England. Noted for his cheerfulness in the grimmest of circumstances, George Salt was the ideal companion for such a long passage.

Another personality who took part in the venture as a junior officer was Captain Robert Ryder, VC, a hero of the famous raid on St Nazaire. Captain Ryder: 'George Salt was a most popular young officer. He was liked and admired by his seniors and those under him. At first sight one would think he was rather irresponsible, but knowing him as I did I realized that behind all the pranks and joking there was a conscientious and very reliable personality. Frequently sailing rather close to the wind, he was a past master at getting out of scrapes. If one was in trouble it was always comforting if George was involved too. He was high spirited, full of adventure, enterprising, and great fun.' Lieutenant-Commander Salt left a widow and young daughter and son.*

The *Enrico Toti* has the distinction of being the only Italian submarine to sink one of HM Submarines. On 23 September 1940 the *Rainbow* (Lieutenant-Commander L.P. Moore) sailed Alexandria for a patrol off Calabria. The battle that took place when *Rainbow* encountered *Toti* was a memorable one. What follows is an account by Giovanni Cunsolo, *Toti*'s first lieutenant. Intended for public consumption, it was written within days of the battle.

---

* Captain J.F.T.G. Salt was CO of the destroyer *Sheffield* when she was sunk by an Exocet missile in the 1982 Falklands war.

*15 October 1940.* An Italian submarine is in passage for an assigned area in the Ionian Sea. She is one of the *Balilla* class, a type not very modern but distinguished by the name of our great hero who, although maimed in one leg, did not want to remain behind the front line.

It was a little after midnight on 14 October. The second detail is on watch. On the bridge with the captain is the officer on watch and a look-out. The captain is Lieutenant-Commander Bandino Bandini. The submarine is proceeding on the surface with the conning tower hatch open and with vents ready to blow for a rapid dive. Dark low clouds hide the horizon as if a thick curtain of fog has been cleverly spread around the unit. The sea is calm and there is no wind. The moon diffuses a gloomy light across the clouds which hide it. Suddenly the officer on watch sights something dark to port which has a shape resembling that of the bow of a submarine. A few moments later he confirms the sighting with the cry: 'A submarine is heading towards us!'. It is the *Rainbow*. There is not a moment to lose. The captain immediately puts into action the plan agreed the previous night with the General Staff in the eventuality of a surface action at night. Through the speakers his voice, clear and resolute, reaches all corners of the ship: 'Surface battle stations'. The Chief ERA, always ready, calm, and smiling, executes a manoeuvre and the boat partly submerges. The Second Officer, the officer in charge of the weapons, the machine-gun crew, and those in charge of the gun, hurry to their posts, climbing up the central ladder like squirrels.

Hard to port! Bow on the enemy! The *Toti* turns rapidly as the signal from the navigator, at the tiller-indicator, is implemented by the helmsman observing the pointer on the assiometer from inside the submarine. Now the two units race towards each other, bow to bow, with the distance reducing rapidly. Aware of the manoeuvre the enemy opens fire with his gun. The shells pass over the top of our unit, or go hissing at the sides. The *Toti* responds with hellish fire from the machine-gun and the rifles, which according to a previously established plan have been placed on their relative supports on the deck ready for use. A real hail of fire raged against the adversary, which had a gun positioned on the conning tower. The officer in charge of the weapons was really splendid in this phase and, together with the Second Officer, was a shining example to the men.

The enemy fire is slower. It then ceases completely. Is their gun damaged, or is it injury to personnel? Who knows! Anyway, the captain, who is standing on the bridge seat so as to get a better understanding of the situation, at once takes advantage of the circumstances to execute the manoeuvre in his mind.

The enemy advances at full speed and, taking advantage of a moment of silence from *Toti*'s machine-gun, crosses the stern of *Toti*'s course at a distance of about 4 metres and fires at point- blank range, from high to low, shots which could have been fatal to our unit. There was, however, a slight delay in the firing and the submarine was hit only a grazing blow, receiving light damage to the casing and to some items of no importance. Immediately after this the *Toti* slackens speed, approaches to port and moves to a position of advantage. It is now our gun – by now loaded – which is aiming, whilst that of the enemy is out of range. Damnation! The shot does not explode! A furious sailor takes off a boot and throws it at the enemy, now so close that we can hear voices speaking English.

Tube number one ready for firing . . . Fire! The torpedo runs directly towards the target, but does not explode. The distance is not long enough to give the rpms necessary to release the striker. Under the menace of the gun and torpedo, the enemy attempts a rapid dive. But before he can dive completely, he is hit by two quick shots from our gun. Multi-coloured rockets burst from the black cloud which envelops the stricken boat. Evidently these were the rockets used by the submarine for identification signals to aircraft and were kept in the side of the conning tower ready for use.

The submarine sinks; then in a desperate attempt to escape she tries to surface stern-first, but soon after she disappears forever under the surface of the sea. The duel is over. A moment of silence hangs over the spectators in a salute between fighters. The entire crew of another submarine would never see light again, shut in a coffin of steel lying 3,000 metres at the bottom of the sea.

## Commander Bandino Bandini, *Toti*'s captain, further states

(1) the fight lasted approximately forty-five minutes (2) from what I know, it was the only fight in submarine history fought between two submarines on the surface as they approached each other (3) from *Toti*'s conning tower we could see (the night was lit by a full moon) the *Rainbow* men and I could see clearly the commander, who was giving orders, wearing white overalls. It is always alive within me the memory of the heroic behaviour of *Rainbow*'s crew. They fought valiantly to get success but the hard and merciless war laws prevented this. For that crew, disappeared in the depths of the sea, I keep an admired and mourned thought.

Commander Bandini had entered the Naval Academy of Livorno in 1922 as a cadet, leaving in 1927 when a midshipman. He joined submarines in 1935 and from then on, except for a short period as captain of the destroyer *Folgore*, served as a commanding officer in submarines. Bandini and his entire crew received an award for their success. Bandini retired from the Navy on 30 November 1949. He now lives in Milan. His first lieutenant, Captain Giovanni Cunsolo, also survived the war and has his home in Livorno.

Lieutenant-Commander Lewis Moore had entered Dartmouth in September 1921. In 1929 he joined the Submarine Service. His first submarine command (*H34*) was in 1936. Lieutenant-Commander Moore left a widow.

*

The original intention to complete six 'R' class submarines was not fulfilled. Two of the class, *Rupert* and *Royalist*, were cancelled. Of the four which eventually entered service (*Rainbow, Regulus, Regent, Rover*) only *Rover* survived the war.

*Regulus* was serving in Hong Kong at the outbreak of hostilities in Europe. She arrived on the Mediterranean scene in early August 1940. Commanded by Lieutenant-Commander F.B. Currie she sailed Alexandria on 18 November. Ordered to the Adriatic, she was to patrol south of latitude 42°N. *Regulus* was not heard of after leaving Alexandria. She was listed as overdue from 7 December. *Regulus* is thought to have been mined in the Straits of Otranto.

Frederick Currie, the younger son of a Cape Town doctor, had entered Dartmouth in 1922. He joined submarines in 1930 and took his Perisher course in 1937. That same year he was appointed captain of *Seahorse*, his first command.

With the loss of twenty-four submarines in 1940, the year became the most costly in men and submarines in the history of the Submarine Service. The curtain on this disastrous year was lowered in December with the loss of *Triton*.

By the time *Triton* was ordered to the Mediterranean she had already gained North Sea battle honours in the hands of Lieutenant-Commander Pizey. In due course command of *Triton* passed to Lieutenant G.C.I. St B.S. Watkins.

The loss of *Triton* is open to speculation. Watkins put to sea from Malta on 28 November for a patrol in the lower Adriatic and Straits of Otranto between 40°N and 42°N. At 0540 on 6 December an SOS from the Italian merchantman *Olimpia* was intercepted. *Olimpia*, steaming for Brindisi, gave her position as 41°06'N 18°39'E, thus making her the probable victim of *Triton*. The *Olimpia*'s escorts (the torpedo boats *Altair* and *Andromeda* and the 13th MAS Squadron) carried out an A/S hunt but there was nothing to suggest that this was successful.

Two other possibilities for *Triton*'s loss remain: mining and an attack by the torpedo boat *Clio*. Lieutenant (later Rear-Admiral) Pasquale Giliberto reports having attacked a submarine in *Triton*'s area on 18 December. It must be said that Giliberto's attack was unlikely to have been against *Triton* as Guy Watkins should have cleared the area by 13 December to arrive Malta on the 17th. During *Triton*'s patrol two signals relating to convoy movements were passed to her. No signals were received or expected from *Triton* during the course of the patrol. It would appear that *Triton* was sunk on or after 6 December. Although *Triton* had only been some three months away from the UK, she was due to refit after the patrol.

Within a week or so of *Triton*'s loss the year came to an end. Britain had survived a year of heartbreaking disasters. After France had given up the fight, Britain had fought on in Europe almost alone. The unwillingness of the French to take their fleet to British ports (or even to American ports for internment) when the defeat of France was imminent had done nothing to make the fight against Nazism any easier.

# 1941

Although commanded by Lieutenant G.V. Prowse at the time of her loss, *Snapper* had hardly ever been out of the care of Lieutenant-Commander W.D.A. King. When war broke out King was twenty-seven and serving in the Mediterranean, where he had been appointed to *Snapper* a few months previous. *Snapper* was ordered home. Throughout her first patrol in Home Waters, North Sea conditions were at their worse. At one stage of the patrol she was driven ashore on the Dutch coast. As if this was not enough, dawn was not far off. Furthermore, with a falling tide it looked as if *Snapper* would be stranded. But by good fortune the helm had been turned hard to port just a moment or so before *Snapper* had struck bottom. The helmsman's action had turned *Snapper*'s bows seawards. This, and Lieutenant-Commander King's six years' experience of submarines, saved the day. King was able to coax *Snapper* into deeper water, even after admitting to himself that she was done for.

In January 1941 *Snapper* was ready to resume patrols following a refit. Bill King was in hospital at the time, and so command was given to Lieutenant Geoffrey Prowse. When *Snapper* sailed the Clyde on the morning of 29 January it was for her thirteenth patrol, and Prowse's first as a commanding officer. *Snapper*, in company with *Tuna*, was escorted by the *La Capricieuse* as far as Bishop's Rock, where she arrived on the morning of the 31st. Routed through 47°48'N 6°39'W *Snapper* proceeded unescorted to her patrol area, which was the Bay of Biscay north of 46°43'N. She probably arrived at her billet on the night of 1/2 February. On 3 February Captain S2 instructed *Snapper*, in a signal of 1128, to remain in the Biscay northern zone, eastern sector, from 1200, 5 February, until 1200, 8 February. Captain S2 next signalled *Snapper* on 7 February when at 1233 he instructed her to vacate her billet after dark on 10 February. She was routed to pass within 30 miles of Ushant to rendezvous with the A/S yacht *Cutty Sark* in 275° Trevose Head seven miles at 0815 on 12 February. *Snapper* failed to complete the rendezvous and did not reply to a signal during the night of 12/13 February.

As *Snapper* had made no signals after parting company with the *La Capricieuse* on 31 January, in view of an incident which took place during her patrol it must be assumed that she was able to comply with her sailing orders, and had also responded to Captain S2's signals. On the night of 10/11 February the German minesweepers *M2*, *M13*, and *M25* were conducting an A/S sweep south-west of Ushant. At 0239, when in position 47°52.5'N 5°47'W, the group was attacked by a submarine which fired three or more torpedoes. The submarine was sighted. An attempt by the minesweepers to ram the submarine failed, although the gear of one of the sweepers caught the submarine and was carried away. The minesweeper force – the 2nd Flotilla – then carried out depth-charge attacks. Fifty-six depth-charges were released but no surface evidence emerged to indicate whether or not the submarine had been sunk or damaged, though it was felt that the submarine had not escaped unharmed. A strong sonar contact had been tracked, but this had suddenly faded and then ceased.

Flag Officer Submarines estimated *Snapper*'s likely position for 0800 on 11 February as 48°40'N 5°50'W. This would place her in the area of the incident at about the time that it had taken place. No other submarines were in the area at that time. That *Snapper* had not made any signals during her patrol might only serve to indicate that her patrol had provided no opportunity for an attack. The absence of any German reports of submarine attacks serves to support this. Further support for this premise is provided by the fact that a patrol by *Taku* in the same area from 16 to 31 January had also proved uneventful. To sum up: there is no concrete evidence as to how *Snapper* met her end, though there is a strong possibility that she was mortally damaged by the minesweepers.

Lieutenant Prowse, *Snapper*'s captain, was the only son of Captain Cecil Prowse, RN. He had entered Dartmouth in September 1925. Promoted lieutenant in November 1934, he then joined submarines. In May 1939 Geoffrey Prowse married, at Alexandria, the daughter of Vice Admiral Sir Geoffrey and Lady Leyton.

Launched on 7 June 1940 HM Submarine *Usk* had a tragically brief career. Lieutenant-Commander P.R. Ward was appointed as her first captain, but it was whilst under the command of Lieutenant G.P. Darling that she failed to return from a patrol off Tunisia.

*Usk* was ordered to the Mediterranean from the west of Scotland as soon as she had completed her work-up. The new submarine set a course for Malta with her crew keen to sample the Mediterranean sunshine. The 2,500 miles journey entailed bringing into use the reserve lubricating oil tank. Up until this point *Usk*'s passage had been normal; after the changeover to the reserve tank things started to go badly wrong. Engine trouble developed to such an extent that when *Usk* eventually arrived at Malta on 17 January, it was on five cylinders of one engine. Subsequent investigation revealed that a considerable quantity of carborundum dust had been put into the reserve tank. *Usk* had almost certainly been the target for sabotage.

On 19 April 1941 *Usk* sailed Malta for a patrol off the north-west coast of Sicily. *Usk*, under the command of Lieutenant Darling, had been assigned a billet in the area 38°00'N 12°00'E. At 2325 on the 25th the following signal was received from *Usk*:

IMMEDIATE. CDR SIO FROM HMS USK. INTENSE A/S ACTIVITY IN AREA. WITHDRAWING CAPE BON SUNDAY MORNING (27 APRIL). MS MESSAGE 752, 753 NOT RECEIVED. TOO 2100 25 APRIL 1941.

Owing to an operation (Salient) that was in progress, Lieutenant Darling was ordered on the 26th to remain north of 38°N until after 0001 27 April, by which time the ships of Salient would have passed through the Sicilian Channel, and then to move to 37°00'N 11°00'E. Darling was also informed that a destroyer had been observed at a large oil patch at 1130 on 24 April and that two explosions had been observed in the vicinity of 37°15'N 11°06'E, that is twelve miles 005° from Cape Bon Light. What happened to *Usk* after her move from the Marettimo area to Cape Bon, eighty miles south, will probably never be known, but it is thought that *Usk* was mined in the vicinity of Cape Bon some time after 25 April. Darling had spent a considerable time studying the available information of the area to which he had been been ordered and there seems no doubt that he was thoroughly conversant with all the known information.

*Usk* was recalled from patrol to arrive Malta at 0600, 3 May, being routed down the known channel from Cape Bon to Kelibia. When *Usk* failed to arrive Malta she was ordered at 1840, 3 May to report her position. No reply to this signal was received, nor to a signal of 2356, 5 May ordering her to report her position.

Between 10 and 14 April *Upholder* carried out several attacks on shipping north-east of Cape Bon. Furthermore, although *Ursula* passed through the dangerous area between Cape Bon and Kelibia on 25 March without detecting any mines (she observed that a convoy escort zigzagged all over the area as if no mines were present), an aircraft reported having seen a ship blown up approximately half-way down the eastern side of this area. *Unbeaten*, on passage from Gibraltar, operated off Capo Marettimo very soon after Lieutenant Darling should have left, and she sighted nothing. On the morning of 30 April *Unbeaten* heard what sounded like heavy depth-charging in the direction of Cape Bon, but by this time *Usk* may have already been sunk.

Adding weight to the favoured premise that *Usk* had been mined was the discovery two weeks later of a new minefield. During an operation (Tiger) a mine was cut by HMS *Gloucester* as she steamed west. Several more mines were cut by a force passing east on the night of 8/9 May, resulting in the loss of a ship. All the mines seem to have been cut on an approximate line of 040° from Cape Bon. It appears probable that this minefield was laid subsequent to *Usk* passing west on patrol and before her movement south on 27 April. This new minefield covered a previous known enemy convoy route between Cape Bon and Naples, running north-west of Marettimo, and it is possible that *Usk*, in order to miss no opportunity of attacking the enemy, retired southward down this route and was lost on this new minefield.

Lieutenant Godfrey Darling was first lieutenant of *Rover* for almost two years, that is up until June 1940. He then took his COQC. After a brief spell as captain of the training submarines *H44* and *H33*, Darling took passage to Malta where on 2 February 1941 he relieved Lieutenant-Commander Ward as captain of *Usk*. Godfrey Darling was described as an 'Outstanding personality with all those qualities that lead to . . . complete confidence [in him].'

Vickers, Sons, & Co. Ltd was the original 1867 name of this great shipbuilding and armaments firm. By the time the firm had begun constructing submarines for the Royal Navy it had become Vickers, Sons, & Maxim, Ltd. April 1911 saw the giant firm established as Vickers Ltd. But it was as Vickers-Armstrong Ltd that the firm launched *Undaunted* at Barrow on 20 August 1940.

*Undaunted* (Lieutenant J.L. Livesay) sailed Malta on 1 May for her first Mediterranean patrol. Her patrol area was off Tripoli. It was from Tripoli that the torpedo boats *Clio*, *Orione*, and *Pegaso* put to sea at ten o'clock on the morning of 12 May as escorts to the merchantmen *M. Odero* and *N. Odero*. The convoy was to make passage along the coast of Tripolitania until in the vicinity of Zuara. It would then set a course for Trapani, Sicily. At 1840 on the 12th, the convoy's escort aircraft signalled the presence of a submarine to seaward. The *Pegaso*, several miles from the convoy, left formation and made for the area indicated by the aircraft as harbouring a submarine. At 2028 *Pegaso* returned to the formation and signalled *Clio*, the escort leader, that she had attacked a submarine with depth-charges and had afterwards observed a large patch of oil on the surface.

The claim that *Pegaso* sank *Undaunted* has never been fully substantiated. Against such a likelihood is that *Undaunted* should not have been in the area at the time of the attack, but on her way back to Malta. In favour of a sinking by *Pegaso* is that a submarine was sighted by the escorting aircraft and that a large quantity of oil was seen on the surface after *Pegaso*'s attack. Mining off Tripoli is also a strong possibility for *Undaunted*'s loss.

The loss of *Umpire* (Lieutenant-Commander M.R.G. Wingfield) in July 1941 was totally unexpected. *Umpire* and *Una* were the only two 'U' class submarines not built by Vickers-Armstrong, both being launchings of the Royal Dockyard, Chatham. It was mid-July when Wingfield eased *Umpire* free of bustling Chatham. His destination was the Clyde, where *Umpire* was to commence trials and training with the 3rd Flotilla at Dunoon. After an overnight stop at Sheerness, *Umpire* joined the north-bound convoy EC4, though she was not a part of the convoy's escort group. The convoy made its way up the east coast without trouble until nearing Aldeburgh on the Suffolk coast. At this juncture a lone Heinkel attacked the leading ships. *Umpire* had never dived at sea before, so Wingfield and his first lieutenant, Peter Bannister, were pleased when the response of the crew was first class. When the German had finished his solo and unprofitable effort, *Umpire* returned to the surface.

Shortly before nightfall *Umpire*'s port engine became so trouble-some that it had to be shut down. Over a period of time this loss of power had a telling effect on *Umpire*'s performance and she began to lose touch with the convoy. A signal reporting the situation was sent to the convoy leader. The response was that a motor-launch was detailed to accompany *Umpire* until such time that *Umpire* could rejoin the convoy.

Although weather conditions were favourable, the night was dark and even at close quarters *Umpire*'s low profile was difficult to distin-guish. In the blackness of night the submarine's escorting motor-launch lost contact.

Some time around midnight convoy EC4 was due to meet and pass a south-bound convoy (FS44) in the same swept channel. The proce-dure for vessels meeting in a swept channelway was that each should keep to their starboard side of the channel, passing each other port to port. Wingfield, aware that a southbound convoy was due, was sur-prised to find that the two convoys must have passed starboard to starboard, as directly ahead of him he could make out the silhouettes of the south- bound convoy, which of course displayed no lights. A move to starboard by Wingfield, which in normal circumstances would have been the correct procedure, would have entailed *Umpire* crossing the path of the oncoming ships. Wingfield eased *Umpire* to port in the hope that the convoy would pass down his starboard side without incident. At a distance of about 200 yards the first half-dozen ships did precisely as Winfield had hoped. Then things began to go terribly wrong.

With binoculars Wingfield saw that a trawler, which he took to be one of the escorts, was on a collision course with *Umpire*. Whenever possible the accepted course of action for vessels in imminent danger of a head-on collision is to alter course to starboard with all speed. Unfortunately for Wingfield, 200 yards to starboard were several long straggling columns of blacked-out ships. The odds to starboard did not look good. Wingfield called for hard to port. The trawler, the *Peter Hendriks*, must have suddenly caught sight of movement ahead, for at the same time as *Umpire* made her move to port, the trawler's skipper instinctively made a rapid change of direction towards star-board.

With a grinding crash the *Peter Hendriks* struck *Umpire* some 25 feet aft of her starboard bow, tearing a large gaping hole in the process. *Umpire* at once plunged towards the bottom. At the moment of impact Lieutenant Bannister was in the wardroom with Lieutenant Edward Young. Bannister promptly ordered the shutting of all watertight doors. By good fortune *Umpire*'s bow-first descent caused the conning tower hatch to slam shut, and thus the control room was saved from being swamped.

*Umpire* lay silently on the seabed. The control room depth-gauge registered 60 feet. From the angle of the deck it was deduced that the bow was resting on the bottom at 80 feet. Both Bannister and Young knew that *Umpire* had been in full buoyancy at the time of the collision. Nevertheless they thought that an attempt should be made to raise *Umpire*, even though the likelihood of her regaining the surface was remote. All tanks were blown. The response from *Umpire* was negative. She would never leave the bottom. They would have to escape.

There were two groups of survivors. The larger group comprised twenty men and was to attempt an escape from the engine room hatch. Lieutenants Bannister and Young and two ratings, an engine room artificer and an able seaman, would try to clear *Umpire* by utilizing the conning tower as an escape chamber. It was estimated that the upper hatch was 45 feet from the surface. After the two officers and ratings had squeezed into the conning tower the lower lid was closed and flooding began. When flooding was completed Bannister pushed hard against the upper hatch cover. As the cover was heaved open a torrent of icy water entered the conning tower. Its occupants fought their way out and clear of the submarine. With lungs almost bursting, the escapers clawed their way towards the surface. Then quite suddenly they found they were taking in great gulps of fresh air and looking up at the stars twinkling their welcome.

Lieutenant Young counted two heads bobbing in the calm sea. By calling out he discovered that the ERA, who had been vomiting and very shaky on his feet, was nowhere to be seen. Sighting a number of vessels at no great distance, they called out in the hope of attracting attention. When this failed they began to swim towards the nearest vessels, which were scanning the sea with searchlights. After a few minutes Young turned expecting to see Bannister and the able seaman. He saw neither, though from time to time he could hear them shouting. Young was nearing exhaustion when he heard voices. The searchlight of a motor-launch then settled on him. A few minutes later he was hauled aboard the launch. Half an hour later he was told the crew in the engine room had begun their escape bid.

Under the guidance of Chief ERA George Killen all the engine room party cleared the submarine. Two of the party failed to survive. The last man to leave *Umpire* was Chief ERA Killen. The chief's conduct throughout the ordeal had been exemplary and he was later awarded the British Empire Medal, though the feeling was, and is, that his conduct merited a higher honour.

Of the four men on the bridge at the time of the collision (Lieutenant-Commander Wingfield, Lieutenant Tony Godden, and two lookouts), only Wingfield survived. The four had remained together as best they could but, as their strength gave out, first one lookout and then the other left the small circle. Mervyn Wingfield helped support Godden until Godden was too exhausted to remain afloat; releasing his hold on Wingfield, he disappeared. Wingfield lapsed into unconsciousness. On regaining his senses he found that he was aboard the trawler's boat.

It was only after his arrival at Yarmouth that Edward Young, an RNVR officer, learned that Lieutenant Bannister had not been saved with the able seaman, who when being rescued had thought that Bannister was close behind. Young went on to become one of the few RNVR officers to captain a submarine, serving with distinction in the Far East as captain of *Storm*.

Lieutenant-Commander Mervyn Wingfield was appointed captain of another submarine. It was whilst under Wingfield's command that *Taurus* became one of only two Royal Navy submarines to sink a Japanese submarine.

Within hours of the loss of *Umpire* in the North Sea, *Union* (Lieutenant R.M. Galloway) was attacked by an Italian torpedo boat in the Mediterranean and sunk with the loss of all hands. Robert Galloway sailed Malta at 0100, 14 July with orders to proceed to position 36°40'N 12°E and to be there by noon of the 15th to intercept a convoy previously reported as steaming to the north of Tripoli. Galloway, in the Mediterranean less than four months, was expected to make contact with the convoy on the 15th.

The 'U' class submarine *P33* (Lieutenant R.D. Whiteway-Wilkinson) was in an area through which the convoy was expected to pass. On the afternoon of the 15th, *P33* made contact with the convoy eight miles south of Punta Sciaccazza, Pantelleria. The convoy consisted of four Italian motor-vessels (*Barbarigo, Rialto, Sebastino, Andrea Gritti*) and the German steamer *Penier*. Escorting the merchantmen were the destroyers *Alpino, Fuciliere, Malocello*, and the torpedo boats *Procione, Orsa*, and *Pegaso*. Air cover added further strength. Out of this array of targets Lieutenant Whiteway-Wilkinson selected the *Barbarigo*, a vessel of 5,300 tons that had been working the seas since 1930. At about two o'clock *P33* emptied her tubes. *Barbarigo* was hit and sunk. The escorts were quickly on the offensive. *P33* was heavily depth-charged but managed to slink away.

If *Union* had joined in the attack on the convoy, she had scored no hits. Attacks, if any, on *Union* by the escorts were not heard by White-way-Wilkinson. When *Union* failed to reply to signals, and had not returned to Malta by 22 July, it was thought that she might have been mined off the Tunisian coast. In actual fact *Union* was sunk on 20 July after having unsuccessfully attacked, again off Pantelleria, a convoy heading north from Libya.

The convoy had sailed Tripoli at 0800, 17 July. Its destination was Trapani. Comprising the Italian tug *Ciclope* and the German tug *Max Berandt*, both towing the damaged German steamer *Menes*, the group had air-cover and the Italian torpedo boat *Circe* (Lieutenant-Commander Carlo Unger Di Lowemberg) in attendance. At 1100, 20 July, the group was at position 36°26'N 11°50'E. *Circe* was zigzag-ging ahead of the convoy, the speed of which was 5 knots. At 1118 the torpedo boat sighted the wake of a torpedo about 3,000 yards north-west of the convoy. *Circe* made for the point of firing.

A thin oily layer was observed on the surface. While the convoy altered course to starboard, *Circe* increased speed to 20 knots and attacked. From the vantage point of his bridge *Circe*'s captain caught sight of *Union*'s periscope: 'But the periscope was not out of the water,' reports Unger Di Lowemberg. 'I sighted it under us very well at a few metres, because the water was so limpid. Naturally I went there quickly to ram but it was already too deep.' At intervals, six depth-charges were launched, regulated to 165 and 330 feet.

At 1131 a large bubble of air was seen 600 yards off *Circe*'s bow. This was taken by *Circe*'s captain to mean that the submarine was expelling air from her tanks in a rapid dive following a depth-charge attack. *Circe* crossed the disturbance at speed and released three 100kg charges at very short intervals. At 1135 *Circe* broke off the attacks to rejoin the convoy which was closing a mined area. Around noon *Circe* left the convoy and returned to the area of her attacks. A large oil patch was seen. In concluding his report of the incident, *Circe*'s captain states, 'I can affirm that the enemy submarine was certainly hit by the depth-charges of this unit, and that she was sunk.'

The observer in the escort seaplane says of the incident: 'At 1142 I

saw to port of *Circe*'s course a large circular bubble of water with a
diameter of about 20 metres and at a distance of at least 150 metres
from the point where *Circe* had launched two depth-charges a few
moments before. I went immediately to the point where the bubble of
water had been and released a bomb from 200 metres. It exploded
exactly at the point wanted. After thirty seconds there came to the
surface a very large quantity of oil. The oil continued to rise to the
surface in great abundance and in a short time had reached a length
of 200 or 300 metres and a remarkable width. Observed the oil fuel
assuming greater and greater proportions and decided to return to
base.'

As no Allied submarine made an attack 25 miles SSW of Pantelleria on the day in question and under the circumstances described,
the submarine was probably *Union*. Regrettably *Union* had not survived long enough to have established a reputation of note. During
her first Mediterranean patrol she had sunk the Italian merchantman *Pietro Querini* south of Pantelleria on 22 June. Lieutenant
Robert Galloway was aged thirty and on his second patrol when lost.

Axis commitments in Tripolitania were heavily dependent on
supplies arriving at North African ports regularly and in reasonable
quantities. Allied submarines gave Axis shipping to Libya and
Tunisia a most difficult time. The Central Mediterranean position of
Malta meant that submarines of the 10th Flotilla were able to make
punishing attacks on convoys. Apart from its strategic position
Malta had a further value. Alexandria could offer only limited
facilities to submarines requiring major repairs or servicing. Malta
with its extensive workshops was able to undertake almost any submarine work. It therefore followed that part of the answer to reducing Allied submarine activity in the Mediterranean lay in the subju-
gation of Malta, which in effect meant unmerciful bombing and the
prevention of supplies reaching the island by sea. Any convoy or
blockade runner attempting to reach Malta was attacked incessantly
and, more often than not, sunk. For a time the only way in which
supplies could reach Malta was by submarine. One of the submarines used regularly as a supply ship to Malta was *Cachalot*.

During July 1941 materiel and personnel continued to arrive at
Malta in submarines from Alexandria, and by new submarines joining station from Gibraltar. At Alexandria *Cachalot* took on a cargo of
petrol and stores similar to a cargo she had taken to Malta the previous month. *Cachalot* (Lieutenant-Commander H.R.B. Newton)
sailed Alexandria on 9 July. Arriving at Malta on the 16th, she left on

the 26th with stores and personnel for Alexandria. *Cachalot* had been instructed to be on the look out for an escorted enemy tanker *en route* from Taranto to Benghazi. On the 29th a periscope sighting of a merchantman was made. The action which followed this sighting, and the sinking north of Benghazi of *Cachalot* in position 32°49'N 20°11'E, begins with a report by *Cachalot*'s captain.

'At sunset July 29, being anxious to obtain an accurate fix, I surfaced for star-sights. Weather conditions at the time were: Sea, calm and smooth; Visibility, clear overhead but patches of mist on the horizon. On surfacing I sighted the lights of a hospital ship (northbound, distance 5 miles) which had not been visible through the periscope. I dived immediately. I did not think *Cachalot* had been sighted as the submarine had been on the surface with low buoyancy for one minute only. As soon as the hospital ship was up sun of me, I surfaced to take sights and to ensure that my position was not being reported by W/T. I had read signals in Malta from the C-in-C Mediterranean saying that he was anxious for an Italian hospital ship to be captured and brought in for examination. Although I had on board an adequate boarding party I considered that the merchant ship was of greater importance and accordingly took no action against the hospital ship. The sighting of this ship had delayed me one hour.

'It was my intention, in view of the weather conditions and the silhouette of *Cachalot*, to avoid night action. Accordingly I adjusted my course to arrive on the enemy's track two hours ahead of him, then to turn and proceed on his course, charging and adjusting my position, so that on diving before dawn, I should be eight miles ahead of his estimated position and could attack him submerged. Having obtained an accurate fix I found it necessary, if I wished to conform to my plan, to proceed at 320 revs until I reached the enemy's line of advance. My expected time of arrival at this position was 0230. It was my practice to sleep on the bridge; so, expecting a long delay next day, I turned in, ordering that I was to be called in accordance with my standing orders and at 0200.

'At 0155 the officer on watch, Lieutenant R.D.C. Hart, RNVR, sounded the night alarm and called me, reporting a destroyer very close. I asked him if we were closing, and on his reply of "Yes" I ordered "Dive! Dive! Dive!" I personally did not sight the destroyer before *Cachalot* had dived. Despite my most particular orders that bow-caps were always to be shut on diving at night, a report was received in the control room, when *Cachalot* was passing 100 feet, that the bow-caps were open. The order was immediately given to shut them but, owing to another mistake in drill in the fore-ends, in that number five tube drain had been left open, the submarine was out of control, being approximately 1,400 gallons heavy in the WRT. The first lieutenant corrected the trim, and the order to grouper down* was given. A new rating was operating the grouper telegraph. On diving he had neglected to alter the telegraph to grouper up and had not been challenged by the motor room. When the order grouper down was given some thirty minutes after dive he, seeing that the telegraph had grouper down, made no alteration to it nor reported the matter. The foremost hydroplanes were then reported to be functioning incorrectly. Some time was spent in rectifying them and in the course of this it was found that the motors were still running grouper up. Finally, after fifteen minutes diving HMS *Cachalot* was in trim and under control, though the battery was very low and the fore hydroplanes still under suspicion, water having been found in the replenishing tank.

'During this dive I had time to interrogate the OOW. I ascertained that we were on the bow of the destroyer, running in, and that he had not sighted the merchant vessel. No HE had been reported by the HTD, either before diving or after. As the HTD, Leading Telegraphist Dunn, was most exceptionally efficient I concluded that the A/S set had broken down. I had served in the 1st Submarine Flotilla in peacetime and knew the peculiarities of the water in the Mediterranean in the summer, but had never before met a case in which the HE of a destroyer had not been detected at 400 yards. Subsequently it was proved that the A/S set was in order and that *Cachalot* must have been in a particularly bad patch of water.

'On surfacing, two courses of action seemed apparent. Firstly, to abandon the attack; secondly, to continue it by following down the enemy's course, hoping that with double his speed I could catch him up in sufficient time. I decided to continue the attack, taking especially into consideration the effect on morale and efficiency, as proved during this dive, a sinking would have. My own and the crew's efficiency had suffered considerably from three months' store running, always with passengers on board and with every prospect of so continuing for an indefinite period. The time being now approximately 0250, with only three hours till dawn and with a very low battery and inefficient fore planes, I decided to weave down the enemy's track for one hour only, at full speed, and if nothing had been sighted

* Grouper up: batteries in parallel for high speed. Grouper down: batteries in series for low speed and conserving battery power.

in that time, to abandon the action. Accordingly the best lookouts were closed up, the crew kept at diving stations, and *Cachalot* proceeded, weaving down the course in full buoyancy and at 340 revs. It appeared certain to me that the merchant ship was in station astern of the destroyer. Little change had taken place in weather conditions, visibility being slightly more patchy.

'After running for forty-five minutes the starboard lookout, Petty Officer Davies, reported an enemy tanker Green 120°. The OOW, Lieutenant Hart, the stern lookout, Chief Petty Officer G. Lanhan, and I sighted the ship immediately. It appeared to all of us to be a heavily-laden tanker with a highish poop, distance off track 1,500 yards. Being very favourably placed, I ordered: "Stand by the tubes. Hard to starboard." Within thirty seconds of sighting, the enemy made smoke and turned away. I concluded from the action that I had been sighted. I therefore turned to follow, closing up all lookouts temporarily to search for the escorting destroyer of which nothing had been heard nor seen. A further twenty minutes' chase ensued through the patches of mist, and I considered the escort to have lost track. Owing to the patchy visibility I decided that the enemy, if I was to keep him in sight, must be slowed down at the earliest moment; I ordered the gun's crew up and on the next occasion of sighting from the bridge, through binoculars, I ordered four rounds to be fired on a bearing of Green 30°, range 1,500 yards. I was on the quarter of the ship. After the fourth round the gun's crew sighted the target and fire was continued independently. The eleventh round appeared to be a hit. Dense clouds of smoke appeared amidships and the enemy appeared to be altering course towards us as if to ram. Having a considerable excess of speed on hand, still being on main engines, I commenced to turn away to counter this threat and place myself in a more favourable position. The enemy was lost to sight almost at once in the smoke. One minute later a destroyer appeared coming towards us at full speed and firing with all available guns. The maximum range was 800 yards.

'In anticipation of a similar situation I had given the gunnery officer, Sub-Lieutenant C.E.S. Beale, RN, orders that whenever gun action took place the whistle was to be kept on the bridge and the gun's crew were to be trained to consider a blast on the whistle to mean "Clear the gun with the greatest emergency". The whistle was blown but owing to the smallness of the gun tower and the insufficient training, a jam occurred in both the upper and lower hatches. I do not consider that the delay caused by this influenced in any way the loss of the submarine. By the time it was safe to commence diving the enemy destroyer was not more than 300 yards away. I alone was on the bridge. There did not appear to me to be the faintest possibility of being able to dive or to avoid being rammed. I gave the order to abandon ship, hoping that some four or five men would get up on deck in time. The enemy destroyer, realizing that I was not diving, and not wishing to collide with a larger ship at full buoyancy and at high speed, had gone full speed astern and finally rammed *Cachalot* in Z tank at about 4 knots. She then remained stopped 20 feet astern with all her main armament trained on *Cachalot*, whose own gun would not bear.

'The crew continued to abandon ship. The pressure hull had not been punctured but there is little doubt that Z tank was holed. Owing to the special service in which *Cachalot* was being employed an abnormal trim was in use. (Every after tank with the exception of Z, which contained approximately 300 gallons, being empty, including the after mine compensating tanks.) It was therefore certain that no trim could be obtained should it be possible to dive *Cachalot*.

'On returning to the bridge I decided with the first lieutenant to attempt a static dive, giving the appearance of having scuttled the ship, with key ratings only on board and hoping to get away on a main ballast trim. In the abandoning of the submarine all hatches had been opened, which greatly complicated this evolution. Whilst it was being organized the enemy opened fire with his entire anti-aircraft armament. Fortunately all shots went high, causing no casualties and only breaking the W/T insulators. It would have required several minutes to organize and carry out my scheme and I realized that the enemy was becoming very impatient and would never allow me so long. Accordingly, to avoid useless waste of life, I flashed at him my lamp to discourage another, heavier burst of fire. The after hatch was then shut to avoid anything floating on the surface, and main vents opened. HMS *Cachalot* sank bows first in 200 fathoms and no debris appeared on the surface. The conduct of the officers and men, in particular that of the first lieutenant, Lieutenant J.E.F. Dickson, RN, and the engineer-officer, Lieutenant (E) E.H. Player, DSC, RN, had been excellent throughout the abandonment of the ship and continued to be so in the water.

'All the passengers were non-swimmers and, with the exception of the Maltese steward Muscat, all were saved, even though it took about one and a half hours to complete the rescue. No explanation can be found as to how Muscat drowned. Leading Stoker Bull fitted him with a DSEA set. He and Chief Petty Officer Lanhun then saw

Muscat into the water, but he was never seen again.'

Leading Stoker C.S. Osmond recalls: 'I was outside the ERAs' mess helping to pass up shells. We had fired eleven rounds when the next thing I heard was a huge bang. Then came the order to abandon ship. I went up through the gun tower hatch. By the time I reached the casing a lot of the crew were already in the water. Stood on the casing was the Maltese steward. "I cannot swim," he said. I told him to come over with me as there was enough of us to hold him up, but he declined. As the boat was going down by the bows, I jumped over the side into the water and got away from the submarine. Turning on my back I saw Muscat make the sign of the cross. I never saw him with a DSEA set on. The steward and I got on very well together. He had told me that he was captains' steward in *Medway*, that he'd some leave to come and had been given permission to take passage with us to Malta. He had had his leave and was on his way back to Alexandria when we were sunk. The Italians put out a boat to pick up survivors but it was very small and by the time I reached it, it was full. I then swam over to the destroyer itself. I was helped out of the water by an Italian sailor who, to my surprise, spoke to me in perfect English: "Hard luck, mate," he said. "It may be our turn next." He told me had owned a cafe in Cardiff and that he was on a visit to his parents in Italy when war was declared and he had been called up in the Navy.'

Lieutenant-Commander Hugo Newton continues: 'Once on board the destroyer *Papa*, which had lowered boats, we were very well treated. The commanding officer sent for me and, on finding that one man was missing, kept me on the bridge with him while he carried out another search, finally asking my permission to give up. In conversation with him the following facts in connection with the loss of HMS *Cachalot* were established. Our presence was suspected, though I could not obtain definite proof that the hospital ship sighted on July 29 had reported us. *Cachalot* had never sighted a tanker or any other merchant ship. The "tanker" was in fact the destroyer *Papa* on her northward course. This error in identification was due to three causes (1) the certainty in my mind that after the first sighting at 0155 any ships subsequently sighted on that course must be southward (2) the possibility of a single destroyer sweeping up and down 70 miles off Benghazi all night had never entered my head (3) at the second sighting the enemy was only in sight thirty seconds. Had it been any longer it would have been apparent at once from the change of bearing that it was in fact a destroyer on an opposite course. The alteration of course and the smoke she had made had been coincidences and although we had known of her pesence since 0155, the first indication she had had of us was when two shells passed between her funnels. The smoke thought to be caused by a hit was in fact a smokescreen. When sighted and reported as a tanker, no signs of her funnels had been seen, though carefully looked for. Consequently smoke coming from amidships conformed with my idea that a hit had been scored on a tanker.'

The survivors were landed at Benghazi. They were then taken by road to Tripoli, where they boarded a merchantman for Taranto. From Taranto they were sent to a POW camp near Naples. After his liberation in 1943, Lieutenant-Commander Newton went on to command *Selene* against the Japanese.

The *Generale Achille Papa* had been in service twenty years at the time of her attack on *Cachalot*. At one time a destroyer – she had been reclassified as a torpedo boat – *Papa* was scuttled at La Spezia on 9 September 1943. Raised by the Germans, she was used as a blockship at Oneglia. Her captain, Lieutenant-Commander Gino Rosica, retired from the Navy in January 1948. He now lives at Pescara on Italy's Adriatic coast.

In December 1957 Mrs M.D. Wanklyn, widow of *Upholder*'s VC captain, launched a second HM Submarine *Cachalot*.

\*

The Sicily area had been relatively free of interference from the 10th Flotilla when Lieutenant Whiteway-Wilkinson's *P33* sailed Malta on 6 August to patrol Sicily. She had been on patrol for six days when a second 'U' class sailed Malta. *P32* (Lieutenant D.A.B. Abdy) had been ordered to form part of a submarine net with *P33* and Lieutenant A.R. Hezlet's *Unique*. The three submarines were under orders to intercept an Italian convoy bound for Libya. Lieutenant Whiteway-Wilkinson was to patrol west of Tripoli. Twelve miles north of Tripoli Lieutenant Hezlet was in a position eight miles from *P33* and twelve miles from *P32*.

At about noon on 18 August Lieutenant Abdy heard explosions to the west. The explosions seemed to occur at regular intervals, and it was clear that enemy vessels were dropping depth-charges. As some of the explosions appeared to be nearer than others it looked as if Italian A/S craft were carrying out a sweep off Tripoli just prior to the arrival of a convoy. Abdy thought it possible that the enemy were attacking *P33*. The Italians persisted with their depth-charging for two hours. When they finally departed Lieutenant Abdy had his asdic operator call *P33*. The echoing call was heard going out for some time, but there was no reply from *P33*. Nothing further was heard from her or of her.

Lieutenant Robert Whiteway-Wilkinson, DSC, had been first lieutenant of *H32* prior to the war. He then became *Truant*'s number one until August 1940 when he took his COQC. Two months later he was appointed captain of *H31*. When the new *P33* had been ordered to the Mediterranean, Lieutenant Whiteway-Wilkinson was her commanding officer.

Lieutenant David Abdy (*P32*) continued with his patrol. At 1530 that same afternoon, engine noises were heard. Abdy raised the periscope. He saw a convoy of five merchantmen under escort in the swept channel and heading for Tripoli Harbour. Abdy, too late to intercept the convoy outside the minefield, decided to run under the minefield, and so to attack in the swept channel. Diving to 60 feet Abdy ran at full speed under the field for ten minutes. Then, believing he was in the swept channel, he ordered *P32* to periscope depth. The submarine was just rising when on the port side forward she struck a mine. The explosion put out all lights. With the forward control room door jammed shut, *P32* took on a heavy list to port and sank towards the bottom. Though the tanks were blown and the hydroplanes set at hard to rise, *P32* struck the seabed with force enough to send the crew sprawling. The impact broke a bottle of hydrochloric acid, used for destroying secret papers. To prevent the vapour from the acid contaminating the air, Acting Petty Officer E.A. Kirk, the coxswain, put on DSEA and cleaned up the mess. Emergency lighting was switched on.

Abdy called for damage reports. The reports were not encouraging. The bow compartments were flooded completely. The whole forward part of the submarine had been destroyed, killing the eight crew forward. Work on raising *P32* was put in hand. This progressed until Abdy was certain that *P32* would never regain the surface, 70 feet above. DSEA were distributed. Rescue on the surface would depend on whether the convoy had seen or heard the explosion.

Ships of the convoy had certainly witnessed the explosion. On their port side a plume of water had leapt from the sea. As the explosion had occurred near the mined area, none of the escorts had left station to investigate. An escort aircraft, a Cant Z501, had also seen the explosion. Its observer sighted a 65 feet high column of water, obviously the result of an explosion. The Cant orbited the area of the sighting for about twenty minutes in an attempt to establish the nature of the disturbance. The plane then left for Tripoli, eight miles away.

Concerned that the jammed control room door might 'give' and release the water from the forward compartments, Lieutenant Abdy ordered the twenty-three survivors to the engine room, from which they would attempt their escape. When the whole crew was crammed into the engine room, Abdy could see that it was doubtful whether all of them would live long enough to escape from this one hatch. Clearly, whilst waiting for the pressure to build up for the escape, they would all be breathing the air of this single compartment. As *P32* had been dived for several hours prior to striking the mine, the carbon dioxide level must already had been at an advanced stage. If a delay should interrupt the usual procedure for escaping, the survivors might have to resort to using oxygen from their DSEA, with the possibility that they might survive only a short time before succumbing to the effects of oxygen poisoning. Whether the danger of oxygen poisoning was realized or not, Abdy proposed that some of the crew should return to the control room, flood that compartment, and follow this with an escape through the conning tower hatch. The jammed forward control room door presented a certain risk, but even one or two fewer in the engine room would increase the chances of a successful escape. When Abdy called for volunteers Petty Officer Coxswain Kirk and ERA W.H. Martin elected to try their luck with Abdy in an escape via the conning tower. After ensuring that his first lieutenant, Lieutenent R.L.S. Morris, understood the drill for a compartment escape Abdy and his two companions returned to the control room, securing the watertight door behind them.

Abdy went through the escape drill with Kirk and Martin: ERA Martin would be first through the hatch followed by Kirk. Abdy had opened the floodvalve to flood the compartment when Petty Officer Kirk discovered that the breathing bag of his DSEA had a small hole in it, probably caused when he was cleaning up the broken bottle of hydrochloric acid. Not wishing to disturb his companions, Kirk said nothing; instead, he opened his DSEA mouth-cock and shut the exhaust valve thus enabling him to draw in air through his nose and then to blow it into the bag. By doing this Kirk would be able to use the bag to help his ascent and, once on the surface, as a lifebelt.

As soon as the water had risen sufficiently to put the actual escape into practice Martin, Kirk, and Abdy climbed up into the conning tower. When Abdy thought the moment was right to open the upper hatch, ERA Martin climbed the conning tower ladder and began to release the clips. Kirk took a last few gulps of air. Then Martin opened the hatch cover and made for the surface. Kirk went up holding his breath. Unable to hold it all the way to the surface, he gulped several mouthfuls of water before he found himself gasping for air in the Mediterranean sunshine. Abdy had an easier time of it and before long he too was splashing around on the surface. Most regrettably Martin was seen to be dead. The ERA's body disappeared soon afterwards and was not seen again. Abdy thought that he and Kirk were five or more miles from Tripoli. They began to swim towards land. It was between 1630 and 1700 on a fine, warm and sunny afternoon.

After reporting the explosion the convoy's escort plane refuelled for the return flight to Pisida. Once airborne the Cant again flew over the area where it had witnessed the explosion. This time the crew saw 'Two survivors waving their arms and two corpses afloat in the water'. For some reason, perhaps fears of mines, the airmen considered the condition of the sea unsafe for a landing. They informed Tripoli of their observation and requested that a boat be sent to rescue the survivors. Soon afterwards a MAS' boat arrived and picked up Abdy and Kirk. When it was explained to the Italians that more of the crew were expected to escape, the MAS captain motored back over the area swum by Abdy and Kirk. The launch remained in the vicinity for some time but none of the engine room party appeared on the surface.

A fishing boat had followed the MAS boat to the position of *P32*, thus enabling the launch to return to Tripoli with the prisoners. Abdy and Kirk were taken to a hospital for examination. They were then separated and interrogated. When this phase had been completed the two survivors were taken to a POW transit camp at Tarhuna. There they met up with the *Cachalot* survivors. Lieutenant-Commander Abdy, he had been promoted during his captivity, and Petty Officer Kirk had been prisoners for eighteen months when they were selected for prisoner exchange. In March 1943 they were taken to Bari with other prisoners. At Bari they embarked on the Italian hospital ship *Gradisca* for the journey to the Turkish port of Mersin. Both eventually returned home. Surprisingly, of eight 'U' class sunk on patrol in the Mediterranean Abdy and Kirk were the only survivors.

There appears to be some doubt as to the origin of the mine which sank *P32*. It was assumed that *P32* had struck a mine in the Italian barrage, and just prior to her arriving in the swept channel. There is just a suspicion that this was not so. There were occasions when Allied aircraft laid mines in the swept channel leading to Tripoli. As Abdy believed that he was clear of the minefield when he started to raise *P32*, it might be that she struck an Allied mine in the swept channel.

David Abdy, who had celebrated his thirty-first birthday during the patrol, had joined submarines in January 1934. He retired from the Navy in November 1951. Chief Petty Officer Kirk left the Navy shortly after the war.

*

Lieutenant-Commander R.G. Mills had taken *Tetrarch* into battle almost before the builder's paint had finished drying. This was early 1940 and every submarine was desperately needed. By October Ronald Mills had taken *Tetrarch* to join the Mediterranean war. When Mills left *Tetrarch* in January 1941, his position was filled by Lieutenant-Commander R.M.T. Peacock and then, in July, by Lieutenant-Commander G.H. Greenway. George Greenway was captain of *Tetrarch* for only three months when she became due for a refit. Greenway, who had not been short of success during his brief time with *Tetrarch*, sailed Alexandria on 17 October 1941 for the UK, where she was to adjust complement as required before undergoing a refit in the United States. In accordance with normal practice the opportunity was taken to load *Tetrarch* with fuel, stores, and personnel for Malta. *Tetrarch* arrived at the beleaguered island on 24 October and sailed on the 26th with Gibraltar as her destination. She would have to pass through the minefield known as QBB65 by a route used by all submarines proceeding through the Sicilian Channel at that time.

*Monday 27th.* Between 1337 and 1500 a dived *Tetrarch* communicated with *P34** by SST. Courses, ranges, and bearings were interchanged. At 1400 *P34* was in position 37°27.5'N 12°35.5'E, 270° eight miles from Capo Granitola, Sicily. By range and bearing by SST, *Tetrarch*, at 1440, was in position 37°28.5'N 12°35.5'E; she must therefore have passed about 2½ miles to the northward, inshore of *P34* and only 5½ miles from Capo Granitola. This 1440 position is

---

* Later named *Ultimatum*.

the last known position of *Tetrarch*.

Captain S10's orders for *Tetrarch*'s passage to Gibraltar included a one-day patrol off Cavoli Island, Sardinia, during daylight of the 29th. It was the practice in the Mediterranean, where distances to patrol areas could be lengthy, that every advantage should be taken by submarines on passage to encounter the enemy. *Tetrarch*'s one-day patrol off Cavoli Island was in accordance with this principle. Flag Officer Commanding North Atlantic Station (FOCNAS) was informed that *Tetrarch* would pass 38°10'N 08°40'E, midway between Capo Spartivento and Galita Island, at 0001, 30 October, and was requested to route her on to Gibraltar. *Tetrarch*'s onward route was ordered in FOCNAS's signal of 1408, 25 October, and she was told to arrive at Gibraltar not later than 1800, 1 November, or else 0800, 2 November. The signal also ordered *Tetrarch* to report her position, course, and speed of advance as soon as practicable after crossing the meridian of 7°E. *Tetrarch* had not replied to this signal by 1908, 2 November. At 1236, 4 November, *Tetrarch* was ordered to report her position, course, and speed. This signal was not acknowledged. The most likely cause of *Tetrarch*'s loss was mining in the Sicilian Channel, probably within hours of her 1440 signal of 27 October.

Lieutenant-Commander Greenway was the eldest son of Lieutenant-Colonel T.H. Greenway. He had entered Dartmouth in May 1923. In early 1938 he qualified for command and was appointed captain of *H49*. At the outbreak of war George Greenway was serving a commission in General Service in the East Indies with the cruiser *Liverpool*.

\*

HM Submarine *Perseus* had joined the 1st Flotilla at Alexandria in early August 1940. From the tragic loss of this old war-horse and her crew in December 1941 came one of the most courageous submarine escapes of the war. Leading Stoker John Capes had served in Malta before the outbreak of war. During that period Leading Stoker Capes had been involved in a minor traffic accident involving a hired car and a horse-drawn cab. The affair had dragged on and it was not until September 1941 that John Capes, a submariner serving with the 1st Flotilla, was able to work his passage in a submarine carrying supplies to Malta to settle the matter. By November the affair had still not been resolved so Capes was ordered to return to Alexandria.

On 24 November Capes joined *Perseus* as a passenger for his return to Alexandria. *Perseus* (Lieutenant-Commander E.C.F. Nicolay) sailed Malta on the 26th. As part of her passage east she was to patrol to the east of Greece.

Dawn of 3 December found the submarine's crew at diving stations. Two torpedoes were fired and it is believed the target was hit. By the 6th *Perseus* was off the island of Cephalonia, largest of the Greek Ionian Islands. What took place on that Saturday night, and of events that followed, is related by John Capes.

'At 2200 on 6 December there was a terrific explosion, which I believe was due to the submarine striking a mine. All starboard buoyancy was lost and the submarine assumed an angle of 90°. She sank rapidly and touched bottom, bow-first, at a perpendicular angle. Finally she settled full length on the seabed, still retaining a starboard angle. At this time I was standing on the steering wheel in the after end. From some object I received a considerable blow on the posterior. Every pipeline and valve in the after ends rear compartment was broken. All lighting failed within fifteen seconds of the explosion. I found that of the crew of fifty-five, only five beside myself showed life after the submarine had finally settled. There were no

---

OPPOSITE:

(Top left)  Lieutenant-Commander C.B. Crouch, lost in *Thunderbolt*

(Top right)  Lieutenant J. Edgar, lost in *Thunderbolt*

(Centre)  When *Thetis* was salved and repaired, the two upper external bow tubes were removed making her more elegant than her bulbous-nosed sisters. Here she is returning to Alexandria after a successful patrol. Under her new name, *Thunderbolt*, all of her fifteen patrols were under the command of Lieutenant-Commander C.B. Crouch

(Bottom left)  Lieutenant Augusto Migliorini was commander of the corvette *Cicogna* when he sank the *Thunderbolt*

(Bottom right)  Survivors from a sunken ship in the Atlantic watched with trepidation as a submarine approached, thinking it might be a U-boat, but were delighted to find that it was the *Thunderbolt*. The *Torbay* probably held the record for the number of survivors rescued, when 180 soldiers were picked up from Crete after the German invasion

(*Top left*) One of the outstanding submarine captains of WWII, Commander J. W. Linton commanded *Pandora* with distinction but he will always be associated with the *Turbulent*. Like Lt-Cdr Wanklyn, Commander 'Tubby' Linton was sunk on his last patrol and, like Wanklyn, was awarded the VC.

(*Top right*) Lt R. G. Sampson DSC, lost in *Tigris*, 1943.

(*Centre*) *Turbulent* in Algiers on 12th February 1943, flying her Jolly Roger after a successful patrol off Sicily. A month later she fell victim to Italian anti-submarine craft off Bastia. The inboard boat is possibly *Tribune*.

(*Bottom*) Because of the Admiralty's inability to absorb the bitter lesson of not using large, unwieldy 'China' boats in the Mediterranean the *Regent* (Lt W. N. R. Knox) leaves Algiers for Malta in March 1943 for her second commission in dangerous waters. Three weeks later she had, in submariners' slang, 'batted'. *Trident* alongside has her periscopes and compass covered with steel helmets against bomb splinters.

(*Right*) The crew of HM Submarine *Splendid* at Algiers around Christmas 1942. Lt Ian McGeoch, seen with hands on guardrail, commanded with success until April 1943 when *Splendid* was sunk by the German destroyer *Hermes*. Eighteen of the crew pictured here failed to survive.

(*Centre right*) Germans attending to the survivors of the *Splendid* on the quarter deck of the German destroyer *Hermes*. The British crew were surprised at the youth of the German crew who, in turn, thought the British rather mature!

(*Bottom right*) The *Splendid* had the unpleasant distinction of being sunk by a British-built destroyer, the German *Hermes*, originally the Greek destroyer *Vasilev Georgios*, built by Yarrow at Scotstoun in 1938. The *Splendid* was forced to the surface after thirty-six depthcharges had made her uncontrollable and was met by a hail of gunfire. Eighteen of her crew were lost.

(*Top left*) Cdr J. H. Bromage, DSO, DSC, RN. This 1941 study was taken shortly before his appointment as captain of *Sahib*. (*Top right*) Leading Seaman A. G. E. Briard, DSM, the gunlayer of *Sahib*. This picture was taken on 4 November 1944, the day he returned home following his escape from captivity.

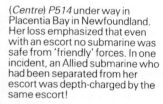

(*Centre*) *P514* under way in Placentia Bay in Newfoundland. Her loss emphasized that even with an escort no submarine was safe from 'friendly' forces. In one incident, an Allied submarine who had been separated from her escort was depth-charged by the same escort!

In this posed photo (the depth gauges only read four feet) Lt G. M Noll, the first lieutenant of the *Tribune* oversees the coxswain and second coxswain on the hydroplanes. Lt Noll, a very charming officer, was lost in command of *Untamed* in May 1943.

officers, petty officers, or sailors, but five other stokers all from the after end and rear compartments. I believe that all forward personnel must have been instantly killed by the explosion and subsequent flooding.

'Eventually two lamps of the secondary lighting were found and switched on. The DSEA equipment was taken from the lockers and donned. The submarine was then flooded by means of the underwater gun, water rising rapidly to about 3½ to 4 feet. The hatch trunking was then pulled down. A pipe was then disconnected from the high-pressure airline and the valve cracked slightly open to allow air to enter the after end compartment. It was felt that the compartment would be completely flooded without a chance of escape, since water was rising rapidly owing to punctures of the exterior hull. The DSEA hatch-clips were taken off and the trunking was then attached to the deck. All this was extremely difficult to accomplish, the starboard ship's side being used as a deck and the fact that a drum of oil and a drum of enamel had burst and greased the water, making it hard to keep the DSEA nose-clip on. At this point only one other stoker besides myself remained. The submarine settled itself on the bottom, taking a still steeper starboard angle. Pressure on the 'Z' tank first showed at 60 pounds but, on the submarine resettling, the gauge was on the FULL stop and showing 70 pounds or more. I attempted to leave with the DSEA torch, but owing to the blast of air coming through the DSEA canvas trunking and dislodging my nose-clip I was forced to return to the compartment. I refitted my nose-clip, etc., and re-entered the outside hatch. The jumping wire was not visible. I proceeded to the surface. The DSEA apron controlled speed very efficiently. The time taken to ascend was about one and a half minutes. A few feet from the surface I saw a mine, which I judged to be 10 to 15 feet down.

'On surfacing I used the torch to SOS towards land; there was no answer, neither was there any sign of other survivors in the sea. I judged the time taken to reach the surface from the time of the explosion was about one and a half hours. I began to swim towards shore, about five or six miles away, reaching it some six hours later at dawn. I was extremely weak, and fearful lest a sentry whom I had sighted on a hill a mile distant should see me. However, I safely reached a small cave. At 1000 two villagers entered the cave and seemed extremely surprised to find me there. After some discussion one left, returning later with dry clothes which I donned; thereupon the two villagers dug a shallow hole in which I lay until nightfall. At night I was removed by donkey to the village of Navrata, about two miles away. There, in the house of Gerasinos Vallianos, I remained for fourteen days. The villagers were generally suspicious of me, thinking me a German spy, but nevertheless I was well treated and a doctor was brought to treat me. In addition to Vallianos, the two Phokas brothers were very helpful.

'At the end of fourteen days I had sufficiently recovered to make a journey on foot of three miles to Hionata, escorted by Vallianos. At Hionata I remained four days in the house of a family who would not reveal their name. On the fourth day Italians came to the house in search of food. I was passed off as an invalid. I was then removed to the house of Nicolas Baldas where I remained two days. On my seventh day in Hionata I was taken by car to the house of Yianni Kritikos in Rosata, about twenty miles from Hionata. The same evening I journeyed on foot to Pharaklata and stayed there four days in the house of Yianni Pollatos. On December 24 Italians came to occupy the village and I left on foot.'

During the course of the next eighteen months John Capes was hidden and well-cared for in different villages at considerable risk to the Greeks. He was in hiding in Argostoli when the news he was hoping for finally arrived.

'On 25 May 1943 Cleo Pollatos came to the house and told me I would be leaving Cephalonia, since she understood arrangements had been made for my escape. On 26 May I was taken to the house of George Metaxas where an unknown Greek showed me a note from Major Parish. On 27 May I was taken by car to Poros with Cleo Pollatos, Metaxas and his wife, and a further unknown man. Outside Poros I was met by Gerasimos Kanthoros. I was introduced to Evangelatos and Captain Milton, who gave me details for my escape. On the early morning of the third day I was taken to an empty house overlooking the quay, where I remained until 30 May. On the morning of 30 May I was taken to a small bay, about three miles distant, by Vanthoros and his brother Nicholas. Sentries had been posted on the hill behind the bay, and at each end of it to warn the escapers if the Italians came. At 0930 an Italian MTB swept round the headland and proceeded close inshore and at slow speed in the direction of Argostoli. I and my companions hid in the rocks and were not observed. At 1000 a caique appeared and hoved-to close inshore. A boat was lowered in which I and Nicholas Vanthoros were taken to the caique. The caique then sailed and arrived safely at Kioste on 2 June 1943 after a three days voyage.'

John Capes was fortunate to have been in the after end when *Perseus* struck the mine – but from that point onwards it was Capes's iron resolve and courage which had saved his life. Remember that even after clearing *Perseus* Capes was still five or more miles from help. Throughout the ordeal Capes had kept a steady nerve. Had this inner toughness not been present, Capes would not have survived. John Capes returned home and in time assumed naval duties. Awarded the British Empire Medal, Chief Petty Officer Capes remained in the Navy until the 1950s.

Lieutenant-Commander Edward Nicolay, *Perseus*'s captain, was the only son of Colonel B.U. Nicolay. He had entered Osborne in September 1920 and had joined submarines as a sub-lieutenant eight years later. In 1935 he was appointed to his first command, *H33*. Later came *Seawolf*, *Otus*, and *Taku*. In December 1941 he was awarded the DSO for successful patrols in *Taku*. Lieutenant-Commander Nicolay left a widow.

In December news was received that *Scharnhorst, Gneisenau,* and *Prinz Eugen* were close to a possible breakout from Brest into the Atlantic. Eight submarines were ordered to the area in expectations of an attack on one or more of these ships. The breakout did not materialize. From this fruitless expedition Lieutenant Frank Gibbs' *H31* failed to return. Lieutenant Gibbs had sailed Falmouth for an area of patrol approximately 250° north of Cape Finisterre and was due to return on 24 December. After parting company with her escort near Wolf Rock on 19 December, nothing further was heard from or of *H31*. On the night of 24th/25th Gibbs was ordered to report his position. As stated, there was no answering signal. *H31*'s loss is believed to have been due to mining some time between 19 and 24 December.

Lieutenant Frank Gibbs had been third hand in *Rorqual* prior to the outbreak of war. For a brief spell he was first lieutenant of *H44* before taking up an identical appointment in *Unbeaten*. In early 1941 he stood by Lieutenant Abdy's *P32* at Barrow before taking his COQC in May. Gibbs had taken command of *H31* in August. The patrol from which he failed to return was to be his last as he was shortly to have taken up another appointment.

The odds against a submarine surviving after striking a mine are almost zero. Nevertheless when mined in the Skagerrak in December 1939 *Triumph* did just manage to survive, though her motto of We Shall Triumph looked rather shaky for a time.

*Triumph* arrived at Malta on 14 January 1941. She was in the hands of Commander (later Admiral Sir) W.J.W. Woods when she encountered the Italian submarine *Salpa* off Mersa Matruh on 27 June. Woods engaged *Salpha* with the gun until she was able to sink her by torpedo. At the time of her loss command of *Triumph* had changed and Lieutenant J.S. Huddart was captain. *Triumph* had sailed on her first war patrol on 24 August 1939. For her last patrol she put to sea from Alexandria on 26 December to patrol the Aegean. Huddart reported having landed a small party at Bireans on 30 December. He was then due to patrol 36° to 39°N 23° to 25°E and then to pick up a party of escapers on about 9 January 1942. *Triumph* failed to make the rendezvous and nothing further was heard of her.

Lieutenant John Huddart had entered Dartmouth in September 1924 and had joined the Submarine Service in 1934. Popular with officers and ratings alike, he had served in *Orpheus* and *L27*, both appointments as first lieutenant.

\*

For Britain the closing weeks of 1941 marked the beginning of what many now consider to be possibly the worst six months of the whole war. British fortunes in all theatres were at their lowest ebb, with the situation in the Mediterranean so grave that on occasions it looked to be only a matter of time before the Axis Powers took control. The torpedoing of the carrier *Ark Royal* in November by *U81* had been a near fatal blow to Malta as it meant not only the loss of aircraft reinforcements for the island, but also that Force 'H'\* could no longer beat a passage through to Malta for vital convoys. The loss, also in November, of the battleship *Barham* in the Mediterranean and the sinking of the battleships *Repulse* and *Prince of Wales* by the Japanese in December, plus the damaging of the battleships *Valiant* and *Queen Elizabeth* at Alexandria by Italian frogmen in the same month, had caused considerable dismay. British naval resources in the Mediterranean were stretched to their limit and beyond. With Axis planes dominating the Mediterranean skies it seemed as if the Royal Navy would be overwhelmed by the enormity of its task.

---

\* This force was based at Gibraltar and comprised 2 battleships, 1 battle-cruiser, 2 cruisers, 1 aircraft carrier and 17 destroyers.

# 1942

In January the 10th Flotilla at Malta welcomed the following additions to its strength: *P35** (Lieutenant S.L.C. Maydon), *P36* (Lieutenant H.N. Edmonds), *P38* (Lieutenant R.J. Hemingway), *P39* (Lieutenant N. Marriott), and *Una* (Lieutenant D.S.R. Martin). In her first patrol from Malta *Una* was involved in an unhappy incident.

It was early February when Lieutenant Martin put to sea with *Una* to patrol the approaches to the Gulf of Taranto. On the afternoon of the 12th an Italian tanker was sighted. *Una* attacked with torpedoes. The ship was hit and soon in flames. At 1524 a signal from the burning tanker was received by the duty officer at the operations room of the HQ for Marittimo, Ionian, and Southern Adriatic. It told of the attack and gave the position as fifteen miles east of Punta Alice, near the Gulf of Taranto. At 1545 a second message from the tanker stated that the fire was serious and that help was needed urgently. The torpedo boat *Lince* was ordered to prepare for sea. In the meantime an aircraft was sent aloft to fly the area. Also the naval base at Crotone was ordered to help the tanker, and to make a search of the area. Crotone had intercepted the tanker's signals and was already taking measures.

The *Lince* and the tug *Atlante* sailed Taranto at 1800. At 2020 the torpedo boat *Circe*, south of Crotone and on a heading for the Gulf of Taranto with the merchantman *Bosforo*, was instructed to divert *Bosforo* to Crotone and proceed alone to carry out an A/S sweep between 39°10'N-39°30'N and 17°40'E-18°00'E.

At the southernmost extremity of *Circe*'s intended patrol area lurked HM Submarine *Tempest* (Lieutenant-Commander W.A.K.N. Cavaye). *Tempest* was a newcomer to the Mediterranean. She had sailed the UK on the morning of 1 January 1942 and had arrived at Malta in early February. On the night of 10 February she sailed Malta for the vicinity of the Gulf of Taranto. By late morning of the 11th she arrived at her patrol area. That afternoon the tanker *Lucania* was sighted. Lieutenant-Commander Cavaye was halfway through an attack on *Lucania* when he realized that his target was a tanker which had been granted a safe passage through the Mediterranean. This tanker was the one which Lieutenant Martin had torpedoed in error.

---

* Later named *Umbra*.

About forty-five minutes after *Tempest* had broken off her attack on the *Lucania* two loud explosions were heard. Cavaye went to periscope depth. He saw Lieutenant Martin's victim down at the bows with smoke and flames pouring from her. Cavaye did not know whether the tanker had been torpedoed or mined. At that point he decided to move to the southern end of his patrol area.

That evening *Tempest* received a signal from Captain S10 to the effect that the Italians had reported a submarine (*Una*) in a position very close to her own, and that the patrol must be considered very close to her own, and that the patrol must be considered compromised. On receipt of this signal Cavaye gave thought as to whether he should move south of his patrol area to charge batteries, returning to his billet next morning, or to remaing where he was. He decided to remain in the area. Proceeding on the surface, charging as he went, Cavaye set course towards the *Lucania*, a British built vessel of 1902 vintage. Cavaye closed sufficiently to observe searchlights around the tanker. It appeared that salvage or rescue was taking place. The batteries not being fully charged, Cavaye turned away. At 2315 the tanker sank. About four hours later (*Tempest* was then ten to twelve miles south-east of *Lucania*) Cavaye and his OOW, Sub-Lieutenant Michael Neel-Wall, sighted what they took to be a small destroyer. This was *Circe*.

*Circe*'s captain, Lieutenant-Commander Stefanino Palmas, had raced at 20 knots towards his area of search. He entered the area at 0015, the 13th. Reducing speed to 14 knots he began a pre-arranged ECG* search pattern: this entailed running north to the limit of his zone, then east for a few minutes before heading south, then again east for a few minutes before heading south, then again east for a few minutes before heading south, then again east for a few minutes, and so on and so forth until his area had been thoroughly searched. By 0136 Lieutenant-Commander Palmas had reached the limit of his first run north. He then made an eastward track for nine minutes before turning south on a parallel course to that of his northern run. He arrived at the southernmost extent of his zone at 0302 and was on an eastward heading preparatory to moving north again when he was sighted by *Tempest*, which dived on sighting *Circe*. Palmas was still on an easterly heading when at 0315 a good ECG was registered at 1,770 yards. Palmas reports: '0332. Executed first launching of depth

* *Ecogoniometro* (Echo Protractor). This apparatus performed a function similar to asdic.

charges. Learned from the prisoners that this first discharge produced considerable damage'.

*Tempest* was at about 100 feet when the first depth-charges exploded. As she made her first run in to attack, *Circe* was heard on the hydrophones and by the crew. The accuracy of the attack surprised the submariners as they had thought that they had dived without being seen. And this had indeed been the case: the torpedo boat had not seen *Tempest* – but the sound of her klaxon had been heard by *Circe*'s hydrophone operator. *Circe*'s attack had had a certain measure of success: lights, clocks, and instruments had been wrecked; the fore planes had been damaged, as had a propeller shaft which had shifted in its housing and was making a loud knocking noise.

*Circe*'s attack of 0332 was to be her last for nearly four hours. There were several reasons for this (1) the sea had become very rough, which made the launching of depth-charges with precision something of a problem (2) as *Circe* had on deck only enough charges for two or three salvos it meant that a fresh supply would have to be brought up from the store below and then rolled along the deck to the launcher, a tricky operation in wheather growing worse by the minute (3) the blackness of the night was another factor to be considered as it made it extremely difficult to check for positive results of an attack: oil, air-bubbles, wreckage on the surface. All things considered, Stefanino Palmas decided that his wisest course would be to sit tight and await daylight. With the ECG maintaining a relentless hold on the submarine, and assisted by lighted marker buoys, Palmas prepared to await the dawn.

A report of this phase of the proceedings, as viewed from inside *Tempest*, states: 'The destroyer passed overhead with almost clockwork regularity. She appeared to be using two different kinds of electrical transmissions, both of which were clearly audible inside the submarine to those people who could hear rather high-pitched noises. The main transmission, which appeared from its regularity to be constant and automatic, was a high-pitched ping very much like ours; it naturally got much louder as the destroyer approached, and continued as the destroyer passed overhead and away on the other side. The other transmission, which was only heard occasionally and which appeared to be the prelude to the other run in, went on through the first noise and sounded exactly like our ordinary echo sounder.'

At 0630 the sky began to display signs of brightening, though a thick layer of cloud persisted. The sea was described as 'very agitated'. Lieutenant-Commander Palmas had not lost touch with *Tempest* for an instant. At 0716 he attacked for a second time with depth-charges. Ten minutes passed. When Palmas closed in on *Tempest* he noticed a patch of oil fuel. The oil was observed by those of *Circe*'s crew who had arrived on deck to view the action, thus satisfying Palmas that the oil patch was not a cloud shadow. When at 0755 two bluish-colour bubbles were noticed close to ˙*Circe*'s bow, Palmas ordered another attack. More oil was seen. *Circe* drew close enough to the oil for an attempt to be made to draw up a sample in a bucket, but the bucket was carried away. The air-bubbles and oil convinced Palmas that the submarine was gravely damaged; consequently at 0840 he informed Taranto of his observations, and also that he had only enough depth-charges for one further attack.

*Tempest*'s asdic had been out of service since 11 December, the day after sailing Malta. This had resulted from a seaman hanging an oilskin over an electric heater to dry. The oilskin had caught fire, causing the forward torpedo compartment to fill with smoke. One of the hands had rushed in and emptied the contents of a fire extinguisher over the asdic motor, thus inadvertently putting the motor out of use. With no asdic *Tempest* did not know how many vessels were attacking, nor of what type they were. But from propeller noises it was concluded that a destroyer was involved. When *Tempest* hydrophones were put out of action, by the second or third attack, it was possible to tell only that a vessel was overhead but not from which direction it had approached, nor where it was going. Though the damage caused by individual attacks was not crucial to survival, they did have a cumulative effect; most of the fittings welded directly to the pressure hull were fractured and came away. The hydroplanes appeared to be working satisfactorily but trimming became increasingly difficult and after the third attack trimming had to be done with main ballast. In one of the attacks an oil fuel bulkhead connection in the control room was damaged. Oil fuel poured into the compartment until Chief Stoker George Spowart managed to stem the flow. Though shut off, depth-gauges were affected and showed considerable discrepancies but, as far as could be made out, *Tempest* had been forced down to at least 400 feet for a long period.

The Italians were very capable. *Circe* dropped a total of forty-five depth-charges: 16 of 50kg and 29 of 100kg. Their depth settings were quite accurate and it was never possible for the submariners to say with certainty whether a charge had exploded either below *Tempest* or above. They all appeared to be very close. At 0917 Lieutenant-Commander Palmas launched his final attack. For *Tempest* this attack was far worse than any of the others. In fact it was decisive. The battery boards of No 3 Battery burst open and chlorine gas appeared in large quantities. Cavaye realized that the position was now hopeless and ordered the confidential books put into a weighted bag, ditched later by Sub-Lieutenant Neel-Wall who failed to survive the sinking. DSEA was issued.

At 0942 the Italians observed two enormous bubbles of air break surface about a thousand yards off. Three minutes later the submarine's stern was sighted.

Lieutenant-Commander Cavaye had waited until *Circe* had made a run without dropping depth-charges. The moment *Circe* had passed by, he ordered *Tempest* surfaced. Cavaye tried to gain control of *Tempest* at periscope depth, but damage and a high-breaking sea drastically affected her trim. With a signalman holding tightly on to his legs, Cavaye opened the conning tower hatch. He then scrambled out.

The Italians were watching events with interest. At 0949 they saw two ratings approach *Tempest*'s gun. *Circe* at once opened fire with her machine-gun, spraying the conning tower. She also opened fire with heavier armament. Within two minutes the men had abandoned their attempt to use the gun. *Circe* stopped firing.

*Tempest* was moving forward as the crew leapt into the sea. From a rating: 'The main line was opened, the fore planes were put hard to dive, and the motors were left at half speed grouped down. The crew abandoned through the conning tower. As soon as the destroyer saw the submarine she opened fire with machine-guns and a few rounds from her larger armament. When she realized that the submarine was being abandoned she ceased fire. By that time two casualties had occurred on the bridge. Everybody else got into the water but owing to the submarine still going ahead, the survivors were strung out in a long line and it was very hard to keep them together in the rough sea.'

The crew left the ship under the supervision of the first lieutenant, Lieutenant-Commander H.D. Bowker, RNR, and Lieutenant (E) R.W.B. Blatchford. When the last man had gone through the hatch, Bowker and Blatchford left, the latter opening the main auxiliary vents and Kingstons. As they went topside, water was seen splashing over No 3 Battery. Chlorine gas was prominent in the control room. There was still telemotor pressure. The vents were seen to open by Lieutenant M.V.H. Caplet, RNVR, who found himself right next to one as he floated in the water. Lieutenant Blatchford, last out of the submarine, encountered five ratings on the bridge, one of whom was Petty Officer Campbell, the torpedo gunner's mate. The TGM informed Blatchford that he had ignited the scuttling charges in the fore ends. Although they had appeared to be all right, the fore hydroplanes were seen to be badly damaged; the port hydroplane was bent into the hard to rise position. From the outside of the submarine an unsuccessful attempt was made to open the engine room hatch. One of *Tempest*'s officers observed: 'After the last man had left the submarine, it was still going ahead with a considerable proportion of the bow and conning tower above water. The destroyer followed her, there being no attempt, as far as I could see, to board. The destroyer then turned back and steamed along the line of survivors, picking them up in reverse order. The last people to be picked up were in the water about two hours. The crew had not shown the slightest signs of panic all through the attack, but they had got excited when it came to jumping into the sea. A number were lost through the misuse of their DSEA as lifebelts. Others were lost because they made no attempt to swim but merely floated and made no effort to keep together, and so drifted away in the heavy seas.'

For the Italians the sight of *Tempest* wallowing on the surface was a delight. As Stefanino Palmas so aptly put it: 'Six hours and thirty-one minutes of a hunt had been crowned with success!' *Circe* had rescued the submariners between 1010 and 1212. During this period the body of ERA Cameron was recovered. Lieutenant-Commander Palmas noted: 'The behaviour of the prisoners was calm and dignified, only one in the sea had shouted desperately when the torpedo boat approached to rescue. All were given refreshments and covering. Nothing of importance was reported, except the hint to the effect of the first attack. They also referred to the violence of the last depth-charge attack, but not to the precise damage.'

*Circe* lowered a small boat with an armed officer and several ratings. Their orders were to carry out an examination of *Tempest* and to make her ready for towing to Crotone, thirty miles away. At 1240 the boarding part returned. Because of the rough sea and the submarine's leeway, they had been unable to get aboard. Three hours passed. For some reason the scuttling charge had failed to detonate.

# NAVAL MESSAGE

To: ADMIRALTY 999        From: C IN C MEDITERRANEAN
   (R) F.O.S.
     S.1.
     V.A.MALTA
     S.10.

---

Much regret to report TEMPEST (now?) 3 days overdue has not replied to signals ordering her to report expected time of arrival and must be considered lost. TEMPEST left MALTA 10th February to establish patrol line by a.m. 12th February N.E. of CAPE COLONNE in GULF OF TARANTO with UNA and UPRIGHT, TEMPEST in centre. UNA and UPRIGHT both report hearing about 70 depth charges in their vicinity between 0355 and 0955 13th February. On 1(?)th. February she was ordered to patrol Southern Approaches to CORFU but while proceeding there was diverted to a position 5 miles west of LEVKAS ISLAND. She was ordered to leave patrol on 18th February and should have arrived ALEXANDRIA dawn 23rd February routed South of CRETE. As TEMPEST was always operating in deep water compromise of documents is unlikely. S.10 is requested to report casualties and documents carried.
Admiralty pass to F.O.S.

0823/28/2
NORMAL DISTRIBUTION

S.H.M.       T.O.R. 1015.      1.3.42.

By 1310 Palmas thought that *Tempest* might be about to sink, as her stern was completely submerged. He considered that the hatches had been left open or had been damaged by his attacks. As *Tempest* appeared about ready to sink, Palmas decided to speed the inevitable by using his guns. More than a dozen hits were registered without tangible result.

*1430. Tempest* remained stubbornly on the surface. As sea conditions were by now less violent Palmas again gave thought to the possibility of taking *Tempest* in tow. A boat was lowered and sent across to *Tempest*. Conditions were still far from ideal but by choosing a moment when *Tempest*'s bow dipped low, three men were able, at no small risk, to jump onto the starboard bow hydroplane, which was horizontal. Whilst two men set about preparing the tow, a petty officer mechanic made for the interior. On entering the control room via the conning tower, he observed that the forward watertight door was shut and that from behind it came the faint odour of gas. After examining as much of the submarine as he was able, he returned to the control room. Two flags were found.

At 1605 *Circe* manoeuvred to take up the tow from the whaler. Six minutes later *Tempest*, quite suddenly, began to sink stern-first. Then the bow disappeared vertically. The cable was quickly released. Those still aboard *Tempest* jumped into the sea. At 1640 *Circe* set course for Taranto. The survivors were treated very well by the Italians. Though at first they were kept together, the three officers were later accommodated in the wardroom, where they were provided with an excellent meal. On arrival at Taranto the twenty-four prisoners (thirty-nine of the sixty-three crew had died) were taken by motor coach to the naval hospital and given a dish of hot bread-and-milk. The officers were put into separate rooms. The next morning they were given an exchange of clothing before being taken to an office block for interrogation, which turned out to be a relaxed affair. After seventeen days at Taranto the survivors, less the three officers who were sent on to Bari, were taken by truck to Campo 85 at Tuturano near Brindisi. Before leaving Taranto the crew had attended the funeral of ERA Cameron, who was buried with full military honours.

It is to be regretted that Lieutenant-Commander William Cavaye was not among the survivors. The nephew of a general, Cavaye entered the Navy in 1924. After successfully completing his COQC in 1936, he was appointed captain of *Snapper* in the Mediterranean.

At the time of his loss Cavaye was aged thirty-five and had been in the Submarine Service for almost thirteen years.

As a sequel to the loss of *Tempest* we return to the sinking of the tanker *Lucania*. Once it was recognized that Lieutenant Martin had sunk the tanker he was immediately ordered to return from patrol. It transpired that Martin was running a temperature. He proved to be so ill that he had had to take to his bunk and allow his first lieutenant to return *Una* to harbour.

Later Martin was to take command of *Tuna*. In April 1943 Martin torpedoed and sank *U644* south-east of Jan Mayen Island. The following day he went after another U-boat, but this second target dived before he could attack. A week later Martin attacked *U302* at long range. Unfortunately for *Tuna* the torpedoes were sighted and *U302* dived to be sunk a year later by the Royal Navy frigate *Swale*.

\*

As the Germans and Italians continued to pour men and materials into the North African campaign, so their need for supplies assumed new dimensions. Targets for Allied submarines became more prolific, a fact of life of which submarine captains, not known to lack enthusiasm even in the most depressing circumstances, took full advantage. Though suffering severe losses, Royal Navy submarines at no time wholly released their stranglehold on Axis lines of communication. It is recognized that the disruption of vital supplies and reinforcements to the shores of Africa was crucial in enabling Montgomery's Eighth Army to achieve final victory over General Rommel's much-vaunted Afrika Korps.

Lieutenant P.R.H. Harrison (*P34*) sailed Malta on 14 February 1942 for a patrol off Kerkenah. Two days later he was ordered to form a patrol line to the north of Ras el Hamra with three other submarines: *P39* (Lieutenant N. Marriott), *Una* (Lieutenant D.S.R. Martin), and *P38* (Lieutenant R.J. Hemingway), the latter leaving two days later to intercept a convoy reportedly bound for Tripoli. All three submarines were in position by the morning of 18 February. On the 20th, intelligence having been received that the convoy had been delayed, the submarine patrol line was withdrawn 60 miles to seaward of its inshore position to rest for forty-eight hours.

On the evening of the 20th the convoy in question put to sea from Taranto. Comprising of four merchantmen the convoy was escorted by six warships of which only the *Circe* was equipped with ECG.

By the 23rd the three submarines had reformed the patrol line. During the early hours the convoy passed through the line. The oft-used deterrent depth-charging was heard by Lieutenant Martin, though he sighted nothing. Norman Marriott (*P39*) had a similar experience. Martin attacked the convoy but failed to score and was heavily counter-attacked for his troubles. At 0800 the destroyer *Antonio Pigafetta*, the escort leader, informed all units that submarines were in the area. As a consequence of this signal Lieutenant-Commander Palmas, fresh from his sinking of *Tempest* ten days earlier, called for enhanced vigilance from *Circe*'s lookouts and the ECG operators. At 1014, when in position 32°48'N 14°58'E, *Circe*'s ECG picked up a good contact 1,630 yards off the starboard bow. This was Lieutenant Hemingway's *P38*. *Pigafetta* ordered the convoy to change course. Having in mind to upset any move by Hemingway to attack, Palmas increased speed to 18 knots as he closed the object of contact. '*Periscopio!*'

The sighting was a little off *Circe*'s starboard bow and at a distance of about a thousand yards. Within seconds the periscope had been replaced by a large bubble of air as Hemingway ordered *P38* deeper. He had obviously seen *Circe* making speed towards him.

*1022.* Assisted by ECG signals, and the air-bubble, Palmas was able to order his depth-charges away with precision. The charges, regulated to 250 feet, exploded at a depth lower than *P38* as she was forced to the surface with her bow facing towards the convoy and well out of the sea. *Circe* moved to starboard in preparation for another attack but whilst executing this manoeuvre the destroyer *Antoniotto Usodimare* opened fire on *P38*, forcing Palmas to check his run. The escorting aircraft opened fire with its machine-gun, and dropped a bomb when *P38* began to submerge. At this stage the destroyer *Emanuele Passagno* intervened and with *Usodimare* began dropping depth-charges. Because of the activities taking place Palmas found it impossible to obtain any kind of bearing on *P38* and was obliged to ask the escort leader to order the two destroyers to break off their action and withdraw.

*1040.* With calm restored the ECG search for the submarine was continued. Suddenly, about 30° off *Circe*'s port quarter, *P38*'s bows appeared high out of the water with hydroplanes clearly at rise. Her bows remained suspended a few moments before crashing back into the sea to send her stern out of the water at a steep angle and with propellers turning wildly. *P38* then dived sharply from view and was not seen again. The *Passagno* returned to the attack with depth-charges.

*1044. Circe* informed *Passagno* that her presence disturbed the ECG search. When the offending destroyer had moved away *Circe* approached the area of *P38*'s disappearance. A large oil stain was easily distinguished.

*1050.* Obtaining an ECG contact on *P38*, Palmas observed a large air-bubble mixed with oil fuel. A few pieces of wood were seen. As was a small cloth bag. Three pieces of wood were recovered, one of which had linoleum attached. The other pieces appeared to be part of a cabinet. The small bag was found to contain three Union Flags and two black flags. The ECG showed that the submarine remained motionless. Bubbles and oil rising to the surface confirmed this lack of movement. Deciding that the evidence pointed beyond doubt to the submarine having been destroyed, after passing slowly over *P38* to honour the dead, Lieutenant-Commander Palmas rejoined the convoy.

What took place in *P38* on that Monday morning will of course never be known, but it would seem that apart from the attacks on her as she appeared briefly on the surface, *Circe*'s attack of 1022 had almost certainly damaged *P38*. Damage reports might have told Hemingway that *P38* was done for and that his best course would be to surface and save the crew. It might be that *P38* was in the process of surfacing when she became uncontrollable. Breaking surface wildly she then plunged a thousand feet to the bottom and broke up.

Of the escorts which attacked *P38* none survived the war. *Pigafetta* was scuttled at Fiume in September 1943. Raised by the Germans, she was sunk at Trieste by the RAF. The *Passagno* survived *P38* by only three months. On 29 May she was sunk by *Turbulent*. Within weeks of sinking, *P38 Circe* was also sunk. On 27 April she was in collision with the merchantman *Citta Di Tunisi* in the Gulf of Castella-mare. Lieutenant-Commander Stefanino Palmas did not survive the incident.

Lieutenant Rowland Hemingway, DSC, had served in *Tigris* and *Regent*. In April 1941 he had taken command of *H31*. His appointment to the new 'U' class *P38* dated from 15 September 1941. Bright, intelligent ('He was always very studious during his schooldays,' comments his brother), and of charming manner, there is every indication that once having got into his stride this fine young officer would have done exceptionally well in the Mediterranean. Lieutenant Hemingway left a widow.

Submarines at Malta were a high priority target for the Luftwaffe and the Regia Aeronautica so it was perhaps inevitable that submarines would sustain damage or even be sunk as a result of prolonged and fierce aerial assaults. The 'U' class *P39* was a bomb victim. How she came to be sunk is narrated by Chief ERA W.G. Wright. The account opens with events leading up to his joining *P39*:

'I arrived back in England on 28 January 1941 in HM Submarine *Pandora* following three years and ten months abroad. Part of that long commission was spent with *Otus* in China. On the outbreak of war I was in *Odin* to help bring her to England; but instead we went on patrols around the Sunda Strait, where we could hear Krakatoa rumbling underneath us, and around Batavia (now Jakarta), Java. In Batavia some German ships were hiding. When we went in close to see if they were still there, Dutch aircraft came out and harassed us. I bet they regretted that later. We then went on very long patrols around the Chegos group of islands looking for *Graf Spee* which was loose around that area. (In the First World War the *Emden* had used some of the remote islands in the Indian Ocean to coal ship.) With Mussolini becoming more belligerent, we went off to Malta. Not bad going for a boat we had started to bring home for scrapping. Fortunately I was sick on shore when *Odin* went to her war station. Soon after war was declared she was sunk off Taranto.

'During these first weeks I managed a Lewis gun in one corner of Fort Manoel. My instructions were to aim at the feet of parachute troops. When the destroyer *Jervis* paid a quick visit I was transported to Alexandria. In Alexandria I was drafted as Chief ERA to *Rorqual*. I made a couple of minelaying trips in her. Then someone must have thought that I had been away from home long enough. I was sent to *Pandora* to work my passage home. We sank two pseudo hospital ships on the way. As already stated, I arrived in England in January 1941.

'After a week or two's leave I was sent to Barrow-in-Furness to stand by the building of *P39*. Her captain, Lieutenant N. Marriott, greeted me when I arrived. I had to follow the construction of the boat, and report on progress daily. She had just been launched when I first saw her, so I had soon to go to Lincoln to see the building and trials of her Paxman engines, being built by Ruston Hornsby. After a small disagreement over the engine trials, I returned to Barrow for the main job. The systems and engines were now being put in at a bewildering rate. I kept a sketchbook with all of the pipe systems, telemotor operated diving valves, steering, hydroplanes, pumping and flooding sytems, and so forth, so that I would know the boat intimately. The crew arrived in Barrow in dribs and drabs and found lodgings in Barrow, as we all had. Most of them were HOs (Hostilities Only) and had had very hasty training. After some early squabbles we had a well trained crew. We finally completed our speed trials, noise trials, etc., and left for Gibraltar on 16 December 1941.

'Our arrival at Gibraltar – where the parent ship was HMS *Maidstone*, which was fairly comfortable – gave the HOs a chance to go ashore in 'foreign' parts. From Gibraltar we made a couple of patrols up the Spanish coast to the French Riviera. We fired no torpedoes but took the names of several merchant ships and noted their nationality and, where possible, the ports they were using. These patrols were on a strict war basis with emergency dives at night and a strict periscope watch, i.e., periscope up only for a few seconds for a quick look round then down for several minutes or more. These were our "breaking-in" patrols. We then left for Malta where the war was really dangerous. However, I felt that we now had a good crew and we would acquit ourselves with honour.

'Malta had quite a well organized base in an ancient but spacious infectious diseases hospital on Manoel Island, where one tied up to a catwalk floating on empty oil drums. We carried out two short patrols from Malta. In the first we could not get near a well-escorted convoy (we were probably spotted from the air). *P39* received sixty depth-charges in as many minutes. Around this time the Germans had brought an air fleet from Russia to deliver a knockout blow to Malta. Consequently air raids became very frequent. A boat could only enter harbour by surfacing and identifying itself. Then nets would be drawn back to allow entry. I should mention that a boat could not surface if a red flag was flying from the citadel to indicate that an air raid was in progress. Our second patrol was fruitless. On our return to Malta a single Messerschmitt fighter jumped us "out of the blue" as we were entering harbour on the surface. The red flag was down of course. The plane put a line of bullet holes along our casing. The pressure hull was not pierced, but the ventilation trunking under the casing from the conning tower to the fore-ends was punctured and this naturally had to be repaired.

'The boat was lying at a catwalk well down the creek when there was an air raid. I was ashore in the mess. I was told that *P39* had been hit. I rushed to the catwalk and down to the boat where I found the coxswain attending to a stoker who had had an artery cut in his wrist. Quite a lot of damage had been done in the fore-ends (1) where their supporting brackets had broken, pipes were hanging down from the deck-head like clothes-lines (2) the torpedo tubes were bent to such an extent that the tail was pulled off a torpedo during an attempt to withdraw it from its tube (3) there was a large dent in the side of the hull where, presumably, a near miss had exploded. I hurried through the boat noting what other damage had occurred. When I came to the control room I noted that the damage was slight, only lighter items such as gauge-glasses having been broken. As I advanced through the boat the damage became progressively worse, so that I arrived in the after end to find that the steering motor and pump, and the hydroplane motor and pump, were all broken off their robust mountings and pouring out their operating oils. The electrician then called that there was water in the battery tanks. I sent a young ERA to get the main ballast pump working in the engine room whilst I broke the lock on the battery tank suction valve and started to pump out the battery tank. If the sea-water had got up to the cell tops it would have produced chlorine gas, a submariner's nightmare. Then the electrician checked the "sea-water" and reported that it was acid and not sea-water. We immediately stopped pumping. I then jammed the battery suction valve shut and wired it shut. The pump must have been running on a battery with common acid between the cells because most of the cells in the battery had had their casings badly cracked and in some instances shattered. I then went back to the after end and hunted around for another near miss but could find no signs of one. Then it dawned on me that the boat had probably "whipped", thus causing the more serious damage at each end*. I wondered if a boat at a depth of 300 or 400 feet would whip like this from a near miss by a depth-charge.

'That afternoon the boat was towed over to the dockyard where our crew had the nasty job of taking the battery cells out of the boat. At the same time as the battery cells were being taken out of the boat the first lieutenant had to keep making adjustments to the trim because such a lot of weight was being taken out. When they finished removing the batteries the boat was quite high out of the water. After this no attempt was made to defend ourselves or deter aircraft with

* *Turbulent* once made such a pronounced whip during a depth-charge attack that an ERA was observed to be 'airborne' (Author).

our twin Lewis guns, so everyone was ordered into the shelters on receipt of an imminent air raid warning. Various signals were given as to where an air raid appeared to be heading (usually towards the dockyard or the various airfields on the island) and only when a raid was imminent on the dockyard did we shut all watertight doors, ventilation valves and hatches before fleeing to the shelters.

'At about 1800 on 26 March 1942 we came out of the shelters to find our boat in a very sorry state. A Stuka had planted a bomb right under the ERAs' mess. This had virtually broken *P39* in halves. Thanks to our systematic shutting of all watertight doors and hatches, she still floated. The two halves appeared to be attached by the keel.

I swam down the side of the boat and noticed that the crack, which was about fifteen inches wide at the top of the hull, progressively decreased as it went down towards the keel. However, I was afraid to go under the keel to see the attachment. The boat creaked and groaned from the slightest of waves. Had the batteries been in her I am certain that she would have sunk.

'Sitting on the casing with the CPO TI and the PO Telegraphist, and finding that *P39* did not sink, I gained courage. Ascertaining that there was about eighteen inches of headroom, and hence airspace, between the top of the pressure hull and sea-level, I went down into my mess and retrieved my photograph album containing photographs of my wife and daughter. The next day the CPO TI and the PO Telegraphist went into the boat through the crack. We had noticed some oil about. To reach their mess they had farther to go than I had been. They quickly came out plastered with black tarry oil fuel. The oil, possibly from the *Legion*, must have been swept in and then out, with the exception of the inner pocket of their mess, by what little wind and tide there was.

'There was always the fear that the ends would part company and sink; but by carefully opening the watertight doors one at a time, and using the bulkhead test cocks (shades of *Thetis*), we found that we could go down the after hatch and through to the forward engine room bulkhead, and from the forward hatch to the torpedo tubes and the forward crew-space bulkhead. We intended to cannibalize the boat for spare parts for other boats. However, instead of attracting bombs to the dockyard *P39* was carefully towed up the Grand Harbour to Kalkara and beached. We then spread fishing nets over her and cut down nearby trees (an act of vandalism in Malta where trees are scarce) and garnished the nets with branches. The local inhabitants were horrified, as well they might be. The Germans soon found out where we had gotten to and smashed up the boat and everything around her. I liked that boat and had had great aspirations for her, the poor thing. Her life had been shorter than the time taken to build her. Her captain and first lieutenant, Marriott and Owen, were both from the Merchant Navy, but they were good. I understand that Owen, a New Zealander, had a master's certificate in sail. Not many of them around.'

As stated by Chief ERA Wright, Lieutenant Norman Marriott was ex-Merchant Navy. Marriott was appointed a midshipman, RNR, in April 1930. In December 1936, as a sub-lieutenant RNR, he was appointed for nine months' training in submarines. Marriott was subsequently transferred to the Royal Navy as lieutenant. Before the war he served in *H32* and *Seahorse*. In 1941 he was awarded the DSC for 'Outstanding zeal, patience, and cheerfulness, as well as devotion to duty'.

The *P36* (Lieutenant H.N. Edmonds) arrived at Malta the same time as *P39*. She survived a little longer. Petty Officer Fred Mathews knew the submarine well and tells of his experience with her in the following account:

'HM Submarine *P36* had a very short life, leaving Portsmouth for Gibraltar in December 1941 on her first patrol, and being sunk by a Junkers 88 on 1 April 1942 at Malta. I was the stoker petty officer, joining her at a moment's notice before she left Portsmouth because her own SPO had reported sick. At Gibraltar we collected a couple of agents, one of whom I believe to be Peter Churchill, and put them both ashore near Monte Carlo. We then proceeded to join the famous 10th Flotilla at Malta.

'Our third patrol found us dived outside Taranto on the morning of 22 March 1942. We observed units of the Italian Navy putting to sea. These units included a battleship of the *Littorio* class, a number of cruisers, and several destroyers. This took place during the early hours of the morning. Changing course and poking our aerial just above the surface, we were able to signal Admiral Vian, who had put to sea from Alexandria with a large force to escort a convoy of supply ships through to Malta. *P36* then set about manoeuvring into position to deliver our own attack. Also in the area at the time were *Proteus* and *Upholder*, while farther south near the Messina Straits were *Unbeaten* and *Ultimatum*. When in position we fired our torpedoes, and then immediately dived deep to await the expected counterattack, which was not long in coming. Although we could not stay near the surface to observe results through the periscope, we did hear what we believed to be four hits by our torpedoes. We were then depth-charged incessantly. In six hours we recorded well in excess of two hundred charges. When we ventured to the surface after dark, various units were still sweeping the area with searchlights. Although we had reloaded our torpedo tubes, we did not hang around. Being badly shaken and in need of repair, we headed for Malta.

'The practice at Malta during this period was for submarines in harbour to remain dived during the day, with perhaps just one submarine allowed alongside for repairs or urgent maintenance to be carried out. On 1 April we went alongside.

'That afternoon we were attacked by the Luftwaffe. Several bombs were dropped quite close, with one particularly heavy one exploding right alongside and holing us. We began to sink. Being only a small boat of some 650 tons, this did not take very long. Contrary to orders from the captain to clear the boat, the coxswain and myself were drinking a couple of tots of Navy Rum in our mess, situated immediately aft of the forward torpedo space. When the heavy bomb exploded we both made it to the control room and up the conning tower in about ten seconds flat. Then we scrambled ashore.'

Every effort was made to keep *P36* afloat, even to the extent of strong wires being passed from the submarine to the piers of the Lazaretto arches to prevent her heeling over. But the effort was in vain. *P36* continued to settle lower in the water until there was a likelihood that her weight would cause the arches to collapse. To avoid two disasters taking place, the wires supporting *P36* were cut. It was just prior to this that Harry Edmonds, her captain, was heard to say that it was bad enough losing a submarine without being sued for destroying an ancient monument as well. Once the wires had been severed it was not long before *P36* rolled over and sank. Divers reported that *P36* lay on a narrow shelf 70 to 80 feet below the surface. It was quickly appreciated that salvage would entail a full-scale operation, not possible under the prevailing circumstance. And so *P36* was left until such time that a major salvage operation could be put in hand. Until that day arrived, she would continue to deposit on the surface a fine film of diesel oil from her fuel tanks and, on occasions, to send up a stream of air-bubbles.

Sixteen years had passed when in July 1958 work on raising the 1942 wreck got underway with Mr P.F. Flett, the senior salvage officer at Malta, in charge of the operation. To rise *P36* Peter Flett made use of two special lifting vessels. These vessels normally required the use of the ebb and flow of tides to assist their operation but with the absence of a tide in the Mediterranean, the raising of *P36* would be accomplished by the taking of and discharge of ballast. The actual work of lifting the wreck began in July with *P36* slung in a cradle of heavy wires between the lifting vessels. After some nineteen separate lifts, *P36* arrived on the surface on 7 August. She was then beached near the Royal Malta Yacht Club. Two weeks later she was towed out to sea and sunk for a second time.

Lieutenant Harry Edmonds had entered the Navy in January 1932. Promoted lieutenant in April 1936, he joined submarines. In May 1940 he was awarded the DSC for 'Daring and resource in the conduct of successful hazardous operations against the enemy' when serving in *Sunfish*.

Stoker Petty Officer Mathews continued in submarines. He now lives in Devon.

*

The heavy bombing of Malta on 1 April 1942 also accounted for the loss of *Pandora*. It had been May 1940 when *Pandora*, commanded at that time by Lieutenant-Commander John Linton, arrived at Alexandria from the Far East. By June she was off on her first Mediterranean patrol, to the Aegean. During the course of the next eleven months *Pandora* spent much of the time at sea; in fact she was at sea 251 days, 196 of which were spent patrolling. By the end of this period (May 1941) *Pandora* was in need of a refit. She was dispatched to Portsmouth, New Hampshire, in the United States. Shortly after this refit, command passed to Lieutenant R.L. Alexander.

On 31 March 1942 *Pandora* arrived at Malta with stores for the island and torpedoes for the Fleet Air Arm. She went first to Marsamxett Harbour to discharge oil. By dawn the following day, she was secured alongside at Hamilton Wharf. As it was urgent that her cargo be discharged, it was decided to risk unloading her during the bombing so that she would be free to leave that night to join the 1st Flotilla at Alexandria. During a heavy raid on the harbour area between 1430 and 1500 on 1 April, *Pandora* received two direct hits. In less than four minutes she had sunk with a loss of twenty-five crew. She was raised and then beached at Kalkara Creek. Some bodies were recovered. *Pandora* remained in being until 1957 when the wreck was sold for scrap. Towards the end of June workmen dismantling the submarine discovered the skeletons of two submariners in a small compartment where they had died fifteen years previously. At 0840 on 1 July 1957, the remains of the two crewmen were buried at sea four miles off Grand Harbour. Captain R.L. Alexander was present to read a short prayer before the flag-draped coffin was committed to the deep from the gun platform of HMS *Tudor*.

Despite the bombing and the acute shortage of supplies the 10th Flotilla continued to do battle. One of the Malta submarines which gained an enviable reputation for successful attacks was *Upholder* (Lieutenant-Commander M.D. Wanklyn). Wanklyn and *Upholder* were a deadly combination, even though captain and submarine were a team for only some fifteen months of actual patrols (24 January 1941 to 14 April 1942). A Dartmouth entrant of 1925, David Wanklyn was twenty-five and a lieutenant when in September 1932 he was appointed to his first submarine, *Oberon*. In August 1940 Wanklyn was given command of *Upholder*, then nearing completion at Barrow. By the winter of 1940 *Upholder* was ready for war. On Tuesday 10 December she sailed England's shores never to return. By 23 December *Upholder* was tying up at Gibraltar. After attending to minor defects she sailed the Rock on 3 January 1941 for passage to Malta, arriving on the 12th. Twelve days later Malta and *Upholder* parted company as she set forth on her first patrol, west of Tripoli. Four attacks were made, and several hits claimed. By 1 February *Upholder* was back at Malta.

On 18 May 1941 *Upholder* sailed Malta on her seventh patrol. It was after sunset on the 24th that Wanklyn carried out a difficult attack on the 18,000 ton liner *Conte Rosse*. Two torpedoes hit the liner. *Conte Rosse*, transporting troops to the desert war, sank with a loss of 2,300 lives. For this attack on a heavily escorted convoy, Lieutenant-Commander Wanklyn was awarded the Victoria Cross, the first submariner VC of the war.

*Upholder* put to sea from Malta on 6 April 1942 for what was intended to be her twenty-first and her final patrol before returning to the UK. David Wanklyn headed south towards the African coast, where he was to land a party of agents. After setting ashore the agents on the night of 9/10 April, Wanklyn set a course for a rendezvous the following night with *Unbeaten*. When the two submarines met at the rendezvous point, an Army officer who had been in charge of *Upholder*'s agents transferred to *Unbeaten* for passage to the UK. *Upholder* then continued with her patrol.

On 12 April *Upholder* was ordered to 33°N 14°E. She was to form part of a patrol line with *Urge* and *Thrasher* to intercept a convoy. It was not known if *Upholder* received this signal. A report by one of the submarines of the patrol line states that heavy depth-charging was heard on the afternoon of 14 April. This report conflicts with that of the Italian destroyer-escort *Pegaso* which claims the sinking of a submarine on the same afternoon but in position 34°47'N 15°55'E, a little farther to the north and east of Tripoli of the position where *Upholder* had been ordered to intercept the convoy. Lieutenant-Commander Francesco Acton, *Pegaso*'s captain, reports:

> On April 14 *Pegaso*, with other units, was escorting an important convoy from Naples to Tripoli. At 1547 the convoy was attacked by eight English torpedo planes. At 1615, in consequence of a sighting by an aircraft of the escort, I proceeded immediately, helped by a bearing from the ECG, to the area of contact for an attack against the submarine. After the launching of depth-charges the ECG contact ceased. I then resumed the A/S and A/C defence of the convoy. There had been no wreckage or survivors in the sea.

This swift and brief attack by Lieutenant-Commander Acton is believed to have been decisive. *Upholder* had almost certainly perished as a result of this attack.

If we accept that there is an element of doubt that *Upholder* and *Pegaso* did actually meet, then there must be an alternative cause of her loss. Apart from the probable sinking by *Pegaso*, two other possibilities need to be examined. It is possible that *Upholder* struck a mine in the area of Tripoli on the night of 11/12 April. In support of this is that a submarine was sighted on the evening of the 11th, two to three miles from the mine barrage. Also, no attacks had been made at any time on convoys or isolated units, which would have been out of character for Wanklyn. Another point is that nothing was heard from *Upholder* after the transferring of the Army officer to *Unbeaten*. Against this hypothesis is that German MTBs leaving Tripoli on the 12th to operate in the area of the submarine sighting of the previous evening did not sight any tell-tale oil patches nor anything else to suggest the sinking or damage of a submarine. A maritime reconnaissance plane also failed to observe anything that warranted closer investigation. Furthermore, ships and other vessels using Tripoli did not report anything that would connect with a submarine having been sunk or damaged. Lastly, Lieutenant-Commander Wanklyn was too experienced to have ended up on a mine barrage, especially a barrage of which the existence was known. The second supposition is that *Upholder* fell victim of an A/S hunt near Tripoli. This hypothesis is only supported by the fact that the submarines in the area adjacent to *Upholder* heard numerous underwater explosions on 14 April, as if a submarine were under attack. As no wreckage was sighted near the coast, these explosions might have been *Pegaso* attacking *Upholder* farther north.

The brief duration of *Pegaso*'s attack would tend to cast doubts of a successful outcome, considering that an A/S hunt quite often went on for hours. Nevertheless, the rapid appearance of an attacking unit at a submarine's position, followed by an accurate release of depth-charges either by design or chance, might have been all that was required to sink the submarine. That no wreckage, oil, or air-bubbles came to the surface when one might reasonably have expected some positive sign of a successful attack may have perhaps been because the submarine had not been destroyed, but damaged in a manner such as to have prevented her surfacing after *Pegaso* had departed. Neither *Pegaso* nor the aircraft had remained in the area to search for the submarine. Neither had they waited to witness possible signs on the surface, which might only have developed hours later from a damaged submarine.

Very much in favour of *Pegaso*'s sinking of *Upholder* are two certain facts: a submarine was sighted by the convoy's air escort, and shortly after this sighting an ECG contact was made by *Pegaso*. A submarine was in all probability in the vicinity of the convoy. But if this submarine was *Upholder* then she was about a hundred miles north of her assigned position. Perhaps Wanklyn had moved north, thereby encountering the convoy, on noticing the increased air and naval activity which had taken place in the approaches to Tripoli. Though none of the three hypotheses can be dismissed with absolute certainty, of the three it would seem that the attack by *Pegaso* offers the most reliable verdict.

Lieutenant-Commander Francesco Acton was of course unaware that he had sunk a submarine. It was not until much later that he learned that his attack had been successful. Acton came from a family which for generations had served in the Navy. Born at Castellamare di Stabia, Naples, on 24 August 1910, Acton was the son of Admiral Alfredo Acton. In 1926 he entered the Navy Academy of Livorno, graduating in 1930. Between 1934 and 1939 he served in submarines. In September 1941 he had been appointed to the *Pegaso*, remaining her captain until July 1942, two months after sinking *Upholder*. Decorated many times during his naval service, he retired from the Navy in January 1947. Captain Francesco Acton has his home in Naples.

Lieutenant-Commander David Wanklyn, VC, DSO, was eminently successful as a submarine captain. *Upholder*'s record of tonnage sunk and damaged was unsurpassed by any Royal Navy submarine.

\*

The heavy bombing and the mining of Malta's harbours and their approaches eventually made submarine operations from the island too hazardous. In April the decision was made to continue operations from Alexandria until such time as it was feasible for the 10th Flotilla to return. The first submarine to leave (*P31*) sailed on 26 April. She was followed by *Urge* on the 27th and *P34* on the 29th. *Una*'s departure on 4 May was followed on the 10th by that of *P35*, the last to leave. With the exception of *Urge*, the flotilla arrived safely at Alexandria.

Lieutenant-Commander E.P. Tomkinson, captain of *Urge*, was also in the top ten of 'submarine aces'. Tomkinson had been appointed to *Urge* when the craftsmen at Barrow were putting her together with skills acquired over many decades. In April 1941 *Urge* sailed for the Mediteranean. During the passage south Tomkinson took the opportunity to sink the tanker *Franco Martelli* as she made for Brest. After a brief stay at Gibraltar *Urge* sailed to join the 10th Flotilla.

It was mid-December 1941, when Tomkinson was presented with the rare chance to attack a battleship. *Urge* was patrolling south of Messina when on the 14th Tomkinson got a periscope view of the *Vittoria Veneto*. A torpedo hit the battleship and put her out of action for months. The light cruiser *Bande Nere* did not fare so well. On the morning of 1 April 1942 Tomkinson scored two torpedo hits on the cruiser. In three minutes she had disappeared beneath the sea.

As already stated the 10th Flotilla's exodus from Malta had begun on 26 April, with *Urge* leaving on the 27th. Expected at Alexandria on 6 May, she failed to arrive. Two possibilities exist for her loss (1) mining soon after sailing Malta (2) an attack off Libya by Fiat Falcon aircraft. At 0810 on 29 April a submarine used its gun to attack the motor vessel *San Giusto, en route* for Derna, in the neighbourhood of Ras el Hilal. The submarine was then attacked by the Italian Falcons. These aircraft were single-seater fighters but were often employed on sea patrols as fighter-bombers by the addition of underwing racks loaded with two 220-pound bombs. There is some cause for believing that the submarine in question was *Urge*. Given that she left Malta on 27 April, *Urge* could have been off Ras el Hilal by the morning of the 29th. *Thorn*, the nearest submarine to the area of the attack, was operating in the Gulf of Sirte, 200 miles to the west, and had not made an attack on the *San Giusto*. Also, no other submarines claim to have attacked the ship. This being so, there is a strong possibility that *Urge* had been the attacking submarine and in turn was attacked by one or more of the patrolling Falcons.

The loss of Lieutenant-Commander Tomkinson, DSO and Bar, was a harsh blow. The burly skipper of *Urge*, married with a young daughter, was a popular CO. With the exception of one patrol by Lieutenant Joe Martin, Tomkinson had commanded *Urge* in all eighteen of her patrols. Quite apart from special operations (the landing of agents, saboteurs, etc.,) Tomkinson had accounted for 26,000 tons of shipping sunk and a further 37,000 tons damaged. Lieutenant-Commander 'Tommo' Tomkinson was the Royal Navy tennis champion for several years.

From June 1941 to November 1942 submarines were used to ferry stores and personnel to Malta. Their use as supply ships probably saved the island from defeat. Several of the larger submarines were adapted to carry supplies. *Olympus* (Lieutenant-Commander H.D. Dymott) had been in regular service ferrying supplies from Gibraltar to Malta when she arrived at Malta on 5 May with stores. Once the supplies were safely ashore, passengers for the UK boarded *Olympus*. These passengers, six officers and thirty ratings, were mostly crew of the bombed submarines *P36*, *P39*, and *Pandora*. In all, when *Olympus* sailed Malta on the morning of 8 May 1942 she had about ninety-eight souls on board.

Though without a submarine of their own the crews of the bombed submarines had not been idle. They had helped to protect submarines against daylight air attacks by diving submarines to the bottom of the harbour, where they carried out maintenance work until nightfall. On surfacing after dark, they refuelled the submarines and worked on repairs that could not be undertaken when dived. Chief ERA W.G. Wright, of the bombed *P39*: 'When it was eventually realized that *P36*, *P39*, and *Pandora* had beached three well-trained crews it was decided to send us back to Barrow to take over boats nearing completion. On *Olympus* arriving one night, and being quickly unloaded, we prepared to go aboard. One of her three batteries had been removed to make room for stores. Into this battery space a layer of copper ingots had been placed over the floor. Also, scaffold tubing had been erected to form hammock rails. This was where the major part of the passengers would live. When *Olympus* attempted to carry out her trim dive, she would not dive. As daylight was approaching, she had hurriedly to put more ballast on board and dive. Remember, the Germans owned the air above Malta at that time. The next night *Olympus* surfaced, adjusted her trim, and then carried out a trim dive successfully. We embarked and settled in. At four o'clock in the morning, we set sail. I had seen the engineer-officer (EO) of *Olympus* and had arranged that I would keep a watch with his ERAs (on leaving harbour I took the first watch) as a refresher to my previous experience in "O" class submarines.

'On board *Olympus* were three submarine captains: Captain Dymott of *Olympus*, Captain Marriott of *P39*, and Captain Edmonds of *P36*. There were also three submarine first lieutenants, one of whom was from *Pandora* and had been wounded. Finally there were three Chief ERAs and at least two of every other grade of submariner, all experienced.

'At five o'clock in the morning, that is one hour after leaving harbour, there was a big bang followed by the boat shuddering. Being "bomb happy" from my experience in Malta, I thought that we were being bombed, and so rushed into the control room to see if I could be of any assistance in diving the boat; however, the Outside ERA*, "Geordie" Talbot, whose job it was to dive the boat, was already there. I went back into the engine room. The port engine room telegraph went to STOP. Sammy Plant, the other ERA with whom I was keeping my refresher watch, stopped the engine and then said, "Shall I shut it down for diving?" I replied "I would." The other engine was still going at half speed. It seemed to me that we were going round in a tight circle. Then the telegraph went to STOP. I stopped the engine and told the others to shut it off for diving. I then nipped into the control room to see what was happening – as we had heard from one of a number of stokers, coming from their mess aft, that it was abandon ship. When I got into the control room it was ankle-deep in water. The rolling action of the boat caused electrical flashes, and also caused the lights to go out and then on again. The lights continued to do this with increasing periods of darkness. The EO of *Olympus*, Bill Keeping I think his name was, was at the bottom of the control room ladder ushering men up the ladder. Shouting "Abandon ship", I rushed back into the engine room. I saw the stoker, at the far end of the engine room, on his way out.

'When I returned to the control room there was more water about.

---

* This rating is responsible for all machinery outside the engine room (Author).

Being "free surface" it made the rolling linger longer at the extremes, and it was this lingering that was causing the shortings and the blackouts to last longer. The EO was still ushering men up the control room ladder. There were about fifteen to go. I looked for'ard along the gangway. It appeared to me that the galley had been displaced into the gangway; water was pouring in alongside it. I also thought that I saw yellowy chlorine gas. With fifteen or more men in front of me, it seemed that I had not much time to get out; so I went for'ard to the gun tower hatch, that is towards the chlorine. At the bottom of the gun tower ladder I found young Lieutenant Bulmer of *P39* doing the same job as the EO of *Olympus*. He had apparently sent his last man up the ladder when I appeared. "Hello, Chief. Up you go," he said cheerfully. And up I went. I think some other men followed me up the gun tower ladder. When I got to the platform around the gun, a 4-inch Mk4 semi-automatic, an attempt had just been made to fire it. Unfortunately the sliding breech would not close because the brass cartridge of the fixed ammunition would not go home. Someone said: "Give us a hand here to pull the cartridge out." Three or four of us each put in one hand with the tips of our fingers over the rim of the cartridge, which would not go home by about three-eighths of an inch, and heaved. I nearly pulled off the tops of my fingers, but we pulled the cartridge out. Unfortunately as we had pulled the cartridge clean off the shell, which was now left jammed in the barrel, our efforts were to no avail.

'When I looked up to the conning tower I saw my captain (Marriott) signalling with a hand torch towards Malta, a dark shape on the horizon and over which an aeroplane with a faint yellow light was flying. Lieutenant Edmonds, the captain of *P36*, was on the gun platform. As the bows of the boat began to slip deeper into the sea he said to us: "Keep your submarine sweater on as long as you can. It will keep a layer of warm water next to your skin." We all took off our boots or shoes and placed them neatly in pairs on the platform before making our way down off from the saddle tank and into the sea. I swam about 20 yards and then turned to see *Olympus* take her last dive. I did feel lonely. (Later a consensus estimated that the time between the big bang and the sinking was about nine minutes. The survivors also estimated that about ninety men had got out of *Olympus*.) Most of the survivors were standing on the fore casing; others were on the gun platform and conning tower. It appears that the recognition flares attached to the periscope standards would not ignite and that the Aldis signalling lamp was out of action.

'At first there was a lot of shouting for the whereabouts of friends, and also a few shouts from non-swimmers calling for help. No doubt some people used up their energy helping others. Quite soon things quietened down and we were able to set out as a group for Malta where we expected help to come from, especially when daylight arrived and they could see us. I slowly discarded my clothing, with the exception of my short pants and belt. I had decided to keep my belt as at one point I had found a small piece of wood which I tucked under my belt to add to my buoyancy. After an hour or so the wood had chaffed my skin and so I had thrown it away, but I had kept my belt in the hope that a more comfortable item of buoyancy would come along.

'The number of swimmers got less as time went by. We saw a float-ing mine with a sort of whip aerial on it. One swimmer started to swim towards the mine but we all shouted at him and he came away from it. We saw the breakfast time raid on Malta. This was a regular feature but we had an irregular view of it. I thought that if one of the planes looked like pointing its nose down towards me as it made its way back home, I would dive under and put a few feet of water bet-ween me and its bullets. How long I would have been able to hold my breath in the state I was by then in, we had been swimming for two hours, I don't know; but if they saw us they disdained to shoot at any-one. We saw two or three air raids on Malta.

'At ten o'clock in the morning, by which time I was close to the shore, I saw an ambulance on a low cliff. I then saw two soldiers watching me from the beach below. When I got quite close to them I shouted "*Help*" and put my feet down. But there was no bottom. I came up spewing out water. I thought: "You fool . . . After all this you are going to drown yourself." I then swam breaststroke until I grounded on the sand, grazing my knees and elbows. As I got to my feet the soldiers came and put their arms under mine. I knew then that I was safe. I fainted. I came to trundling along in an ambulance. A soldier was rubbing me down. I looked down at myself and saw that I was blue. The soldier said: "Are you cold?" I thought, "You fool." I then fainted again. The next time I came to I was in a milit-ary hospital with six other survivors. It was an emergency hospital and appeared to be a large commandeered private house. We soon learned that two other survivors had gone straight to Lazaretto, so there was a total of nine survivors: three from *Olympus* and six from *P39*.

'A picket boat was dispatched to where oil and air were seen to be rising. A fix showed that *Olympus* was seven miles from Malta. During its journey the picket boat recovered one or two bodies that were found floating in lifebelts or DSEA. Apparently these men could not cover the distance before being overcome by cold and exhaustion. The Outside ERA of *Olympus*, Geordie Talbot, had stood up on reaching the shore, and had then fallen down dead. The temperature of the water had been 51° Fahrenheit, not bad for a quick dip but not for a long swim without training or grease.

'Within a few days we were on our way back to England in HMS *Welshman*, a 39-knot minelayer. She was disguised as a French *Simoom* class destroyer and flew a large French tricolour. She came out of Malta at night and went like a greyhound all night at 39 knots; then when daylight arrived she went down to 12 knots, the economical speed of a *Simoom* class destroyer, and lolled along the Vichy-held North African coast. This was most frightening to us submariners; lolling along at 12 knots in broad daylight, there could easily have been a boat down below preparing a torpedo. As soon as it was dark, it was up to 39 knots. We were soon in Gibraltar. Then on to Milford Haven. The kind and pleasant tea-ladies at Milford Haven's railway station gave us bagged sandwiches for our journey, which in our case was to Portsmouth and HMS *Dolphin*. Following our arrival at *Dolphin*, I was given a few days' leave during which Petty Officer Coxswain Selby, Petty Officer Electrician Seymore, and myself (we three being the senior survivors), had to go to Swiss Cottage, Northwood, to give Admiral Sir Max Horton our account of the loss of *Olympus*. The admiral asked if we wanted to carry on the fight in submarines. To this there was only one answer, and I think we all gave him the truthful answer "Yes".'

Lieutenant-Commander Herbert Dymott, the captain of *Olympus*, had joined the Navy in 1924 and the Submarine Service in 1929. Qualifying for command in 1935, he had been appointed captain of *H50*.

Chief ERA Wright later joined *Tactician* and fought against the Japanese. Chief ERA Wright, one of the pluckiest and resourceful of men, has made his home in Hampshire.

The name of *Olympus* was perpetuated in the Submarine Service when on 14 June 1961 the Royal Navy launched the patrol class submarine *Olympus*.

\*

The loss of a submarine by accident or error is an occasion of particular regret. In 1942 the Royal Navy lost two submarines by means other than enemy action. One of them was the *P514* (Lieutenant-Commander R.M.E. Pain). The *P514* was one of nine United States Navy submarines transferred to the Royal Navy under the Lend-Lease Agreement of 1941. She had been launched as the *R19* in January 1918. In June 1919 she arrived at Pearl Harbour to begin almost twelve years of training submariners and testing equipment. On 9 March 1942 she entered the service of His Majesty King George VI.

The *P514* spent her remaining days operating with the Royal Canadian Navy, largely in the capacity of a training vessel. A Ship's Movement Card of two months into her service with the Royal Canadian Navy states: 'Arriving Argentia May 27. Will divide time between B and C Groups till *L27* arrived in July. Then to B Group only.' On Canada's eastern seaboard, the fishing village of Argentia was where in August 1941 the Atlantic Charter was signed by Roosevelt and Churchill aboard ships off shore. And it was from Argentia that 32-year-old Lieutenant-Commander Richard Pain put to sea on the afternoon of 20 June. Escorted by the flower class corvette *Primrose*, *P514* had been routed along the 'safest inshore route' to St John's, Newfoundland, 65 miles to the north.

HMC Minesweeper *Georgian* lay alongside at St John's. Her log for 20 June shows that at 0815 hands were fell in to secure ship ready for sea. At 0945 the steering gear, telemotor, telegraphs, etc., were tested and found to be in order. By 1030 *Georgian* had slipped her lines; thirty minutes later she was passing the harbour entrance and making for a designated area to await the arrival of the six-ship convoy (CL43) she was to escort the 300 miles to Sydney, a small township of Cape Breton Island off Nova Scotia. The latest summary of U-boat dispositions had shown that two U-boats were in the vicinity of Cape Race. By 1430 that afternoon, convoy CL43 had arrived and the passage to Sydney was begun.

During the early hours of the 21st Lieutenant-Commander Stanley, RCN, *Georgian*'s captain, picked up unmistakable diesel HE whilst listening for hydrophone effect of the convoy. At the same time sound signals from another convoy (SC88) were heard. Convoy SC88, routed along a line approximately eight miles southward of that followed by *Georgian*'s convoy, was proceeding eastwards escorted by five RCN ships and was about ten miles to the north of its correct course. The two convoys and *P514* with *Primrose* had arrived

Lt E. P. Tomkinson with his wife who launched the *P31*, later to become the *Uproar*, a boat which survived two commissions in the Mediterranean. It was felt very strongly in many quarters that Lt-Cdr Tomkinson deserved a VC for his prowess in *Urge*.

Pictured during Far East duty with HM Submarine *Tactician* are two survivors of *Olympus*: to the left of Chief ERA W. G. Wright, DSM, MBE, is PO Syd Seymour.

*Thorn* in September 1941, prior to leaving for the Mediterranean. Four ships fell to her torpedoes including the Italian submarine *Medusa* but in August 1942 she in turn became a victim of the Italian destroyer *Papa* off Crete.

Despite her name, *Talisman*'s luck ran out in September 1942. A month before this she had been attacked by a British aircraft and had suffered extensive damage which may have contributed to her eventual loss. In September 1941 she had been damaged by a Sunderland aircraft and in an early patrol a Junkers 88 had wounded her Officer of the Watch. (*Inset*) Lt-Cdr M. Willmott lost in *Talisman*.

The Spare Crew postman waits as *Traveller* ties up in Beirut after a successful patrol where she sank a ship off Benghazi and recovered two agents from Crete.

(*Above*) *Utmost* comes home after a successful Mediterranean commission. Lt-Cdr R. D. Cayley, sitting on the bridge rail and his Yeoman of Signals, PO Moon, nearest the camera, both went down on the *P311*. His first lieutenant, in the very strange headgear, Lt Oxborrow, was washed overboard from *Unshaken* later when in the Gulf of Lyons with two lookouts in very rough weather. *Utmost* returned to the Mediterranean and was lost in November 1942.

(*Left*) Submarine hatches were sometimes bolted from the outside before going on patrol to prevent their lifting when the boat was under attack.

Lt-Cdr C. B. Crouch of *Thunderbolt* and Cdr R. D. Cayley of *P311* with his engineer officer, Lt J. H. Gordon, at Malta just before Operation Principal, the Chariot (Human Torpedo) attack on Italian naval bases. *P311* was lost on this operation and the other two participants, *Thunderbolt* and *Trooper* were lost later. *Traveller*, involved in reconnaissance duties for the operation, was lost, strengthening submarine officers' dislike of such work.

The new *P311* forms up behind her escort en route to Holy Loch for her working up period. Unusually, she flies a Jolly Roger, normally flown only by returning successful submarines, but sadly she never returned from her first patrol to fly it again or to take up the strange name allotted to her, *Tutankhamen*.

The *Trooper* (Lt R. P. Webb in temporary command) leaves Malta on 3rd February 1943 for a patrol off the Ionian islands. In the background the *Rorqual* nurses a damaged periscope, the result of shore battery fire when she was engaged in bombarding a railway bridge on the Italian mainland at the same time in position 46°33'N 53°40'W. Visibility was about 400 yards. Immediately after hearing SC88's sound signals, *Georgian* also picked up asdic transmissions. These were probably from an escort of SC88 as *P514*'s oscillator frequency was too low to have been picked up by *Georgian*. The minesweeper's log records what happened next on that early morning encounter:

0303. Observed hydrophone effect and transmissions (bearing 260°).
0305. Action stations.
0306. Hydrophone to starboard.
0306. Stopped engines.
0307. Full speed ahead. Stand by to ram.
0310. Rammed submarine.
0311. Half ahead.
0312. Slow ahead. Observed convoy to starboard.
0314. Full astern.
0320. Searching for survivors of submarine. East- and west-bound convoy scattered.
0410. Unable to locate submarine wreckage, or survivors.

Except for the corvette *Primrose*, no vessel in the area knew that *P514* was at sea. *Georgian* had therefore assumed that the darkened shape crossing her bows from starboard to port was an enemy, especially when the vessel made no recognition signal. Consequently the minesweeper had rammed the submarine midships on the port side, broadside on. An attempt to locate and possibly rescue survivors was put in hand. *Primrose*, after dropping a buoy, made a search. From St John's the duty ship *Dianthus* was dispatched and by mid-afternoon had joined *Primrose*. The two vessels failed to establish contact with the submarines by A/S or hull tapping and after dusk they returned to St John's. The body of a man dressed in British submariner's clothing had been sighted but could not be recovered.

Lack of information by the ships at sea as to what vessels they could expect to encounter was a contributing factor of the accident. A disposition report warning *Georgian* of the presence of a Royal Navy submarine failed to reach her. One of the recommendations of an inquiry into the circumstances surrounding *P154*'s loss was that up-to-date details of ship movements should be given to vessels prior to sailing, and that relevant information received too late to be included in sailing orders or the nightly situation report should be promulgated by special signal to those concerned. Considering the circumstances the action of *Georgian*'s captain would appear to have been appropriate to the occasion.

*Thorn* was another of the Mediterranean losses. Launched in March 1941, she was completed five months later and commissioned under the command of Lieutenant-Commander Robert Norfolk. By the end of September *Thorn* had completed her various trials in the Clyde area and had taken passage to Gibraltar. On 3 October she sailed Gibraltar for a work-up patrol whilst *en route* to Malta. Five days into the patrol a small merchantman in company with a destroyer was sighted. An attack was made but no hits claimed. *Thorn* put in at Malta on 10 October. Norfolk remained at Malta for three days and then sailed to join the 1st Flotilla. During the passage east Norfolk's sailing orders entailed patrolling off Cephalonia. This part of his orders was cancelled on the 20th and he was directed to form a patrol line with *Trusty* and *Truant*. An enemy convoy was expected on the Taranto-Benghazi route. When nothing materialized the three submarines resumed their respective patrols, with *Thorn* arriving at Alexandria on the 27th.

*Thorn* sailed harbour on 10 November for her second Mediterranean patrol. Passing through the Kaso Strait, on the 15th she landed stores and personnel on a small island of the Paros group. It was fortunate that later in the patrol a night attack by Norfolk on a fully lighted ship failed. The vessel turned out to be a Turkish Red Cross relief ship. On the 20th an unsuccessful attack was made on a small convoy. A pursuit to arrive at a position for a second attack was frustrated by aircraft. Norfolk's next action was a bombardment of a warehouse and a power-station at Voudia Bay. He then returned to the Paros group to pick up agents and twenty-one British troops, escapers from mainland Greece. By 27 November *Thorn* was back at Alexandria.

A collision in harbour on 5 December with the Admiralty cable ship *Bullfinch* necessitated *Thorn* having to spend time at Port Said for repairs. By 18 December *Thorn* was again at sea. Christmas Day found her off Cephalonia. Two days later Lieutenant-Commander Norfolk carried out a torpedo attack on a tanker. Scoring no hits he surfaced to bring his gun into play. Gun action continued until the tanker, after suffering two hits, managed to work up sufficient revs to escape. During the same patrol the 3,000-ton German (ex-Romanian) tanker *Campink* provided *Thorn* with her first real success. The *Campink* was encountered off Cape Dukato, Greece, as she made passage between Taranto and Patras. The *Campink* was sunk on 30 December with three torpedoes. As luck had not readily favoured *Thorn* during her three months in the Mediterranean, the sinking was all the more welcomed by her crew. *Thorn* returned to harbour on 5 January 1942.

Lieutenant-Commander Norfolk was soon back on patrol, this time to the Adriatic. He passed through the Straits of Otranto on 22 January to put ashore two agents at Port Sablonara on the Yugoslavian island of Mljet. This task was completed on the 22nd. The landing of a second party of agents in the area had to be postponed. The next day Norfolk made an unsuccessful gun and torpedo action on a 4,600 tons vessels, the *Ninnuccia*. During this action *Thorn* grounded, damaging her bows and putting her three starboard torpedo tubes out of action as a result. In a second torpedo attack the target was sunk. It was on this fourth patrol that Robert Norfolk sank a submarine. Norfolk sighted the Italian submarine *Medusa* off the naval base of Pola, Yugoslavia, and sent her to the bottom. After this attack of 30 January, Norfolk moved south and set ashore the second party of agents.

*Thorn*'s sixth patrol produced little activity. Her seventh and eighth patrols were also uneventful. It was from this last patrol that she returned on 21 June to the new base at Haifa in Israel, a result of Rommel's success in Egypt. And it was from Haifa that *Thorn* departed for her ninth and last patrol. She had been tied up alongside *Otus*, due to sail the next day for England. Last-minute letters were passed to *Otus* for posting on her arrival home. *Thorn*'s lines were cast off and she moved away to cries of good luck. It was Tuesday 21 July. *Thorn*'s orders assigned her to a billet off Tobruk. They also entailed a move north to Cape Matapan. On 29 July Norfolk requested permission to remain in the Tobruk area. He was instructed to remain off Tobruk until 6 August and then proceed to Cape Matapan. Nothing further was heard from *Thorn* after her request and she failed to arrive at Haifa on 11 August when due.

Four months had passed since Francesco Acton and *Pegaso* had sunk *Upholder*. During this period command of *Pegaso* had passed to Lieutenant Mario De Petris. On the afternoon of 6 August *Pegaso* sailed Benghazi as escort to the steamer *Istria*. At 1255 the following day, a Ju88 escort aircraft was seen to machine-gun an area of the sea's surface. *Pegaso* at once moved to investigate. Lieutenant De Petris saw quite clearly 'A periscope which left a wake visible at a considerable distance despite the ruffled surface of the sea'. For some reason the periscope remained visible even after the action of the Ju88. *Pegaso*'s crew saw the periscope move at speed to cut across the track of the convoy to arrive on its port side. The periscope remained exposed for about two minutes before disappearing from view. By this time the *Pegaso* was closing on the submarine fast. About four minutes after the action of the Ju88 a good contact was obtained off the bow at 1,500 yards. Between 1258 and 1347 *Pegaso* maintained a good contact and carried out seven attacks. After the seventh attack ECG contact was lost. But, significantly, oil fuel and air-bubbles appeared on the surface. Lieutenant De Petris stayed at the point of the suspected sinking for some time before leaving to take up escort of the *Istria*. In his report of the encounter De Petris states: 'The submarine manoeuvred in a lively manner to try and avoid the hunt but after the second bombardment her speed had reduced noticeably and shortly afterwards traces of oil were seen.' It had been after the sixth attack that De Petris gained the impression that the submarine was attempting to come to the surface. Oil and three notable bubbles of air apeared in succession on the surface. Lieutenant De Petris thought it worthwhile to mention that in his opinion there had been something the matter with the submarine because prior to the initial attack the periscope had been exposed too long to justify the situation. This is of interest as there is a slight suspicion that *Thorn* had earlier been attacked by Allied aircraft.

There can be no doubt that the submarine attacked had been *Thorn*. Lieutenant-Commander Norfolk had remained in the vicinity of Tobruk as on 3 August he had sunk the 5,300 ton motor vessel *Monviso* eight miles off Sidi Suetcher. On the night of 5/6 August he had moved northward. Then on the 7th he had encountered *Pegaso* thirty miles south-west of Gavdhos Island, off southern Crete.

Rear-Admiral Mario De Petris retired from the Navy in January 1969. He died in Turin on 23 April 1978.

Lieutenant-Commander Robert Norfolk was the son of Captain S.B. Norfolk, RN. He entered Dartmouth in May 1923. In May 1940 he had been awarded a DSO for 'Bravery and resolution in successful patrols'. Lieutenant-Commander Norfolk was thirty-three. He left a widow.

*

Towards the end of July 1942, air attacks on Malta had eased sufficiently to permit the resumption of submarine operations. Events in Russia had forced Hitler to transfer a large portion of his bomber force to the Russian Front, thus reducing the aircraft available for the air offensive on Malta. Though the easing of Axis air raids made the future seem a little brighter, Malta was still desperately short of basic necessities.

Launched by Cammell Laird in January 1940, *Talisman* was completed three months later and commissioned under Lieutenant-Commander Philip Francis. By July 1940 she was ready for action. Her first duty was to help maintain a continuous patrol off the French west coast with *Tigris* and *Cachalot*. *Tigris* carried out the first of these patrols. She was relieved by *Talisman* which landed two agents off Hourtin Lighthouse on 2 August, but otherwise had an uneventful patrol. These patrols became the Biscay Patrol in September and the three submarines became part of the 2nd Flotilla. On 12 September *Talisman*, *Utmost*, and *Upright* were lent to the 5th Flotilla to reinforce patrols in the English Channel during the period of threatened invasion. On 20 November *Talisman* entered her patrol area off St Nazaire with orders to try and capture a tunny fishing boat with the object of using this prize to observe the movements of U-boats in and out of Lorient. A prize crew had been embarked for this purpose. After an unsuccessful long-range attack on a tanker on 25 November, *Talisman* accomplished her special task and the tunny vessel *Le Clipper* of 40 tons was intercepted and sent to Plymouth in prize on 27 November.

In February 1941 *Talisman* was transferred to Halifax, Nova Scotia, with the 2nd Flotilla and the depot ship *Forth*. *Talisman* arrived at Halifax on 26 March. She remained in Canadian waters until 7 July 1941 when she sailed St John's for the Mediterranean. Towards the end of July *Talisman*, now commanded by Lieutenant-Commander Michael Willmott, sailed Gibraltar on passage for Alexandria, delivering 5,500 gallons of aviation spirit at Malta in the process. *Talisman* set forth on her first patrol from Alexandria on 21 August. She arrived back at Alexandria from her fifth and last patrol on 17 December. Preparations were then begun for her passage to Scotland for a refit.

It was the beginning of August 1942 when *Talisman*, still under the command of Michael Willmott, sailed Holy Loch for her return to the Mediterranean. During the passage she was attacked by Allied aircraft and damaged. This attack resulted in her having to spend a month at Gibraltar effecting repairs. On 10 September Willmott sailed Gibraltar to reinforce the 1st Flotilla. At 0845 on the 15th he reported the sighting of a U-boat to the northward of Cape Bougaroni. After this signal nothing further was heard from *Talisman*. The cause of her loss is not known. There is no evidence to substantiate the theory held at the time that *Talisman* had attacked a ship off Marittimo on the evening of 16 September and had been sunk in a counter-attack. The most likely cause of her loss is mining in the Sicilian Channel some time around 16/17 September.

Aged thirty-three, Lieutenant-Commander Michael Willmott was described as being 'An alert and resourceful officer'. He left a widow.

*Unique* was one of thirteen 'U' class submarines launched in 1940. She arrived at Malta in January 1941 under the command of Lieutenant A.F. Collett. One of Collett's first successes in the Mediterranean took place on 10 March whilst patrolling 60 miles south-east of the Kerkenna Islands; Collett met up with, and then quickly sank, the 2,500 ton merchant vessel *Fenicia*. When in August 1941 Collett was rested for a patrol, command of *Unique* was given temporarily to Lieutenant Arthur Hezlet. This was the patrol in which Lieutenant Hezlet had teamed with David Abdy's *P32* and Robert Whiteway-Wilkinson's *P33* to attack a convoy of four liners transporting troops from Italy to North Africa. Of the three submarines, only *Unique* had had any success against the convoy, her victim being the liner *Esperia*. At 10 o'clock on the morning of 20 August Lieutenant Hezlet attacked *Esperia* when eleven miles off the Libyan coast. With several of the escorts busy saving troops from the sea, Hezlet was able to retire without having to contend with a really determined counter-attack. It was soon after this patrol that *Unique* sailed to Scotland for a refit.

*Unique* was in the UK for a short period only, as by 7 October she had sailed Holy Loch under the command of Lieutenant R.E. Boddington for a return to the Mediterranean. After bidding farewell to her escort on 9 October, nothing further was heard of *Unique*. Lieutenant Boddington had been ordered to spend some time patrolling off northern Spain. *Ursula*, under similar orders, was in the same area as *Unique* when on 10 October she heard underwater explosions which led her to believe that *Unique* was under attack. Although the Germans made no claim as to having sunk a submarine in October, the failure of *Unique* to arrive in the Mediterranean would seem to point towards her having been sunk by the explosions of the 10th.

Lieutenant Robert Boddington had entered Dartmouth in January 1930. In August 1932 he joined submarines. Boddington had married in Singapore Cathedral in October 1939.

*Unbeaten* joined the 10th Flotilla in April 1941. Under Lieutenant-Commander E.A. Woodward and Lieutenant D.E.O. Watson she gave an active three years' service. *Unbeaten* was one of six Royal Navy submarines that sank two enemy submarines. Lieutenant-

Commander Woodward sighted the *U374* off Catania, Sardinia, at 0810 on 12 January 1942. Three minutes later he sent her to the bottom. On 17 March just three months after sinking *U374*, Woodward sank the Italian submarine *Guglielmotti* off Calabria. It was shortly after this patrol that *Unbeaten* came near to being bombed out of the war. The bombing incident took place on the same day that *Pandora* and *P36* were bombed at Malta. *Unbeaten*, her conning tower just awash, was submerged in Lazaretto Creek when a stick of bombs fell close enough to cause serious distortion to her torpedo tubes. Though still seaworthy *Unbeaten* could not fire torpedoes. This was of course a totally unsatisfactory state of affairs. Arrangements were thus made for *Unbeaten* to proceed to Gibraltar, after which she would steam for the UK. On 9 April *Unbeaten* put to sea on the first leg of her journey. The night of 10/11 April saw the meeting between Woodward and Wanklyn. When the Army officer had been transferred to *Unbeaten* the two submarines parted company.

In Scotland work on rectifying the distorted torpedo tubes was put in hand. On 23 October *Unbeaten*, now commanded by Lieutenant Donald Watson, sailed Holy Loch for patrol. On the evening of 2 November Watson signalled that he had completed a successful landing operation in the vicinity of Vigo, in northern Spain, on the previous evening. In view of this signal, Donald Watson was ordered to carry out a normal Biscay patrol. On the morning of 6 November *Unbeaten* was ordered to intercept an outward bound enemy supply ship attempting to breach the blockade. Watson sighted the vessel, which had already suffered attacks from aircraft, and reported its position. Lieutenant Watson was then ordered to rendezvous with a submarine which was escorting vessels off Bishop's Rock. *Unbeaten* failed to make the rendezvous. Though it is by no means certain, there is a possibility that *Unbeaten* was attacked and sunk in error by a Wellington aircraft of 172 Squadron.

'F' Freddie had taken off at 1745 on 10 November. The aircraft's report states:

At 0030 in position 46°55'N 08°43'W a message from base was received diverting 'F' to attack a submarine reported in position 46°13'N 07°40'W at 2120 and steering 040° true. Speed 15 knots. At 0129 in position 48°00'N 07°44'W aircraft set course for the estimated position of the submarine. At 0216 a S/E contact was obtained 8 miles 20° to port. Aircraft then homed to within 3 miles when severe S/E interference was encountered. A course of 180° true was held and at a ¾ mile range a submarine was sighted by L/E dead ahead.

The submarine was fully surfaced and on a course of 347° true. Speed 12-15 knots. 'F' was flying at 200 feet and at 0222, in position 46°50'N 06°51'W, made a steep dive to starboard down to 75 feet in an endeavour to drop the depth-charges ahead of the submarine. The full turn was not completed and the depth-charges were released at 75 feet at the moment when 'F' was approaching from a starboard beam, heading about 20 yards ahead of the U- boat. A column of water was observed to envelope the stern and it was estimated that at least two explosions straddled the submarine which made a 90° turn to port and remained stationary at right angles to its original course. Aircraft then made three further runs on the target and the rear gunner fired approximately 200 rounds. 'F' remained in area for 33 minutes after attack and then set course for base.

The Wellington reported landing at 0525, 11th. Whether the submarine had been *Unbeaten* was never fully established.

After the launching of *Ursula* in February 1938, two years went by before the next 'U' class submarine was sent down the slipway. This had been *Utmost*. In October 1940 *Utmost* was ordered to the Mediterranean. She was a week into the passage when HM Destroyer *Encounter* rammed her off Cape St Vincent in mistake for a U-boat. *Utmost* limped into Gibraltar for repairs. *Utmost* remained in the Mediteranean until January 1942. She then returned to Britain but after two months was back at Malta to continue the offensive under the command of Lieutenant J.W.D. Coombe. Unfortunately this second tour in Mediterranean waters did not last long.

*Utmost* sailed Malta on her last patrol on 17 November 1942 for a billet in the vicinity of Bizerta, Tunisia. At ten o'clock on the night of the 23rd Lieutenant Coombe signalled that he had fired his remaining torpedoes in a successful attack. He stated his position and intention of returning to Malta on a direct course. Evidence suggests that Coombe might not have taken a direct route to Malta, but instead had moved farther north to make his final signal. The successful attack referred to by Coombe had been against the Italian auxiliary cruiser *Barletta* at 1215 on the 23rd. *Utmost* had attacked *Barletta* with three torpedoes at a position three miles north of Cape Blanc. Although John Coombe had reported the attack successful, none of his torpedoes had scored a hit. The *Barletta* had counter-attacked, launching three depth-charges in the process. The destroyer-escort *Groppo* began an ECG search which was to last twenty hours and produce negative results.

At 1210 on the 25th the *Groppo* (Lieutenant-Commander

Beniamino Farina) was escorting a convoy to Bizerta. When in position 30°31'N 12°01'E, north-west of Marittimo, Farina's attention was drawn to the convoy's escorting aircraft, which had dropped a bomb some 4,000 yards from the convoy. Farina then received a SUBMARINE TO PORT signal from the aircraft. *Groppo* left station to make a search. An ECG contact was quickly established. Farina's first attack was repeated at speed. These attacks were judged to have sunk the submarine. *Groppo* resumed her position in the convoy. Two hours after Farina's attack, the aircraft dropped another bomb to signal the position of a submarine. At the same time the wake of a torpedo (*Utmost* had no torpedoes) was sighted by *Groppo*. Farina at once attacked with depth-charges. The contact was quickly lost. *Groppo* rejoined the formation. Beniamino Farina had the impression that between 1210 and 1530 he had attacked two different submarines and had sunk the first.

As is so often the case with submarine losses, how *Utmost* actually met her end is uncertain. It is known that the attack on the *Barletta* at 1215 on the 23rd was made by Lieutenant Coombe. The long search by *Groppo* following this attack may have driven him north. That night Coombe surfaced and transmitted the signal in whch he reported having sunk a ship with three torpedo hits (Coombe possibly confusing the three depth-charges dropped by *Barletta* as torpedo hits). His quickest route to Malta would have taken him across one or more minefields. An alternative was to move some 15 miles north of Cape Blanc and then east to skirt the mined area. This would have taken him to Marittimo, after which he would head south through the swept channel. It seems likely that Coombe took this second route and whilst moving eastward encountered *Groppo*. *Utmost* approaching the convoy when she had no torpedoes might have been for observation purposes for a transmission of its disposition. Against the supposition that John Coombe took the northern route for his return to Malta is that he went farther north than would appear necessary. Also, it must be remembered that Lieutenant Coombe gave the impression that a direct course to Malta was his intention.

On 25 May 1943, six months to the day of her having possibly sunk *Utmost*, the *Groppo* was sunk by aircraft at Messina. Rear-Admiral Beniamino Farina retired from the Navy in September 1968. He died in Turin on 23 April 1978.

Lieutenant John Coombe had entered Dartmouth in January 1929. He had joined the Submarine Service in 1937. Aged twenty-seven, Coombe left a widow.

*

The December 1941 attack at Alexandria on *Queen Elizabeth* and *Valiant* by Italian frogmen stung the British into making similar attacks on Italian shipping. One such attack was directed towards Taranto. As part of the preparations for the Taranto attack, *Traveller* (Lieutenant-Commander D. St Clair Ford) sailed Malta 28 November for a patrol which would take in a reconnaissance of the approaches to Taranto, known to be heavily protected by anti-ship and A/S mines. *Traveller* failed to answer signals after 8 December and did not return to harbour. The most likely cause of her loss was mining some time around 4 December. Lieutenant-Commander St Clair Ford was actually the captain of *Parthian*. For the patrol with *Traveller* he was a temporary replacement for Lieutenant Michael St John who had been taken ill.

Lieutenant-Commander Drummond St Clair Ford had been a well-known rugby player before the war, representing the Navy over several years. He had joined the Submarine Service in 1929. St Clair Ford left a widow.

The loss of *Traveller* made no difference to the planned attacks of the British chariots, as the two-man torpedo-like craft with their detachable warheads were called. The three 'T' class submarines *Thunderbolt*, *Trooper*, and *P311* had each been fitted with a large cylindrical container to enable them to transport the chariots on deck. Operation Principle involved chariot attacks on targets in Sardinian ports – Maddelena for *P311*'s chariots and Cagliari for *Thunderbolt*'s – and at Palermo in Sicily for *Trooper*'s chariots. First away from Malta was *P311* on 28 December. The next day *Trooper* and *Thunderbolt* left harbour. The outcome of Operation Principle was that the chariots from *Trooper* and *Thunderbolt* met with some success. For *P311* the operation was a disaster. At 0130 on 31 December, *P311* transmitted a signal in which she gave her position as 38°10'N 11°30'E, attributed as her position at 1830 the previous day. Nothing further was heard from her and she did not return to harbour. There is no evidence to suggest that her two chariots had been launched. It might be that *P311* had safely navigated the east coast of Sardinia only to be mined in the Straits of Bonifacio on or shortly after New Year's Day. Apart from *P311*'s crew, the ten skilled and adventurous chariot operators were also lost.

The captain of *P311* had been Commander Richard Cayley. Educated at Clifton College, Bristol, Cayley had entered the Navy in June 1925, and the Submarine Service five years later. His first command, August 1937, had been *Sunfish*. On 31 January 1941 he arrived at Malta by aircraft from Alexandria to take command of *Utmost*. With *Utmost* Cayley destroyed almost 70,000 tons of shipping, a feat which caused him to become known as 'Dead-Eye Dick'. In July 1941 he was awarded a DSO. On 5 May 1942 he was awarded a Bar to his DSO, and a week later a second Bar to his DSO. Cayley was promoted commander in June 1942 and appointed captain of *P311*. An accomplished harmonica player, Commander Cayley often appeared on stage at base concerts, a practice which led to him being known affectionately throughout the Service as 'Harmonica Dick'. An officer of great ability and courage, Richard Cayley was thirty-five at the time of his loss.

The 'S' class submarine *P222* (Lieutenant-Commander A.J. Mackenzie) was lost with all hands in December. She had sailed Gibraltar on 30 November for patrol off Naples. Expected at Algiers on 21 December, nothing was heard of her after 7 December. George Colvin (*Tigris*), patrolling in an adjacent area, heard heavy depth-charging on the evening of 12 December; it is believed that this depth-charging was Mackenzie suffering an attack which proved fatal. If *P222* had been under attack at this time, her assailant was probably the Italian escort-destroyer *Fortunale*.

The regular captain of *Fortunale* was Lieutenant (later Rear-Admiral) Alfredo D'Angelo. On 11 December Lieutenant D'Angelo was injured in an American air raid on Naples. Temporary command of *Fortunale* was given to Lieutenant Edoardo Manacorda. At 1300 on 12 December, *Fortunale* and the escort-destroyer *Ardito* sailed Naples with the merchantmen *Onestas* and *Castelverde*. The convoy was to make for Trapani where after a brief stop it would leave for Tunis. At 1522, by which time the convoy had crossed the Bay of Naples and was off Punta Campanella, a signal was received from Capri reporting a submarine sighting three miles to the west of the island. At 1734 and when six miles south of Punta Campanella, *Fortunale* sighted in the fading light of evening, but in good weather conditions, a submarine surfacing 3,500 yards off the bow. Whilst *Fortunale* made to attack, the *Ardito* ushered the merchantmen eastwards. *Fortunale* closed the submarine at speed. Diving did little to help the submarine evade her enemy, as shortly after the Italians established ECG contact and carried out an attack, to be quickly followed by two further attacks. After the third attack there were observed 'Columns of clear water about 15 metres high with a short distance between them, and at a few seconds interval'. ECG contact was resumed and Lieutenant Manacorda carried out a fourth attack. Contact was then lost.

It is probable that the submarine sighted to the west of Capri was Mackenzie's *P222*. Realizing that the convoy was going to pass east of Capri, Mackenzie manoeuvred to accomplish a surface interception after dusk. *P222* surfaced west of the convoy, which had then turned eastwards. The submarine was probably silhouetted against the lightest part of the horizon, the sun had set less than an hour before, when she was sighted by *Fortunale*. Thirty-one depth-charges had been launched. If signs that *P222* had been damaged or sunk had risen to the surface, they were not seen in the darkness. *P222* had been on her fifth patrol.

The 'U' class submarine *P48* (Lieutenant M.E. Faber) had a brief and, as regards sinkings, uneventful career. Launched at Barrow in April 1942 by the wife of *Unbroken*'s captain, Lieutenant Alastair Mars, *P48*'s first patrol had been off Algiers, and subsequently off the Marittimo patrol line, between 31 October and 17 November, *P48* again put to sea, this time for billets off Bizerta and Tunis. Ten days later she was back in harbour. *P48* had on both patrols expended all torpedoes but had failed to sink any targets. This lack of success must have been very disappointing for captain and crew and in no way indicated a lack of effort or commitment. It was just the way things went in the submarine war.

Lieutenant Michael Faber put to sea from Malta on 21 December for his third patrol. His billet was the approaches to Tunis. On 31 December Faber was ordered to report his position. Nothing had been heard from *P48* for more than a week. There was no reply to this signal and *P48* failed to arrive at Malta on 5 January 1943.

There seems every likelihood that *P48* was attacked and sunk by the Italian destroyer-escort *Ardente*. The *Ardente* and the *Ardito* sailed Palermo on 24 December as escort to the steamers *XXI Aprile* and *Carlo Zeno*. At 1120 on Christmas Day and at a point 16 miles north-west of Zembra Island in the Gulf of Tunis, *Ardente* registered an ECG contact at 2,600 yards. She signalled *Ardito* to continue escorting the convoy while she herself tracked the submarine. On obtaining a firm ECG contact *Ardente* launched a salvo of twelve depth-charges. In a second attack she launched another dozen. Lieutenant Rinaldo Ancillotti, *Ardente*'s captain, then waited fifteen minutes to allow the surface to calm. The ECG echo indicated that the submarine was stationary. Oil was then seen to come to the surface. Ancillotti attacked for a third time, again dropping a pattern of twelve charges. Soon after this attack a large area of the sea's surface became a mass of bubbles. The Italians were certain that the submarine was attempting to surface and directed their armament in preparation for when she broke surface. But no submarine appeared, and the bubbles soon died away. The ECG indicated that the target had not moved since the second attack. In a fourth and final attack Ancillotti dropped a further twelve depth-charges, bringing the total to forty-eight. *Ardente* then rejoined the convoy. Less than three weeks after this Christmas Day encounter *Ardente* was sunk in a collision with the Italian destroyer *Grecale*. From this incident of 12 January 1943, Lieutenant Rinaldo Ancillotti failed to survive.

# 1943

February saw the loss of one of the improved 'U' class submarines. *Vandal* (Lieutenant J.S. Bridger) was a new submarine. Launched by Vickers on 23 November 1942, she was to survive only three months from that date. On completion of her acceptance trials *Vandal* sailed Barrow on 20 February 1943 to join the 3rd Flotilla at Holy Loch. Two days later John Bridger cast off from the depot ship *Forth* to carry out a three-day independent exercise in the Clyde area. This exercise programme was performed by all submarines joining the 3rd Flotilla immediately after construction and trials. *Vandal*'s programme consisted of an independent exercise in Kilbrannan Sound on 22 and 23 February. The programme included a deep dive in Upper Inchmarnock on the 24th. Lieutenant Bridger had instructions to carry out a deep dive only if satisfied as to the watertightness of *Vandal* and the standard of crew training reached by the third day of the exercise. The three-day period was considered of the greatest value and importance. It was regarded as a form of work-up patrol in which a commanding officer could get his new crew together and give them a thorough training. To help simulate war conditions a commanding officer was under no obligation to communicate by W/T, and had a comparatively free hand to use the occasion as he saw fit. Bridger had been directed to anchor as convenient on the nights of 22 and 23 February and, on completion of the exercise programme, to return to Holy Loch at about 1900 on the 24th. On the evening of the 23rd *Vandal* was observed to anchor at Lochranza, a small village in the north of the island of Arran. At about 0830 the following morning *Vandal* was seen leaving her anchorage. She then disappeared.

Owing to an oversight the failure of *Vandal* to return to Holy Loch by the evening of the 24th was not known to the officer commanding the flotilla. It was not until the morning of the 25th that the submarine's absence was recognized. A search was at once put into effect. Another 'T' class (*Templar*) was exercising in Lower Inchmarnock on the afternoon of the 24th. *Templar* reported having sighted a single white smoke-candle over the sea about 2½ miles 282° north of Inchmarnock. As the smoke-candle was not a distress signal, an investigation was not made by *Templar*. It is thought that the smoke-candle might have been fired by *Vandal*. A second report, that of *Usurper*, states that hull tapping was heard by her at 1630 on the 24th in position 183° 1 mile More Light. These two positions were three miles apart. *Severn* was sent to confirm, but returned with negative results. The area in which *Vandal* had been exercising contained very deep water, so even if she had been speedily located salvage might not have been possible. *Vandal*'s crew, and the submarine herself, were considered above average.

Twenty-five years old, John Bridger was the son of a doctor. He entered Dartmouth in September 1931, and the Submarine Service in April 1939.

Lieutenant-Commander G.R. Colvin was captain of *Tigris* at the time of her loss, also in February. To George Colvin, a splendid officer and one of the most likable of men, had been entrusted the command of the captured German submarine *U570* (known under her Royal Navy colours as *Graph*) for her passage from Iceland to Britain in October 1941. Colvin then commanded *Sealion* until his appointment to *Tigris* in March 1942. Seven Italian submarines were sunk in 1942 by Royal Navy submarines in the Mediterranean. One of them was the *Porfido* and she fell victim to Colvin in December. But for *Tigris* time was also at a premium.

*Tigris* sailed Malta on 18 February for a patrol to the south of Naples. A submarine, probably *Tigris*, was sighted at 0730 on 24 February at a point 39 miles 204° from Capri. On the morning of the 27th *Tigris* was again the object of enemy attention. The *UJ2210* was escorting a convoy six miles south-east of Capri when at 1050 she made an ECG contact with a submarine. At 1114 the *Unterseejäger* attacked with fifteen depth-charges regulated between 150 and 400 feet. At 1135 *UJ2210* launched another fifteen depth-charges, this time regulated to maximum depth. A copious quantity of air-bubbles and oil appeared on the surface. At 1150 contact, which had been lost for a few minutes, was regained and ten minutes later the German carried out a third attack, also of fifteen depth-charges. A large mass of air-bubbles and oil was again noted. At 1225 the ECG revealed that the target was stationary. A further fifteen charges were dropped over the submarine at 1235. The UJ then observed on the surface 'A huge bubble of air about 30 metres long and 3 metres wide. Then came four large bubbles of air. Pieces of wood were seen.' On 6 March *Tigris* was ordered to Algiers. There was no reply to this signal and *Tigris* failed to return to harbour.

*

March 1943 brought the loss of a submarine which had at one time been the most widely known warship in Britain – *Thetis*. Eighteen months had passed since that horrific moment when *Thetis* had been swamped by water entering through number five torpedo tube. *Thetis* had been raised, refitted, renamed *Thunderbolt* and sent into battle.

It had taken five months of difficult salvage operations before *Thetis* was beached at Moelfre Bay, Anglesey. After removal of the bodies, *Thetis* had been subjected to intensive scrutiny before being towed to Holyhead for dry-docking. When Holyhead had finished with her in mid-July, she was taken back to Birkenhead under her own power. Opinions were expressed that in view of her tragic past, *Thetis* should be scrapped. The urgent need for submarines outweighed opposition to her commissioning, and so it was as *Thunderbolt* that she was readied for war. Command of *Thunderbolt* was given to Lieutenant C.B. Crouch. A ship's company was drafted in the usual manner, but with the exception that anyone not wishing to serve in her could request a transfer to another submarine. By October 1940 *Thunderbolt* was ready for her acceptance trials. Unlike *Thetis* she passed with flying colours. The following month she joined the 3rd Flotilla at Dunoon.

On the afternoon of 3 December 1940 *Thunderbolt* slipped her moorings and set off on her first war patrol. Lieutenant Crouch, who had joined the submarine from *Swordfish*, had been patrolling the Biscay area for almost a week when on the morning of 15 December he sighted the Italian submarine *Tarantini* in company with two German trawlers. Crouch had no sooner set up an attack when *Tarantini* made a change of track, so that she became a stern-on target. The first of a salvo of six torpedoes was fired. In just over sixty seconds all the tubes were empty. A minute passed . . . Another dragged by . . . Then another. After what seemed an eternity Crouch ordered the periscope raised. He had a terrible feeling that he had missed the target. The glass cleared just in time for him to observe a column of water heading skyward. *Tarantini* sank with less than a half-dozen survivors.

After completion of a negative second patrol *Thunderbolt* was ordered to Canada where for the next six months she operated out of Halifax. In early 1941 *Thunderbolt* put Halifax astern and sailed for the Mediterranean. Apart from her cloak-and-dagger activities, by March 1943 *Thunderbolt*'s Mediterranean service had resulted in an impressive list of sinkings. For his fifteenth and last patrol Cecil Crouch put to sea from Malta on 9 March for an area off the north-west coast of Sicily.

During the afternoon of Friday 12 March the torpedo boat *Libra* sailed Palermo to reinforce the escort of a four-ship convoy bound for Tunisia. At 1600, having joined the convoy off Capo Cefalu, the *Libra* took up her position in the formation. Towards 2000 the convoy was illuminated by the Leigh light of a British aircraft. The aircraft reported the convoy's position and at 2100 the Italian force came under aerial attack. At 2130 the tanker *Sterope* was hit by an aircraft torpedo. The tanker was detached and ordered to make for Palermo.

At 2210 that night, the merchantman *Esterel* was torpedoed two miles north of Capo San Vito. The aggressor was *Thunderbolt*. The convoy leader ordered the destroyer-escort *Orione* and the corvette *Persefone* to give assistance to the *Esterel*. The *Libra* was ordered to hunt for the submarine. After less than an hour's search in position 38°17'N 12°57'E, the *Libra* obtained a good ECG contact at 1,200 yards. This contact was held for two hours and during this period *Libra* carried out seven attacks. After the final attack *Libra*'s captain sighted in the darkness something floating on the surface which led him to believe that he might have damaged the submarine.

*Saturday 13th.* At 1345 the corvette *Cicogna* sailed Trapani to search for the submarine which had been hunted and possibly damaged by the *Libra*. At 1845 *Cicogna* was met by the *Persefone* in the area pre-scribed for the A/S sweep. Weather and sea conditions were ideal.

*Sunday 14th.* At 0516 the *Cicogna* obtained an ECG contact. A buoy was dropped in the sea. The other corvette could not confirm the contact; *Persefone* left shortly after to assume escort of the steamer *Pegli*, in transit from Trapani to Palermo. For the next two hours Lieutenant Augusto Migliorini, *Cicogna*'s captain, continued with the ECG search. At times the signal was quite good, but on occasions it would fade and then disappear altogether. However, Migliorini's persistence was rewarded when at 0734 the echo became very good. Shortly after this a periscope was sighted off the bow at 2,000 yards. Migliorini did not attack, possibly wanting the submarine's captain to think that *Cicogna* was without depth-charges. At 0845 the echo became particularly strong. Then an excited cry from the bow informed Migliorini that the periscope had been sighted again. Leaning over the wing of the bridge he was startled to see the periscope's wake less than seven feet from his ship. The order was at once given to release a salvo of depth-charges and twenty-four of them went hurtling into the sea. *Cicogna* had increased speed to clear the vicinity and to come in for another attack when a huge explosion thrust the submarine's stern out of the sea to an angle of at least 90° (the Italians could see the keel). The submarine then sank in a boiling discharge of air and oil. Two further depth-charges were dropped. Air bubbles and oil, the latter in large quantities, came to the surface. After about four minutes a whitish-colour smoke appeared all around the point of sinking. *Cicogna* remained in the area for another hour but no further contact was made.

Lieutenant-Commander Cecil Crouch had been awarded a DSO and Bar for his service in submarines. His leaving of *Swordfish* and *Seahorse* just prior to their loss had caused him to become known as 'Lucky' Crouch. Crouch had entered the Navy in 1927, and had joined submarines in May 1932. In April 1939 he took his COQC and three months later was appointed captain of *Swordfish*.

There is a likelihood that *Turbulent* (Commander J.W. Linton) was sunk on the same day as *Thunderbolt*. *Turbulent* sailed Algiers on 24 February 1943 for a patrol in the Tyrrhenian Sea in an area east of 14°E and south of 40°N. She was expected to arrive at her billet on 28 February. On 1 March *Turbulent* was sighted off Paola, Calabria. She was engaged in an action reported as follows:

At 0945 in the neighbourhood of Paola a submarine attacked with a torpedo the steamer *Santo Vincenzo* of 865 tons which was *en route* from Naples to Milazzo. The torpedo hit the beach. The submarine then surfaced and used her gun on the steamer, hitting her repeatedly. The coastal battery at Paola opened fire on the submarine, causing her to dive. At 1000 the

submarine launched another torpedo, sinking the steamer 1 mile 330°
from the lookout station of Paola. The torpedo boat *Dezza* carried out an
A/S search from 1220 until 1040 the following morning, but without
result.

*Turbulent*'s patrol was extended to 40°N after sunset that same day.

During the early hours of 6 March five Italian warships sailed
Naples as escort to three merchantmen bound for Trapani. A report
by the captain of the *Ardito* indicates that *Turbulent* was in the vicinity
of the convoy.

> At 0745 March 6 at a point 34 miles 264° from Punta Licosa, a JU88
> dropped a bomb about 3,000 metres from my ship. I immediately moved
> to attack, whilst the convoy turned to port. The aircraft continued to cir-
> cle the point of sighting. At 1,300 metres I picked up an echo off the bow.
> I then approached and launched the first carpet of depth-charges. I
> turned about and made for the point where I had launched a buoy. The
> ECG picked up an echo at 1,000 metres and I set course to launch a sec-
> ond carpet. I was on the position and was about to launch when the ship
> suddenly reduced speed owing to loss of steam pressure. For reasons of
> safety this loss of speed made it impossible to launch depth-charges.

The number of attacks and the total charges dropped by *Ardito* is not
known, but it is known that at 0935 the contact was lost without any
visible signs that the submarine had been sunk or damaged.

*Turbulent* was ordered to patrol north of 40°N and east to 13° from
eight o'clock on the evening of 6 March up until the afternoon of the
12th. The next likely sighting of *Turbulent* occurred on 7 March. With
several other warships the destroyer *Lampo* sailed Bizerta for Naples
as escort to three merchant ships. From her captain's report:

> At 1557 on March 7 at a point 15 miles 240° Punta Carena (Capri) the
> convoy's escort aircraft signalled the presence of a submarine to port. I
> ordered a course alteration to 90°starboard. As a merchantman and a
> torpedo boat had been delayed a few hours, and as *Lampo*'s ECG
> apparatus was not functioning, no unit was detached from the convoy to
> make a search to verify the validity of the sighting.

As this was to have been his last patrol before returning to the UK,
Commander Linton had requested before sailing that, after leaving
the Naples area and circumstances permitting, he might proceed
north along the coast to Giglio Island. As the date of *Turbulent*'s refit

had been postponed a fortnight, the request was agreed to, particularly as Commander Linton had patrolled in that area previously and he seemed confident that targets would not prove elusive. Linton had then been told to report his expected time of arrival at a position off the south-east coast of Sardinia, when an onward route would be signalled.

An unsuccessful submarine attack with two torpedoes on the mail-ship *Principessa Mafalda* was probably conducted by *Turbulent*. The attack took place eight miles from Bastia, Corsica, on 11 March as the 850 tons mail-ship made her regular call between mainland Piombino and Bastia. At about 0910 on the morning following the attack, the A/S trawler *Teti II* sighted four miles ESE of Punta d'Arco first the periscope and then the emerging conning tower of a submarine. The submarine was attacked without signs of success. There were several other sightings, true or imagined, of a submarine in the north-east area of Corsica. These sightings were probably of *Turbulent*. At 1400 on 14 May a submarine sighting was reported some fifty miles south of Bastia. If this sighting was of *Turbulent*, then it was the last seen of her for she was not seen again during her expected passage south towards Sardinia. *Turbulent* was expected to arrive off south-east Sardinia not earlier than 16 March. She was ordered to patrol about fourteen miles off the east coast in latitude 40°13'N from 2100 on 19 March to 0001 on the 20th and then to withdraw and report her ETA south-east of Sardinia. No reply was received to this signal. On 20 March *Turbulent* was given an onward route to Algiers and ordered to acknowledge receipt of the signal. No reply was received and *Turbulent* did not arrive at Algiers on 23 March.

Evidence suggests that *Turbulent* might have been mined some time after 14 March at a position off eastern Corsica or, and this is more probable, in the vicinity of Maddalena or Olbia, Sardinia. *Turbulent*'s first move after being attacked by the Ju88 and *Ardito* off Punta Carena on the afternoon of 6 March was to move north towards Giglio Island. From there she made for north-east Corsica, probably arriving off Bastia on the evening of the 10th or the morning of the 11th as no attacks were made in the vicinity of Bastia until the attack on the *Principessa Mafalda* on the 11th and Commander Linton, who had expressed a determination to fire off all his torpedoes if circumstances favoured, would have been unlikely to allow targets to pass without making use of his torpedoes or gun. The attack on *Turbulent* by the A/S trawler *Teti II* on the 12th probably did nothing to harm the submarine. No visible signs of a successful attack had been observed, and a possible submarine sighting had been made a few days later. Also, the position of the incident is known and no sonar exploration has yet revealed the presence of a submarine wreck. Until such time as firm evidence comes to light, whether *Turbulent* had been mined or had been sunk by A/S craft is a matter for conjecture.

Commander John Linton was born at Newport, Gwent. The son of an architect, he had entered Osborne in May 1919. Then came Dartmouth, where he remained until December 1922. In 1927 he joined submarines. Apart from duty in *Iron Duke* from 1936 to 1938, Linton spent the whole of his naval service in submarines, thirteen years of which eight were as a commanding officer. At the advent of war Commander Linton was in China as captain of *Pandora*. In May 1941 he was awarded a DSC. A few weeks later he took command of the new submarine *Turbulent* and on 3 January 1942 sailed her to the Mediterranean. In September 1942 he was awarded the DSO. Linton sank some thirty vessels, totalling about 100,000 tons, and was in the top echelon of submarine commanders. After his promotion to commander in December 1941, Linton asked to be allowed to continue serving in submarines instead of taking a staff or training appointment. His final patrol would have been his last in submarines. During the course of his twenty-one patrols his skill and courage had been put to the test many times. On 25 May 1943 he was posthumously awarded the Victoria Cross. Commander Linton was married with two sons. He was thirty-seven.

*

Lieutenant W.N.R. Knox had been captain of *Regent* for two years when on 11 April he put to sea from Malta on what was to be his last patrol. Knox was under orders to patrol the southern Adriatic before moving on to join the 1st Flotilla at Beirut. Sightings of a submarine off the coast of Calabria on the 13th, 15th, and 16th were thought to be that of *Regent*. By the 18th she was north of Monopoli. At 1545 that afternoon, she was then 5 miles 45° from the port, *Regent* fired a torpedo at the merchantman *Balcic*, in convoy from Bari to Patrasso. The torpedo passed *Balcic*'s stern and went on to explode on shore. That evening in the area of Monopoli a heavy explosion was observed. This is thought to have been *Regent* striking a mine.

If *Regent* had struck a mine off Monopoli it must have been a mine that had broken adrift from the mine barrage which extended for ten miles south of Bari as there was no mine barrage for fifteen miles north and south of Monopoli. On 1 May, thirteen days after the suspected sinking, the body of an engine room artificer clad in blue overalls was found on a beach at Brindisi. The man, who was wearing DSEA, was believed to have been dead for between six and eight days. The Italians thought that he might have been part of a squad of saboteurs. On 15 May on a beach at Santa Andrea di Missipezza another body was discovered, also wearing DSEA. The next day a third body was recovered in the neighbourhood of Torre Santo Stefano, two miles north of Otranto. This body was in an advanced state of putrefaction. From the man's clothing and insignia he was taken to be an officer or a petty officer. On the same day a fourth body was found a few miles farther south at Castro Marina, 120 miles south of Monopoli. It was judged that the death of the last three men had taken place twenty-five days prior to recovery of their bodies. The current flowing along the Apulia coast flows towards the Mediterranean at no more than half a knot. At a speed slightly less than this a dead body might cover a distance of about six miles a day. This would mean that the men had died some time between 18 and 25 April.

On pure supposition it might be that after his attack on the *Balcic* Lieutenant Knox moved a little farther north, striking a mine off the Bari field. Most of the crew who had survived the explosion might have escaped; on the other hand it might be that only a few, the strongest swimmers, cleared the submarine in hope of attracting a vessel to the area.

If doubts exist as to whether *Regent* was sunk on 18 April there are no doubts whatsoever that *P615* was sunk on that day. *P615* was one of four submarines under construction for the Turkish Navy by Vickers-Armstrong in early 1940. Subsequent events ensured that for a time all of these submarines found their way into Royal Navy service: two of them, *P611* and *P612*, were handed over to Turkey in 1942 whilst *P614* and *P615* were used for training purposes at Freetown, West Africa. *P614* eventually returned to Home Waters and continued her role as a training submarine before being handed over to Turkey to become the *Burak Reis*. *P615* never left the tropics.

On the afternoon of 17 April the *P615* (Lieutenant C.W. St C. Lambert) put to sea from Freetown, Sierra Leone, bound for Takoradi 900 miles south in Ghana. Though every eventuality was always considered by the authorities at Freetown, her loss next morning still came as a nasty surprise. The route selected for *P615*'s passage was similar to those in general use in that area, and which had previously been free of U-boat attention. When available, air cover had been supplied to convoys and independent sailings. On the day of *P615*'s departure from Freetown, a Catalina flying boat searched the area without result. Furthermore, the general trend of U-boat dispositions as indicated by the tracking plot suggested that no U-boats were in the area. It was thought, also, that *P615*'s own asdic equipment would provide adequate protection against under-water attack. For this reason no close air-escort was considered necessary. The demands for air and sea escorts were very heavy at this time, so these were only provided for individual sailings when conditions appeared essential. The advisability of *P615* taking passage with a convoy had been considered but it was thought that the danger from the convoy's own escorts would outweigh any advantages if the convoy should be attacked and scattered at night. It was eventually decided that for her journey south the submarine would have as escort the *Motor Minesweeper 107*.

As *P615* and *MM107* headed south Lieutenant Lambert informed the minesweeper's captain that he intended to maintain a continuous A/S watch and would contact him if anything was heard. During that night submarine and minesweeper lost contact owing to poor visibility, but at 0400 the following morning, 18 April, the watch officer of *MM107* sighted a submarine, believed to be *P615*, on the port quarter. Heavy rain had reduced visibility to under a thousand yards and *P615* was no longer in sight when fifty minutes later the minesweeper's OOW saw the track of a torpedo pass under the bridge from port to starboard and then break surface. No U-boat was sighted. When at 0700 A/S touch was regained between *P615* and *MM107*, the following messages were exchanged:

TO P615. AT 0450 OFFICER ON WATCH OBSERVED WAKE OF MOVING OBJECT APPEAR FROM UNDER BRIDGE ON STARBOARD SIDE, TRAVELLING 210 DEGREES AT 40 MPH. 18/0700.

TO MM107. REF. 18/0700. SUSPECT PORPOISE. UNABLE TO CONFIRM TORPEDO AS I LOST TOUCH FROM 0340 TO 0600 INVESTIGATING SUSPICIOUS VESSEL WHICH I THINK WAS A TRAMP. I FEEL IT WAS A TORPEDO. I WILL MAKE AN 'ENEMY REPORT'. 18/0805.

As no Enemy Report was received at Freetown, it is assumed that none was made. The suspicious vessel investigated by Lieutenant Lambert was not sighted by *MM107*. After making his 0805 signal

Charles Lambert closed *MM107* and took station 300 yards on her starboard quarter.

At 0905 *MM107* sighted the merchant vessel *Empire Bruce* fine on the starboard bow. *MM107* signalled *Empire Bruce*, noticing at the same time that the submarine was calling either the merchantman or *MM107*. A few minutes after this, *P615* was seen to blow up. The explosion took place in position 6°49'N 13°09'W and *P615* is reported to have sunk in just five seconds. There were no survivors. Observations suggest that *P615* was hit on her starboard side by a torpedo under her conning tower. No torpedo track had been sighted by *MM107*.

The minesweeper closed *Empire Bruce* and challenged her. No reply was received. At 1020 the sweeper passed a signal to *Empire Bruce* warning of a U-boat in the area. Although the signal went unacknowledged and the merchantman apparently continued on the same course, about 300°, she started zigzagging. Experiencing difficulty with her radio, *MM107* made towards the coast in hopes of finding more favourable conditions for transmitting an Enemy Report to Freetown. Whilst engaged in this act an explosion at 1050 was seen to erupt on the port side of *Empire Bruce*. At midday *Empire Bruce* blew up and sank.

At 1600 *MM107* succeeded in passing a message to an aircraft. It was whilst thus occupied that she observed a stretch of heavy brown oil and green paint, together with a few pieces of timber, floating over an area roughly half a mile by three miles. After rescuing survivors of *Empire Bruce*, *MM107* returned to Freetown.

Though only indirectly related to the sinking of *P615*, one or two points have never been adequately explained: the reason for a large cloud of smoke, similar to a smoke-screen, observed eight to ten miles off *MM107*'s port beam, and the area of oil and paint seen later. *MM107*'s captain thought that the smoke had reminded him of the occasion he had witnessed a burning tanker. No ship had been sunk in this area prior to *P615*, and the oil could not have come from *Empire Bruce*. The mystery remains.

*P615*'s signal timed 18/0805, in reply to the attack on *MM107*, appears to be corrupt as received by the sweeper. As no Enemy Report was received at Freetown from *P615*, it seems likely that the last sentence as transmitted by *P615* should have read: 'IF YOU FEEL IT WAS A TORPEDO I WILL MAKE AN "ENEMY REPORT" '. This of course is just conjecture.

The captain of the U-boat had made three attacks between 0450 and 1050 and had had success with two of them. The U-boat, which had been *U123*, survived the war and later served in the French Navy as the *Blaison*.

As a brief note on *Empire Bruce* and *MM107* it can be said that the merchantman was built in 1941 by Sir J. Laing & Sons and was of 7,459 tons, and *MM107* was one of four minesweepers built at Port Quebec by Brunton & Co, and that she survived the war.

Lieutenant Charles Lambert was the son of Major-General H.P. Lambert, CBE, DSC. He had entered the Navy as a cadet in 1937. After service in the minesweeper *Selkirk* in 1940, he joined *Unbeaten* and served in her with distinction in the Mediterranean, rising to first lieutenant and being awarded a DSC and Bar for 'Courage, skill, and coolness in successful submarine patrols'. In November 1942 he was appointed to command *P615*. Married in April 1941, Lambert had celebrated his twenty-fourth birthday a week prior to his loss.

*

On the morning of 17 March 1943 a five-ship convoy sailed Palermo for Trapani. The convoy comprised the tankers *Devoli* and *Velino*, and the corvettes *Persefone, Antilope*, and *Cicogna*. At 1055, and at a point 6½ miles from Capo San Vito Lighthouse, the 3,300 tons *Devoli* was hit by two torpedoes. The *Persefone* immediately raced down the torpedoes' wakes to the point of firing. She was followed in this action by *Antilope*, whilst the *Cicogna* set about rescuing the crew of the sinking tanker. Fearing that the submarine would again strike, the *Persefone* and *Antilope* departed for Trapani with the *Velino*. After putting *Devoli*'s survivors aboard a tug, the *Cicogna* began a systematic search for the submarine. At 1525 *Cicogna* obtained a good sonar contact 2½ miles 340° from the lighthouse at Capo San Vito. She carried out an attack, launching twenty-four depth-charges. *Cicogna*'s captain believed he had damaged the submarine and carried out two further attacks. Observation of the area, bubbles were seen, convinced the Italians that the submarine had been damaged but not sunk. The submarine had indeed escaped destruction and four days later she sank another tanker, the *Giorgio* of 4,887 tons. These successes were scored by the captain and crew of HM Submarine *Splendid*.

Launched at Chatham in January 1942, the fighting life of *Splendid* lasted barely a year, but under the command of Lieutenant I.L.M. McGeoch she brought honours to those who took her into battle. In 1943 McGeoch was awarded a DSO for:

Outstanding zeal, efficiency, and daring as commanding officer during three successful submarine patrols in which he sank two enemy destroyers and three supply ships totalling 10,000 tons. He also sank an A/S trawler and two A/S schooners. Many of these attacks have been on screened targets and his coolness and skill in handling his submarine enabled him to avoid damage during the subsequent depth-charge attacks. The fact that these successes have been achieved in *Splendid*'s first three patrols in the Mediterranean reflects great credit on Lt McGeoch's leadership and daring, and on the forethought and skill he has devoted to the maintenance of a very high standard of fighting efficiency.

An officer of courage and genuine ability, Lieutenant McGeoch was to have an outstanding career.

After a period in dry-dock *Splendid* sailed Malta on 18 April for patrol. By the morning of Wednesday 21st she was about three miles SSE of Capri. At 0838 a lookout of the German destroyer *Hermes* (ex-Greek *Vasilefs Georgios I*) sighted a periscope some 3,000 yards off the port bow. The destroyer, *en route* from Salerno to Pozzuoli, turned towards the sighting. Almost immediately *Hermes* established good sonar contact. She at once closed the submarine and attacked with depth-charges. Between 0843 and 0924 *Hermes* made three attacks, launching in total forty-three depth-charges. The efficiency of Commander Rechel, captain of *Hermes*, and his crew is apparent from Lieutenant McGeoch's account of *Splendid*'s loss.

'The immediate cause of my being attacked by *Hermes* was the sighting of my periscope. Asdic (sonar) contact was then made. The sea was flat calm and the strong sun was behind the *Hermes* as she approached at 20 knots. In an attempt to identify the destroyer, which did not correspond with any I knew of, I was still using the high-powered periscope by the time the range was down to 3,000 yards or so. I had just come to the conclusion that she was probably an ex-Yugoslav British-built (Yarrow) destroyer which was in Italian hands – I had no intelligence report of any German-manned destroyer in the Mediterranean – and decided to take a range, with the periscope, before ordering "Down periscope". That delay was fatal. But I needed a range for a special reason: because our Mk VIII torpedoes were air-driven they left a bubble-track which was easily seen by an alert lookout in time for a fast-moving manoeuvrable ship like *Hermes* to take effective avoiding action. The submarine would then have revealed her position to no purpose, as potential targets could be routed clear of her patrol area. It was my policy, therefore, not to fire in daylight at warships such as destroyers when the sea was glassy calm, unless the running range of the torpedoes would be less than 2,000 yards. Sadly, in determining the range of 21 April, I left the periscope up for too long, especially as it was the larger (high-powered) one. Furthermore, owing to the sun being low and behind the target it probably caused the top-glass of my periscope to glint as I moved it round. It so happened that the crew of the *Hermes* was at that moment at action stations; also, as her captain was a senior commander who had seen much action in Norway, etc., the lookouts were certainly on their toes.

'Having been sighted, the next thing was the asdic attack. In this the snag was, from my point of view, that the sonar detection conditions in the Tyrrhenian Sea in April tend to be ideal – that is to say the sea is isothermal with no "temperature gradient" to cause a layer effect and bend the sonar transmission beams, which would have provided some safety from detection to the lurking submarine. Meyer-Abich, *Hermes*'s sonar officer, subsequently to become a rear-admiral in the Federal German Navy, told me that he never lost contact with *Splendid* and that after his first two depth-charge patterns had produced no visible results he set the third to go off at 100 metres. As by then the *Splendid* had been taken to 300 feet (the maximum operational diving depth was 250 feet), and was going as slowly as possible in order to avoid making hydrophone effect, Meyer-Abich scored a bull's eye. Our after hatch was torn from its seating and water came in fast, while the submarine took up a steep stern-down angle. She also began to go down rapidly, although I had begun to speed up when I heard the propellers of *Hermes* getting louder as she came in to the attack – in fact I said to the people in the control room: "Hold your hats on!"

'*Hermes*'s third attack resulted in serious damage to the submarine. Only one shaft would turn, the other having been jammed by hull distortion caused by the depth-charge explosions being so near. Both main motors were on fire. The depth-gauge went to its maximum reading of 500 feet. As we stayed at a steep angle, stern down, I knew that the stern must already be nearly at the crushing depth of the submarine and that I had to make an immediate decision to blow the main ballast tanks in order to prevent disaster. I had always said to my ship's company that whereas the submarine herself must be regarded as expendable, they were not and their safety would, *in extremis*, be my first consideration. This mental preparation for a circumstance which in view of the wartime submarine losses could not be regarded as unlikely no doubt helped me to take the decision quickly enough when the moment came. It certainly seemed an age from my order to blow main ballast to when I saw the depth-gauge show that we were on our way to the surface. I told the crew to be ready to abandon ship.'

Leading Signalman R.W. Auckland was on duty at the fore hydroplanes. He quite clearly heard *Hermes*'s sonar pinging off the hull 'almost like the squeak of a mouse'. Auckland says that there then came 'One hell of a crash and a flash and blast right through the boat'. Lieutenant McGeoch had given the order to blow main ballast but, owing to the steep angle of the submarine, only half the water was leaving the ballast tanks. As *Splendid* was not responding, full ahead was ordered to drive her upwards. All eyes were fixed on the depth-gauges; the needles, slowly at first, left the 500 feet mark and then gained momentum as *Splendid* left the great pressure of the deep behind. Leading Signalman Auckland: 'I went to my bunk where my lifebelt was stowed. I strapped it on and tried to inflate it, but it seemed as though the valve was blocked with French chalk. I proceeded to the control room. There was a queue waiting to go up the conning tower so I moved on to the gun tower hatch, situated in the officers' mess. I opened the lower hatch and then clambered to the upper hatch. It was pitch-black and I had great difficulty in releasing the safety-pins. By this time other members of the crew had followed me. They shouted for me to hurry up, etc. I replied in appropriate nautical terms that I was doing my best. Eventually I met with success and proceeded to open the hatch and clamber out.

'The destroyer was firing at us. I took shelter behind the gun mounting. As the rudder had been jammed, and as the motor was driving us on, we were going round in a wide sweep. This manoeuvre probable made the Germans think that we were going to fire a torpedo at them, and so they opened fire with their main armament. A shell went through the conning tower, killing members of the crew who were climbing up it, so I decided it was time to abandon ship. And this I did. Telegraphist Boulton jumped with me. He said: "I can't swim." Before I could assist him he disappeared in the water. As my own lifebelt was useless I asked Stoker Marshall to swim with me. He had on DSEA, so if we were in the water for any length of time I could hang on to him. Having heard of German atrocities I didn't fancy them running me down in the water; so Marshall and I, and five others, swam away from the main body of survivors. Thankfully I was wrong in my presumption and I later learned the German crew had picked up the other survivors and treated them very well. The destroyer radioed the Italians at Capri. An Italian MTB came out and picked up our party. They pulled us aboard and at pistol point made us strip. They gave us blankets to wrap round ourselves. We were then taken to a cabin. When they saw we were in no condition to threaten them they relaxed and gave us a small nip of Cognac. The Cognac was welcomed but the bread with condensed milk which was also offered was politely refused, our stomachs being in no state for such fare. They landed us at Capri with only the blankets wrapped around us, quite embarrassing really as the news of our capture had circulated and all the village had turned out to see us.'

Lieutenant Ian McGeoch completes the account: 'As *Splendid* levelled off, my crew scrambled out of the conning tower hatch and out of the gun tower hatch, forward of the conning tower. While abandon ship was taking place the first lieutenant, Lieutenant Robert Balkwill, RNVR, and I seized the emergency hand-levers and opened some main vents in order to let water into the ballast tanks again as quickly as possible so as to ensure that the submarine slipped under the surface before there could be any chance of a boarding party getting control of her. Meanwhile the 5-inch guns of *Hermes* had scored some direct hits, and had had some near misses, killing or severely wounding several of the crew either before they could get clear of the submarine or as they swam nearby. The *Hermes* was also firing with lighter guns and as I followed the first lieutenant through the conning tower hatch, making sure I was the last to leave the submarine, I saw *Hermes*'s German ensign for the first time. Then my right eye ceased to function. (Later I found that I had received a small splinter in my eye. This had penetrated the lower part of my eye and severed the retina. In the end I had to have the eye removed.) I jumped into the sea, where I joined Robert Balkwill. I remember us agreeing that we should swim towards Capri as it was known to be a most attractive place!'

When Robert Auckland was taken from the sea by *VAS 226*, an A/S launch, it was to begin a term as a POW in Italy and Germany. He had joined the Navy in May 1934 and submarines in March 1941. Prior to *Splendid* he had gone to the United States to help crew the obsolete *P511* to the UK in what Auckland describes as 'An extremely perilous voyage which we survived only by the grace of God.'

Lieutenant Ian McGeoch had entered the Navy in 1932. Following pre-war service in *Clyde* as navigating officer, he was appointed to

*H43* as first lieutenant in February 1940. Six months later he was performing first lieutenant duties in *Triumph*. McGeoch's first command came in December of 1940 when he returned to *H43*. In April 1941 he arrived in Malta as a Spare CO. During this period he captained *Ursula* for one patrol. McGeoch was twenty-eight when in July 1942 he was appointed to command *Splendid*, then nearing completion at Chatham. Less than a year after the loss of *Splendid* the enterprising McGeoch escaped captivity. After a harrowing time he arrived in England in May 1944. Vice-Admiral Sir Ian McGeoch, KCB, DSO, DSC, retired from the Navy in 1970 after a distinguished career of almost forty years.

Although the active life of *Splendid* had been but a short while, her Mediterranean Battle Honour had been richly deserved. She had sailed Britain for the Mediterranean at the end of September 1942. Between October 1942 and April 1943 *Splendid* completed five patrols:

| | |
|---|---|
| 1st Patrol: | Auxilary schooner sunk |
| | Destroyer *Velite* severely damaged by torpedo and took no further part in the war. |
| | Supply ship sunk by gunfire |
| 2nd Patrol: | Supply ship sunk. |
| | Destroyer *Aviere* sunk. |
| 3rd Patrol | Supply ship sunk. |
| | Schooner sunk. |
| | Armed trawler sunk. |
| | Special operation (landing of agents in Sardinia) |
| | Supply ship sunk. |
| 4th Patrol: | Supply ship sunk. |
| | Supply ship sunk. |
| | Tanker sunk. |
| 5th Patrol: | Tanker sunk. |
| | Fishing vessel sunk. |

It will be noticed that after each patrol *Splendid* returned to harbour having sunk at least two vessels; this was by no means a common occurrence and captain and crew deserve full credit for their professionalism.

Eighteen of *Splendid*'s forty-five crew were lost with her. On 21 April 1981 a Memorial was held in the Italian warship *Alloro* over the position where *Splendid* had been sunk thirty-eight years before. Of the occasion Sir Ian says: 'The Memorial Service could not bring the dead back to life, but it helped to keep alive their memory. They were fine men.'

The *Hermes* survived *Splendid* by only a few weeks, being sunk ·at Bizerta by Allied aircraft. Commander Rechel survived the war and died in Germany in the 1970s.

In 1971 the first of the six nucleared-powered *Swiftsure* class submarines was launched. Among the class was the second HM Submarine *Splendid*.

The loss of *Splendid* on the Wednesday was followed on the Saturday by the loss of *Sahib*. What follows has been compiled from an account by her captain, Lieutenant J.H. Bromage, and a crewman, Leading Seaman A.G.E. Briard.

*Leading Seaman Briard*: 'To me those few days in Algiers, the base to which we had been detached from the 10th Flotilla at Malta, had been quite memorable. First there had been the glitter of Algerian night life, so different from the smoke-filled cellars and caves of Malta. Then the frantic buying of perfumes, nylons, and cosmetics – all seldom seen back home in the battered shops of war-torn Britain. But all good things come to an end and at 1900 on 16 April we slipped our moorings and proceeded on our next patrol. The following morning, we were proceeding on our first day's dive, our skipper mustered us in the control room, as was his custom, to put us in the picture. We were informed that our destination was the vicinity of the Lipari Islands and the northern entrance to the Messina Straits. It was a familiar hunting ground to us. We had made several sinkings in that area and had become quite a thorn in the side of the Italians. On the morning of the 22nd, *Sahib* was then five miles south of Capo Vaticano, we sighted our first target. Prior to surfacing about a thousand yards off the starboard quarter of the target, the skipper allowed me a quick glance through the periscope. I observed an armed tug towing a large barge with some sort of high lifting tripod mounted on it. We broke surface on a beautifully calm sea with just a slight swell running. By the time I had set the range and my telescopic sight my trainer, Able Seaman "Hooky" Hook, had already trained the gun bang on target. At that range, something under half a mile, I had to put the gun out of action fast. My gun's crew were well trained and had already experienced a number of actions.

'My first shell fell just short of, but in line with, the bow of the target. The second shell exploded on its bow, a few feet below the place where her gun was mounted. My third shell was a little slower and very deliberate. Through my high-powered telescope I could see that her gun was trained directly on us. I was looking down a large black hole. On the right of the gun was a man whom I presumed was the gunlayer. As *Sahib* straightened out after a down swell, I brought the gun up slowly. Just as the cross-wires reached the point on the enemy gun where the barrel joined the mounting . . . I fired. A 3-inch gun gives a mighty kick when fired so I had to settle the sights before I was able to see that I had achieved all I could have wished. The enemy gun was tilted at a crazy angle with its muzzle pointed skywards. Its crew had disappeared completely. After that it was little more than a training exercise for our gun crew. I put shell after shell into the tug until the skipper ordered me to shift target to the barge, which had slipped its tow and was slowly spinning in a circle. After many hits on the barge, the skipper gave the order to cease fire. We immediately dived. The entire action had taken less than ten minutes. Out of seventy-two rounds fired, we had scored seventy hits, about forty-five of them on the tug. The tug's gun, possibly a 3-pounder, had been put out of action by our third round. According to the Italians, the tug *Valente* had been so badly damaged that she was forced to beach herself along with her pontoon.'

Two days after the incident with the tug, *Sahib* arrived off Capo Milazzo, Sicily. Lieutenant Bromage was at breakfast when shipping was reported on a westward course and two miles from Capo Milazzo. At 0450, it being half an hour before sunrise, *Sahib* was dived from the northward. The ships, five in number, were a convoy four hours out from Messina. One of the convoy was the heavily laden merchantman *Galiola*. A brief scan through the periscope informed Bromage that the *Galiola* had the corvettes *Gabbiano* and *Euterpe* positioned off either bow. Off her starboard and port quarters were the torpedo boats *Climene* and *Bassini* respectively. With such a strong escort the *Galiola* must have been of some importance.

*Leading Seaman Briard*: 'Throughout the boat there was an air of increased awareness as 'enemy in sight' was passed round. From the asdic cabinet where Ted Cook and John Townsend were huddled came reports of HE on several bearings. Obviously we were closing a convoy. The skipper was now using the periscope very sparingly, taking only quick glimpses. He was also keeping us informed of what was happening on the surface. Then suddenly the moment arrived to commence the attack. The skipper snapped the handles of the periscope against its sides. The column slid quickly back down its well. Then the orders came at speed: "Sixty feet. Group up. Half ahead

together. Steer 1-6-0. Stand by 1, 2, 3, and 4 tubes. Put me on a
hundred track." *Sahib* began to vibrate slightly as the increased pitch
of her propellers forced her faster through the depths. I was at the
helm. I turned the wheel to bring her on the ordered course. Then
from the asdic cabinet the voice of Ted Cook broke the silence:
"Enemy in contact, sir. Transmitting on – ." I forget the frequency.
Being now steady on course 160° I cast a furtive glance behind me.
The captain was standing behind the first lieutenant, who was
absorbed with the two planesmen. The skipper's face was expressionless. "Well, they now know we're here." He spoke slowly and
calmly. "We'll press on regardless." Moving to the close-attack
periscope he ordered: "Slow ahead both. Bring her up to periscope
depth, Number One." Crouching on his knees, the captain ordered
the periscope raised, placing his eyes to the eye-piece as soon as it
cleared the well. "Dammit! She's turned away. Steer 1-8-0. Down
periscope." I gave the wheel full helm knowing that the captain, who
came and stood behind me, would want to get onto a new firing track
immediately. As it was, we would now have to fire from a position on
the target's starboard quarter. As I reported "Steady 1-8-0, sir," the
captain, back at the periscope, ordered that the torpedoes would be
fired independently. Then: "Up periscope. Prepare to fire number
one tube." The captain's voice was the only sound in an electric
silence. "Fire 1 . . . Fire 2 . . . Fire 3 . . . Fire 4. Down periscope.
Hard to starboard. Steer 0-2-0. Shut off for depth-charging." '

*Lieutenant Bromage*: 'At 0458 four torpedoes were fired, aimed individually and spread two-thirds of a ship's length apart on an estimated 100° track with range 2,800 yards, *Sahib* then being about 700
yards 15° on the starboard bow of the *Climene*. Though the sea was
flat calm the attack was unobserved. One hit was obtained. The merchant ship sank almost instantaneously, without survivors according
to the captain of the *Climene*. After firing, *Sahib* nearly broke surface
and the swirl of her propellers was observed by aircraft after the torpedo had hit the target. One bomb was dropped which did no damage but which indicated our position to the *Climene*. She immediately
obtained A/S contact.'

*Leading Seaman Briard*: 'The first lieutenant's voice came sharply:
"Keep her down." Then suddenly: "Open 'A' Kingston." I was
holding the wheel hard to starboard when the sense of urgency of the
last order made me turn my head. The coxswain and second coxwain both had their planes pushed over to hard to dive but the
pointer on the shallow diving-gauge was oscillating crazily between

24 and 26 feet. At that depth I knew that all our periscope standards, and perhaps part of the conning tower, would be plainly visible to the enemy. At this moment there came two unmistakable explosions – the crunch of torpedoes hitting a ship. Our corresponding cheer was hearty, but perhaps a little muted. It might be our turn next to suffer attack. The captain went to the forward periscope and ordered it raised. He swept the area astern several times before the periscope descended into its well. "She's gone! She's disappeared!" He sounded almost surprised. *Sahib* had taken a sharp bow-down angle as we strove for more depth. I still had the wheel pressed over. *Sahib* seemed to be coming round slowly when two violent explosions occurred within a few seconds of each other. "Probably the Junkers having a go at us," observed the skipper. By now we had reached a hundred feet and had begun to level out. We switched to deep diving-gauges. We were all very much aware of the relentless BEEP . . . BEEP . . . BEEP . . . BEEP of the enemy's asdic.'

*Lieutenant Bromage*: '*Sahib* had by this time turned and was proceeding north at 4 knots and at 300 feet. The *Climene* took up a position on the starboard quarter and maintained contact without difficulty in perfect A/S conditions, breaking off only to carry out an all round sweep every five minutes or so. However, no attack developed and no other HE could be heard. The Italians at this time had coastal escorts which had a form of submarine propulsion: they hunted on electric motors operating off batteries but changed over to diesels when they went into attack. At the time I was unaware that such vessels existed. For some three-quarters of an hour I was well aware that I was being hunted because asdic transmissions in contact could be heard. Nevertheless I was mystified because I could not hear any hydrophone effect from the engines of the attacking craft. The submarine was at 250 feet and going very slow to minimize noise when, quite suddenly, hydrophone effect which was clearly audible to the naked ear in the control room started up directly overhead. Very shortly afterwards the asdic office reported the unmistakable sound of depth-charges hitting the water.'

*Leading Seaman Briard*: 'Word that the enemy were preparing to attack came from Ted Cook in the asdic cabinet: "HE on Green 1-2-0, sir. Revs increasing." One of the enemy vessels was building up speed as she approached for an attack. The beeping increased to a steady tattoo. Then, faint at first but rapidly increasing in intensity, came the swish, swish of racing propellers. As was usual in these circumstances, I just gripped the wheel a little tighter and stared unblinkingly at the lubbers line in the compass in front of me. The pattern of depth-charges was right on target and it felt as if some giant hand had taken a hold of the submarine and was continually slamming it down. The shock waves inside the boat seemed to burst inside my head and dim my sight. The stunned, shocked silence which followed the attack was punctured by a sort of hissing roar coming from the engine room department.

' "All compartments report damage to the control room." The captain's voice contained a note of urgency. The gyro in front of me was spinning wildly. When I attempted to put correction on the helm, the wheel spun loosely through my hands. Glancing at the tele-motor pressure-gauge I saw that it read zero. "Steering out of action, sir," I reported. As I sat idly spinning the wheel through my hands, I listened to the reports coming in.'

*Lieutenant Bromage*: 'Quite suddenly, at about 0545, very loud HE started directly overhead. *Sahib* was put full ahead group up and con-sequently, by the time the depth-charges exploded, the centre of the salvo must have been astern of the submarine. Nevertheless the result inside the boat was fairly spectacular (1) the compressor outlet valve, behind the starter on the port side of the after ends, was blown clean off the ship's side, leaving a hole about 1½ inches in diameter. The water that was entering through the hole looked like a 1½-inch-thick steel bar, and no little Dutch boy could have put his finger in that hole (2) every depth-gauge in the ship gave a different reading, anything from 0 to 500 feet (3) all normal emergency lighting in the fore-ends was broken (4) 'A' Relief had lifted (5) 'Q' outboard vent had opened (6) the mainline flood in the magazine space opened (7) the Chief ERA reported that the pressure hull itself was holed under the after-end bilges but the engineer-officer could not confirm this (8) some of the fore-ends crew reported that water was entering for-ward. I considered this to be most unlikely as had the submarine been damaged forward we must inevitably have sunk. In the dark-ness they must have mistaken the loose water caused by "A" Relief lifting for further damage. Numbers 3, 4, 5, and 6 of the faults as listed were soon dealt with but, owing to its position behind the star-ter, attempts to plug the compressor outlet valve proved to be quite impracticable. In the meantime *Sahib*'s stern had dropped, so to cor-rect this I increased speed and blew number five main ballast to bring the boat on an even keel. The control room depth-gauge was fairly steady at about 270 feet at this time, and so the depth was kept by that gauge. More and more buoyance had to be given to keep the

(*Left*) AB Webb, lost in *Parthian* just after his eighteenth birthday. (*Right*) Lt C. A. Pardoe RNR lost when in command of *Parthian*.

(*Left*) Lt Michael Lumby is seen emerging from *Saracen*'s fore-hatch to be greeted by Captain G. B. H. Fawkes, Captain S8, at Algiers in 1943. The depot ship *Maidstone* is in the background. (*Right*) Rear-Admiral Mario Baroglio, pictured here in 1940 when first lieutenant of the submarine *Settimo*. After a year with *Settimo*, he was appointed CO of the submarine *Galatea*, but it was as CO of *Minerva* that he sank Lt Mike Lumby's *Saracen* in August 1943.

(*Above left*) Lt H. B. Turner commanded the small *Unrivalled* with distinction in the Mediterranean in 1942 and 1943 but in November 1944 was appointed to the worn-out, lumbering minelayer *Porpoise* which disappeared in January 1945 after laying a minefield off Penang. (*Above right*) Midshipman R. F. Drake, aged 18, was serving in the *Queen Elizabeth* when he volunteered for submarines. He served in the *Torbay* (Lt-Cdr A. C. C. Miers) and when the first lieutenant of *Torbay*, Lt D. S. Mc. Verschoyle-Campbell obtained his own command the *Stonehenge*, Sub-Lt Drake joined in him as the 'third-hand'. *Stonehenge* disappeared off Northern Sumatra in March 1944.

(*Centre*) *Turbulent* 'doing a trot fob' in Alexandria harbour; these were local harbour movements which could be carried out by any of the boat's officers holding a 'driving licence', that is, being competent to move the boat without supervision from the captain. In the background is the Greek depot ship *Corinthia* with the Greek submarine *Nereus* alongside. *Nereus* completed eleven operational patrols.

(*Bottom*) *Sickle* under way in Algiers harbour. Her captain, Lt J. R. Drummond was jokingly known as 'The man who broke the bank at Monte Carlo' after an errant torpedo had exploded on the cliffs under the famous casino there. An ace of spades on his Jolly Roger commemorated the incident.

boat manageable so, when the engineer-officer reported that there was nothing he could do about the damaged aft, the order to stand by to abandon ship was given and DSEA issued.'

*Leading Seaman Briard*: 'The captain was in the favoured submarine commanders' pose, a stance between the two periscopes with an arm hooked through the lower conning tower ladder. His face was still expressionless but his words, when they came, seemed to hold infinate regret.

' "I'm sorry, lads . . . Stand by to abandon ship." '

'The silence which followed this announcement was itself followed by a burst of frenzied activity as we complied with the order to destroy everything that might be of use to the enemy. DSEA were issued for use as lifebelts when we reached the surface. When the captain was satisfied that all the correct measures had been taken, he told me to open the lower gun tower hatch. The gun tower would serve as an extra exit. While these events were taking place *Sahib* had developed a marked stern-down angle. This the captain had already countered in part by putting a blast of high-pressure air in to number five main ballast tank. But water was still thundering through the hole in the pressure hull and we had either to go upwards or to go down for ever. At this point the captain gave the order to blow all main ballast. As air hissed in to the ballast tanks most eyes were fixed on the useless depth-gauges. Then from the wireless office was heard: "We're on the surface, sir." Apparently a shallow water-gauge which had been switched off for depth-charging had been found to be functioning.'

*Lieutenant Bromage*: 'It was then reported from forward that the boat was breaking up, and at the same time it was reported from aft that we were on the surface. I solved this problem by hitting the periscope wires with my hand and, finding them slack, was happy to agree with the after ends. The control room gauge still said 270 feet. I proceeded onto the bridge. The situation was then as follows: *Sahib* proceeded at about 13 knots with her after casing awash and her bow well up. The *Climene* was on her starboard quarter and the two corvettes on her port quarter, all about 2,000 yards away and firing their forward guns (I later thanked the CO of *Climene* for not firing to hit but he said that he had been). Two Ju88s were machine-gunning the submarine and it was their bullets on the pressure hull that had made the breaking up noises. I then ordered the motors to be stopped and the crew to abandon ship.'

*Leading Seaman Briard*: ' "*Abandon ship!*" The captain's order had been sharp and decisive. I went up the ladder of the gun tower hatch towards a circle of blue sky and hauled myself onto the casing. As I stood shakily near the gun I squinted at the sun sparkling on a calm blue sea. Then, on a course parallel to ours, I saw an Italian destroyer racing along slightly ahead of our starboard beam and at a range of not more than 2,000 yards. A sudden flash came from her forward guns and a pillar of smoke and water shot up about a hundred yards off, and in front of, our bow. The gun flashed again and a second shell landed in almost the same spot. Most of *Sahib*'s crew were now crowded on the casing, all seemingly reluctant to take the first plunge into the sea. The captain called from the conning tower for all hands to keep clear of the main vents. He then disappeared below. There was another flash from the destroyer's gun but I saw no fall of shot as my attention had been drawn to another menace. A Ju88 had wheeled and then banked along our starboard side in preparation for an attack. I saw the plane go into a shallow dive and then come straight towards us low and very fast. As the plane grew rapidly in size, the sound of its engines swelled to a howling crescendo. There was a series of flashes on its wing tips and lines of splashes in the water came racing in our direction. This one definitely wanted us dead. The tracers appeared to move leisurely towards us. One that went past my head at less than a foot made a crack on my left eardrum that tingled for more than a minute. I then heard a clunk, clunk followed by a rush of air from both saddle tanks as *Sahib*'s main vents opened. I stepped down to the saddle tanks. Taking a deep breath I plunged head first into the sea. The water was surprisingly warm. I struck out vigorously to put a few yards between myself and our stricken submarine.'

*Lieutenant Bromage*: 'When I thought all hands were out I looked down the conning tower. I saw a stoker pushing up a leather dhobi basket* which he had bought at Fez when on leave and which he had no intention of leaving behind. Having eventually got this stoker out – without his basket – I went down into the control room. After satisfying myself that the boat was empty, I opened main vents and went up again – *fast*. I had just got over the side from the gun platform when the stern went down and the bows went up. *Sahib* sank at a 90° angle in 600 fathoms at a position approximately 10 miles north of Capo Milazzo. I have had recurrent nightmares about what I would have done if the main vents had not opened! Ju88s continued to

---

* Used for stowing soiled clothing (Author).

machine-gun survivors in the water and it was at this point that Electrical Artificer E.G. England must have lost his life, as he was seen to enter the water with DSEA on. Two ratings had their DSEA hit by bullets but themselves were uninjured. Survivors were picked up promptly by *Climene* and a corvette and after good treatment taken to Messina where we were given dry clothes. Later that night we were taken to Rome for interrogation. The commanding officer of *Climene* informed me that one of the torpedoes passed under the corvette that made the damaging attack. I arrived on board *Climene* at 0615, seventy-seven minutes after firing.'

*Leading Seaman Briard*: 'There were quite a number of bobbing heads around me and from one of them came a yell: "She's going down, lads!" As though ordered, all crew stopped swimming and turned to look back at *Sahib*, now some 30 yards away. Her conning tower had almost disappeared. Her bow was perpendicular, pointing almost to the zenith. Slowly, quietly, she began to sink from sight. Someone called for the traditional three cheers – and then *Sahib* slipped beneath the surface to a thunderous farewell from her crew.'

The Italians report that the merchantman *Galiola* had sunk five minutes after being torpedoed. The *Gabbiano*, *Euterpe*, and *Climene* had turned and made towards the direction of the attack whilst the *Bassini* occupied herself in the rescue of survivors. Of the sinking of *Sahib* it is reported that at 0506 a Ju88 had dropped a bomb 700 yards north of the corvette *Euterpe*. The three units then steered north and began an ECG search. At 0526 the *Gabbiano* (Lieutenant Nilo Foresi) picked up a clear echo a thousand yards to the north. Four minutes later Foresi launched a pattern of twenty-one depth-charges. This attack was followed by the two escorting Ju88s each dropping a bomb at the point where *Gabbiano*'s depth-charges had exploded. At 0537 *Euterpe*, which had drawn towards *Gabbiano*, also obtained ECG contact, at 1,100 yards 005°. At 12 knots she closed to attack. At 0540 *Euterpe*'s captain, Lieutenant Antonio March, ordered away a pattern of thirty depth-charges. It was this attack which caused so much damage to *Sahib*. When *Sahib* appeared on the surface it was about 6,000 yards from where she had torpedoed the *Galiola*, and 800 yards from *Gabbiano* and *Euterpe*. The corvettes opened fire with their main armament and machine-guns. From 2,000 yards the *Climene* opened fire. The ships maintained fire for about two minutes, ceasing when they realized that the submarine was being abandoned.

If, as seems possible, *Sahib* broke surface after firing her torpedoes, this almost certainly was the cause of her being counter-attacked so

quickly; though the Italian ships appear to have seen nothing of
*Sahib*, the Ju88 that dropped a bomb at 0506 probably saw a disturbance and was thus able to attract the attention of the escorts to the
submarine's position. With so little time to distance herself from the
searching warships, the end for *Sahib* was almost inevitable. In a
period of less than ten minutes, *Sahib* was attacked twice with a total
of fifty-one depth-charges. Fortunately for the submariners, the
enemy's gunfire was rather poor; in good visibility and from a range
of 800 to 2,000 yards not one of about fifteen shells hit the target. The
forty survivors rescued by *Climene* included John Bromage and five
officers. Six ratings were rescued by *Gabbiano*. Twenty-three of
*Sahib*'s crew were later to escape captivity, twelve of them reaching
Allied lines.

The *Gabbiano*, the name means seagull, was the name-ship of her
class of sixty corvettes completed after September 1942. She continued in service long after the war. Six months after the sinking of
*Sahib* the *Euterpe* was scuttled at La Spezia. Raised by the Germans,
she served as the *UJ2228* before being scuttled on 24 April 1945 at
Genoa.

Lieutenant Nilo Foresi (*Gabbiano*) survived the war and remained
in the Navy. On 8 March 1958 Foresi died in a car crash at
Louveciennes, France. He was at that time serving with NATO in
Paris. Lieutenant Antonio March, whose attack had been responsible for forcing *Sahib* to surface, retired from the Navy in January
1960. Commander March died in Rome on 25 October 1966.

Leading Seaman Briard had joined HMS *Ganges* in June 1935.
Returning home from overseas he passed through Chatham Gun-
nery School. He then applied to join submarines. In March 1939 he
arrived at HMS *Dolphin*. Within four months he was serving in
*Triumph*. *Sahib* was nearing completion at Birkenhead when Bobby
Briard joined her on 5 May 1942, following duty in *Trident*. As a
POW he escaped captivity and reached Allied lines. Leading Sea-
man Briard had been Mentioned in Despatches in December 1940.
Just prior to the loss of *Sahib* he had been awarded the DSM.

Lieutenant J.H. Bromage, DSO, DSC, had taken *Sahib* to the
Mediterranean in August 1942. Among his successes was an attack
in January 1943 against the *U301* off Capo Bonifacio, Sardinia,
which destroyed the U-boat. Commander John Bromage now lives
in Devon.

*

The loss of *Untamed* in May 1943 seemed all the more tragic by its total unexpectedness. *Untamed* (Lieutenant G.M. Noll) was launched at High Walker on 8 December 1942 and left the yard on 29 March 1943. Two months later (29 May) she drew alongside at Campbeltown, Kintyre, to be greeted by Commander Tom Jenks, Commander S (Campbeltown). With his submarine secured, Noll retired to Jenks's office for a friendly chat. Jenks asked Noll if *Untamed* had any defects, troubles, and the like; he also inquired as to how the crew had so far shaped up. Gordon Noll expressed himself satisfied with submarine and crew, and said that he was looking forward to the exercise planned for the morrow with the A/S training yacht *Shemara*.

The A/S exercise which *Untamed* and *Shemara* (Commander H. Buckle) were to undertake was a standard type known as AST6. During this most elementary of training practices a submarine dives to a safe depth, usually 80 to 90 feet. Throughout the dive the submarine is marked by fisherman's buffs secured to her bridge to indicate her position. The submarine's underwater duration, track, etc., was predetermined and known to the surface vessel taking part.

*Sunday 30th. Untamed* sailed Campbeltown and headed south for the exercising area which in this instance was to be near Sanda Island south of Kintyre. At 0950 *Untamed* dived and commenced her first practice run. In *Shemara* Commander Buckle put the trainees through their paces. After three hours the practice dive drew to an end and *Untamed* came to the surface. Orders were passed for a second practice run to take place. Lieutenant Noll was informed that hedgehog practice would be carried out during the course of the exercise and, if he had no objection, two practice projectiles would be fired on each run. When Noll agreed to the proposals he was informed, also, that he would probably be surfaced before the end of the time specified for the exercise to enable him to comply with his further orders for night exercises. Just before the resumption of the exercise a signal was made by Noll stating that his periscope was leaking and that he wished to make a signal to Captain S3 before diving. This signal was relayed and the exercise resumed. What follows are *Untamed*'s movements as noted by *Shemara*.

*1345.* Submarine reported ready to proceed.

*1348.* Black flag down. Submarine commenced to dive. *Shemara* 087° 5.8 miles from Ship Light House.

*1355.* Commenced the exercise. Range of submarine approximately

1,500 yards. It was intended to give the CO of each team under training two runs each, and further runs if time permitted. The buffs of the submarine were being towed from the conning tower and not from the bow as is the usual practice. The CO of the submarine notified me before diving that he could not tow from the bow.

*1400.* Fired two practice hedgehog projectiles. Increased speed from the attacking speed of 10 knots to 14 knots in order to open range quickly.

*1412.* Second run. Two practice projectiles fired. Buffs sighted. Speed increased after crossing track to open the range quickly.

*1418.* Sighted white smoke-candle, fired by *Untamed*. Position of ship 098° 4.7 miles from Ship Light. Stopped engines and tapped hulls. I was informed there appeared to be a swirl of water around the candle. If there was I did not see it. Estimated distance 1,800 yards.

*1431.* Continued practice. According to A/S reports submarine appeared to be continuing on her course and speed.

*1436.* Fired two practice projectiles. Buffs not sighted, so at 1440 fired one 'INDICATE POSITION' charge. Stopped and tapped hulls. No answering candle.

*1450.* Yellow smoke-candle, fired by *Untamed*, sighted astern about 1,000 yards. I also sighted a yellow smoke-candle in area 'Y'. I made interrogative Uncle Edward One to *St Modwen*, in area 'Y'. Reply was negative. Ship's position 106° 5.2 miles Ship Light House. *Shemara* turned towards smoke-candle. Stopped and tapped hulls. A swirl of water was seen by people on the bridge and by myself, near where the candle had been fired. One of the COs under training and an ex-submarine officer considered that the submarine had fired a water shot. I considered it most unusual and decided to surface the submarine. *Shemara* in A/S contact.

*1458.* Fired three charges to surface submarine. Ship's position 108° 4.8 miles from Ship Light. No answering candles.

*1510.* Fired three charges. In A/S contact. No reply to charges. No buffs seen. Stopped transmitting and listened for HE.

*1515.* HE bearing 145°. Resumed asdic sweeping.

*1526.* Fired one 'INDICATE POSITION' charge and then tried to communicate with submarine on asdic.

*1542.* Fixed position when passing over what was believed to be submarine. 124° 4.6 miles from Ship Light House. No buffs sighted.

*1602.* HE bearing 028° from *Shemara*. Decided all was not well with submarine and made out a signal to Naval Officer in Command to be coded and sent.

*1615.* Resumed transmitting. Echo 360° 600 yards. Fired one 'INDICATE POSITION' charge. Stopped and tapped hulls. 1623. Course 355°. Speed 5 knots. Echo 020°, 1,000 yards. Altered course to 020°.

*1628.* Stopped transmitting. Listened to whistle effect.

*1637.* Strong whistle effect heard right ahead.

*1648.* Zero time. No smoke-candles. Whistle effect. All round lookout.

*1706.* Slow ahead. Echo 080°, 1,900 yards. *Shemara* steering 080°.

*1710.* Reduced range to 1,300 yards. Fired three charges.

*1712.* Echo 075°, 800 yards. Buffs sighted bearing 080°. Proceeded towards buffs to pass astern. Course 063°.

*1713.* Stopped. Echo 077°, 700 yards.

*1716.* Echo 135°, 300 yards. HE and sound of blowing tanks. Continuous whistle effect and sound of blowing tanks until

*1720.* Echo 155°, 150 yards. Echo sounder showing 24½ fathoms. *Shemara*'s position 105°, 4.2 miles Ship Light House. Buffs bearing 164°, 150 yards.

*1721.* Submarine working engines and blowing tanks.

*1724.* Echoes bearing 170°. Submarine's engines stopped and starting.

*1730.* Echoes 175°, 250 yards. HE ceased and restarted. Ship's head 095°.

*1733. St Modwen* and submarine *Thrasher* arrived. *Thrasher* trying to communicate with *Untamed*.

*1735.* HE strong.

*1737.* HE ceased.

*1738.* HE.

*1745.* HE heard for about a minute and from then onwards no more sounds came from the submarine.

Commander Buckle dropped a dan buoy 400 yards from *Untamed*'s buffs and dispatched a boat to the position of the buffs with orders to look out for any object on and in the water. Two hours later Commander Buckle dropped a second dan buoy a hundred yards from the submarine. The sea at the time *Untamed* had dived had been calm but as the day drew towards its close the weather showed a marked deterioration. At 2200 Buckle took the precaution of dropping a 5 hundredweight sinker and some floats alongside *Untamed*'s buffs as insurance against the buffs being carried away. Around this time some large air-bubbles were seen. At 2333 *Shemara* dropped anchor 800 yards from *Untamed*'s position. An asdic watch was maintained. Ten minutes into the watch the Royal Navy diving ship *Tedworth* arrived. The submarine's crew had by this time ceased to exist.

During the night conditions became very difficult for boat work. With tidal conditions making operations hazardous for divers, it was not until 1115 on the morning of 1 June, forty-five hours after *Untamed* had dived, that divers found *Untamed* lying on an even keel on a hard, flat sandy bottom. There was no response to a diver tap-

ping on one of the hatches. A quick examination of *Untamed* showed
no obvious damage.

When it became clear that there were not going to be survivors,
thoughts were directed towards raising *Untamed*, particularly in view
of recent acts of suspected sabotage. By the evening of 1 June the raising of *Untamed* had been turned over to a salvage company. All naval
craft with the exception of *Tedworth* were ordered to withdraw. On 7
June *Tedworth* reported one lifting craft in position. Further operations had to be suspended when a southerly gale compelled a return
to Campbeltown, so it was not until 1530 on the 9th that the first of
the four 9-inch lifting wires was placed on *Untamed*'s bows. The
intention was to place two wires forward and two wires aft, each wire
passing in a bight under the keel and up to the lifting vessel. By the
15th all four wires were in position and the task of lifting *Untamed*
from the seabed was put into operation. On the afternoon of 19 June,
*Untamed* had by then been manoeuvred into 115 feet of water, a halt
had to be made owing to the onset of rough weather and the need to
replace worn cables. It was another week before *Untamed* was safely
inside the boom at Campbeltown. An investigation into the cause of
her failure to surface was immediately got underway.

When *Untamed* was pumped out it was found that, other than
spaces left by overhead air-locks, the entire vessel had been flooded
with the exception of the central compartment which comprised the
control room, wardroom, and wireless office. After studying the evidence the investigating committee was able to piece together the
most likely reason for *Untamed*'s foundering – which appeared to be
not entirely the cause of a single accident or mistake but of a series of
errors and misfortune, i.e., misuse of the Ottway log, failure of the
crew to respond quickly with the correct action during the initial
stages of flooding, distortion of a water-tight door in the bulkhead
separating the torpedo stowage compartment from the crew space,
and the incorrect assembly of a valve used for rapid flooding.

The routine aboard *Untamed* during the first half hour of her second dive had been pretty much the same as her previous dive, with
the exception that shortly after 1400 Petty Officer Welford, the torpedo gunner's mate, had entered the auxiliary machinery space at
the after end of the torpedo stowage compartment to withdraw and
examine the Ottway log.

As this log is crucial to what occurred later, a few words as to its
function may be helpful. Basically the Ottway log was an electro-
mechanical device used for measuring a ship's speed through the

water by means of a small propeller spinning in a tube which, because the propeller required a flow of water over it to make it spin, protruded through the bottom of the pressure hull and into the sea. For the spinning action to take place the log had to be lowered from its normally stowed position. This operation was carried out by opening the hull valve, or sluice, and winding down the log tube by hand. To raise the log back into its stowage, or log tank, for whatever reason (shallow water, shutting off for depth-charging, maintenance, etc.,) the process was reversed, the log would be raised and the hull valve beneath it shut, thus making it safe to lift the whole log clear.

It is thought that Petty Officer Welford – it was presumed to have been Welford – raised the log, but just failed to raise it completely. He then shut the sluice valve but, as the bottom of the log was not fully clear of the valve, the sluice valve only partially closed. When Petty Officer Welford felt the sluice valve operating wheel go hard home he mistakenly thought that it was shut, when in fact it was only two-thirds shut. It is believed that Welford failed to take proper note of an indicator which would have shown the state of the sluice valve. Welford's next move must then have been to open the hinged watertight cover over the log tank in order to have access to the log. He then unscrewed the three bolts securing the log to its raised crosshead. The moment he did this, and as the pressure of the sea-water had access to the bottom of the log, it must have been forced upwards and partially clear of the tank by the pressure. This at once opened up the auxiliary machinery space directly to the sea; a jet of water of more than 35 pounds per spare inch entered the fore-ends through an opening of approximately three square inches. Water would have entered the compartment at about two tons a minute.

The situation for *Untamed* was serious but at that stage was not completely damaging. It is believed that had immediate steps been taken to blow number one main ballast tank (capacity 16 tons) *Untamed* could have been raised to a shallower depth or even to the surface where the danger would have been less pressing. There was no direct evidence to show that this was not done, but the fact remains that *Untamed* settled at 160 feet. As there was no way of stopping the rapid inflow of water – the cover of the log tank could not be shut owing to the log protruding – the compartment was abandoned and the hatch shut and clipped. It is not easy to see what took place after this, but as fourteen DSEA were found in lockers in the torpedo stowage compartment it is certain that the tube space and torpedo stowage compartment were evacuated hurriedly by all except Petty Officer Welford and Sub-Lieutenant Acworth, the latter possibly engaged in superintending the examination of the Ottway log.

During this hurried evacuation no effort seems to have been made to shut a watertight door between the torpedo space and the torpedo stowage compartment. But the forward watertight door of the control room had been shut and fastened. On one side of this control room door were thirty-four men; on the other side were Sub-Lieutenant Acworth and Petty Officer Welford. Attempts were made by Acworth and Welford to shut the watertight door of the bulkhead separating the crew space from the torpedo space compartment. However, after salvage this door was found to be open and swinging; furthermore it was also found to be slightly distorted at its bottom, but that had the door been held shut by hand this distortion was not sufficient to prevent a pressure building up in the torpedo space compartment and finally forcing the door on to its seat, regardless of whether or not the locking gear was in operation. In the type of watertight door in question were a large number of dogs with sliding wedges that fitted into corresponding holes in the frame of the door which rotates and binds all these wedges. There is also a leading clip to catch the first hole of the door; when the door is shut the leading clip would grip and hold the door nearly shut. In *Untamed* the wedges at the top of the relevant door would start to ride up correctly on the wedges of the door, but they were not doing so at the bottom. The door had been distorted in such a way that the lower half was pressed outward – that is to say, forward – about a quarter of an inch. It was never satisfactorily determined whether this door had been damaged before or during the flooding of *Untamed*, or what had caused the damage. It was, however, considered that the distortion may have been caused by some foreign matter having fallen between the moving wedges and the lower coaming of the door, and that some considerable force had been used to try and shut the door against this obstruction. The finding of tackle in the crew space tends to add weight to the theory that some abnormal force may have been used to try and shut this door. No obstruction was found after salvage, but it may have been a piece of wood which had floated away when pressure on each side of the door had equalized. This equalization would also allow the door to open and swing freely during salvage operations.

A period of approximately three hours forty-five minutes, that is until about 1815, seems to have been devoted to attempts to get

*Untamed* back to the surface. At 1745 it was reported that all sounds of machinery working had ceased, although oil was seen coming to the surface as late as 1815. It is presumed that at about this time the idea of saving *Untamed* was given up and preparations made for escaping. The control room was abandoned and shut off. All but two of the crew, Acworth and Welford, made their way into the engine room for an exit through the after escape hatch. The process of escape was rapidly to flood the compartment through a special large flooding connection fitted for this purpose. This connection had in it a screw-down valve on the hull and a flag valve immediately below it. Unfortunately, and tragically as things turned out, this flap valve was defective. A subsequent examination of the flap valve showed that though it was in an apparent open position as indicated by the pointer, the lever was in actual fact assembled 90° from its correct position. This caused the indicator to show OPEN when the flap valve was shut and it also meant that the lever could not appreciably be moved when the pin was removed. How the valve came to be in this condition is not known. One theory was that the valve had been incorrectly assembled from the outset; but this view appears to have been dashed when a petty officer stated that he was certain he had worked the valve on 16 March during an examination of *Untamed*'s escape apparatus – and it does seem unlikely that if the valve had been incorrectly assembled it would not have been discovered on installation, and certainly during one of the inspections carried out before final acceptance. The most likely explanation is that the lever was removed, possibly for cleaning, and wrongly replaced by a member of the submarine's crew. For whatever reason the flap valve had become defective, the fact remains that the special means of rapid flooding was denied to *Untamed*'s crew, though it is not quite understood why they did not remove the access cover to the flap, which would have given the necessary flooding aperture.

Such a large number of personnel crammed in the darkened engine room must have made the location and operation of alternative means of flooding extremely difficult. After discovering that the flap valve was inoperative other ways of flooding were tried during which some of the more obvious methods were overlooked or half completed, an indication that by this time mental process had been drastically affected by the $CO_2$ content. The flooding of the engine room continued at a slow rate. This slow flooding was the result of the underwater drain-gun cock, situated in the after ends, having been left open. The underwater drain-gun cock had a tray beneath it for catching and holding water when the gun was drained down after firing a smoke-candle. The tray had a small pipe leading through the engine room bulkhead to the bilges. The pipe was fitted with a cock for shutting off in the engine room side of the bulkhead. The engine room pressure could not be equalized with the pressure outside the submarine until the after compartment was also equalized through this small quarter-inch-bore pipe. The long delay was fatal. Not all the crew waiting to escape had DSEA. The DSEA from the control room, together with two DSEA from the crew space, had been brought into use but as this amounted to only twenty-four of all the DSEA on board, ten of the crew were without DSEA. The danger of carbon dioxide poisoning must have been acute. Several of the crew had vomited into their DSEA. In view of the congestion in the engine room, it might have been desirable for a party to have chanced an escape via the conning tower. There is no doubt that a conning tower escape was at some time contemplated as instructions for escaping by this means were found on the wardroom table. Possibly it was thought of as being too difficult.

It is not possible to say with precision when death overcame the crew; watches worn by several men had stopped between 2130 and 2200. The engine room clock, situated high in the compartment, had stopped at 2207.

On 16 June, the day after *Untamed* was reported ready for lifting off the seabed, Lieutenant A.J.W. Pitt of the submarine *Taku* arrived at Campbeltown. Arthur W. Pitt had been appointed to assist the salvage company in technical matters concerning *Untamed* and to take special note when the submarine was 'get-atable' to see that nothing was touched which could have materially affected her sinking. Lieutenant Pitt eventually remained with *Untamed* until after she had been examined by a committee and had been towed to Barrow. His experience with *Untamed* makes his views on the submarine's foundering of special interest. Arthur Pitt's account is taken up from where the crew hurriedly evacuate the torpedo stowage compartment.

'It is my personal opinion that the bulkhead door leading into the crew space was known to be defective and that the bulk of the crew immediately went straight through into the control room, shutting that compartment's forward bulkhead door. In the meantime Sub-Lieutenant Acworth and Petty Officer Welford shut down the auxiliary machinery space hatch and themselves went into the crew space where they attempted to make this defective bulkhead door as watertight as possible by securing a tackle somehow on the door and onto the bulkhead in the POs' mess. Whether or not they were in communication with the control room I do not know, but it appears that they must have opened the bilge suction to the auxiliary machinery space. On the other hand, if the rest of the crew had not immediately gone into the control room perhaps one of them did it. At any rate, it was open, which made any pumping of two and three main ballast tanks ineffective. Quite what happened to this officer and rating after that is difficult to say. They were found sitting facing each other on opposite bunks in the POs' mess. The petty officer was naked with a blanket wrapped around him which seems to suggest that he had got thoroughly soaked during the initial flooding and had taken off his wet clothing. From the way they were sitting it seems that death must have come rather suddenly to them. The petty officer had a DSEA round his ankle and there was one other DSEA close to Sub-Lieutenant Acworth; otherwise no attempt nor preparation had been made to escape through the DSEA hatch in the torpedo stowage compartment, the clips of which were tightly secured and twill trunk lashed in the stowage position. I consider both this officer and rating could have had very little idea of what they were doing from the start of the flooding for they made no attempt to shut the tube space door and they made no attempt to get into communication with the control room through the bulkhead voice-pipe.

'Now considering the crew who were in the control room; there was no evidence either way as to whether they tried to blow the flooded compartments through the salvage blows. It seems they did not. Presumably they were not quite sure as to the condition of the next compartment, i.e., whether it was flooded or not, whether the officer and rating were in there or not. If they had tried to pump out two and three main ballast, they would not have been successful unless they had done it before shutting the bulkhead door. Also, if they had tried to blow them before shutting the bulkhead door, this being necessary as two and three master blows and Kingstons were shut, they would still have no success as the blower drain was found to be open and there would have been no way of shutting this in the auxiliary machinery space as it was one of the first to be flooded and "unget-atable". It seems that they made every attempt to lighten the vessel – there was no high pressure air left in the bottles – and also it appears that number five main ballast, which was, I believe, full of fuel, had been pumped at least two-thirds out.

'On getting into the engine room they shut the bulkhead door and ventilation into the control room completely and effectively, so that the control room remained dry until it was entered after the submarine was salvaged. They also shut off the after ends but unfortunately left the underwater gun drain-cock open. This drain passes through from the after ends, through the engine room bulkhead and into the bilge. They started to try and flood the engine room but found that no water would come in; this was owing to the fact that the flap valve in the emergency flood system was shut when the indicator read OPEN. It was found during the investigation that the handle of this valve had been secured 90°wrong and that this flap valve could only read in the OPEN position. It was immovable and was actually always shut. They may have wrestled with the actual hand-wheel and flap valve for a bit, because the hand-wheel was found to be off and lying on top of the engines. They then set about flooding the engine room through other means, the main method being to flood through the engine room mainline hose connection suction valve. All manner of other valves were opened but without much system. It seemed to me to indicate that in the general congestion and worry of the moment there was no reasoning brain directing their efforts. The only other places where I found a small amount of water coming through in the engine room when trying to make it tight was through the after heads, whose valve and intermediate valve were open (a trickle was coming through when she was on the surface, presumably more would come through at 150 feet), and through the underwater gun drain, but this was only draining down the after ends which had been flooded because the engine room was flooded. It appears from looking at water marks that there would only be about two feet of headspace when the engine room could be fully flooded. I think that in the general congestion of thirty-four people in that space, some of the crew would find that when the water began to get up to that level it would be difficult for them to keep their heads above water owing to projections sticking down from the top of the compartment, such as DSEA lockers and valves. These people began to get a bit worried and wanted the Chief ERA, who had obviously been detailed off, to open the hatch before the compartment was fully flooded; the clips were off and the hatch was easy to lift, as found by divers three days later, but the Chief ERA himself could not raise it against the outside pressure.

'I consider that the final thing that defeated their efforts to escape was that the drain of the underwater gun was open, so that up to the time taken to flood the engine room there was also the time taken to flood-up the after ends, of which the crew were unaware, through a very small pipe, and this would have taken a considerable time. It is probable that until this after end was nearly flooded up there could not be any chance of the Chief ERA pushing open the engine room hatch and that they all began to drown or die before it was open. It had been made complicated for the Chief ERA to open the hatch by the fact that people were crowding up behind him on first getting into the engine room, we found the head of the next man after him only six inches from the coaming, then only two feet below the coaming were two other bodies jammed absolutely tight trying to get out.'

The conclusion drawn as to why *Untamed* was not saved by her crew, and why they themselves failed to escape, was disconcerting. It was considered that her loss was directly attributable to the crew failing to take immediate, obvious, and adequate steps to prevent unrestricted flooding. The fact that such an obvious measure as the shutting of a watertight door was neglected, plus the leaving of fourteen DSEA in the torpedo stowage compartment, indicates that for a short time a certain amount of panic must have prevailed. It seems that the great danger was not immediately realized, so that emergency measures to surface were left until too late. Numbers one and six main ballast tanks had apparently been blown, but it is not clear whether two, three, four, and five had been blown as their Kingston valves were found shut, which may have been done after an attempt to blow when pumping had been resorted to, as it had been in the case of four and five ballast tanks. All high pressure air had been practically expended, so that although it is not certain whether all main ballast tanks had been blown it is clear that a good deal of blowing had taken place. Efforts by the crew to save *Untamed* were continued long after it should have been realized that these efforts were futile. This indicated a lack of appreciation of the situation and deficient technical knowledge, attributed in part to the comparatively short time allowed for training. The failure of the crew to escape was put down to poor drill, ignorance, and lack of leadership, which no doubt was accentuated towards the end by $CO_2$ poisoning.

Mishandling of the Ottway log had of course set the whole tragic train of events in motion. The Ottway log remained in regular use in Royal Navy submarines until the early 1960s when it was replaced by the more reliable electronic log. As for *Untamed*, she eventually went to war as HM Submarine *Vitality*. She was scrapped at Troon in March 1946.

August 1943 saw the loss of *Parthian*, a stalwart of the China Station.

Lieutenant-Commander M.G. Rimmington was her captain when towards the end of April 1940 she arrived at Alexandria from the Far East and secured alongside *Medway*. Her first Mediterranean patrol was off Tobruk and took place shortly after Italy's entry into the war. At midnight 19/20 June, Rimmington received a signal reporting an enemy submarine *en route* for Tobruk. The enemy was sighted through the periscope on the afternoon of the 20th. Rimmington was able to manoeuvre for an attack with four torpedoes. The submarine was hit and she sank with the loss of all hands. This attack on the Italian *Diamente* made *Parthian* the first Royal Navy submarine to sink an enemy vessel in the Mediterranean.

Another sinking by *Parthian* of an enemy submarine took place in June 1941. Allied naval forces operating off the Syrian coast had experienced trouble with Vichy submarines. On 21 June Rimmington sailed Alexandria to see what could be done about the matter. It was Wednesday 25th when Rimmington sighted the Vichy French submarine *Souffleur* on the surface. The Frenchman dived before *Parthian* could attack. For three hours Rimmington tracked the enemy. When *Souffleur* again came to the surface, Rimmington was ready with four torpedoes. *Souffleur* was hit under her conning tower and sank at once. As the attack had taken place within two miles of the coast road and less than four miles from an airfield, Michael Rimmington rightly withdrew seawards and did not attempt a rescue of survivors. The attack on *Souffleur* brought *Parthian*'s Mediterranean activities to a close. She had been away from home for more than three years. In mid-August *Parthian* sailed Alexandria. She survived attacks by Allied ships off Gibraltar and arrived at Fort Blockhouse to an enthusiastic reception.

After a refit in the United States *Parthian* returned to the Mediterranean. She sailed Malta under the command of thirty-one years old Lieutenant Cyril Pardoe, RNR, on 21 July. Pardoe had been briefed to keep off shore and to operate on cross-Adriatic routes. On 26 July when Taranto battleships were showing signs of activity, Pardoe was ordered to patrol in the vicinity 090° Capo Otranto 10 miles. This order was cancelled on 28 July and he was ordered to patrol between 40°N and 41°13'N. Lieutenant Pardoe was ordered to leave patrol on 6 August and to make a brief patrol summary when south of 36°N. No signal was received and *Parthian* did not arrive at Beirut on the morning of 11 August, the date of her expected arrival. Her loss is thought to have been the result of mining in the Adriatic some time after 6 August.

With Lieutenant Michael Lumby at the helm *Saracen* had an

eventful twelve months as a warship. *Saracen* had been launched in February 1942. She was on her work-up patrol when on 3 August Lumby torpedoed the *U335* north-east of the Shetlands. It was shortly after this that *Saracen*'s bows were heading south to do battle in the Mediterranean. Lieutenant Lumby was quickly on the offensive. An early victim was the Italian submarine *Granito*. On 9 November Lumby attacked and sank her with three torpedoes off Capo San Vito, Sicily.

*Saracen* had two patrols remaining when in early July 1943 she sailed for a billet off Tuscany. On the morning of 6 July Lieutenant Lumby was patrolling to the west of the island of Monte Cristo when he sighted a steamer on a heading for Bastia. Five minutes later he attacked with torpedoes. The *Tripoli* was hit and sunk. The Italians dispatched ships in search of *Saracen*. The search continued for days. The corvettes *Danaide* and *Cormorano* had been carrying out A/S sweeps for five days when at 0545 on the 10th, at 070° 15 miles Bastia, the *Danaide* obtained a submarine contact and attacked. Michael Lumby saw the Italian approaching at speed and was at 300 feet when the depth-charges exploded, forcing *Saracen* down even farther. Luckily for *Saracen* two aircraft intervened and drove off the Italians. After effecting repairs Lumby was able to continue the patrol, claiming the German steamer *Tell* as a victim. *Saracen* was again counter-attacked and damaged. Lumby retired to a quieter area to carry out repairs and rest the crew. On 16 July he was able to begin the return to harbour, arriving at Algiers on the 20th. Badly shaken by the counter-attacks, *Saracen* required extensive repairs before she was able to put to sea on her next patrol, her last before leaving the Mediterranean.

On 5 August, the day before departing on her final patrol, *Saracen* was taken into the swept channel for engine trials. On her return the steamer *Fort Lamont* was seen to be ablaze in the harbour entrance with HM Destroyer *Arrow*, also on fire, lashed alongside her. As the *Fort Lamont* was expected to blow up, Lieutenant Lumby was invited to sink her. At a range of twenty yards *Saracen*'s gun duly obliged. This was the last ship sunk by *Saracen* and was never shown on her Jolly Roger.

*August 6. Saracen* put to sea from Algiers. Steering an easterly course she passed into the Tyrrhenian Sea and crossed to the Naples area before cruising northwards along the coast, finally arriving off Bastia, Corsica, on the 13th. Lieutenant Lumby takes up the story: 'We were ordered to proceed on the surface to patrol in the vicinity of Bastia. The passage was without incident but had one novelty to us:

we had just been fitted with a pair of dipoles on the side of the bridge. These were to pick up enemy airborne radar. They certainly picked up radar transmissions continuously and of varying degrees of loudness, but gave no bearing or distance. It quickly became apparent that we would never reach our patrol area if we took any notice of these unless they became very loud. This they never did and, fortunately, on diving for trim on the second morning, the system flooded up and the worry was removed from us.

'The patrol area was well known to us. I had seen Bastia through the periscope many times and knew what it looked like. On Friday 13 August we dived in what we had come to believe was the approach channel to Bastia. During the night we had received a signal alerting us to some activity in the Bastia area. It was a hot, still day, with the sea like glass, and rather hazy. Asdic conditions were appalling. We headed in towards Bastia. As we got closer it appeared that there was a large merchant ship in the harbour. We spent the day patrolling quite close in, watching for any movement in the harbour. The odd patrol vessel was seen but with the bad Asdic conditions no HE was heard, nor were any Asdic transmissions. Once a seaplane landed with its floats astride the periscope. But no one seemed to suspect our presence. As evening approached, the haze cleared and I realized I had been fooled by a mirage. The 'ship' in Bastia Harbour had become a building and a chimney! So we set off out to sea again, surfacing to charge, I suppose, at about 2230 when well clear of the land. We surfaced to find an enormous full moon bearing south, and a glassy sea still. We had no choice but patrol up and down the moon. This we did, starting in a northerly direction. At about 2345 the watch officer sighted two MTB-like craft and two larger vessels to the north. These must have had us silhouetted against the moon. We dived straight to 400 feet and put our faith in the bad Asdic conditions. Strangely enough we seemed to have dived into a pool of fresh water. The HE of the four vessels was very clear and Asdic transmissions very loud.'

The two larger vessels sighted were the Italian corvettes *Minerva*, commanded by 29-year-old Lieutenant Mario Baroglio, and *Euterpe*, still under the command of Antonio March. Baroglio had sailed Bastia that morning (13th) with the intention of hunting *Saracen*, sighted earlier at a point 6 miles from Bastia. Baroglio had passed Bastia's mine barrage at 1028. Once free of the barrage he started an ECG search whilst awaiting the arrival of *Euterpe*. Throughout the remainder of the 13th the Italians hunted *Saracen*. It was not until after midnight that the A/S hunt produced positive results. Lieutenant Mario

Baroglio's log entries for the early hours of the 14th are reproduced together with Lieutenant Michael Lumby's account of *Saracen*'s loss.

*Lieutenant Baroglio*: '14/0014. The ECG recorded an obstacle 270°, distance 700 metres. Turned 90° to port and ordered the engines slow ahead. At the end of the turn the ECG beat again at 310° and at a distance of 750 metres. Turned to port a further 50° and at the end of the turn stopped engines to avoid cutting the distance of the obstacle to less than 400 metres. From 0022 to 0040 the ECG continued to beat on the obstacles while I maintained practically a constant course.

'14/0040. Having obtained with certainty the identification of an enemy submarine moving at a speed of about 3 knots on a course equal to mine and at a distance of about 700 metres, I increased speed to 14 knots and started the attack.

'14/0046. I started the bombardment and discharged four salvos of eight depth charges plus two more salvos of four depth-charges each.'

*Lieutenant Lumby*: 'After a short time one of the vessels came in to attack and dropped its carpet of thirty-six depth-charges. All seemed close, but the last one made the boat whip alarmingly, a lamp bulb landed in my coffee cup and the steering wheel sheared off. Then a report came that the after ends had been evacuated (the watchkeeper in the after ends left so quickly that he could not give a description of the damage). Attempts to get back into the after ends were unavailing, they being full of water; otherwise all systems appeared to be functioning correctly. The boat of course assumed a considerable bow-up angle. We attempted to correct this with main ballast trimming but it was not very successful. We porpoised up and down and used up a lot of air.'

*Lieutenant Baroglio*: '14/0049. I reversed the course and approached the zone marked by our two flares. At the end of the approach I stopped making way.

'14/0053. At about 650 metres I saw the highest part of the submarine's conning tower emerging almost in line with the corvette *Euterpe*, which had reached me in the zone and was on the opposite side of the submarine. I put the engines at full speed to ram. After a few minutes the conning tower of the submarine submerged again. I stopped the engines. Almost instantly the ECG regained contact with the submarine at about 450 metres. I manoeuvred the corvette to maintain the bow on the target as the ECG was fading rapidly to port. I ordered preparations for a second bombardment.'

*Lieutenant Lumby*: 'I was quite determined not to be sunk on Friday 13th. Once it was past midnight I began to wonder how long we could continue porpoising up and down. I was kept informed of the HP air situation. Fairly soon, I have no idea how long as it seemed ages, I decided we were on a losing game. Hands were ordered to muster in the control room with DSEA. Sadly many of the DSEA burst on being inflated. I suppose twelve months in the Mediterranean had caused them to perish. Those without DSEA were told to hold on to men with DSEA when they got into the sea. Everyone was told to gather on the casing and jump into the sea together when the main vents were opened. The order to surface was given at 400 feet. It seemed to take a very long time and a lot of HP air before the depth-gauges started moving in the right direction. Once started the gauges moved very fast.'

*Lieutenant Baroglio*: '14/0059. On about 310° distance 500 metres I saw the submarine emerging slightly on her side. I ordered the gun and machine-gun to open fire. The shooting was bang on target. I got the impression that the submarine was in motion. I continued to approach to port. Then I noticed the enemy unit on 15° and continued to chase. At that moment we heard the shouts for help from the survivors, who moved along the side of the corvette.'

*Lieutenant Lumby*: 'My Italian captors told me that we cleared the sea like a salmon leaping. A marvellous sight in the full moonlight. I came up the tower last, having opened the main vents, and was relieved to see that the boat was diving. Everyone had jumped off the casing but there were still three figures on the bridge. Then we four jumped. The sea was very warm. There was some 5-inch gunfire going on but I never saw any splashes and certainly nothing hit us.'

*Lieutenant Baroglio*: '14/0105. I was just going to signal the *Euterpe* to stop firing, to allow me to go close to the submarine, when I saw the enemy unit sliding strongly and sinking rapidly. I gave the order to stop firing and to prepare the motor-boat. I returned to the survivors, who were about 500 metres astern from the point of sinking.

'14/0107. Whilst some survivors were being rescued directly from the sea, I launched the motor-boat. To facilitate and hasten the salvage operations I used the searchlight to light the surrounding area. A similar operation was carried out by *Euterpe*.'

*Lieutenant Lumby*: 'We four who had jumped last were some way from the main body of the ship's company when the corvette *Minerva* came past. Loud whistles attracted her attention and she stopped and picked us up. Had I not been very good at whistling through my fingers I do not think she would have stopped as she was going quite fast. Once aboard *Minerva* I directed her to where the main group was and they were duly picked up. Two men were missing: Acting

Stoker Petty Officer Ward, who I knew was a non-swimmer, and Able Seaman Downer of the spare crew, who also may have been a non-swimmer. When being led through the mess decks of *Minerva* I saw a number of wounded men. Assuming they were members of my ship's company I demanded to be allowed to speak to them. However, I was hurried forward and assured they were Italians, members of *Minerva*'s crew who had been hit by gunfire from the other corvette. We were very well treated aboard *Minerva*. I was put in the engineer-officer's cabin and brought brandy and coffee. My clothes were taken away to be dried and I was amused to find when they came back that the sheets of periscope paper in my shirt pocket had been dried individually!'

Now to the experience of Stoker Edward Metcalfe. Having joined the Submarine Service the previous January, Metcalfe was a relative newcomer to submarines. He can still recall the shattering explosive force of the depth-charging: 'The submarine suffered a direct hit in the after ends. In the stokers' mess deck the plates sprung above the compressors and water poured in. The bulkhead door was ordered shut, and the after ends were then sealed off. With the weight of water in the stern, the captain had great difficulty in holding trim. In order to keep any sort of buoyancy full ahead was ordered. This sent the boat through the water stern-down at 45°.'

In compliance with Lieutenant Lumby's orders all hands had assembled in the control room. 'Come on, skipper. It's up to you,' Metcalfe remembers hearing uttered in the gloom. Lumby ordered *Saracen* to the surface. The first lieutenant stood poised on the ladder ready to fling open the hatch at a moment's notice. The instant the hatch cleared surface, the first lieutenant leaped smartly through. Behind him came the clatter of feet as the crew made a speedy exit up the ladder. 'On getting into the conning tower I experienced a tremendous blast of air,' reports Stoker Metcalfe. 'Looking over the top I saw it was as colourful as Blackpool. Tracer was coming from all over the place. I jumped on top of the conning tower and, seeing people lying on the saddle tanks, I decided to dive off the top of the conning tower and get away from the saddle-tanks. I landed in the water. There was quite a bit of swell running. The next thing I knew there were crew all over me. Eventually I was picked up by a boat. When we got alongside the Italian ship I looked up and saw the name at the bottom of the gangway: MINERVA. I thought – Blimey! That was the name of an auxiliary ship for coastal forces at Gosport. I had climbed aboard and was walking along a passage when I caught sight of myself in a mirror. I was covered from head to foot in blood. I looked like a Red Indian. I hadn't realized I'd been hit. They sat me down and gave me a cigarette; then they began pulling bits of some 20mm shrapnel out of me from all over the place.'

Engine Room Artificer F.K. Hutchings also has clear recollections of *Minerva*'s devastating attack: 'We had great difficulty in keeping our trim and depth. Due to the efforts of our captain we managed to surface. As the boat was in no condition to proceed as a fighting unit, the captain ordered abandon ship. Before leaving, the captain ordered me to open all main vents. The motors were still running when we left the control room and went up the conning tower to leap into the sea. The *Saracen* continued to run for a short distance before she took her last dive. The Italians treated us very well and gave us brandy, cigarettes, and blankets.'

*Lieutenant Baroglio*: '14/0150. Having rescued all the survivors the two units set course for Bastia.

'14/0333. Manoeuvred to enter port.

'14/0410. Moored at North Dock. Disembarked the prisoners and handed them over to the military authorities.'

The whole operation had taken 17 hours and 22 minutes. *Minerva* had steamed 188 miles and had taken twenty-six prisoners, including two officers. The *Euterpe* had returned with twenty prisoners, three officers among them.

Bastia had not yet awakened when the submariners were marched from *Minerva*, through the town, and up a hill to what resembled an old fort. They were given a change of clothing and put into cells. 'I was taken to a hospital which was run by nuns,' recalls Stoker Metcalfe. 'There were two of us wounded: apart from myself there was Stoker Petty Officer Paddy Ryan, who I think was wounded in the leg. I had a few fairly heavy shrapnel wounds, four or five through the chest. We were in hospital for quite some time. When they let us out for a walk we were exercised in a yard which looked out at the waters where we had been sunk. It was no surprise to me that we had been sighted in that sort of water, as from there I could have seen a periscope ten or twelve miles away owing to the placidness of the water.'

After four days at the fort the crew were taken to the dockyard for the journey to Piombino, sixty miles away on the Italian mainland. On arrival in Italy they were ushered into lorries and taken to a railway station. After a night at the station they boarded a train for Rome. At the Italian capital they transferred to another train. Its destination was Manziana where on a hill overlooking the town was situated the interrogation centre known as Campo No 1 Marina. 'We were interrogated by a German and an Italian officer, kept in separate cells, and had our hair and beards shaved,' states ERA Hutchings. 'When we were let out for exercise we hardly recognized shipmates with whom we had lived with for two years. We were kept in that camp until the Italian surrender.'

When the Germans began their move to take control of prisoner of war camps which were under Italian supervision, some prisoners, fearing a move to Germany, made their escape. Edward Metcalfe had a whole series of adventures while on the loose. He was never recaptured and eventually met up with the Allies in Italy. ERA Hutchings – awarded a DSM for his service in *Saracen* – also remained free from recapture, and at one time worked with the Gurkhas. For his assistance to escaped POWs he received a Mention in Despatches. Hutchings had been in the Navy since 1938 and had joined *Saracen* when she was under construction at Cammell Laird.

Lieutenant Mario Baroglio was born at Casale Monferrato, Piedmont, on 3 January 1914. In October 1928 he entered the Naval Academy at Livorno as a cadet. In November 1939 he joined submarines. His first command, the submarine *Galates*, came in December 1940. Baroglio was appointed to *Minerva* on 4 February 1943. At this time *Minerva* was still in the hands of her builders, Cantieri Riuniti dell'Adriatico, at Monfalcone. Lieutenant Baraglio remained *Minerva*'s captain until 24 February 1944. Between September 1957 and November 1959 Captain Baroglio was with SHAPE* in Paris. Rear-Admiral Baroglio retired from the Navy on 15 January 1964 after almost thirty years distinguished service. He now lives in Livorno.

*Minerva* had been in service only five months when she sank *Saracen*. At the time of the Italian armistice she had completed over fifty operations. This *Gabbiano* class corvette was still giving faithful service in 1969.

Lieutenant Michael Lumby had been a submariner since 1938. A Dartmouth entrant of 1931, prior to joining submarines he had served in *Rodney* and *Norfolk*. Lumby left *Sturgeon*, his first submarine, in 1940 for duty in *Ursula*. In 1942 he was appointed to his first command, *L23*. His appointment to *Saracen* followed shortly after. On returning from captivity Lumby resumed active service, becoming captain of *Truncheon* and *Astute* between 1947-48. His last sea-going

* Supreme Headquarters Allied Powers Europe.

command was the cruiser *Belfast*. Between 1964-66 Michael Lumby was Captain S3 at Faslane. Captain Lumby, DSO, DSC, retired from the Service in October 1966.

*Saracen* was the last Allied submarine to be sunk by the Italians. Two weeks later (3 September) the Allies landed in Italy. On 3 September General Pietro Badoglio, the Italian Prime Minister, agreed to the unconditional surrender of Italy.

The loss of so many Royal Navy submarines to Axis mines would seem to justify the extensive use of the mine as an A/S measure. With a minimum of 54,000 mines having been laid in the Mediterranean by the Italians it is hardly surprising that when Italian records became available for examination such wide-spread use of strategically positioned mines prompted Captain S10 (Captain G.C. Philips) at that time to comment: 'Had we known of all these minefields, it is difficult to see how we could have operated our submarines in the Mediterranean at all.' Though at times handicapped by a severe shortage of torpedoes the Mediterranean submarines had fought a hard and unrelenting campaign. Although never a really a large force, submarines had had a major influence on events in that theatre: their success in helping Malta to stave off defeat and their contribution to the Allied triumph in North Africa has already been acknowledged. All things considered, submarine activity in the Mediterranean had been most rewarding.

Although the main sea enemy in the Mediterranean had surrendered there were still the Germans to contend with. During the remaining months of conflict in the Mediterranean, a further four submarines were sunk. Launched on the Tyne in September 1942, the *Usurper* (Lieutenant D.R.O. Mott) had only a matter of months at war before being sunk with the loss of all hands. For his last patrol Mott put to sea from Algiers on 24 September for an area off La Spezia. On 3 October Lieutenant Mott was ordered to move farther north and to patrol the northern part of the Gulf of Genoa. What happened to *Usurper* after 3 October is not known. She did not answer signals on the 11th and failed to arrive at Algiers the following day when expected to do so. As always when the definite cause of a submarine's loss was unknown, mining was considered a possibility. Adding substance to the theory of *Usurper*'s loss by mining was the later discovery that the minefield QB192 was in the vicinity of her billet. However, in the case of *Usurper* another possibility exists for her loss: the German A/S vessel *JU2208* reports having attacked a submarine in the Gulf of Genoa on 3 October.

Aged twenty-five and married, Lieutenant David Mott, DSC, was on his third Mediterranean patrol with *Usurper* when lost. Mott was regarded as 'A splendid commander whose full potential was yet to be realized.' *Usurper* was the last of the great little 'U' class to be sunk during the war.

HM Submarines *Unruly*, *United*, and *Trooper* all sank Italian submarines in July 1943. *Unruly* and *United* were scrapped in Scotland in 1946. *Trooper* never left the Mediterranean. *Trooper* was on her sixth patrol when she sank the enemy submarine. Under the command of Lieutenant G.S.C. Clarabut, *Trooper* sailed Port Said on 7 July to patrol the Adriatic and western Greece. On 15 July Captain S10 ordered her to proceed to the Gulf of Taranto. At 0300 on the 22nd Clarabut started to attack a submarine. The attack was abruptly terminated when Clarabut realized that the enemy was in fact a 'T' class (*Tactician*) in a neighbouring billet. Considering the nearness of their billets it would perhaps have been wiser had they been ordered not to attack submarines. Clarabut was three weeks into the patrol and was about to leave his billet for the return to harbour when on the 29th he noticed that the lighthouse at Capo Santa Maria had been switched on. This aroused Clarabut's curiosity and he decided to investigate. He was rewarded when at 0646 the large minelaying submarine *Pietro Micca* put in an appearance. An attack at long range was made. The enemy was hit and sunk. By 2 August *Trooper* was back in harbour.

At the time of his attack on the *Pietro Micca* Lieutenant Clarabut had been in temporary command of *Trooper* while her regular captain, Lieutenant J.S. Wraith, was away ill. Wraith was back in command when *Trooper* sailed Beirut on 26 September for patrol west of the Dodecanese and later to the east of Leros. No signals were received from her and she failed to return to harbour on 17 October. Mining was strongly suspected.

Lieutenant John Wraith was the son of an Army officer. He had entered Dartmouth in January 1927. On completion of his course for lieutenant in December 1934, Wraith joined submarines. He became well known for his excellent command of *Upright*. On returning home from the Mediterranean with *Upright* in March 1942, Wraith went on a morale-boosting lecture tour of factories before taking command of *Trooper*, then nearing completion at Scotts. John Wraith was awarded the DSC in November 1940, and the DSO in April 1942 for 'Courage, skill, and coolness in successful submarine patrols'.

\*

A simoom is a hot, cyclonic wind which blows across the African, Arabian, and Syrian deserts. It often raises heavy sandstorms. When launched by Cammell Laird in October 1942, His Majesty's Submarine *Simoom* was named after this wind. *Simoom* had done her 'warm-up' patrol off Sardinia in June 1943. She joined the 1st Flotilla at Beirut in October 1943. After battery repairs and a brief docking in Port Said, *Simoom* (Lieutenant G.D.N. Milner) left that port on 2 November for patrol in the Aegean. Passing through the Kaso Strait on the 4th to patrol between the islands of Naxos and Mykoni, *Simoom* was diverted on the 5th to the Dardanelles' approaches. As the currents in the vicinity of Cape Helles were so unpredictable, Milner was advised to operate five miles to the west of Tenedos. *Simoom* was ordered to leave patrol on the 15th. Her return route was designed to give passage between Psara and Khios, and then on through the Kaso Strait. A German radio broadcast of 15 November, the day *Simoom* was ordered to leave patrol, announced that an Allied submarine had been sunk in the Aegean and that several of the crew had been rescued. German records show that from a range of 2,000 yards the *U565* had attacked a submarine east of Kos Island at 2345 on the evening of the 19th. After three or four minutes an explosion had been heard and all HE had ceased. A sinking could not be confirmed but had nevertheless been claimed. This claim must be balanced by the fact that three hours after this alleged sinking the steamer *Trias* was sunk by a submarine whilst taking passage from Mudros to Mitylene.

It seems unlikely that the U-boat had sunk *Simoom*. Unless *Simoom* for reasons unknown had left her patrol area prematurely, she could not have been in the vicinity of Kos Island at the time of the attack by *U565*. If *Simoom* had been sunk by the U-boat, Lieutenant Milner was some way off from his ordered return route. There seems to be no foundation to the claim that survivors from the submarine had been rescued, as had been stated in the radio broadcast, which in any case had been made before *U565* had made her attack. In view of the lack of more definite information the loss of *Simoom* due to mining cannot be ruled out.

Lieutenant Geoffrey Milner was aged twenty-five and married. Though *Simoom* had not been in service long enough to impress by tonnage sunk, she had disposed of the Italian destroyer *Vincenzo Gioberti* three months earlier.

*

It is not proposed in this history to relate in detail the loss of midget submarines and other small submersible craft; nevertheless the opportunity is taken to say a few words concerning their loss, if only to mention the outstanding bravery of their crews and operators under extremely hazardous circumstances. The first midget submarine to be sunk was the *X3*. This class of submarine, they were usually called X-craft, had an overall length of about 50 feet. Launched in March 1942, the *X3* was the first of her class. Six months after her launching she sank when exercising in Loch Striven. Her 3-man crew survived and she was later salvaged. In September 1943 six X-craft sailed their Scottish base to attack German capital ships in the fiords of Norway. Nine crewman were lost and none of the X-craft returned from what was a brilliantly executed operation.

Another type of small submarine were the one-man operated *Welmans*. These submarine craft began to appear on the scene in July 1942. With an explosive charge fitted to the bow, these craft were 17 feet in length and had a displacement of almost 3 tons. These ingenious little craft were hampered by their limited range and by having no periscope, which made navigation difficult as it meant the commando operator had to break surface and look through the window of a tiny conning tower to gain his bearings. Five *Welmans* were lost: one on exercise in September 1943, and four the following November during an attack on Bergen Harbour.

# 1944

Including one X-craft five submarines were lost in 1944. Lieutenant B.M. McFarlane, RANVR, was captain of *X22* when she was sunk in an accident of 7 February. *X22* was involved in a towing exercise which continued during winds of gale force. The heavy seas whipped up by the gale washed the OOW from the bridge of *Syrtis*, the towing submarine. *Syrtis*, turning suddenly in a rescue bid, collided with *X22* and the X-craft sank at once with the loss of McFarlane and three crewmen. It was three weeks after this unhappy incident that *Syrtis* (Lieutenant M.H. Jupp) sailed Lerwick on 16 March for a billet off the Norwegian coast. On 20 March *Syrtis* was ordered to an area near Bodo, some seventy miles inside the Arctic Circle. It is known that Michael Jupp with gunfire sank a small ship on the 22nd. Jupp was

ordered to leave patrol on 28 March. This signal was not acknowledged by *Syrtis* and she failed to put in an appearance at Lerwick.
Though German reports indicate the sinking of a submarine by
shore batteries in the Bodo area about this time, mining was the most
probable cause of *Syrtis*'s loss.

With HMS *Adamant* as depot ship, the build-up of Royal Navy
submarines in the Far East began in October 1943. *Adamant* was still
depot ship of the 4th Flotilla when in March 1944 *Maidstone* arrived
in Ceylon (now Sri Lanka) to serve as depot ship to the newly formed
8th Flotilla, comprising 'S' class submarines of recent construction.
The *Stonehenge* (Lieutenant D.S. McN. Verschoyle-Campbell)
arrived in Ceylon towards the end of 1943. She was to become the
first of three Royal Navy submarines to be lost in the war with Japan.
Very little is known of events leading up to, and during, the loss of
*Stonehenge*. She sailed Trincomalee on 25 February for her third patrol in the Far East. Her billet was in the northern part of the Malacca
Straits and in the area of the island of Great Nicobar. Nothing
further was heard from *Stonehenge* and she failed to arrive at Ceylon
on 20 March. As the Japanese made no claim regarding her loss,
*Stonehenge* is presumed to have been mined some time between 2nd
March and 16 March.

Lieutenant David Verschoyle-Campbell was the youngest Royal
Navy officer to gain command of a submarine. He joined submarines
in 1940. After completing his Perisher in 1943, he was appointed to
command *Sealion*. Verschoyle-Campbell was just twenty-one when
on 28 July 1942 he arrived at Buckingham Palace to receive his DSC
and Bar from King George VI.

*Sickle* (Lieutenant J.R. Drummond) was the last of HM Submarines to be sunk in the Mediterranean. For her tenth and final patrol *Sickle* departed Malta on 31 May for an area in the northern
Aegean. By 4 June she was off the island of Mitylene. At 2015 that
evening she fired two rounds at shipping in Mitylene Harbour, causing little or no damage. The German patrol vessels *GA76* and *GA91*
engaged *Sickle* with their 3.7cm armament. *Sickle* took hits on her
conning tower and her gun. One man was killed, a further two men
were wounded, and a fourth blown overboard; this fourth man, Able
Seaman Richard Blake, was rescued by the Germans, thus becoming
the only survivor of the patrol. *Sickle* was able to dive her way out of
trouble. James Drummond then headed south-west towards the
Doro Channel, a hundred miles away, where he attacked a convoy,
sinking the motor vessel *Reaumur* of 550 tons. Lieutenant Drummond

then turned north and by 9 June was off Lemnos. On this day he attacked another motor ship but failed to score a hit.

*June 12, 1255*. Lieutenant Drummond reported the sighting of a convoy in the northern approaches to the Steno Pass. The convoy had passed eastwards through the Steno Pass at noon that day and was proceeding towards Leros. *1400*: The torpedo boat *TA19* investigated a trail of oil reported by an Ardo of the air escort. *1418*: A 'SUB-MARINE SIGHTING' was signalled. *1441*: The submarine alarm was cancelled when the torpedo boats failed to confirm a sonar contact in the area of the oil sighting. *1753*: Two bombs were dropped ahead of the convoy. In order to avoid the possibility of an attack the convoy made a sharp alteration of course away from the area. *1935*: Distant and unexplained underwater explosions were heard. No attacks were made on the convoy and it arrived at Leros at 0800 the following morning.

After Drummond's signal of 1255, 12 June, nothing further was heard from him. On 12 June he was ordered to patrol north of 38°N. On the 14th he was ordered to terminate the patrol. The exact cause of *Sickle*'s loss has yet to be established. There is a possibility that she was mined in the Kythera Channel some time around 16 June.

*Stratagem* was under the command of Lieutenant Clifford Pelly when she became overdue on 3 December after failing to acknowledge signals. She is believed to be the only Royal Navy submarine lost in a direct confrontation with Japanese forces. Her fate after leaving Trincomalee on 10 November remained unknown until the surrender of Japan nine months later. Lieutenant Pelly's orders had taken him to the vicinity of Malacca. Intelligence reports had referred to a pier which the Japanese were thought to have in use for the loading of ships with bauxite ore, used in the manufacture of aluminium. During the six-day journey to the Malacca Straits, Pat Pelly had plenty of time to reflect on the circumstances which had brought him command of *Stratagem*, and a role in the Far East war. *Stratagem*'s regular captain had been Mike Willoughby. When Willoughby had been forced onto the sick list by doctors, Lieutenant Pelly had stepped in to take command of *Stratagem* just prior to her departure for the Far East.

It was on 16 November, with *Stratagem* well advanced into the Malacca Straits, that Pelly came upon a junk. The passage up till then had been without incident, and without the slightest sign of the enemy. The junk was approached and investigated, and then allowed to continue its business, Pelly having been satisfied that all

was in order. However, Pelly from then on dived *Stratagem* during the
hours of daylight. The closer *Stratagem* got to Malacca, the more
numerous became the junks. The activities of a Japanese Zero aircraft gave Pelly the feeling that the enemy may have had some idea
that a submarine was in the region. For most of the 17th and 18th
Pelly searched for the reported pier but met with no success. On the
night of the 18th he moved farther south and by dawn the following
morning was some thirteen miles from Malacca. Nothing of any
importance was noted until about three o'clock that afternoon when
a convoy was sighted.

'Down periscope. Sixty feet.' The greased shaft descended into its
well. Evidently absorbed in assessing what he had seen, it was several moments before Pelly addressed the crew. 'Well, there's five
ships and they all appear to be in ballast. They're in line-ahead and
on a steady course with one destroyer out front and another on either
side.' *Stratagem* was manoeuvred for an attack. Thirty minutes after
the sighting, the range having been reduced to 2,500 yards, Lieutenant Pelly sent three torpedoes racing towards the convoy. The target
was the second ship in line, the tanker *Nichinan Maru* of 2,000 tons.
The tanker took a torpedo well forward. The escorts at once went
chasing wildly in all directions, dropping about twenty depth-
charges in the process. *Stratagem* was taken deep and turned through
180°. The destroyers were still scattering depth-charges when Pelly
decided to chance a quick look through the periscope. He saw that
although stopped and considerably down by the bows, the *Nichinan
Maru* was still afloat. A shot from the stern tube at a thousand yards
broke her in two and sent her to the bottom. *Stratagem* then cleared
the area.

*November 22.* Dawn found Lieutenant Pelly near Malacca and close
inshore. By 0830 he was positioned three miles south-west of
Malacca. At about this time a Japanese aircraft began a strict surveillance of the area. Pelly, at the periscope for much of the morning,
informed the crew that a destroyer was also patrolling in the vicinity.
It was approximately 1210 when diving stations was ordered. Then
came: 'Shut off for depth-charging.' Shortly after this a destroyer
passed overhead. Almost immediately a depth-charge exploded so
close that *Stratagem*'s stern was forced up and her bow struck the seabed quite hard. The explosion left *Stratagem* in near darkness. Less
than ten seconds later another depth-charge, exploding midships,
left *Stratagem* totally blacked out. Water was heard entering the submarine at a fast rate. Certain that *Stratagem* was flooding, Pelly

The sad end of the beautiful *Truculent*. *Truculent* had the reputation of being a 'Happy Boat' but the happiness died in the Thames estuary on a dark January evening in 1950.

The last few minutes in the life of a gallant man. With his back to the periscope standard is Surgeon Lt C. E. Rhodes RNVR who was not a submarine officer, before venturing down into *Sidon* to help injured men. He died in the wrecked boat and was awarded a posthumous Albert Medal.

Lt-Cdr H. T. Verrey, in the white shirt, waits dejectedly for *Sidon* to sink, knowing that there has been heavy loss of life amongst his crew.

(*Top left*) The luckiest man in the Submarine Service! CPO Gordon Selby left the *Upholder* after its 24th patrol, joined the *P39* five days before she was sunk alongside the submarine base, was one of the survivors from the *Olympus*, left the *Sickle* before she sank, served in *Storm* in the Far East, left *Truculent* before she sank and having been taken ill when boarding the *Affray* with his officers' training class was left ashore! (*Top right*) Sub-Lt J. Blackburn, seen here on the bridge of the *Safari* in the Mediterranean in 1942, became the captain of the *Affray* which was lost in May 1951. Incredibly, amongst the seventy-five people onboard here, there were twenty-five officers! There were also four Royal Marines who were going to be landed in a commando exercise.

(*Centre*) The top of the fin of the *Artemis* just shows above the water alongside the jetty at HMS *Dolphin* with divers about to start the work of recovering her.

(*Bottom*) Captain H. P. K. Oram with Commander R. C. Whiteside, Flag Officer Submarine's Escape and Rescue officer, at HMS *Dolphin* in February 1986. Ninety-one years old and the last of the *Thetis* survivors, Captain Oram's dramatic stories of life at sea under sail, submarine life in the first war and escapes and adventures held his modern submariners' audience enthralled.

ordered the main ballast blown. His orders were carried out but *Stratagem* made no response.

Forward in the torpedo stowage compartment the torpedo officer, Lieutenant D.C. Douglas, directed his torch towards the after door of the compartment. Water was flooding into the compartment from amidship. Calling for the watertight doors to be shut, Douglas then satisfied himself that all hands had cleared the tube space before ordering those doors shut also. The water in the compartment was very soon more than a foot deep, and flooding through the after doorway so strongly that the door could not be shut against the torrent. The position of the door-stop (the stop held the door in the open position) on the after door was such that for it to be removed it was necessary to stand in the doorway, owing in this instance to the port side of the door being blocked by stores. As the force of the water passing through this doorway was so great, no one could stand in its path to remove the stop.

The survivors in the torpedo space compartment were amazed at how rapidly their fortunes had changed for the worse. As an aid to morale, they began to sing; Lieutenant Douglas ordered them to stop singing and to put on DSEA. Lieutenant Douglas found that his own DSEA had a defective valve on its oxygen bottle. Taking up another, which worked efficiently, he placed this over the head of one of the older ratings who had become distressed owing to the pressure effect on his eyes. The air pressure in *Stratagem*, and also the chlorine content, was very high. One of the hands, Leading Seaman Gibbs, cleared the escape hatch and set to trying to ease back the clips. Unable to remove one of the clips he called to Douglas for help. After what seemed a considerable time, but in actuality was probably about a minute, Douglas managed to remove the obstinate clip by striking it with his fist. Unfortunately by this time all chance of lowering the twill trunk had gone because the rising water, which had become saturated with oil fuel, had reached the coaming which housed the twill trunk. Douglas, with Gibbs alongside him, had continued working on the hatch clips. Immediately the last clip was freed, the hatch cover was blown open by the extreme internal pressure and Gibbs went hurtling through the open hatch at such speed that it was a moment or so before Douglas realized that Gibbs had gone. The heavy hatch then dropped shut again, striking Douglas on the top of his head – but it at once blew open and he too went speeding towards the surface in an air-bubble.

'Ten of the fourteen men in the torpedo space compartment are known to have left the submarine alive, although only eight were picked up,' reports Lieutenant Douglas. 'The ship's cook was later seen to be floating face downwards on the surface and was obviously drowned. Another rating was seen while in the submarine to have on a DSEA set and apparently working it correctly; although he was observed to leave the boat he was not seen on the surface. The Japanese destroyer had dropped two more charges after we were hit, but they were not so close and did not seem to harm us, although they probably accelerated the flooding. Throughout the unwelcome experience the behaviour of the crew in my compartment was mangificent. I should specially like to mention Weatherhead, the ship's cook, who kept up the cheerful narrative of the wonderful fruit cake which he had recently cooked, and who had shown great bravery and coolness throughout the dreadful experience in the flooded submarine. This rating was responsible for the singing and by his behaviour greatly assisted in preventing panic. It is with the deepest regret that I have to say that this extremely brave rating failed to survive the ascent to the surface.

'The destroyer circled· us for about three-quarters of an hour, dropping a lifebelt and baulks of timber. All of us were suffering from the bends. I do not know how the ratings felt but I myself was scared "pea green" at the sight of the Japanese ensign flying from their masthead. This was more or less justified as we later found out. However, I managed to overcome this somewhat by swimming around and seeing to the ratings. Able Seaman Westward was just on the verge of sinking. His eyes were full of oil and he could hardly keep himself afloat. I fixed him in the lifebelt and then went to the assistance of Able Seaman Philips. He was in a similar plight but a puff of air into his DSEA kept his head above water and he was all right, although he was almost delirious with shock. The Japanese eventually lowered a cutter and picked us up, clubbing us as they hauled us into the boat. Then we were each compelled to pull an oar. This was practically impossible owing to the bends but we reached the destroyer, assisted by their clouts and unpleasantness. By this time another destroyer of similar design had arrived on the scene. The Japanese were certain there was another submarine in the area and got furious with us when we denied this. On being hauled on board we were bound, blindfolded, and beaten. We were not given food at any time whilst on board the destroyer and spent the night on top of a hatch, which was about three feet square, all bound together. We were not clothed and the night was extremely cold. The pains from the bends were now at their worst and every time someone murmured, the guards would come and hit us over the head with their clubs. We were being taken to Singapore, where we arrived at about 2100 on 23 November. No food was given to us and we were locked in separate cells still bound and blindfolded. We remained in this condition for twenty-eight days.

'Our first meal arrived on the evening of the 24th. It consisted of a small rice ball. When I stated that I did not like rice I was informed that I should soon learn to like it. Little did I know at the time how true this statement was to prove. However, I eagerly devoured my first rice ball after returning from six hours' extensive interrogation by a Japanese captain. My first interrogation had taken place about midnight on the night of my arriving in the base. At this time I was in very bad shape and refused to give them any information except that permitted by international law. However, I was informed by the interpreter that I had better give some sort of answer or otherwise I should be shot. That brought to mind a lecture I had attended in England on the subject of being taken prisoner where the lecturer had told us that the Japanese would never recognize international law and that they would probably use all manner of torture for extracting information. Daily interrogation varying from two to six hours at a time continued, all manner of Japanese individuals being employed for the purpose. The ratings were also being taken away for interrogation, although not for such long periods. I was greatly assisted in misinforming my captors by the Japanese interpreter. This individual had no pro-Japanese tendencies whatsoever. Prior to his coming to Japan in 1940, he had lived in Kingston Grammar School. He was born of an English mother. He had been brought to Japan, against his mother's will, by his father and, being unable to return before the Pearl Harbour episode, had been conscripted into the Japanese Navy. Being employed on a short-wave radio he was able to bring me the BBC news each night and in this manner I was able to keep up with world affairs. He also took messages to my shipmates and brought me cigarettes and sweets, etc., and kept me well informed as to the others being interrogated later on. I always knew what to expect when I went before my questioners, and also if they had any idea of the answers to their questions.

'After about a week I was interrogated about every third day or so, the Japanese being particularly interested in codes and radar. However, at every questioning, both in Singapore and in Japan, I denied any knowledge of these subjects, stating that I was a torpedo officer and those subjects did not concern me. To my relief I managed to get away with this answer. I found that as long as I gave them *some* sort of answer, regardless of its true nature, they were satisfied. On one occasion, sometime in March 1945 whilst in Japan, I was nearly baffled in this respect by the Japanese producing a copy (a photographic copy of the very torn and burned original) of one page of the Special Submarine Secret Cypher. However, I looked at it in blank amazement for one afternoon and the nine men who had come all the way from Tokyo, at a time when transport was unobtainable, walked away disappointed. On another occasion I was badly shaken by the Japanese producing copies of one of our back signal logs. They could not understand the abbreviations and apart from gaining knowledge of some of the flotillas' names this was of little value to them.

'After a month of starvation diet in the cells of Singapore, Leading Seaman Gibbs, Able Seaman Robinson and myself were flown to Japan, bound and blindfolded throughout the trip. We were allowed to remove our blindfolds while in the aircraft. Leaving Singapore on 19th December, we called at Saigon, Shanghai, and some other ports in the south of Japan before reaching Tokyo on the 23rd. We were then taken to Ofuna prisoner of war camp. In spite of being assured by the Japanese that we should be recognized as fully qualified prisoners of war on arrival in Tokyo, we were never treated as such (we were never registered) and were imprisoned in a camp the existence of which remained unknown to the Red Cross throughout the whole time we were there, hence we were never reported as prisoners of war. The treatment in this camp was particularly brutal and at times almost beyond endurance. Our food, nine parts barley and one part rice with very watery vegetable soups, was given to us three times daily and varied very much in quantity. It was never sufficient to keep us in health and very soon we contracted beriberi and other illnesses. We were not permitted the use of writing materials, razors, books (although we received a supply of these in April), or anything which might have helped our morale to hold body and soul together. In the warmer months we lacked soap. The camp became lousy and we spent the greater part of the day removing foreign bodies from our own bodies and clothing.

'My interrogation still continued frequently in Ofuna. On arrival there I was questioned most days, but as the weeks went by this dropped off to once or twice a week. Being a regular naval officer I was supposed to be able to answer all the questions put to me. At this stage in the interrogation they were getting short of questions and I never knew what to expect next. Sometimes it was a question about the RAF or the Royal Navy; or it might be about England's political outlook. In fact it appeared that any questions which cropped up in their stupid heads were put to me. Towards the latter months of the war it was very noticeable from the questions that the Japanese were putting out peace-feelers. They expected me to be able to give them an answer to these. It was quite obvious to me that if the Japanese were willing to waste their time, and I had plenty of time in which to entertain them, on such ridiculous subjects they must have abandoned all hopes of victory.'

The winter of 1944-45 was one of the coldest Japan had experienced for many years. For the POWs the hardship became almost unendurable as they continued their miserable existence clad only in Japanese ragged cotton uniforms and poor quality gym shoes, and this during the heaviest snowfalls for forty years. It is hardly surprising that most of the prisoners suffered from frostbite. Lieutenant Douglas, Gibbs and Robinson had been anxious to get word home that they had survived *Stratagem*'s sinking. In April 1945 it looked as if an opportunity had arrived to do so when the Japanese moved Able Seaman Robinson from Ofuna to Omori prisoner of war camp in Tokyo*. Unfortunately when Robinson arrived at the new camp the Japanese failed to register him and so nothing came of the move.

It was on 26 August, twelve days after the Japanese surrender, that Red Cross officials arrived at Ofuna after having learned of its existence from prisoners at Omori. The officers were angered by the appalling conditions and ordered immediate changes. On 29 August the United States Navy liberated the camp. Of the eight *Stratagem* survivors taken from the sea nine months earlier by the Japanese, only Lieutenant Douglas, Leading Seaman Gibbs, and Able Seaman Robinson survived the brutality of the Japanese, the other crewmen either having died in captivity at Singapore or from execution.

# 1945

Lieutenant-Commander H.B. Turner was in command of the minelayer *Porpoise* when she failed to return to harbour in January. It had been Hugh Turner who had earned the anger of a certain enemy

---

* Ofuna was not a registered camp, whereas Omori was known to the Red Cross.

minesweeping flotilla when during a Mediterranean patrol he had sunk a ship off the Lipari Islands carrying £18,000 in lire, the flotilla's pay!

Having been in service since 1932 *Porpoise* was well known in the Submarine Service. Her work during the siege of Malta made her name known to a wider audience. She arrived in the Far East towards the middle of 1944. A mine-lay of 8 July in the Malacca Straits sank a Japanese A/S craft. Soon after, the same minefield accounted for the tanker *Taketun Maru* of 3,000 tons. Command of *Porpoise* had passed to Hugh Turner in late 1944. When Turner signalled the completion of a mine-lay off Penang, it was the last of his signals. The exact cause of the minelayer's loss is not known. Japanese reports have led to speculation that *Porpoise* had been sighted in the vicinity of Penang by an enemy aircraft. The plane dropped a bomb which is believed to have caused *Porpoise* to slightly leak oil. A/S craft from Penang were able to track and perhaps destroy the submarine. Lieutenant-Commander Hugh Turner, DSC, was aged twenty-nine.

Delivered in early 1945, the *XE11* was one of the new and improved class of X-craft. On the morning of 6 March she was exercising in Loch Striven under the command of Lieutenant A. Staples, SANF (V). *XE11* was calibrating instruments when she collided with a boom defence vessel busy laying buoys. Staples and two ratings failed to survive the incident.

*XE11* was the last Royal Navy submarine loss of the war. In almost every instance the sinking of a submarine had meant the loss of its crew: 341 officers and 2,801 ratings had lost their lives, and a further 50 officers and 310 ratings were taken prisoner of war. By coincidence these figures combined (3,502) equalled almost exactly the strength of the Submarine Service of September 1939.

# PART V

## 1945-1971

# 1950

The January sinking of *Truculent* was the first peace-time submarine loss since *Thetis* had taken her tragic dive in Liverpool Bay in 1939. Launched at Barrow in September 1942, *Truculent*'s war service included the June 1943 sinking of *U308*. *Truculent* had undergone a refit at Chatham when on 12 January she sailed the Royal Dockyard and made for open water to carry out trials. In addition to her complement of sixty-one, *Truculent* had on board eighteen dockyard employees. On completion of her trials the submarine set a heading for Sheerness. It was during her passage through the Thames Estuary that *Truculent* encountered the 643 tons Swedish coastal tanker *Divina* (Captain Karl Hommerberg) in transit from Purfleet to Ipswich with a cargo of paraffin. A lookout of *Truculent* reported lights fine on the port bow. The OOW, Lieutenant J.N. Humphrey-Baker, directed his glasses onto the approaching lights. The lights did not appear to be the usual arrangement of lights; furthermore, they seemed to be too far over the wrong side of the channel. Humphrey-Baker called the captain, Lieutenant C.P. Bowers, to the bridge. It was seven o'clock on a cold, dark January night.

When Charles Bowers arrived on the bridge he saw three lights, two red and one green, forming a triangle. He was not immediately sure as to the significance of the three lights but eventually they were interpreted as meaning that a ship was stationary to one side of the fairway. As *Truculent* could not pass to the starboard of the lights without risking running aground, Bowers slowly altered course to port. No sooner had *Truculent*'s bow swung away to port than the lights resolved themselves into those of a ship heading down channel with an extra red light to indicate that her cargo was explosive. Bowers suddenly realized that the tanker was very much closer than he had first imagined, and that a collision was likely. Though Bowers at once took emergency measures the *Divina* was so close that a collision could not be avoided. When the two vessels did crash together, the force of the impact was sufficient to hurl Bowers and four of his crew into the sea. *Truculent* and *Divina* stayed locked together for a few seconds. Then *Truculent* sank out of sight. Fifteen minutes had passed since Charles Bowers had been summoned to the bridge.

When the Dutch merchantman *Almdyk* arrived in the vicinity of the sinking, the survivors had been in the sea for more than half an hour. *Almdyk*, homeward bound from New Orleans, sighted Bowers and four others: Lieutenants Humphrey-Baker and J.E. Stevenson, Sub-Lieutenant L.A. Frew and Leading Seaman Headley. After, rescuing all four, the Dutchman gave the first news of the accident in an SOS:

HM SUBMARINE TRUCULENT SANK NORTH-WEST RED SANDS TOWER
BETWEEN X4 BUOY AND E. PILES BUOY. HAVE PICKED UP FIVE SUR-
VIVORS. BELIEVE SUBMARINE IN COLLISION WITH SWEDISH SHIP
DIVINA. ALL SHIPS PLEASE LOOK OUT.

The position given by *Almdyk* was almost mid-channel and roughly half way between Whitstable in Kent and Foulness Island, Essex.

Of the seventy-nine personnel aboard *Truculent* five had been thrown into the sea and about ten had been drowned on impact. This left sixty-four survivors, of which the majority seem to have assembled in the area of the engine room and after end. In the engine room Chief ERA F.W. Hine took charge; in the after end it was *Truculent*'s first lieutenant, Lieutenant F.J. Hindes, who took command. Perhaps it was inevitable that thoughts should stray to the *Thetis* tragedy of ten years earlier; and as both submarines had sunk within sight of land the situations were not totally dissimilar. Over the years since the 1939 disaster opinion had gravitated towards the view that the heavy loss of life in *Thetis* was mainly due to the lengthy delay between the submarine's sinking and her detection. It was reasoned that the time-lapse had been so lengthy that the crew had become too weak to escape when help finally arrived.

The thrashing of propellers above *Truculent* was interpreted to mean that rescue vessels were on hand to receive escapers. But in fact this was not so. The propeller noises were those of a passing vessel which was completely unaware of *Truculent*'s distress. At 1940, twenty-five minutes after the collision, the twill-trunk was extended and flooding of the compartment begun. By 2020 the crew were ready to escape. In the mistaken belief that rescue vessels were on hand to take him from the sea, the first escaper made his way to the surface, where on his arrival he must have been dismayed to discover that he was entirely alone. No rescue craft. No searchlights playing on the water. Nothing but darkness and an ebbing tide that would sweep many escapers out to sea and certain death.

At thirty-six years of age Dennis Brice, coxswain of the Margate Lifeboat, was one of the youngest coxswains of the RNLI. As the first grey light of dawn touched the waters of the estuary Brice noted that the area held more than forty vessels, many of which had raced to the scene following the transmission of: MARKER BUOY FIRED FROM SUB-MARINE HAS BEEN LOCATED. It was believed that several of *Truculent's* crew were still alive, though there had been no indication from *Truculent* that this was so. As the day wore on, the rescue craft waited in vain. The survivors had already made their escape and, with the exception of ten escapers taken from the sea by *Divina*, had suc-cumbed to the cold, currents, and tide. Concerned about delaying their escape too long, they had done the opposite and had left too soon. With darkness upon them, and with an ebbing tide, they should have waited at least a few more hours or until receiving a sig-nal that rescue craft were in position.

It is probable that the last man to leave *Truculent* had been Chief ERA Hine. Without exception the few survivors that had escaped from the engine room were keen to express their praise and gratitude of the manner in which Hine had conducted the escape proceedings. As crew and civilians gathered in the engine room, Francis Hine marshalled them and told them amusing stories to keep up spirits. As each man left the submarine a cheery word from Hine helped them on their way. 'His leadership was magnificent,' commented Robert Stevens, Inspector of Engine Fitters and one of two civilian sur-vivors. Also regarding Hine, ERA E.C. Buckingham states: 'I was the last but one to leave. He was the last man out. We rose to the sur-face almost together and swam together for a while. Then we drifted apart. I did not see him again.' Chief ERA Hine had spent most of his twenty years' naval service in submarines. *Truculent* was the second occasion on which he had been involved in a submarine sinking. Regrettably, Francis Hine did not survive the ordeal.

*Divina* was moored alongside a destroyer in the river Medway. After a sleepless night Karl Hommerberg breakfasted in his cabin. Broad shouldered and stockily built with black thinning hair, Cap-tain Hommerberg spoke to reporters in slow but excellent English of his encounter with *Truculent*: 'We had picked up a pilot. Both the pilot and myself were on the bridge when the collision came. It was dark but clear and we saw the submarine ahead and gave warning of our approach. The crash came with an impact that shook us from stem to stern. We saw the submarine sink immediately – in one minute. We saw men in the water. My crew rushed to get them out. Ropes and lifebelts were thrown to them. We also launched our boat. We managed to pick up eight survivors and two dead men. We gave them a cup of coffee, and then a lifeboat transferred them to a destroyer. We stayed on the scene cruising around for four hours in the search for survivors.'

On 26 January, two weeks after the collision, a Swedish maritime inquiry into the disaster opened in public in London. Conducted by the Swedish Consul-General in London, Mr M. Hallenborge, the inquiry was opened by Mr Hallenborge stating that 'The purpose of the inquiry is to discover what has happened and why it has happened – not to assess any guilt or damage and such matters'. The evidence was taken in Swedish but much was translated into English. Extracts from *Divina*'s log describing the final moments of *Truculent* were read to a hushed court:

A green light could be seen with a white one above it, at about 15° to 20° on the port bow. While occupied in turning to starboard at about 1904, the *Divina* collided with the approaching vessel, which sank almost immediately. The engines were stopped and the lifeboat launched to search for any possible survivors. It could be seen that some men were taken on board an approaching ship. As nothing could be seen or heard, the lifeboat was taken on board again after one hour. The *Divina* crossed backwards and forwards and at 2100 hours a cry for help was heard. The boat was launched and four men were picked up.

The log-book also recorded that another man had later been seen in the water. The boat was lowered again. It returned with two more men, both dead. At 2300 the Southend lifeboat arrived to take the survivors to a destroyer.

Captain Hommerberg, who was forty-seven and lived at Sete in France, then gave evidence. Hommerberg, whose evidence differed slightly from that which he had earlier told the Press, stated that he had gone below at 1830 and was having a meal when the collision took place. He went to the bridge at once. The pilot, Mr D.E. Ellison, told him that they had struck a small vessel, probably a tug or fishing boat. He had ordered the ship's boat lowered. Then the *Almdyk* had arrived and rescued some men. 'As we thought that we had hit only a very small vessel, we believed that the crew had been picked up by the Dutch ship, and so our lifeboat was taken back on board,' stated Hommerberg. 'About an hour later we heard shouts from the water and launched the lifeboat again. This time it picked up four survivors.' When asked if his ship carried a radio Captain Hommerberg replied that *Divina* only carried a telephone, which was difficult to manage, and it was impossible to obtain contact with the shore.

Next to give evidence was Ellison, the pilot. Mr Ellison, white-haired and wearing a row of medal ribbons on his uniform, said that *Divina* was proceeding down river at 7½ knots. 'I did not know what it was we had struck,' continued Ellison. 'It was just a black spot and lights. I saw no shadow at all. It was a pitch black night. I never saw the red light at all.'

Less than a week after the Swedish maritime inquiry had been completed an inquest was held at the Royal Naval Hospital, Gillingham, to determine the cause of death of the bodies recovered. One of the survivors called to give evidence was Sub-Lieutenant A.A. Frew. Anthony Frew was the son of Rear-Admiral Sir Sidney Frew, himself an ex-submariner. In the course of his evidence Frew stated: 'Nothing unusual happened during the trials in the North Sea and we surfaced to return during the early afternoon of 12th January. I went up the conning tower at about 1835 and the commanding officer, Lieutenant Bowers, and the navigating officer, Lieutenant Humphrey-Baker, were there on the bridge. I was followed up by the engineer-officer, Lieutenant Stevenson. It was dark and there was a very slight sea mist, but I should say that visibility was about two miles. I understand that we were travelling at about 9 knots.' Sub-Lieutenant Frew said that he had noticed the lights of a vessel on the starboard bow but was not looking particularly at that point, but astern. As far as he could remember, the vessel was displaying a white light with two red lights beneath it. Lieutenant Bowers gave an order, which Frew believed was 'slow'. Soon after he saw the bows of a ship. Frew got the impression that the ship was steering at right angles and probably coming towards the submarine. When the coroner asked whether anything was done to check what the other ship was Sub-Lieutenant Frew replied: 'Yes. The navigating officer, I think, called for a seamanship manual to be brought to the bridge. It was brought up by Leading Seaman Headley and handed to me. I handed it to the navigating officer.'

CORONER: 'How far do you think the vessel was when the book was being brought?'

SUB-LIEUTENANT FREW: 'I can only guess. About half a mile, perhaps.'

CORONER: 'We will go back now to the time you saw the bows of the vessel. What happened then?'

SUB-LIEUTENANT FREW: 'The captain ordered full astern together, and ordered the helm to be put hard to starboard.'

Frew went on to say that he stood where he was on the bridge when the *Divina* struck. The tanker had hit the fore-end near the torpedo tubes. As the ship fell away, the submarine dipped down. Lieutenant Bowers ordered everyone on the bridge to go below. Before Frew could get through the lower conning tower hatch, the lower hatch closed, thus preventing him gaining access to the control room. Frew had been delayed in his dash below because the upper conning tower hatch had closed on his arm, breaking his arm and trapping him in the conning tower. With the sea pouring in, Frew went down with the submarine. But as soon as the conning tower had filled with water, he was able to open the upper hatch fully and then make his way to the surface. When he arrived on the surface he was joined by someone with a lifebelt. Together they swam towards a lighted buoy. Frew was still clinging to the lifebelt when he was joined by Charles Bowers and Leading Seaman Headley, the latter with a lifebelt thrown from *Divina*. By the time *Almdyk*'s boat arrived to pick them up, Frew had lapsed into unconsciousness.

Lieutenant J.N. Humphrey-Baker opened his account of the sinking by saying that he first saw the *Divina*'s lights fine on the port bow. He estimated them at about two miles distant. He was puzzled by an additional red light and thought that the vessel might have been a dredger. After calling Bowers to the bridge he was ordered to alter course 10° to port. When this had been done he checked the position on the chart to make sure that there was sufficient depth for the submarine's 13 feet draught. While doing this he heard the order: 'Stop together.' 'I jumped to the telegraphs which were about 6 feet behind me and put both to STOP', recalled Humphrey-Baker. 'I then looked round and saw the *Divina* on our starboard bow at a distance of, I would say, under a cable. The next order was "Astern together" and "Starboard thirty". Then came "Shut all bulkhead doors and watertight doors".' When asked if he had observed whether the order was able to take effect Humphrey-Baker replied that no one could tell from the bridge, but he presumed the order was repeated back as Lieutenant Bowers would have given it again and he had not done so. In telling of his final moments with *Truculent*, Humphrey-Baker said that Lieutenant Bowers had given the order to go below. The lookout, AB Powell, went below. Lieutenant Frew then got into the hatch to do likewise. Then everyone was sucked down. When he himself came to the surface he saw the tanker astern with her engines still turning. He shouted for a lifebelt. Two were thrown.

Interest heightened when Lieutenant Bowers took the oath. In evidence he said that after altering course to port sufficiently in his judgement to go clear across the front of *Divina*, he caught sight of the ship's silhouette. 'I could see she was a vessel underway, about one to two cables away. I realized a collision was extremely likely and gave orders to stop both engines and pull full astern. The two ships locked together for ten to fifteen seconds. She then seemed to break clear and go down. I did not hear any sound signals. When I came to the surface I was just about level with the *Divina*'s stern and I thought she was going ahead at the time. I would swear to that.' Bowers went on to say that he did not consider his action in altering course to port was wrong as *Truculent* was too close to the northern side of the channel and the presence of an extra light on the tanker might have indicated it was some kind of moored vessel it was dangerous to pass on the red light side.

Towards the end of the proceedings the coroner stated: 'My prime duty is the simple one of determining whether or nor there was gross criminal negligence. There is no shadow of evidence to support anything so grave as that. It is not for me to say which of these two vessels was at fault in civil law. I am only required to say that there is no gross negligence amounting to criminal negligence.' The coroner further stated that after the collision those in *Truculent* kept calm and their behaviour in every way was in the highest traditions of the Navy. In praising the way in which those who escaped assisted each other, the coroner singled out for special mention Lieutenant Humphrey-Baker, who for some considerable time had held up Sub-Lieutenant Frew. A verdict of accidental death was returned on all the dead bodies recovered up to that time.

On 7 February it was announced that the Albert Medal had been posthumously awarded to Lieutenant Frederick Hindes, *Truculent*'s first lieutenant, and Chief ERA Francis Hine for their gallantry in attempting to save life. After commenting on the exemplary conduct of all who went down in *Truculent*, the announcement continued:

> The splendid example set by Lt Hindes and Chief ERA Hine was beyond praise. Lt Hindes, by calm demeanour and clear orders, maintained perfect discipline and was able to ensure that the greater part of those on board moved safely to the engine room and after end of the vessel before

she sank. When all was ready he opened the escape hatch. Despite having told a crewman to hold on to him, he was blown violently out of the submarine and was not seen again. Yet the sense of order which Lt Hindes had instilled survived him. Chief ERA Hine took charge of the escape arrangements in the engine room. This duty he performed faultlessly, taking care that the limited number of escape sets were alloted to the weakest swimmers and ensuring that the least experienced men were carefully reminded of the correct drill.

It was two days after this welcome announcement that the court martial of 28-year-old Lieutenant Charles Bowers took place at Chatham. Lieutenant Bowers had taken command of *Truculent* in November 1949, so he had been her captain for only a few weeks at the time of the collision, which had happened on the first occasion he had taken *Truculent* to sea. During the course of his evidence Bowers, wearing the 1939-1945 Star, the Atlantic Star and Clasp, the Burma Star, and the War Service Medal, stated: 'I saw a triangle of a green light and two red lights. The next thing that I remember is that I lost sight of *Divina*'s green light and practically at the same time I caught sight of her silhouette. I suddenly realized that she was much closer than I had estimated.'

After deliberating for an hour and twenty minutes the court found that the charge against Lieutenant Bowers of negligently or by default losing his ship had not been proven and he was acquitted of that charge. A second charge, that of negligently or by default hazarding his ship, was deemed to have been proved. The Deputy Judge-Advocate gave the court's reasons for the findings (1) on sighting *Divina*'s lights, which included the lights of a steamship underway, Lieutenant Bowers altered course across the channel and *Divina*'s course – when the rule of the road at sea required, and navigational conditions permitted, *Truculent* to maintain her course – thereby endangering the safety of his ship (2) that Lieutenant Bowers made no sound signal to indicate his ship's alteration of course to port. The sentence of the court was that Lieutenant Bowers be severely reprimanded.

Lieutenant Charles Bowers had seen action with *Tactician* during the war. In 1945 he had taken command of *Satyr*. An experienced submariner, it is to be regretted that he should have lost his command in such sorry circumstances.

Two months passed before *Truculent* was brought to the surface. During a period of slack water on the afternoon of 14 March, water began pouring from valves in the sides of the *Ausdauer* and *Energie*, two ex-German lifting vessels performing the lift. Just as light was failing, the submarine's name became visible on the port side of her conning tower. Forward of the bridge on her starboard side were signs of the collision. *Truculent*, broadside astern of the *Ausdauer* and *Energie*, and in care of four tugs, then set off on the 5-mile journey to Cheney Spit, a sandbank off Sheerness. At 1050 that night *Truculent* was beached. On 16 March she was moved a thousand yards inshore. Bad weather then hampered further salvage operations until the 17th. On that day ten bodies were recovered. On the 23rd *Truculent* was refloated and towed to Sheerness Dockyard. On 8 May 1950, following eight years' service, she was sold to T.W. Ward for breaking up.

## 1951

*Affray* was one of the first of the 'A' class submarines, which came into service in early 1945. Launched at Cammell Laird on 12 April 1945, *Affray* was within a few days of the sixth anniversary of her launch when during Exercise Training Spring she became the last Royal Navy submarine to sink at sea. Exercise Training Spring called for *Affray* to:

(1) Make a surface report between 0900 and 1000 daily.
(2) Signal her position to Air Officer Commanding 19th Group RAF. This signal was to be cleared by 0900 daily.
(3) Land and recover a small party of Royal Marines and their folboats on any suitable beach in the patrol area during the night.
(4) Call at Falmouth at 1700 on Thursday 19 April. If the folboat landings had been completed the marines were to return to Plymouth from Falmouth by rail.
(5) Depart Falmouth 1700 on April 20 to continue the exercise, which was expected to last until the morning of the 23rd.

The orders of Lieutenant Blackburn, *Affray*'s captain, did not bind him too rigidly to any set course of action; they called for him to proceed west and then to spend several days on a simulated war patrol for the benefit of some twenty or so submarine executive and engineering officers who were required to gain experience of a submarine under war conditions. At some unspecified time during the

exercise, John Blackburn was to land the party of four marines somewhere on the Cornish coast.

*Affray* sailed Portsmouth at 1615 on the afternoon of Monday 16
April. Blackburn had indicated his noon position for the 17th before
leaving harbour. On the morning of the 17th *Affray* failed to make
her surface report, scheduled between 0900 and 1000. Rescue
organizations were put on the alert. An hour later a full alert brought
the whole submarine rescue organization into action. Throughout
the morning of the 17th shore radio stations called *Affray*. There was
no reply. The number of vessels joining the search grew with each
passing hour. It was known that *Affray* had dived at 2115 in position
50°10'N 01°45'W, some 30 miles south of the Isle of Wight. As she
was expected to surface about 20 miles south-east of Start Point, the
search was at its most intense in that area. A number of submarines
involved in the search reported picking up faint distorted signals on
their A/S listening apparatus. Hull tapping was also heard.
Attempts to obtain a cross-bearing on the source of the signals and
the sound, both of which were thought to have originated from
*Affray*, were unsuccessful. On the afternoon of the 18th the *Ambush*
picked up the code letters representing WE ARE TRAPPED ON THE BOT-
TOM. On the 19th a submarine was dispatched to investigate the
reported sighting of a large oil patch near the Casquets, a group of
small rocky islands about seven miles west of Alderney which for
centuries have been the graveyard of many unwary mariners.
Nothing came of the investigation. By the evening of the 19th the
intensive search for *Affray* was regretfully terminated. There was no
longer any great urgency to locate the submarine in order to save life.

Although the main requirement for locating *Affray* had ceased, the
search was not abandoned. A squadron of frigates equipped with the
latest sonar apparatus was detailed to continue the search. Discovery of *Affray* might possibly reveal signs of involvement in an accident, though no accident had been reported. And it might also indicate whether any of her crew had attempted to escape. The task for
those who were to continue with the search was extraordinarily difficult. The search area extended over 1,500 square miles of an
expanse of water well known for its vast numbers of wrecks.
Whenever a likely contact was made Navy divers would descend and
investigate the wreck. This took a considerable time. Also, it was
only during the brief period of slack water each day that the diving
ship *Reclaim* could be moored for diving purposes. The search had
been in progress for more than a month, and without the slightest

trace of *Affray*, when it was decided to employ an underwater televi-sion camera on any wreck considered worthy of investigation. The camera proved invaluable. If a picture was received of what was obviously the wreck of a surface vessel, the *Reclaim* could move on to the next located wreck.

By the middle of June the search for the elusive submarine was concentrated in an area north-west of Alderney. On 14 June the TV camera was lowered the 260 feet to a reported wreck. To the delight of all, a picture of a rail of the type round a submarine's gun platform came into view. Then the camera focused on the letter Y. Moving from right to left the camera picked out the letters A-R-F-F-A. After a search of almost nine weeks the *Affray* had been found. Her position was 67 miles 228° St Catherine's Lighthouse, 37 miles south-west of her last reported diving position. She was lying on an even keel near the edge of Hurd's Deep and close to the area where the large patch of oil had been reported off the Casquets. Hurd's Deep – a series of long, narrow underwater chasms which drop sheer from the bed of the English Channel and vary in depth between 300 and 500 feet – begins at the west coast of Guernsey and passes three miles north of Alderney before continuing along the English Channel and past the Casquets to a point north-west of the Cherbourg Peninsula. In Hurd's Deep was dumped the arms (tanks, guns, shells, etc.) of two German divisions which had garrisoned the Channel Islands during the Second World War.

Divers could find no evidence of collision damage. They noted that *Affray*'s radar aerial and a periscope were raised, an indication that *Affray* had been submerged at the time of her foundering. A check at the hatches showed that all were closed. There was no outward sign that an attempt had been made to release the indicator buoy. Further investigation revealed that both pairs of hydroplanes were at hard to rise. This, and the fact that both pointers on the bridge tele-graph were at STOP, might signify that *Affray* had been going down fast and that Lieutenant Blackburn had been trying to correct this.

During the divers' examination of *Affray* an alarming detail came to light – the submarine's snort*-mast had broken off at a point 3 feet above the deck. The break had been so clean that defective material was suspected; but to be completely certain that metal fatigue had caused the snort-mast to snap off, it was necessary to recover the mast for examination by experts. Work on retrieving the mast was

---

* From the German schnorkel=snorkel=snort.

difficult and dangerous but after several days it was recovered and sent to Portsmouth. An examination of the mast produced no indication that it had been struck by a passing ship. Laboratory tests confirmed the suspicion that a weakness in the metal had been responsible for the mast breaking off. The main factors contributing to the break were (1) materials susceptible to brittle fracture in one of the component tubes and (2) the presence of poor welding in the butt joints of the fairing plates connecting the tubes.

The fact that the snort-mast was defective did not in itself explain why it had broken off. Just because a weakness had been discovered by the metallurgical examination did not mean that the snort-mast was about to break off. So the need was to discover what had caused it to do so. Research work in the rapid propagation of cracks suggested not only the need for a starting point, such as a notch – a faulty weld would provide this – but also some exciting force. The metallurgical conditions of some parts of *Affray*'s snort-mast, and those of two other 'A' class submarines, were found to be below standard. Also, some of the welding was rather poor. Tests on all three masts indicated that they were capable of standing up to all stresses other than those associated with an explosive shock. The possibility of a major battery explosion in *Affray* could not be ruled out. Such an occurrence could have started a shock wave in her hull, perhaps comparable with that of a depth- charge. If such an explosion did occur, it could have started a crack in the snort-mast, which might then have snapped off as *Affray* grounded. Against the theory of a battery explosion was the lack of damage to *Affray*'s stern; a battery explosion could be expected to cause some visible damage, yet none was observed by divers.

At the moment the snort-mast had snapped off, the induction valve at the point where the mast entered the pressure hull should have automatically shut. This very important valve was designed to close as soon as the top of the mast was beneath the surface. It may be that the induction valve had stayed open. If this was so, other submarines could, under certain conditions, be in danger. The Admiralty were keen to put beyond doubt the question as to whether the valve had operated as designed, or had failed. The *Reclaim* returned to the wreck in hopes of gaining the relevant information. Although every effort was made, the divers found it impossible to determine whether the valve was open or closed. As *Affray* had taken on a pronounced list to port, the risk to the divers was considered sufficient to halt permanently all work on *Affray*.

The general opinion as to the most likely cause of *Affray*'s sinking was that her snort-mast had broken off while she was at periscope depth. The induction valve had failed to operate satisfactorily and water had entered *Affray* through a 10-inch hole. With her buoyancy destroyed, she had gone quickly to the bottom. It is unlikely that what really happened to *Affray* will ever be known with certainty.

*Affray*'s captain had been a submariner for nine years. His first command (*Token*) was for ten months during 1948-49. Married to an ex-Wren since April 1947, Lieutenant Blackburn had been awarded the DSC in 1943 for 'Great daring, enterprise, and skill' in a successful submarine patrol. Rear-Admiral B. Bryant, under whom Blackburn served in *Safari*, says of him:

> I remember him well. He was my Third Hand (gunnery and torpedo officer) before he became First Lieutenant at my request. Not only was he a first-class officer, but a very pleasant personality, popular alike with officers and ratings. He was typical of those young men who since their schooldays had known nothing but war. He was alert and conscientious knowing that survival depended upon always seeing the other chap first in the submarines of pre-radar days, a requirement alike for officers and ratings on watch on the bridge; and they took easily to responsibility at an early age. Blackburn was one of the best and should have gone far.

Lieutenant Blackburn left a small daughter.

One of the seventy-five men lost with *Affray* was Sub-Lieutenant William Linton, the 21-year-old son of Commander John Linton, vc, the captain of *Turbulent*. Also of the crew was Sub-Lieutenant Anthony Frew, one of the five survivors taken from the sea by the *Almdyk*'s boat after *Truculent* had been sunk in the Thames Estuary. Twenty-two-year-old Radio Electrician Jack Rutter was another lost with *Affray*. Less than two years earlier, on the night of 30 July 1949, Jack Rutter had been serving in the frigate *Amethyst* when Lieutenant-Commander John Kerans had made his epic dash down the Yangtse in the face of strong Communist opposition.

As stated, *Affray* was the last Royal Navy submarine to sink in open waters.

# 1955

When Her Majesty's Submarine *Sidon* sank in Portland Harbour it was the first occasion on which a Royal Navy submarine had been sunk during the reign of a queen.

*June 16.* Sunshine was starting to filter through the morning haze. *Sidon* (Lieutenant-Commander H.T. Verry) was one of five submarines moored alongside the depot ship *Maidstone*. Several of the submarines were about to cast off and proceed seaward for a torpedo firing exercise. The submarine *Springer*, moored on *Sidon*'s starboard side, cast off and got underway. It was 0820.

Surgeon-Lieutenant C.E. Rhodes, a doctor on National Service, sat down to breakfast in *Maidstone*'s wardroom. A few minutes later he heard a dull thud . . . thud. Then came the shrill sound of alarm bells. Without a word the young doctor jumped to his feet and hurried from the wardroom. Arriving on deck he saw smoke belching freely from *Sidon*'s conning tower. It was 0825.

An eye-witness to the explosion in *Sidon* has this to say of the event. 'A sheet of flame shot up through the conning tower followed by more flames and smoke; then bits of equipment and furniture, hats and coats, and clouds of paper were blown into the air.' The cause of this powerful explosion was one of the recently embarked practice torpedoes. These torpedoes had no warheads, but they did have the new volatile hydrogen peroxide propellent.

ERA Peter Leech had served nine years in submarines. ERA Leech states: 'I was at the control panel with "Happy" Day when there was a loud thud and a burst of orange flame. I was tossed about 10 feet through the door of the radio room. We were something like a hundred feet from the torpedo compartment. I guessed what had happened as the yellowish-greenish smoke thickened. I was dazed and it seemed only a matter of seconds before someone shouted, "Everybody out of the boat." I can remember thinking that the blood streaming down my face and hands must have been from somebody else. I walked off *Sidon* across the gangway over another submarine lying alongside.'

'Happy' Day (Petty Officer William Day) reports: 'I was in the control room just below the conning tower. We were checking the control panel instruments to see that everything was all right for when we dived during exercises later. There was a dull sort of bang, and then a blast lifted me off my feet. The next I knew was when I came to in hospital. Somebody must have got me out. I have no idea who it was.' It seems likely that Petty Officer Day was helped from the control room by Surgeon-Lieutenant Rhodes.

Steward Dereck Jones had been on duty in *Maidstone*'s wardroom.

He saw Charles Rhodes jump to his feet and then rush out of the wardroom. 'He removed his spectacles and put on breathing apparatus, and leapt down on to the deck of *Sidon*,' reports Jones. 'I saw him go down the hatch in a cloud of smoke. A minute later I saw him come up half-carrying an injured seaman. Then down he went again. Four times he came through the smoke. Each time he brought up a man. When he went down the fifth time, the submarine was beginning to sink. He seemed to be gasping and struggling with his breathing apparatus. We did not see him again.'

*Sidon*'s captain was on the bridge with engineer-officer Roy Hawkins when the explosion shook the submarine. Hawkins, who had been reporting engines ready for sea, says of the incident: 'We heard the explosion, and then a rush of air came up through the hatch. Some of the hands came up immediately after, very dazed. I went below. You could hardly see anything, although the lights were on. In the engine room I found "Geordie" Pearson; between us we got the blower running to try and get rid of some of the smoke, but the after hatch was open and the air went straight through. I could not breathe anymore and had to come up. I put breathing apparatus on and, with Captain Verry, First Lieutenant Puxley, and Surgeon-Lieutenant Rhodes, went to see if we could get some of the boys out. We did not realize the boat was sinking. We went forward through a lot of smashed equipment until we came across a pile of metal lying in the gangway. We pulled some of it away and I burrowed a 2-foot hole, but when I crawled through I could get no farther than a bulkhead blocked by debris. The nose clip of my breathing apparatus came adrift. I started to choke for breath and I knew I was passing out. Lieutenant Rhodes grabbed me and pulled me back.'

After the explosion *Sidon* dipped noticeably by the bow. The visiting Danish submarine *Saelen*, on *Sidon*'s port side, was towed away from *Sidon*. Though not at first obvious to those inside the submarine, *Sidon* was sinking. When the call to abandon ship came, men blackened by soot and smoke made a dash to get out of and clear of the submarine. One of the last to leave *Sidon* was Jack Gill, a 23-year-old engineer from *Maidstone*. 'I went down to help,' says Gill. 'Through the smoke I heard somebody gasping. I could see Lieutenant Rhodes lying at the bottom of the conning tower. He was struggling with his breathing apparatus and seemed to be trying to work the levers which control the oxygen flow. Just then someone shouted to me to get out. The submarine was sinking. I got clear just in time.'

At 0845 *Sidon*, with ensign flying, sank by the bows.

The mooring vessel *Moordale* was lying just across the harbour when the explosion took place. She at once went in aid of *Sidon*. By the time the submarine's bows sank, *Moordale* had secured a wire round *Sidon*'s rising stern; however, the flooded *Sidon* became too heavy for the 767-ton *Moordale* to hold and the submarine gradually slipped under water, dragging the cable down with her.

From *Maidstone* frogmen clambered into launches before slipping into the muddy water. In pairs they groped along *Sidon*'s hull and hammered a message in morse to those who had gone down with her. There was no reply. A torpedo was seen sticking out of a tube. By early afternoon it was clear that all inside the submarine were either dead or incapable of replying to hull tapping. Aboard *Maidstone* sailors looked in silence at two patches of rising air-bubbles, 20 yards apart. A little way off, a motor-boat with trippers circled.

Three officers and ten ratings had gone down with *Sidon*. Surgeon-Lieutenant Charles Rhodes numbered among the dead. Rhodes had served sixteen months of his National Service and in a further two months would have been back home in Manchester. Part of his medical training had been at a hospital in Harold Wood, Essex. It was whilst there that he had met his future wife, a nursing sister. Charles Rhodes was twenty-eight. He left a three-week-old daughter.

Lieutenant-Commander Hugh Verry, who was thirty, had entered the Navy as a midshipman in May 1944. At one stage he had served in X-craft. Verry's command of *Sidon* dated from 30 March 1954.

On 18 June work began on rigging four large buoyancy cylinders, known as camels, to *Sidon*. After two of the camels had been secured she was raised slightly to enable wires to be positioned beneath her for securing two more camels. When this was completed *Sidon*'s stern rose to the surface. At this point her conning tower was visible just below the surface. Further raising cleared the after hatch. Movement then ceased. *Sidon* had a strong list to port. After twenty minutes she was lowered beneath the surface. The salvage team wanted to try to correct the list so as to bring her up on an even keel.

During the early hours of the 23rd, *Sidon* was again on the surface. By 0430 she was secured. It had been 0200 when *Sidon*, in the glare of dozens of searchlights mounted on *Maidstone* and salvage vessels, began to emerge through swirling mist. Ten minutes later her periscope and bridge equipment were seen. Then came her conning tower with the name *Sidon* in brass letters on the side. At noon the next day *Sidon*, towed by two fishing vessels with two lifting craft at her stern, was moved a mile to an area of shallow water not a hundred yards from the main Weymouth-Portland road which skirts the harbour. Shortly after, on the 28th, the dead were buried in the small naval cemetery on the cliff edge of Portland.

The *Sidon* explosion had occurred because of a material failure in one of her torpedoes. The torpedo's hydrogen peroxide propellent had started to flow and because the torpedo was in the confined space of its tube, with both the tube door and bow cap shut, there was a great pressure set up in the torpedo tube, and intense heat; the pressure and heat built up into a form of explosion. The tube door and bow cap were blown open. The main force of the explosion had dissipated through the door and into the submarine. With the tube door and bow cap open, the sea had direct access to the interior of *Sidon*.

On 14 June 1957 *Sidon* was towed from Portland and sunk for use as an A/S target. She had been only the second Royal Navy vessel to have borne the name *Sidon*, the first having been a frigate of 1846.

# 1971

The 'A' class submarines were in service for thirty years. Designed during the war for service in the Far East, the war came to an end before any of the class could fire a shot in anger. Peacetime requirements were far short of the intended forty-six submarines and so only sixteen 'A' class were completed. The *Artemis* was the first of two 'A's built by Scotts of Greenock. Launched in August 1946, she was completed a year later. *Artemis* was nearing the end of her useful life when on 1 July 1971 she sank whilst alongside a jetty at Fort Blockhouse. Earlier that day she had been moved from dry-dock by a tug and taken across Portsmouth Harbour to the jetty. During this time *Artemis* had been in the charge of Lieutenant John Crawford, her third hand and sonar officer. Crawford was twenty-five and had been in submarines for two years.

There were relatively few hands aboard *Artemis* at the time of her sinking. Chief Petty Officer David Guest was on deck 'enjoying a bit of sunshine' when another crewman yelled that *Artemis* was sinking by the stern. 'I knew there were three sea cadets who had just gone below,' says Guest, 'as I had sent one of the duty watch to show them around the submarine. My first thoughts were for the cadets. I went down below and told them in no uncertain terms to get out.' Having got the cadets clear, Guest ran through *Artemis* to ensure that the few hands aboard were out of their bunks. By the time this had been done it was too late for Guest and two other ratings to escape. David Guest continues: 'We saw we could do nothing to stop the water coming in. We could not shut the bulkhead doors, so we checked that the conning tower hatch was shut and then went forward, making sure that nobody was left behind.' The water was coming in astern. In a torrent it followed the three ratings as they ran to the torpedo stowage compartment. On gaining access to the compartment they slammed fast and secured the door. With Chief Petty Officer Guest, who at thirty-six was the eldest of the three, were Mechanic Engineer Donald Beckett and Leading Mechanic Engineer Robert Croxen, the latter at twenty-two being the youngest of the trio. In time they were able to establish telephone contact with the *Ocelot*, lying alongside *Artemis*, thus making the situation more bearable.

*Artemis* had been on the bottom more than ten hours before the three ratings were able to make a bid to reach the surface. First to leave the submarine was Croxen. He was followed in quick succession by Beckett and David Guest. All three safely reached the surface.

The reason for the foundering was deemed to have been because 'too many people had forgotten the basic principles of submarine safety – ship stability'. *Artemis* had sunk after being flooded through two open hatches while her fuel tanks were being 'first filled' with water preparatory to fuelling. Attempts to stop the submarine from flooding had failed owing to a shore power-cable having been passed through a hatch, thus preventing the hatch cover from being shut, an echo of the *H29* sinking of 1926.

The captain of *Artemis* had not been present when she had sunk. Lieutenant-Commander Godfrey was later to state that the reason for his not being aboard *Artemis* during her undocking and transfer to the jetty at Fort Blockhouse was that he had to be at RAF Boscombe Down for talks on a forthcoming exercise. He had returned to HMS *Dolphin* during the morning of 1 July and had met Lieutenant Crawford and two other officers from *Artemis* in the wardroom bar at lunch-time after the undocking move of *Artemis* had been completed. Godfrey further stated that he had not been aboard the submarine for almost a week, but had asked his officers to furnish him with daily briefings, which was why he had not gone down to *Artemis* after meeting his officers in the wardroom bar.

Lieutenant-Commander Roger Godfrey had entered the Navy in 1959. After *Britannia* he had served in HMS *Chichester* until joining the Submarine Service in 1963. Godfrey was thirty-one and had first served in *Artemis* in 1964.

With the help of the salvage vessels *Golden Eye* and *Kinloss*, *Artemis* shook herself free from the mud of Haslar Creek on 6 July. The following year *Artemis* was sold for scrap.

The sinking of HM Submarine *Artemis* concludes this history.

# HM Submarine Losses 1904-1971

### THE EARLY YEARS

| | | | |
|---|---|---|---|
| *A1* | 18.3.04 | Lt L.C.O. Mansergh. | Sank off Isle of Wight after collision with liner *Berwick Castle*. |
| *A8* | 8.6.05 | Lt A.H.C. Candy. | Sank in Plymouth Sound after an internal explosion. |
| *A4* | 16.10.05 | Lt M.E. Nasmith. | Sank in Portsmouth Harbour. |
| *C11* | 14.7.09 | Lt C.G. Brodie. | Sank in English Channel after collision with SS *Eddystone*. |
| *A3* | 2.2.12 | Lt F.T. Ormand. | Sank off Isle of Wight after collision with S/M tender HMS *Hazard*. |
| *B2* | 4.10.12 | Lt P.B. O'Brien. | Sank off Dover after collision with SS *Amerika*. |
| *C14* | 10.12.13 | Lt G.W.E. Naper. | Sank in Plymouth Sound after collision with a hopper. |
| *A7* | 16.1.14 | Lt G.M. Welman. | Sank in Whitsand Bay, near Plymouth. |

### THE GREAT WAR

| | | | |
|---|---|---|---|
| *AE1* | 19.9.14 | Lt-Cdr T.E. Besant. | Lost off New Britain (cause unknown). |
| *E3* | 18.10.14 | Lt-Cdr G.F. Cholmley. | Sunk off Borkum Island by *U27*. |
| *D5* | 3.11.14 | Lt-Cdr G. Herbert. | Mined off Yarmouth. |
| *D2* | 25.11.14 | Lt-Cdr C.G.W. Head. | Lost off Borkum Island. |
| *C31* | 4.1.15 | Lt-Cdr G. Pilkington. | Presumed mined off Belgian coast. |
| *E10* | 18.1.15 | Lt-Cdr W.St J. Fraser. | Possibly mined in Heligoland Bight. |
| *E15* | 17.4.15 | Lt-Cdr T.S. Brodie. | Ran aground in Dardanelles. |
| *AE2* | 30.4.15 | Lt-Cdr H.G.D. Stoker. | Scuttled in Sea of Marmara. |
| *C33* | 4.8.15 | Lt G.E.B. Carter. | Probably mined in North Sea. |
| *E13* | 19.8.15 | Lt-Cdr G. Layton. | Ran aground off Danish coast. |
| *C29* | 29.8.15 | Lt W.R. Schofield. | Mined in North Sea. |
| *E7* | 4.9.15 | Lt-Cdr A.D. Cochrane. | Scuttled at A/S nets in Dardanelles. |

| | | | |
|---|---|---|---|
| *E20* | 6.11.15 | Lt-Cdr C.H. Warren. | Torpedoed in Sea of Marmara by *UB14*. |
| *E6* | 26.12.15 | Lt-Cdr W.J. Foster. | Mined off Harwich. |
| *E17* | 6.1.16 | Lt-Cdr J.R.G. Moncreiffe. | Scuttled off Texel Island after striking a submerged rock. |
| *H6* | 19.1.16 | Lt R.N. Stopford. | Ran aground off Ameland Island. |
| *E5* | 7.3.16 | Lt-Cdr H.D. Edwards. | Possibly lost off Western Ems. |
| *E24* | 24.3.16 | Lt-Cdr G.W.E. Naper. | Possibly mined in North Sea. |
| *E22* | 25.4.16 | Lt R.T. Dimsdale. | Torpedoed in North Sea by *UB18*. |
| *E18* | 24.5.16 | Lt-Cdr R.C. Halahan. | Lost in Baltic (cause unknown). |
| *E26* | 3.7.16 | Lt E.W.B. Ryan. | Possibly sunk off Eastern Ems. |
| *H3* | 15.7.16 | Lt G.E. Jenkinson. | Mined in Adriatic. |
| *B10* | 5.8.16 | Lt K. Michell. | Sunk in Venice by aircraft. |
| *E4* | 15.8.16 | Lt-Cdr J. Tenison. | Sunk off Harwich in collision with HM S/M *E41*. |
| *E41* | 15.8.16 | Lt A.M. Winser. | Sunk off Harwich in collision with HM S/M *E4*. |
| *E16* | 22.8.16 | Lt-Cdr K.J. Duff-Dunbar. | Lost in North Sea (cause unknown). |
| *E30* | 22.11.16 | Lt-Cdr G.N. Biggs. | Possibly mined off Orford Ness. |
| *E36* | 19.1.17 | Lt T.B.S. MacGregor-Robertson. | Lost in North Sea, probably in collision with HM S/M *E43*. |
| *K13* | 29.1.17 | Lt-Cdr G. Herbert. | Sank in Gareloch during trials. |
| *E49* | 12.3.17 | Lt B.A. Beal. | Mined off Huney Isle, Shetlands. |
| *A10* | 17.3.17 | (No captain). | Sank at Ardrossan after water leaked into the ballast tanks. |
| *C16* | 16.4.17 | Lt H. Boase. | Sunk off Harwich in collision with HM Destroyer *Melampus*. |
| *C34* | 17.7.17 | Lt I.S. Jefferson. | Torpedoed east of Fair Isle by *U52*. |
| *E47* | 20.8.17 | Lt E.C. Carré. | Lost in North Sea (cause unknown). |
| *G9* | 16.9.17 | Lt-Cdr Hon. B.P. Cary. | Rammed in error in North Sea by HM Destroyer *Pasley*. |
| *C32* | 22.10.17 | Lt C.P. Satow. | Grounded in Vaist Bay, Estonia, and blown up to avoid capture. |
| *K1* | 18.11.17 | Lt-Cdr C.S. Benning. | Damaged off Danish coast in collision with HM S/M *K4*. Sunk by HM Cruiser *Blanche* to avoid capture. |
| *G8* | 14.1.18 | Lt J.F. Tryon. | Lost in North Sea (cause unknown). |

| | | | |
|---|---|---|---|
| *H10* | 19.1.18 | Lt M.H. Collier. | Lost in North Sea (cause unknown). |
| *E14* | 28.1.18 | Lt-Cdr G.S. White. | Sunk by shore-based guns in Dardanelles. |
| *K4* | 31.1.18 | Lt-Cdr D. de B. Stocks. | Sank in Forth Estuary after collision with HM S/M *K6*. |
| *K17* | 31.1.18 | Lt-Cdr H.J. Hearn. | Sank in Forth Estuary after collision with HM Cruiser *Fearless*. |
| *E50* | 1.2.18 | Lt R.E. Snook. | Possibly mined in North Sea. |
| *H5* | 2.3.18 | Lt A.W. Forbes. | Rammed in error in Irish Sea by SS *Rutherglen*. |
| *D3* | 12.3.18 | Lt W. Maitland-Dougall. | Bombed in error off Fécamp, France, by a French airship. |
| *E1* | 3.4.18 | Scuttled in Helingfors Bay, Finland, to avoid capture. | |
| *E9* | 3.4.18 | Ditto *E1* | |
| *E19* | 3.4.18 | Ditto *E1* | |
| *E8* | 4.4.18 | Ditto *E1* | |
| *C26* | 4.4.18 | Ditto *E1* | |
| *C27* | 5.4.18 | Ditto *E1* | |
| *C35* | 5.4.18 | Ditto *E1* | |
| *C3* | 23.4.18 | Lt R. Sandford. | Employed as explosives ship to destroy viaduct at Zeebrugge, Belgium. |
| *D6* | 28.6.18 | Lt S.A. Brooks. | Sunk off Irish coast by *UB73*. |
| *E34* | 20.7.18 | Lt R.I. Pulleyne. | Lost in North Sea (cause unknown). |
| *L10* | 3.10.18 | Lt-Cdr A.E. Whitehouse. | Sunk north of Terschelling by gunfire of German ships. |
| *C12* | .10.18 | Lt N. Manley. | Sank at Immingham after collision with HM destroyer. |
| *J6* | 15.10.18 | Lt-Cdr G. Warburton. | Sunk in error off Blyth by Q-ship HMS *Cymric*. |
| *G7* | 1.11.18 | Lt C.A.C. Russell. | Lost in North Sea (cause unknown). |

BETWEEN THE WARS

| | | | |
|---|---|---|---|
| *G11* | 22.11.18 | Lt-Cdr G.F. Bradshaw. | Wrecked off Howich during fog. |
| *L55* | 4.6.19 | Lt C.M.S. Chapman. | Possibly sunk near Kronstadt, Gulf of Finland, by Soviet warships. |
| *H41* | 18.10.19 | Lt-Cdr N.R. Peploe. | Sank at Blyth when holed by propellers of HM Destroyer *Vulcan*. |
| *K5* | 20.1.21 | Lt-Cdr J.A. Gaimes. | Sank SW of Isles of Scilly (cause unknown). |
| *K15* | 25.6.21 | Cdr G.F. Bradshaw. | Sank at Portsmouth when loss |

| | | | of oil in hydraulic system slackened ballast tank vents and allowed air to escape. |
|---|---|---|---|
| *H42* | 23.3.22 | Lt D.C. Sealy. | Sank off Gibraltar in collision with HM Destroyer *Versatile*. |
| *L9* | 18.8.23 | (No captain). | Sank in Hong Kong Harbour during a typhoon. |
| *L24* | 10.1.24 | Lt-Cdr P.L. Eddis. | Sank off Portland in collision with HM Battleship *Resolution*. |
| *M1* | 12.11.25 | Lt-Cdr A. Carrie. | Sank in English Channel after collision with Swedish collier *Vidar*. |
| *H29* | 9.8.26 | Lt F.H.E. Skyrme. | Sank at Devonport whilst surface trimming with hatches open. |
| *H47* | 9.7.29 | Lt R.J. Gardner. | Sank off Pembrokeshire coast after collision with HM S/M *L12*. |
| *Poseidon* | 9.6.31 | Lt-Cdr B.W. Galpin. | Sank in Yellow Sea north of Wei Hai Wei after collision with SS *Yuta*. |
| *M2* | 26.1.32 | Lt-Cdr J.D. de M. Leathes. | Sank off Portland whilst surfacing. Access hatch to aircraft hangar was probably opened too soon. |
| *Thetis* | 1.6.39 | Lt-Cdr G.H. Bolus. | Sank in Liverpool Bay during acceptance trials. |

### THE SECOND WORLD WAR

| | | | |
|---|---|---|---|
| *Oxley* | 10.9.39 | Lt-Cdr H.G. Bowerman. | Torpedoed in error off Obrestad, Norway, by HM S/M *Triton*. |
| *Undine* | 7.1.40 | Lt-Cdr A.S. Jackson. | Sunk SW of Heligoland by German A/S trawlers. |
| *Seahorse* | 7.1.40 | Lt D.S. Massey Dawson. | Possibly sunk by German A/S craft. |
| *Starfish* | 9.1.40 | Lt T.A. Turner. | Sunk SW of Heligoland by German minesweeper trawlers. |
| *Thistle* | 10.4.40 | Lt-Cdr W.F. Hazelfoot. | Torpedoed off Utsira, Norway, by *U4*. |
| *Tarpon* | 10.4.40 | Lt-Cdr H.J. Caldwell. | Probably sunk in North Sea by German Q-ship. |
| *Sterlet* | 18.4.40 | Lt-Cdr G.H.S. Haward. | Sunk in Skagerrak by German escort vessel *M75*. |
| *Unity* | 29.4.40 | Lt F.J. Brooks. | Sunk off Tyne in collision with |

| | | | |
|---|---|---|---|
| | | | Norwegian steamer *Atle Jarl*. |
| *Seal* | 5.5.40 | Lt-Cdr R.P. Lonsdale. | Captured in Kattegat after striking a mine. |
| *Odin* | 14.6.40 | Lt-Cdr K.M. Woods. | Sunk in Gulf of Taranto by Italian Destroyer *Baleno*. |
| *Grampus* | 16.6.40 | Lt-Cdr C.A. Rowe. | Sunk east of Syracuse, Sicily, by Italian TB *Polluce*. |
| *Orpheus* | 19.6.40 | Lt-Cdr J.A.S. Wise. | Possibly sunk off Tobruk, Libya, by a mine. |
| *Shark* | 6.7.40 | Lt-Cdr P.N. Buckley. | Scuttled off Stavanger, Norway, to prevent capture after damage by aircraft. |
| *Salmon* | 9.7.40 | Cdr E.O. Bickford. | Possibly mined in North Sea. |
| *Phoenix* | 16.7.40 | Lt-Cdr G.H. Nowell. | Probably DC off Augusta, Sicily, by Italian TB *Albatros*. |
| *Narwahl* | 23.7.40 | Lt-Cdr R.J. Burch. | Possibly sunk off Norway by aircraft. |
| *Oswald* | 1.8.40 | Lt-Cdr D.A. Fraser. | Scuttled east of Capo Spartivento, Italy, after ramming by Italian destroyer *Ugolino Vivaldi*. |
| *Spearfish* | 2.8.40 | Lt-Cdr J.H. Forbes. | Torpedoed in North Sea by *U34*. |
| *Thames* | 3.8.40 | Lt-Cdr W.D. Dunkerley. | Probably mined in North Sea. |
| *Triad* | 10.10.40 | Lt-Cdr G.S. Salt. | Presumed mined off Libya. |
| *Rainbow* | 15.10.40 | Lt-Cdr L.P. Moore. | Sunk SW of Calabria by gunfire from Italian S/M *Enrico Toti*. |
| *H49* | 18.10.40 | Lt R.E. Coltart. | DC west of Texel Island by German A/S trawlers. |
| *Swordfish* | 7.11.40 | Lt M.A. Langley. | Mined off St Catherine's Point, Isle of Wight. |
| *Regulus* | 26.11.40 | Lt-Cdr F.B. Currie. | Possibly mined in Straits of Otranto. |
| *Triton* | 6.12.40 | Lt G.C.I. St B.S. Watkins. | Lost in Southern Adriatic (cause unknown). |
| *Snapper* | 11.2.41 | Lt G.V. Prowse. | Possibly sunk SW Ushant by German minesweepers. |
| *Usk* | 26.4.41 | Lt G.P. Darling. | Presumed mined off Cape Bon, Tunisia. |
| *Undaunted* | 12.5.41 | Lt J.L. Livesay. | Possibly sunk off Zuara, Libya, by Italian TB *Pegaso*. |
| *Umpire* | 19.7.41 | Lt-Cdr M.R.G. Wingfield. | Sunk off Suffolk in collision with trawler *Peter Hendriks*. |
| *Union* | 20.7.41 | Lt R.M. Galloway. | DC SSW of Pantelleria by Italian TB *Circe*. |
| *Cachalot* | 30.7.41 | Lt-Cdr R.B. Newton. | Scuttled off Benghazi, Libya, to avoid capture by Italian TB *Generale Achille Papa*. |

| | | | |
|---|---|---|---|
| *P32* | 18.8.41 | Lt D.A.B. Abdy. | Mined off Tripoli, Libya. |
| *P33* | 20.8.41 | Lt R.D. Whiteway-Wilkinson. | Presumed mined off Tripoli, Libya. |
| *Tetrarch* | 27.10.41 | Lt-Cdr G.H. Greenway. | Probably mined off Capo Granitola, Sicily. |
| *Perseus* | 6.12.41 | Lt-Cdr E.C.F. Nicolay. | Mined off Cephalonia, Western Greece. |
| *H31* | 20.12.41 | Lt F.B. Gibbs. | Lost off NW Spain (cause unknown). |
| *Triumph* | 31.12.41 | Lt J.S. Huddart. | Lost in Cyclades (cause unknown). |
| *Tempest* | 13.2.42 | Lt-Cdr W.K.A.N. Cavaye. | DC near Gulf of Taranto, Italy, by Italian TB *Circe*. |
| *P38* | 23.2.42 | Lt R.J. Hemingway. | DC north of Tripoli, Libya, by Italian TB *Circe*. |
| *P39* | 26.3.42 | Lt N. Marriott. | Sunk at Malta by aircraft. |
| *P36* | 1.4.42 | Lt H.N. Edmonds. | Sunk at Malta by aircraft. |
| *Pandora* | 1.4.42 | Lt R.L. Alexander. | Sunk at Malta by aircraft. |
| *Upholder* | 14.4.42 | Lt-Cdr M.D. Wanklyn. | Probably DC north of Tripoli, Libya, by Italian DE *Pegaso*. |
| *Urge* | 29.4.42 | Lt-Cdr E.P. Tomkinson. | Possibly sunk off Ras el Hilal, Libya, by Italian aircraft. |
| *Olympus* | 8.5.42 | Lt-Cdr H.G. Dymott. | Mined off Malta. |
| *P514* | 21.6.42 | Lt-Cdr R.M.E. Pain. | Rammed in error off Newfoundland by HMC MS *Georgian*. |
| *Thorn* | 7.8.42 | Lt-Cdr R.G. Norfolk. | Probably DC off Gevdo Island, Crete, by Italian DE *Pegaso*. |
| *Talisman* | 17.9.42 | Lt-Cdr M. Willmott. | Presumed mined south of Sicily. |
| *Unique* | 10.10.42 | Lt R.E. Boddington. | Possibly DC off Northern Spain. |
| *X3* | 4.11.42 | Sub-Lt J.T. Lorimer. | Sank on exercise in Loch Striven, Scotland. |
| *Unbeaten* | 11.11.42 | Lt D.E.O. Watson. | Probably sunk in error in Bay of Biscay by RAF aircraft. |
| *Utmost* | 25.11.42 | Lt J.W.D. Coombe. | Possibly DC off Marittimo by Italian DE *Groppo*. |
| *Traveller* | 4.12.42 | Lt-Cdr D. St Clair Ford. | Probably mined in Gulf of Taranto. |
| *P222* | 12.12.42 | Lt-Cdr A.J. Mackenzie. | Probably DC off Capri by Italian DE *Fortunale*. |
| *P48* | 25.12.42 | Lt M.E. Faber. | Probably DC off Zembra Island, Tunisia, by Italian DE *Ardente*. |
| *P311* | 2.1.43 | Cdr R.D. Cayley. | Presumed mined off Northern Sardinia. |
| *Vandal* | 24.2.43 | Lt J.S. Bridger. | Foundered in Inchmarnock |

|          |          |                        | Water, Scotland, during exercises. |
|----------|----------|------------------------|------------------------------------|
| *Tigris* | 27.2.43 | Lt G.R. Colvin. | Probably DC SE of Capri by German *JU2210*. |
| *Thunderbolt* | 14.3.43 | Lt-Cdr C.B. Crouch. | DC off Capo San Vito, Sicily, by Italian CVT *Cicogna*. |
| *Turbulent* | 14.3.43 | Cdr J.W. Linton. | Possibly mined off Corsica or Sardinia. |
| *Regent* | 18.4.43 | Lt W.N.R. Knox. | Mined in Adriatic. |
| *P615* | 18.4.43 | Lt C.W. St C. Lambert. | Torpedoed off Liberia, West Africa, by *U123*. |
| *Splendid* | 21.4.43 | Lt I.L.M. McGeoch. | DC off Capri by German destroyer *Hermes*. |
| *Sahib* | 24.4.43 | Lt J.H. Bromage. | DC off Capo Milazzo, Sicily, by Italian CVT *Euterpe*. |
| *Untamed* | 30.5.43 | Lt G.M. Noll. | Foundered off Sanda Island, Scotland, during exercises. |
| *Parthian* | 7.8.43 | Lt C.A. Pardoe. | Possibly mined in Adriatic. |
| *Saracen* | 14.8.43 | Lt M.G.R. Lumby. | DC off Bastia, Corsica, by Italian CVT *Minerva*. |
| *Welman 10* | 9.9.43 | (1 Operator). | Sank alongside depot ship in Loch Cairnbawn, Scotland. |
| *X9* | 16.9.43 | Sub-Lt E.A. Kearon. | Lost *en route* to Norway to attack *Scharnhorst*. |
| *X8* | 18.9.43 | Lt B.M. McFarlane. | Scuttled *en route* to Norway to attack *Lützow*. |
| *X5* | 22.9.43 | Lt H. Henty-Creer. | Presumed sunk by gunfire during attack on *Tirpitz*. |
| *X6* | 22.9.43 | Lt D. Cameron. | Scuttled after attack on *Tirpitz*. |
| *X7* | 22.9.43 | Lt B.C.G. Place. | Sank after attack on *Tirpitz*. |
| *X10* | 3.10.43 | Lt K.R. Hudspeth. | Scuttled in North Sea after failure to attack *Scharnhorst*. |
| *Usurper* | 3.10.43 | Lt D.R.O. Mott. | Possibly DC in Gulf of Genoa by *JU2208*. |
| *Trooper* | 10.10.43 | Lt J.S. Wraith. | Probably mined east of Leros Island in the Aegean. |
| *Simoom* | 19.11.43 | Lt G.D.N. Milner. | Possibly mined in Northern Aegean. |
| *Welman 45* | 22.11.43 | (1 Operator). | Lost in attack on Bergen Harbour, Norway. |
| *Welman 46* | 22.11.43 | (1 Operator). | Ditto *Welman 45*. |
| *Welman 47* | 22.11.43 | (1 Operator). | Ditto *Welman 45*. |
| *Welman 48* | 22.11.43 | (1 Operator). | Ditto *Welman 45*. |
| *X22* | 7.2.44 | Lt B.M. McFarlane. | Sunk in Pentland Firth in collision with HM S/M *Syrtis*. |
| *Stonehenge* | 16.3.44 | Lt D.S.McN. Verschoyle-Campbell. | Possibly mined north of Sumatra. |
| *Syrtis* | 28.3.44 | Lt M.H. Jupp. | Probably mined off Bodo, Norway. |

| | | | |
|---|---|---|---|
| *Sickle* | 16.6.44 | Lt J.R. Drummond. | Probably mined in Southern Aegean. |
| *Stratagem* | 22.11.44 | Lt C.R. Pelly. | DC off Malacca by Japanese destroyer. |
| *Porpoise* | 19.1.45 | Lt-Cdr H.B. Turner. | Possibly sunk off Penang by Japanese A/S craft. |
| *XE11* | 6.3.45 | Lt A. Staples. | Sank after collision in Loch Striven, Scotland. |

1945-1971

| | | | |
|---|---|---|---|
| *Truculent* | 12.1.50 | Lt C.P. Bowers. | Sank in Thames Estuary after collision with Swedish tanker *Divina*. |
| *Affray* | 16.4.51 | Lt J. Blackburn. | Foundered NW of Alderney. |
| *Sidon* | 16.6.55 | Lt H.T. Verry. | Sank in Portland Harbour after a torpedo exploded in its tube. |
| *Artemis* | 1.7.71 | Lt-Cdr R. Godfrey. | Sank in Portsmouth Harbour. |

# Principal Systems of Submarine Escape

## THE TWILL-TRUNK SYSTEM

Figure 1 shows a typical submarine compartment, such as the engine room, fitted as an escape-compartment, and in the normal operational state at sea.

The 'Twill-trunk', from which the system derives its name, is made from tough rubberized cotton-twill reinforced with steel hoops. It is shown (1) collapsed concertina-wise under the hatch protected by a short steel skirting against undue wear and tear when the hatch is in normal daily use in harbour. The ladder (2) hooks into the skirting. The hatch itself is secured by screw clips.

The watertight doors (3) in the bulkheads at either end of the compartment are open to allow normal passage through the boat.

In the highest part of the pressure hull so that it cannot be blocked at any angle of heel is fitted the special flood valve (4) backed up by a flap valve (5). From these two valves a large bore pipe follows the curve of the hull down to the bilges. This arrangement ensures that the point of ingress of water into the compartment can never be higher than the hatch, in which case it would act as a vent and no air-lock would be formed.

Conveniently near the flood valve is the 'differential depth-gauge' (6), showing the differences in pressure inside and outside the compartment. Since the pressure in the compartment is at atmospheric, the gauge at present is registering the submarine's diving depth.

It will be seen how little this arrangement of the escape fittings interferes with the normal life of a submarine, and that simplicity is the key-note of the whole method.

Figure 2 shows the same compartment rigged for escape, flooded-up, and the hatch ready to open. The Twill-trunk (1) has been extended and lashed down to special eye plates in the floor plates. The bulkhead doors (3, 3) are shut, excluding the survivors from the damaged and flooded portion of the submarine forward, and from

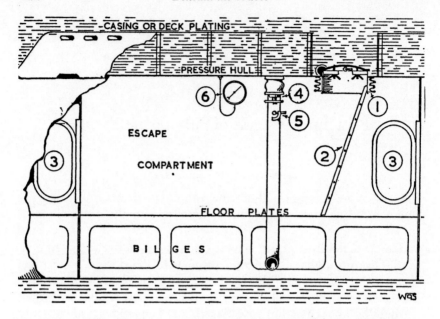

*Fig. 1. The "Twill-trunk" or Compartment Method of Escape*

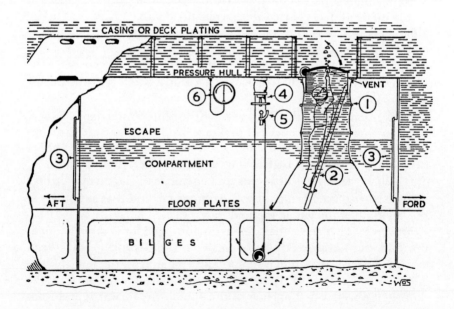

*Fig. 2. The "Twill-trunk" or Compartment Method of Escape*

the empty compartment aft. If this compartment were not isolated it would also have to be flooded before equalization could be achieved, and the flooding-up period would be unduly prolonged.

The flood-valves (4) and (5) are open, and water has flooded in until the pressures equalized. This is shown by the differential gauge which has centralized on the 'Zero' mark. The water level in the compartment suggests a depth of sinking of sixty to seventy feet (3 atmospheres), because the airlock occupies one-third of the height of the compartment. At 300 feet or 10 atmospheres the airlock would be compressed into the top one-tenth of the compartment, and conditions would be very difficult and unpleasant.

The rating wearing breathing apparatus has climbed up into the trunk, and has opened the vent in the hatch, letting out all the air in the trunk which has flooded and formed a 'stairway of water' out of the boat. He has also taken off the screw clips and is about to push open the hatch.

### THE ESCAPE CHAMBER SYSTEM

Figure 3 shows an escape compartment of the type fitted to British submarines immediately prior to World War II. They were fitted

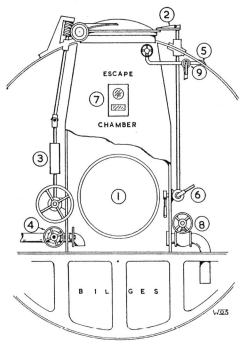

*Fig. 3. The "Escape Compartment" Method of Escape*

between two compartments such as the torpedo stowage, and the crew space or the engine room and the after ends. In some classes of submarine the only gangway through the boat in normal times was by way of a sort of double hurdle through the escape chambers, but in the boats built in 1938-1939 a separate bulkhead door was fitted to 'by-pass' the chamber.

All the controls shown in the diagram were duplicated either side of the dividing bulkhead, so that the chamber could be operated from whichever compartment remained unflooded. Some of them were operable from inside the chamber so that the last group of men to leave could let themselves out.

The drill for escape was as follows:

After the men have entered the chamber, the access door (1) is shut and clipped. The screw clips on the hatch are removed, and the hatch is held down by the external 'toe-clip' (2). The clutch (3) on the hatch operating gear is disconnected so that the hatch is 'free to open' and can be pushed up as soon as the toe-clip is released.

Sea-water is admitted through the flood valve (4), and the air in the chamber is vented overboard through the outboard vent (5). No attempt is made to retain an airlock, and the chamber is flooded as rapidly as possible. The toe-clip is now taken off by the handle (6), and the escapers push open the hatch and go up to the surface.

Watching them through the special port (7), those remaining behind see them go clear, then reconnect the clutch (3) on the hatch operating gear, shut the hatch and replace the toe-clip. The flood and outboard vent are shut, and the drain-valve (8) and inboard vent (9) are opened, allowing the water in the chamber to drain away into the submarine's bilges. As soon as the chamber is 'dry' it can be opened up and a fresh group of men can escape by repeating the process.

The last group must remember to put the hatch to 'Free' before shutting themselves in, and must then operate the flood, the outboard vent, and the toe-clip from inside the chamber.

From the description, the great advantage of the chamber of submitting men to pressure and cold for the absolute minimum of time can well be appreciated. On the other hand the complication of the drill and the multitude of gearing necessary will be equally obvious. The maintenance required on these chambers is beyond the capacity of a submarine's crew at sea for any length of time, and many an escape chamber has been found to be inoperable after the submarine's return to harbour.

# Bibliography

*Straws In The Wind*, Cdr H.G. Stoker, RN. Herbert Jenkins, 1925.
*Take Her Down*, Cdr T.B. Thompson, USN. Sheridan House, 1942.
*One Of Our Submarines*, Cdr E. Young, RNVR. Hart-Davis, 1952.
*The British Submarine*, Cdr F.W. Lipscomb, RN. A. & C. Black, 1954.
*The War At Sea*, Capt. S.W. Roskill, RN. HMSO, 1954.
*Submariner*, Charles Anscomb. William Kimber, 1957.
*The Admiralty Regrets*, C.E.T. Warren and James Benson. Harrap, 1958.
*One Man Band*, Rear-Adm B. Bryant, RN. William Kimber, 1958.
*The Stick And The Stars*, Cdr W.D.A. King, RN. Hutchinson, 1958.
*Subs And Submariners*, Arch Whitehouse. Muller, 1961.
*Will Not We Fear*, C.E.T. Warren and James Benson. Harrap, 1961.
*The K Boats*, Don Everitt. Harrap, 1963.
*The Far And The Deep*, Cdr E.P. Stafford, USN. Arthur Barker, 1968.
*Italian Warships Of World War II*, Lt-Cdr Aldo Fraccaroli, R It N. Ian Allan, 1968.
*A Damned Un-English Weapon*, Edwyn Gray. Seeley, Service & Co., 1971.
*British Submarines At War 1939-1945*, Lt-Cdr A. Mars, RN. Kimber, 1971.
*British Warships 1914-1919*, F.J. Dittmar and J.J. Colledge. Ian Allan, 1972.
*Periscope View*, Rear-Adm G.W.G. Simpson, RN. Macmillan, 1972.
*Warships Of World War II*, H.T. Lenton and J.J. Colledge. Ian Allan, 1973.
*The Anti-Submarine Struggle*, Volume XXII of the Official History of the Royal Italian Navy in World War II, edited by Rear-Adm V. Rauber, R It N, 1978.
*Submarine Boats*, Cdr R. Compton-Hall, RN. Conway Maritime Press, 1983.

# Index